Creative Economy

Series Editors

Stephen Hill, University of Wollongong, Wollongong, NSW, Australia
Kazuo Nishimura, Institute of Economic Research, Kyoto University, Sakyo-ku Kyoto, Japan
Tadashi Yagi, Faculty of Economics, Doshisha University, Kyoto, Kyoto, Japan

This book series covers research on creative economies based on humanity and spirituality to enhance the competitiveness, sustainability, peace, and fairness of international society. We define a creative economy as a socio-economic system that promotes those creative activities with a high market value and leads to the improvement of society's overall well-being. As the global economy has developed, we have seen severe competition and polarization in income distribution. With this drastic change in the economic system, creativity with a high market value has come to be considered the main source of competiveness. But in addition to the improvement of competitiveness, we are required to work toward fairness in society. In the process of developing a mature market, consumers come to understand that what they require most essentially is humanity and spirituality. This cannot be given or bought, but requires sharing with others across cultures and learning and developing further from their richness. Long-term sustainability of a company in this new age also requires building the same values of humanity and spirituality within its own internal organizational culture and practices. Through this series, we intend to propose various policy recommendations that contribute to the prosperity of international society and improve the well-being of mankind by clarifying the concrete actions that are needed.

Series Editors

Stephen Hill, University of Wollongong, Wollongong, NSW, Australia
Kazuo Nishimura, Institute of Economic Research, Kyoto University,
Sakyo-ku Kyoto, Japan
Tadashi Yagi, Faculty of Economics, Doshisha University, Kyoto, Kyoto, Japan

Editorial Board

Nobuko Kawashima, Faculty of Economics, Doshisha University, Kyoto, Japan
Sébastien Lechevalier, École des Hautes Études en Sciences, Paris, France
Yoshifumi Nakata, Doshisha University, Kyoto, Kyoto, Japan
Andy Pratt, University of City London, London, UK
Masayuki Sasaki, Graduate School of Economics, Doshisha University, Kyoto, Japan
Toshiaki Tachibanaki, Faculty of Economics, Doshisha University, Kyoto, Kyoto, Japan
Makoto Yano, Institute of Economic Research, Kyoto University, Kyoto, Japan
Roberto Zanola, Università del Piemonte Orientale, Alessandria, Italy

More information about this series at http://www.springer.com/series/13627

Sébastien Lechevalier
Editor

Innovation Beyond Technology

Science for Society and Interdisciplinary Approaches

Editor
Sébastien Lechevalier
EHESS
Paris, France

ISSN 2364-9186   ISSN 2364-9445   (electronic)
Creative Economy
ISBN 978-981-13-9055-5   ISBN 978-981-13-9053-1   (eBook)
https://doi.org/10.1007/978-981-13-9053-1

© Springer Nature Singapore Pte Ltd. 2019
This work is subject to copyright. All rights are reserved by the Publisher, whether the whole or part of the material is concerned, specifically the rights of translation, reprinting, reuse of illustrations, recitation, broadcasting, reproduction on microfilms or in any other physical way, and transmission or information storage and retrieval, electronic adaptation, computer software, or by similar or dissimilar methodology now known or hereafter developed.
The use of general descriptive names, registered names, trademarks, service marks, etc. in this publication does not imply, even in the absence of a specific statement, that such names are exempt from the relevant protective laws and regulations and therefore free for general use.
The publisher, the authors and the editors are safe to assume that the advice and information in this book are believed to be true and accurate at the date of publication. Neither the publisher nor the authors or the editors give a warranty, expressed or implied, with respect to the material contained herein or for any errors or omissions that may have been made. The publisher remains neutral with regard to jurisdictional claims in published maps and institutional affiliations.

This Springer imprint is published by the registered company Springer Nature Singapore Pte Ltd.
The registered company address is: 152 Beach Road, #21-01/04 Gateway East, Singapore 189721, Singapore

Preface

This book is the outcome of two successful conferences co-organized by the Japan Science and Technology Agency (JST), the Centre National de la Recherche Scientifique (CNRS), and the Ecole des Hautes Etudes en Sciences Sociales (EHESS). The first one took place in Paris on June 2–3, 2015, at the EHESS and the Institut d'Etudes Avancées (IEA) de Paris and was entitled *Engaging Society in Innovation and Creativity: Perspectives from Social Sciences and Humanities*. The second one took place in Tokyo on September 12, 2016, at The University of Tokyo and was entitled *Innovation Beyond Technique*. I would like to thank the three hosting institutions (EHESS, IEA de Paris, and The University of Tokyo), the three members of our consortium (JST, CNRS, and EHESS), as well as the Maison Franco-Japonaise for its support during the Tokyo event. In particular, I would like to express my gratitude to the JST for having believed in the project since the beginning and for having been committed itself until its conclusion. More precisely, my debt is great to Mr. Hiroshi Tsuda and to Ms. Shiho Hamada. Also, I would like to give my warmest thanks to Prof. Tadashi Kobayashi (Osaka University), without whom this project could not have become a reality.

Besides the two events, this book would not have been published without the financial support of JST, Fondation France-Japon de l'EHESS, and Séric. We are particularly grateful to its President, Mr. Christian Polak, for his trust in this ambitious project. The editorial assistance from both Juno Kawakami (Springer) and Sarah Boisard (EHESS) has been crucial and beyond our expectations.

Last but not least, I would like to thank all the contributors to this project for their commitment and the way they took very seriously our critics, comments, and advice. The core of this project is based on a series of convictions: Innovation should be thought, defined, and implemented beyond technology; a contribution from Social Sciences and Humanities (SSH) is required to seriously go beyond a narrow technological view; interdisciplinary approaches within SSH and between SSH and sciences are crucial; a collaboration between Japanese and French institutions and individual researchers will be beneficial because of the complementarities between our approaches. This series of beliefs made things much more difficult than what unidimensional and national perspectives would do, but our bet was that, in case of success, it would be really fruitful. We hope that the readers will agree that it was worth to take this risk.

Paris, France   Sébastien Lechevalier

Contents

1 Innovation Beyond Technology—Introduction 1
Sébastien Lechevalier and Sandra Laugier

Part I Critical Views on Innovation from Economics and History of Science, and Law

2 Reimagining Innovation 25
Pierre-Benoit Joly

3 'Innovation' as an Adaptation of 'Progress': Revisiting the Epistemological and Historical Contexts of These Terms 47
Sayaka Oki

4 The Light and Shadow of the Fourth Industrial Revolution 63
Shinichi Koizumi

Part II Case Studies 1: Health and Medicine

5 How Scientific Breakthroughs and Social Innovations Shape the Evolution of the Healthcare Sector 89
Robert Boyer

6 From Crisis to Reformulation: Innovation in the Global Drug Industry and the Alternative Modernization of Indian Ayurveda 121
Jean-Paul Gaudillière

7 Consortium-Based Open Innovation: Exploring a Unique and Optimal Model for Regional Biotechnology Industry 141
Shintaro Sengoku

vii

Part III Case Studies 2: Environment

8 Environment and Social Innovation: Why Technology Never Was *the* Solution ... 175
Dominique Pestre

9 Post-disaster Community Recovery and Community-Based Collaborative Action Research—A Case of Process Evaluation Method for Community Life Improvement ... 195
Takayoshi Kusago

10 Lessons from Fukushima for Responsible Innovation: How to Construct a New Relationship Between Science and Society? ... 223
Yuko Fujigaki

Part IV Innovation for Whom and for What?

11 Public Participation in the Setting of Research and Innovation Agenda: Virtues and Challenges from a Philosophical Perspective ... 243
Stéphanie Ruphy

12 Innovation for Whom? City Experiments and the Redefinition of Urban Democracy ... 265
Brice Laurent

13 Image of Jurisprudence Reconstructed to Enhance Innovation: Liability Allocation for Improved Predictability ... 285
Takehiro Ohya

14 Science as Care: Science and Innovation in Post-growth Society ... 301
Yoshinori Hiroi

Editor and Contributors

About the Editor

Sébastien Lechevalier is an economist and Professor at EHESS (School of Advanced Studies in the Social Sciences, Paris), specialized in the Japanese economy and Asian capitalism. He is also Associate Researcher at GREThA (Bordeaux University). He is Founder and President of the Fondation France-Japon de l'EHESS (FFJ). He has been Visiting Professor at The University of Tokyo, Kyoto University, Hitotsubashi University, Waseda University, and Doshisha University.

He has published extensively on various dimensions of the Japanese economy in comparative perspective, including *The Great Transformation of Japanese Capitalism* (Routledge, 2014). His research also deals with the issue of innovation in academic institutions, at the corporate level, and from a public policy perspective.

Contributors

Robert Boyer Institute of the Americas, Vanves, France

Yuko Fujigaki The University of Tokyo, Tokyo, Japan

Jean-Paul Gaudillière Cermes3, Inserm-EHESS, Paris, France

Yoshinori Hiroi Kyoto University, Kyoto, Japan

Pierre-Benoit Joly LISIS (CNRS, ESIEE Paris, INRA, UPEM), Marne-la-Vallée, France

Shinichi Koizumi DeNA Co., Ltd., Tokyo, Japan

Takayoshi Kusago Kansai University, Osaka, Japan

Sandra Laugier Université Paris 1 Panthéon Sorbonne, Paris, France

Brice Laurent CSI—Centre de Sociologie de l'Innovation, i3 UMS CNRS, PSL Research University, MINES ParisTech, Paris, France

Sébastien Lechevalier École des Hautes Études en Sciences Sociales, Paris, France

Takehiro Ohya Keio University, Tokyo, Japan

Sayaka Oki University of Nagoya, Nagoya, Japan

Dominique Pestre Ecole des Hautes Etudes en Sciences Sociales, Paris, France

Stéphanie Ruphy Université de Lyon—Jean Moulin, Lyon, France

Shintaro Sengoku Tokyo Institute of Technology, Tokyo, Japan

Chapter 1
Innovation Beyond Technology—Introduction

Sébastien Lechevalier and Sandra Laugier

Abstract For a few decades now, innovation—mainly derived from technological advances—has been considered a driving force of economic and societal development and prosperity. The dominant view is that, in the context of globalization, and the accompanying rise of international competition, OECD countries have a choice between two options: innovate or perish. However, the last two decades, which can be regarded as the golden age of innovation, saw a gradual shift in ideology. There has been indeed growing doubt about the relevance of the dominant model of innovation. This introductory chapter's main goal is to analyze the conditions of a shift from a techno-centric society to a human-centric society, one where technology's potential for positive impact is not disregarded, but where social and human well-being is central to realize this potential. Another goal is to discuss non-technological aspects of innovation and their importance in dealing with complex contemporary societal issues, while also making a critical assessment of the relationship between science, technology, innovation (STI) and society.

1.1 The Paradox of Innovation in Troubled Times

For a few decades now, innovation—mainly derived from technological advances—has been considered a driving force of economic and societal development and prosperity. Innovation driven by science and technology is expected to reduce the general sense of economic and social stagnation felt in some countries and the various risks created by climate change (Joly 2019; Koizumi 2019; Pestre 2019). Thus, innovation enjoys very positive publicity nowadays, to say the least. There is a noticeable shift from science and technology policy to science, technology *and innovation* policy. Few people, or groups of people, would agree to being defined

---

S. Lechevalier (✉)
École des Hautes Études en Sciences Sociales, Paris, France
e-mail: sebastien.lechevalier@ehess.fr

S. Laugier
Université Paris 1 Panthéon Sorbonne, Paris, France
e-mail: Sandra.Laugier@univ-paris1.fr

© Springer Nature Singapore Pte Ltd. 2019
S. Lechevalier (ed.), *Innovation Beyond Technology*, Creative Economy,
https://doi.org/10.1007/978-981-13-9053-1_1

as opponents of innovation, although the contemporary rise of populism goes hand in hand with conservative or reactionary thinking. The dominant view is that, in the context of globalization, and the accompanying rise of international competition, OECD countries have a choice between two options: innovate or perish. From this point of view, innovation can be considered an ideology (Oki 2019).

This effort to innovate shows a clear focus on the technological side of innovation and we should acknowledge its great contributions, best exemplified by information and communication technologies (ICT; e.g. the Internet, smartphones or Internet of things (IoT)), robotics and artificial intelligence (AI), and biotechnologies, all of which have already changed our lives profoundly and made possible things that most people would have still thought impossible three decades ago. Who could have anticipated that progress in robotics would lead to such diversification in the tasks of robots? Their use can be seen in plants, in confined environments, can increase the productivity of manufacturing firms, but they can also interact with human, learn and assist in some service sectors. Who could have imagined that the progress of biotechnologies would allow doctors to regenerate skin? Are we still able to fathom a world without the Internet or mobile phones, which revolutionized our ways of communicating?

From the perspective of economic policy, this focus on the technological side of innovation has important consequences. If, at this stage, we accept that growth is paramount,[1] we must then acknowledge that the true engine of growth is technical progress, not labor or capital. The respective shares of resources dedicated to natural sciences and to social sciences and humanities illustrate this priority in the scientific field, where the latter is clearly marginalized.

It is not surprising that more and more resources are dedicated to innovation at different levels, from basic research to research and development (R&D). The OECD is one of the international organizations that encourage investment in sciences and R&D and even rank countries based on their efforts in this field (OECD 2005). The major justification for these actions is that humanity is considered to have entered a new era, namely the "knowledge economy and society," in which the issue at stake is not access to natural resources or even production of manufactured goods, but production of and access to knowledge.

However, the last two decades, which can be regarded as the golden age of innovation, saw a gradual shift in ideology. We started off by embracing (technological) innovation as the solution to the crises of our times, but ended up seeing our model of innovation become yet another problem to solve. Indeed, there has been growing doubt about the relevance of this model. There are a few factors that contribute to this state of affairs, which we will now review. First, a discrepancy appears between increasing resources dedicated to innovation and decreasing well-being observed in many places. Hospitals are an obvious example, where the technological environment has developed much faster than the attention to care or how to take into account the many ways of mitigating patients' suffering. The role of innovation in increasing inequality is also important. This was a source of controversy for a long time before

---

[1] See Pestre (2019) and Cohen (2018) for a critical discussion of this idea.

1 Innovation Beyond Technology—Introduction

economists more or less reached a consensus confirming it (Card and DiNardo 2002), although there are still many debates about the mechanisms at work.[2] Some obvious cases of detrimental innovation have also been identified. This is the case of planned obsolescence, for example (Joly 2019; Slade 2009).

Second, various scandals have also cast doubt on the benefits of innovation. Pharmaceutical and chemical industries are particularly implicated in these scandals. In France, the infamous case of MEDIATOR, produced by Servier Laboratories, shed a stark light on the practices of some pharmaceutical companies, and eroded patients' trust in these companies and health authorities. This drug, which was developed to reduce the effects of a type of diabetes, was responsible for many deaths over several decades, until a doctor publicly denounced its harmful effect on health. We could cite many other such cases, but we will focus on only two of them. The first case originated in the late nineteenth century, when the widespread industrial use of asbestos began. It was only in the 1960s that asbestos was identified as the cause of a malignant disease called mesothelioma. Its use has started to be phased out in some countries, but not all. It was banned in the EU only in late 2010, and is considered to be responsible for the death of 4,000 people a year in the UK alone. An editorial in *Nature* pointed out that, among the many reasons for this long-lasting scandal, the misuse of "scientific" proof by the industry played a key role: "To support this, industry advocates point to scientific data and studies. Yet although the relevant literature is a mire of conflicting results, this should not be seen as an endorsement of their position. Rather, it reflects a string of industry-sponsored studies designed only to cast doubt on the clear links between chrysotile and lung disease" (Nature 2010).

A second infamous case concerns the use of Roundup, a powerful herbicide commercialized by the US firm Monsanto, which has been cited as the cause of numerous cases of cancer. Monsanto was sentenced by the San Francisco court to pay $289 million to Dewayne Johnson, a gardener, who was diagnosed with cancer after having used the herbicide for years, while Monsanto failed to warn users about the associated risks. Again, scientific studies have been used extensively by Monsanto in this case to create fake scientific controversies and to appeal the sentence.

Finally, the Fukushima Daiichi nuclear disaster in March 2011 and its aftermath were a turning point not only for Japan, but also for the rest of the world in terms of the relationship between nature, technology and society. As it has been well documented, the nuclear industry in Japan was considered one of the safest, but a major earthquake followed by a tsunami proved dramatically that not all risks could be avoided and technology did not, in fact, help avoid a historical disaster. This catastrophe was one of the events that prompted the project that led to this book (see below).

Moreover, besides the negative side effects of innovation-led society and economy, what is increasingly considered problematic is that the priority given to innovation is set without a real public debate on the reasons behind such a decision. This concern

---

[2]For example, skill-biased technologies is a concept that has been introduced to illustrate the fact that technologies are non-neutral and may help those who are educated enough in increasing their productivity, while they may hinder those who are less educated and therefore less able to benefit from new technologies such as computers or Internet.

is not new, and the Budapest Declaration, drafted in the context of the UNESCO's 1999 World Science Conference, was a turning point for this issue, as emphasized by Oki (2019). This declaration is famous for its motto "science in society and science for society." It mentions the importance of pursuing scientific knowledge and the necessity of building institutions that promote innovation as conditions for sustainable progress. However, it recognizes at the same time that the applications of scientific advances and the development and expansion of human activity have led to environmental degradation and technological disasters, and have contributed to social inequality or exclusion. This shows that blind enthusiasm for scientific progress had waned by the end of the twentieth century. The associated risks were well identified. The Budapest Declaration went one step further in calling for 'a vigorous and informed democratic debate on the production and use of scientific knowledge.'

Twenty years later, has the situation improved or even evolved in terms of this democratic debate on innovation? There is certainly room for doubt, as expressed and emphasized by a recent editorial in the journal *Nature*, entitled "Beyond the science bubble" (Nature 2017), cited by Ruphy (2019). The authors of this editorial call for the results of scientific research and innovation to align more closely with the needs and expectations of society. This is a desperate call back to the Budapest Declaration, in a context of rising populism and overall social discontent expressed in various forms: "The needs of millions of people in the United States are not well enough served by the agendas and interests that drive much of modern science. (…) Research leaders in the United States and elsewhere should address the needs and employment prospects of taxpayers who have seen little benefit from scientific advances." This article does not really propose solutions from the perspective of innovation policies or democratic debates, but it is a strong signal of the problems associated with the disconnect between scientific developments and the needs of society.

Some of these solutions are discussed in an article by Schot and Steinmueller (2016), as explained in Joly (2019). The question addressed by the authors is very clear: "How to use science and technology policy for meeting social needs and addressing societal challenges?" Their answer rests on the way innovation policy can achieve system-wide transformation of the food, energy, material, mobility, healthcare and communication socio-technical systems. It is such wide-scale transformations—not competitiveness, or other targets—that should constitute the core of innovation policy (see also Joly 2017). This, in turn, requires an outlook that surpasses traditional innovation policy-making tools, which are based on support for R&D and specific research priorities.

To put it simply, society's expectations of science have changed. The seemingly growing dissatisfaction with scientific research and innovation can be explained as follows: while global contribution to economic growth is still central, it does not satisfy the expectations of today's society; *socially relevant* and *desirable* research and innovation is also expected. What distinguishes our "knowledge society" from the post-war period (which was still relatively optimistic in terms of possible progress, despite WWII), for example, is that our expectations of science have become both more pressing and more precise (Ruphy 2019).

This book's main goal is to give substance to the above reflections. With the Fukushima Daiichi Nuclear Accident as a backdrop, our aim is to analyze the conditions of a shift from a techno-centric society to a human-centric society, one where technology's potential for positive impact is not disregarded, but where social and human well-being is central to realize this potential. It is especially meaningful to us that world-renowned research institutions in natural sciences, such as the Japan Science and Technology Agency (JST) and the National Center for Scientific Research (CNRS), have cooperated on this initiative with a leading school in social sciences and humanities (SSH), the Ecole des Hautes Etudes en Sciences Sociales (EHESS, Paris).

Another goal is to discuss non-technological aspects of innovation and their importance in dealing with complex contemporary societal issues, while also making a critical assessment of the relationship between science, technology, innovation (STI) and society. This book deals with the following questions in particular: What non-technological sources of innovation are there? What can progress in STI contribute to humankind? What role will society be expected to play in this new model of innovation? We argue that the majority of so-called technological innovations are actually social innovations, using considerable resources for financing activities, adapting regulations, designing adequate policy frameworks, and shaping new uses and new users, while properly interacting with society (see also Collingridge 1980). This book compiles articles with multi- and trans-disciplinary approaches on innovation that go beyond technology and take into account the interrelations with social and human phenomena. We show a possible path to more responsible and more inclusive forms of innovation.

1.2 What Is Innovation? A Critical Investigation[3]

1.2.1 Innovation and Progress

In order to reach these goals, it is important to first explore the concept of innovation itself and perhaps dispel certain myths (Joly et al. 2010). What we learn from the history of sciences and ideas (Oki 2019; Godin 2015) is that the use of innovation is in keeping with the notion of progress. Innovation is in fact a concept that historically emerges as a result of the decline of the concept of progress in the 1980s and 1990s. Contrary to popular belief, the turning point is not World War II, which provided the most extreme examples of the negative use of scientific knowledge in service of totalitarianism, but rather the end of the Cold War and the decline of Marxism, which can be considered the Enlightenment's successor in seeking to shape a "better" human

---

[3]This section is mainly based on Oki and Joly's contributions in this volume.

being. The more positive role in the 1970s–1980s of Neo-Schumpeterian research should not be neglected either however, with its diverse contributions from Sydney Winter, Richard Nelson, Richard Freeman or Giovanni Dosi, among others (Freeman 1995; Herman and Avram 2011). This area of research revived Schumpeter's vision of innovation as creative destruction and popularized it in a new technological context (Schumpeter 1943). These researchers' work made innovation central to economists' research agendas, and also economic policies in the US, EU and some Asian countries.

Innovation should also be considered an ideology, much like progress, which it has replaced in various respects. Many countries now rely on the concept of 'innovation' both as a tool and as a fundamental value of society, while the use of 'progress' as a socio-political ideal has faded away in most public discourse. This is why, as stated by Oki (2019), "the concept of innovation is simply the idea of progress adapted for our era."

Indeed, both concepts share some similarities (Oki 2019). The concept of innovation has inherited, or absorbed, social values from the Enlightenment, incorporating a range of modern values, such as originality, utility, rationality and progress. It also appears to have inherited another, more disruptive, aspect of the modern notion of progress, namely, evolution through fierce competition. However, there is also a major difference between the two concepts: innovation differs considerably from progress, especially in that it is based on concepts such as discontinuity and diversity. The ideology of innovation obliges us to count on abrupt and unpredictable changes in order to secure a better future.

Some characteristics of innovation therefore become clearer. In the Neo-Schumpeterian theory of innovation, technological innovation was closely linked with the market, and innovations that were tailored towards consumer needs were favored (Freeman 1974). This new trend implied a shift from the techno-expert-centric attitude of the 1950s to technological innovation comprising a more social nature, involving the wider public and its collective creativity.[4] At the same time, it also fostered industrial/market-centric innovation policy, with a social vision that tended to view citizens as consumers. The main flaw in this outlook is that 'innovation does not contain an implication of a grand path or a grand design of a knowable future' (Siva Vaidhyanathan, cited in Oki (2019)) as was the case for progress.

---

[4]Representative of this approach is Lazonick's work on the innovative firm, in which he shows that innovation cannot be analyzed independently from its social environment (Lazonick 2013).

1.2.2 Innovation as a Tool of Competition Versus Innovation as a Source of Well-Being: A Critical Discussion of the Neo-Schumpeterian Concept of Innovation as Creative Destruction

The influence of Neo-Schumpeterian thinking is most obvious in the concept of innovation as a process of creative destruction. Inspired by Schumpeter himself, this idea suggests that innovation needs to erase past habits and technologies in order for new technologies, which are always better than previous ones, to develop. This outlook recognizes the possible disturbance of innovation, its destructive capacity, but assumes that the costs of this destruction are always more than compensated for by the benefits of new technology, as explained by Joly (2019). This assumption is rarely discussed in the scientific literature and its political implications are never the object of a public debate. Before explaining what we mean by social innovation, it is important to show the limits of this Neo-Schumpeterian view of innovation. A major one is given by Luc Soete, whose contributions have often been associated with the Neo-Schumpeterian school of thought. According to Soete (2013), the creative capacity of innovation does not necessarily make up for its destructive capacity; this means that, in some cases, innovation is simply a process of destructive creation. There are many examples of economic, social and environmental damage caused by new technologies, the most dramatic ones being nuclear accidents such as Chernobyl or Fukushima.

A second—more or less—explicit idea associated with this concept of innovation is that solutions are found in new technology, not in improvements to old ones (Joly 2019). This idea also underlies innovation policies aiming to promote startups. This is inherent to a culture of novelty and disruption, as explained above. However, there are plenty of examples of innovation through incrementalism, recycling and maintenance. The Japanese system is a good example of this type of innovation, which is often criticized as being neither radical nor disruptive enough (Lechevalier 2006; Lechevalier et al. 2014). Other examples include frugal innovation, grassroots innovation, reverse innovation or innovation from the bottom of the pyramid (Prahalad 2005). This goes with a new geography (the "South" as a key source of innovation) and a new cosmology (the "users" at the core) of innovation, also explained by Joly (2019). Von Hippel (2004), among others, mentions several examples: for instance, in some sectors, such as scientific instrumentation and semiconductors, users are the main source of innovation. In this case, innovation is based on neither the push of technology nor the pull of demand; it is the result of interactions among actors with complementary knowledge sets. Users are no longer seen as only using: they learn by using, and, in some situations, they co-innovate. Open Source Software (OSS) is a perfect example of this process. This type of innovation—which takes various forms, such as bottom up innovation, user-centered innovation, distributed innovation, community-based innovation—is the exact opposite of the centralized-delegated model of innovation.[5]

A third problematic idea inherent to the Neo-Schumpeterian concept of innovation is the fact that, more or less explicitly, the focus on technological solutions avoids researching solutions that call for societal changes. Opposed to this idea is the concept of institutional change (Amable 2003; Lechevalier 2014), where institutions are not defined as social technologies, but political compromises, and this concept expects societal changes to occur through a political mediation. This is not a way to deny the importance of technology, but a strategy to better articulate them to social needs. As already mentioned above, this approach is in line with Schot and Steinmueller (2016), who address the issue of science and technology policy aligning more closely with social needs.

Without claiming to be exhaustive, it is important to mention a fourth problem, according to Joly (2019): the Neo-Schumpeterian vision of innovation assumes not only that innovation is always good (destructive creation), but also that actors who are skeptical of innovation are laggards. This is a crude simplification that ignores an alternative vision of innovation, which was developed by Callon (1981). Controversy and contention have played an important role in the innovation process and the current volume gives numerous examples.

1.2.3 Social Innovation and Innovation Beyond Technology

All the criticism against the narrow Neo-Schumpeterian vision of innovation converges inevitably on the need to acknowledge the non-technological sources of innovation. In this context, social innovation—defined broadly as "[N]ew social practices that aim to meet social needs in a better way than the existing solutions" (Howaldt and Schwarz 2010)—is of great interest. The next section presents several examples of social innovation. In all these examples, we do not only consider the results of innovation, but also its process and the diversity of ways to innovate. Innovation is not only a matter of efficiency, but a matter of agency, collective action, empowerment and social relations.

This perspective is more in line with the EU responsible research and innovation (RRI) framework: "RRI means that societal actors work together during the whole research and innovation process in order to better align both the process and its outcomes, with the values, needs and expectations of European society" (cited in Fujigaki (2019)). RRI discourse refers to inclusive and participative forms of governance. The meaning of responsibility embedded in RRI is prospective rather than retrospective, moral rather than legal, and collective rather than individual. It is a way to give serious weight to the desire to *steer* research and innovation towards solving societal problems (Owen et al. 2012).

---

[5]Ruphy (2019) gives an epistemological discussion on this.

1.3 Examples of Social Innovation

Before examining the examples of social innovations covered in this volume, let us first present a case that is not specifically discussed, but is nonetheless relevant to this book's purpose: the nature of innovation in Japanese firms. We believe it is possible to learn from the Japanese experience, provided some myths are dispelled. The paradox, explained in other works (Lechevalier 2014; Lechevalier et al. 2014), is that Japan is one of the most techno-centric countries in the world, but the success of Japanese firms rests on a model of organizational innovation, rather than technological innovation.

The story of this paradox is complex, but it is possible to summarize it as follows. Forty years ago, understanding why the productivity of Japanese manufacturing firms outperformed their US and European counterparts was a priority on the research agendas of economists and management specialists. The conclusion was that the reason for the superior performance of Japanese firms was organizational rather than technological. The concept of "Toyotism" was introduced to express this model that was based on an important corporate investment in training workers and fostering their commitment to the firm. These days, many Japanese firms have forgotten the efficiency of this model.

The major stylized fact that emerged from empirical research in the 1980s was that Japanese firms were more productive than their US or European counterparts (Aoki and Dore 1994; Lechevalier 2012). Several studies revealed this trend by demonstrating that the superior productivity of Japanese firms lay mostly in Human Resource Management (especially on the shop floor) and more generally in the organization of production, rather than in technology itself. It was especially true of the so-called "catching-up period," when the Japanese government's target was to catch-up with leading European economies and then the US, but it was also partly true after the Japanese successfully did so. This policy giving priority to organization is part of what the concept of Toyotism encapsulates. However, once again, there is some misunderstanding about what this concept means. The core of Toyotism is not robotics or mechanization or automation, despite the importance of the principle of *jidoka* (which can be translated as auto-activation) within the system. Rather, the idea behind Toyotism is a form of intensification of human work, through its involvement at each stage of the production. From this perspective, Toyotism shares the same goal as Taylorism. However, it relies on different methods to achieve this goal:

1. (Relative) worker autonomy at the level of the team (team work);
2. Importance of learning, on-the-job training (and therefore re-introduction of skills);
3. Workers' understanding of the whole production process;
4. Innovation and productivity gains on the shop floor, as much as in the engineer offices—smaller productivity gap between blue collar workers and engineers than in European or US firms.

Paradoxically, once the catching-up period was over (end of the 1980s) Japanese firms appeared to forget the lessons from their past success, and even more so during the 1990s when the concept of New Economy, imported from the US and incorporating the ideology of technological innovation, dominated. They have committed to a technological race, with massive investments in R&D, and a HRM race-to-the-bottom, including wage reductions, in the context of competitive pressures from countries characterized by lower labor costs. The results of these decisions have been disappointing to say the least. Over-investment in R&D has led to poor returns (OECD 2005; Lechevalier 2006); some companies such as Sony have discovered that having the best technology is not a guarantee of gaining market shares, if consumer needs or tastes are not taken into consideration. More importantly, a relative decline in labor productivity has been observed. Our explanation for this is that wage stagnation and well-being issues (e.g. long working hours) have led workers to lose motivation. In this context, the solution is not to invest more in technology, but to rebuild a social compromise within the firm (Lechevalier 2014).

This volume presents other compelling examples of social innovation, in which technology features little. Without going into detail, let us review three of them. As mentioned by Boyer (2019), medicine is a particularly interesting example as it is often cited as a field of tremendous technical progress. However, what is often forgotten is the coevolution of medical techniques with definitions of illness and institutions, on which healthcare systems are based. Historians have shown extensively that the recognition of illnesses results from conceptual and social processes and is thus evolutionary by nature. Changing medical techniques are endogenous because they are largely conditioned by the socio-economic context. Medical innovation is shaped by the institutional context. This relationship is examined by Gaudillière (2019), he discusses the case of Ayurveda, the medicine of ancient India, which is based on the oldest and the most complete therapeutic system. More generally, healthcare, education and culture are *exceptions to the concept of innovation* that defines it as a combination of technical progress, increased productivity and lower costs. The least one can say is that these exceptions are not minor ones…

Environmental innovations are another fascinating example. This is another area that suffers from techno-centrism, and Pestre (2019) explains how and why technology was never really the solution to environmental issues. He reviews a number of tools, either economic or legal in nature, the purpose of which is to control technical progress and its negative side effects instead. Kusago (2019) offers a convincing example of the effectiveness of these tools in a context of post-earthquake relief. He shows how community-based action can be applied by extension to a nuclear disaster such as the one that occurred in the Fukushima prefecture.

Last but not least, urban experiments, such as the case of San Francisco described by Laurent (2019), are another example of social innovation, which depends greatly on the ability of citizens to oppose technological innovation and to propose alternatives. More generally, the issue of mobility in urban environment, discussed in Veltz (2017), among others, entails conducting experiments outside the laboratory, as was done by Google in Toronto or Columbus, for example. We cannot deny the importance of technology, but we must relativize its contribution to social welfare, especially when it has not yet been appropriated and adapted by citizens.

1.4 What Is the Role of Social Sciences and Humanities (SSH) in This Discussion? The True Meaning of Interdisciplinarity

The topics discussed in the previous section confirm that creating "real" innovation requires strengths other than the development of science and technology. Innovation must integrate knowledge from human and social sciences (SSH). This is the heart of the change in the role of society and SSH in science, innovation and creativity, but it should be stated clearly. Indeed, the call for SSH to have a greater role is often linked, at best, with advising how to adjust policy to the social demands or human needs or, at worst, with helping to promote the *acceptability* of technology or behavior changes.

The various contributions in this volume defend the idea that the role of SSH need not be limited to pushing a posteriori adjustment and acceptability, but is a useful part of science and creativity, and that the "human factor" should be involved at the outset of scientific policy. Interdisciplinary work comprising natural sciences and SSH is necessary to clearly identify those needs and interests of society that cannot be addressed by the market, and also to anticipate the evolution of these needs and interests, so that scientific research can adjust its goals accordingly (Ruphy 2019; Hiroi 2019). This also relates to the idea that practical knowledge and wisdom, and the involvement of people—what is called "the public"—is not only good for democracy, but is crucial for innovation. Interdisciplinary research—with SSH playing a central role, especially in the preliminary phases—must therefore be set up in order to support actual innovation. A better understanding of the human and social aspects of science and technology improves the understanding of global challenges and their solutions. The point is not just whether science is done "for" society: it is done *in, with* and *by* society.

1.4.1 Science for Society. The Role of SSH in the Progress of Science

There are many important reasons for the increasingly major role of SSH in the progress of science. We identify five of these reasons in the following section.

First, various authors (e.g. Dewey 1981: 94) have emphasized the gap between principles of science and technology, on the one hand, and their human applications, on the other, as well as the risks posed by this gap. These applications emerge from complex social, political and economic contexts and they combine science, technology and society in their implementation. This makes knowledge of both the human side and the scientific side essential for responding intelligently to societal challenges. Thus, while science and technology are at the center of efforts to improve human health and well-being, the application of science and technology has not always contributed as anticipated to these efforts to improve human condition and well-being. It is essential, therefore, that research on the relationship between science, technology and society be integrated into the broader research agenda. Given the fact that, more than any other research field, work in the fields of SSH focuses on the systems that link human and social values and behavior to actual progress, it is easy to see why SSH are fundamental to this approach.

Secondly, and more importantly, SSH can be the tool for introducing an ultimate criterion for choosing different directions of research.[6] A key contribution of this volume, which we will discuss again later in this introduction, is the idea that this ultimate criterion should be well-being (Hiroi 2019). Why? This concept is essential to SSH research and to science in general. It refers not just to data that can be isolated as "impact," or to vague ethical issues, but rather to an element that must be taken into account in any pursuit of knowledge. The issue of well-being is in fact related to the question of progress (Oki 2019).

This leads us to the third, even more fundamental, reason for the importance of SSH. As we saw at the beginning of this introduction, the main reason why societies have been looking so intently to SSH for the last two or three decades is because we are living in a time of crisis. The crisis is twofold: it is simultaneously a crisis of development—catalyzed by both a sense of stagnation (the so-called "secular stagnation" theorized in the post-2009 context by different economists such as Krugman, Summers or Gordon) and the identification of global risks such as climate change—and a crisis of belief—specifically that progress made in natural sciences is the answer to the first crisis. Since the Enlightenment, the West has operated on the conviction that the advancement of knowledge, science and technology (carried out through mathematization) necessarily facilitates social progress and the progress of civilizations (Oki 2019). This conviction has been upheld by an increase in the amount of energy available for human activities, a rise in food and commodity production, and by increased life expectancy at birth—thus, a rise in quality of life and well-being. This causal relation has been broken, even shattered, over the course of the past few decades due to several factors. Crises and disasters in advanced countries, such as chemical and nuclear accidents (e.g. Fukushima), have played a critical role in the rise of SSH.

Also, the positive value inherent in the word "progress" and its universal dimension have been undermined by increasing awareness of the unequal distribution of progress in terms of improved well-being among different populations. The word "universal" itself has become problematic, and newly discovered global (environmental) inequalities have opened a new field of research in both SSH and science (see Piketty 2014; Koizumi 2019).

In this context, instead of having a naive faith in overall progress, we do better to see how we can actually make progress where it is most vital and urgent to do so; how we can make progress in specific ways that will benefit countries other than Western ones. The questions the SSH ask are not intended to hinder scientific progress, nor to criticize the other sciences. Instead, they make it possible to see the importance

---

[6]It can be done, for example, when budgets are allocated to different research fields or approaches. Who makes the decision is another question that is considered by Ruphy (2019).

1 Innovation Beyond Technology—Introduction

and consequences of progress in a certain area and to take people's well-being into account.

Fourth, without succumbing to anti-scientific relativism, we must understand SSH's contribution in its criticism of the positivist universalism that is somehow inherent to the natural sciences. The complexity and uniqueness of different situations mean that there is an irreducible uncertainty about the results of human actions and, therefore, that there are specific difficulties in formalizing these actions: for example, patients' varying reactions to the same treatment (Boyer 2019; Gaudillière 2019), or society's unexpected reactions to events. Unlike science, practical wisdom, deliberation, *phronesis*, cannot claim universality. Considering all relevant elements in any given situation leads to a change in perspective. And having to acknowledge a disturbance or a risk always leads to discovery and innovation when new, neglected elements of the situation must be taken into account. This is the basis of science.

One asset of modern SSH is its capacity for prudence and deliberation, which means including all and any additional variables inherent in human actions and situations. The interesting point here is that taking context into account does not mean research burdened by relativism, but rather carried out with greater precision and accuracy. More generally, as shown by the various contributions collected in Haag et al. (2012), the essence of social sciences can be described by a triple action: to criticize, to compare and to generalize. The first step, the critical aspect of social sciences, is similar to what has been described above. This step is the minimum requirement for prudence and deliberation: "To criticize is one of the activities that all research must start with and without which it cannot start, at least in substance" (Haag et al. 2012, our translation). The second step, comparison, again does not mean that social sciences are intrinsically relativist. However, they tend to explore the limits of universality and postulate that there is no universal law that can be applied to societies, as can be in natural sciences. The third step, generalization, obviously balances out this outlook: recognizing the fundamental diversity of human societies does not mean that it is impossible to accept a certain degree of generality. This intellectual attitude of social scientists is not in contradiction with the epistemology of natural sciences, and should be considered a source of fecundity if properly articulated.

Fifth, another reason for the centrality of SSH is that researchers do not exist outside the world. They do not stand before a readily understandable and tractable reality. From this perspective, the relationship between science and humans has changed over the last century. This co-dependence between the human/social world and the world of "hard" science is referred to as *global change*. Philippe Descola (2005) discusses the fact that, for decades, SSH have been witnessing a change in the relationship between nature and society. The transformation of relationships and hierarchies between cultures; between nature and culture; between the living and the non-living (biotechnologies); social, technological and environmental risks; new social and health risks; and global inequalities... all these shape a new landscape of knowledge, one that integrates the human and the social dimensions into science as a whole. In other words, science is practiced by humans in a world of humans, who are in turn affected by science. This means that, conversely, we can also change and transform this human world. Ancient civilizations differentiated those things that depend on us from those that do not. Today, the realm of what depends on us is enormous, and the climate crisis is the greatest illustration of this.

1.4.2 Science with Society: Data Science and Public Participation

If science is to answer, or *include*, human needs then the public expression of these needs should matter. The same decades that put humans at the center of the global processes explored by science have also witnessed an evolution in the concept of the *public*, which is no longer understood to be the ignorant masses whose irrational fears must be controlled, but rather a community of citizens capable of understanding the practical stakes of science. The current rise of populism observed in several countries makes consulting the public even more urgent. This means accounting for and evaluating the public's ability to organize and acquire collective intelligence on scientific issues. The new requirements of democracy and the complexification of decision-making processes mean science is now a public commodity, which is not reserved for scientists (Ruphy 2019; Laurent 2019; Ohya 2019; Hiroi 2019).

The task today, and probably SSH's new mission, is to work towards this ideal by analyzing *how* the public can become a collective intelligence and contribute to science. One way to explore public participation in science is to study the rise of *crowdsourcing*—i.e. gathering data online by mass, open invitation as a method of discovery—as an example of collective intelligence. Who does not use Wikipedia? Crowdsourcing systems are becoming very popular in a variety of fields and for a wide range of online tasks. Common crowdsourcing scenarios include data gathering (asking volunteers to tag a picture or a video), document editing (online collective writing, Wikipedia), collaborative intelligence (asking residents to identify old city maps). Crowdsourcing has a variety of uses, but for science, it means the process of getting desired ideas or content by asking for contributions from a large group of people, and especially from an online community, rather than from traditional suppliers or sources or experts.

Increasingly, governments across the world are using crowdsourcing for knowledge seeking and civic engagement. Decision-making in building and assessing public policies can no longer rely on purely technical expertise, nor on analytical tools that have demonstrated their unsuitability to contexts with substantial epistemic, ethical, and political imperatives.

SSH research provides a look at new methods and changes in the forms of public decision-making: how inclusion is built through the analysis of Big Data and through the integration of values, which implies citizen participation. Here the advent of Big Data—the mass production of information through scientific experiments, sensors, and populations equipped with communication technology—is not only a technological revolution, it is a *new method of discovery*. Analyses of Big Data focus just as much on major trends as on minor facts emerging from mass data; they change the stakes of social and scientific decision-making by taking into account neglected data or reconfigured indicators. At a time when we hear so much about "changes in behavior," analyses of Big Data make the phenomena and transformations underway in society visible, and the emerging innovations discernible. These are the changes and processes that are at work but not always perceived.

Within this new paradigm for knowledge production, we may envision a sensible concept of *citizen science*. Citizen science is defined as scientific work undertaken by members of the general public, in collaboration with or under the direction of professional scientists and scientific institutions. It has evolved over the past decade from amateur knowledge to an almost legitimate scientific method in itself. Recent projects have placed more emphasis on scientifically sound practices.

Work in SSH has advanced conceptual models of knowledge and decision-making that go beyond the over-simplistic linear and deficit models that characterize prior research and continue to dominate public policy discussions. Understanding these new knowledge and decision-making systems requires conceptual frameworks and methodological approaches drawn from SSH research. This is the condition of the rise of collective intelligence. Of course, this process is not without its drawbacks, as illustrated by the issue of fake news. In this context, it is important to define criteria for prioritizing between different sources of information and to develop a critical discussion on the conditions of this decentralized model of knowledge production. What is certain is that decision-making in building and assessing public policy can no longer rely on purely technical expertise. SSH research allows to look at new methods and areas of transformation in the forms and modes of public decision-making: the construction of inclusion through analysis of Big Data, and through the integration of values, which implies citizen participation.

1.5 Key Contribution(s) of the Book: Well-Being as the Ultimate Criterion for Innovation

This book is far from being the first to focus on social innovation. However, it has some qualities that, we believe, differentiate it from previous contributions such as, Thomas and René (2013), Franz et al. (2012), Nicholls et al. (2015) or Moulaert et al. (2014). These authors have already emphasized the potential contribution of social innovation. Some of the topics covered by their books (such as applications in the fields of health and environment) will also be examined in our book, but we believe our approach broader and more coherent.

This volume is the unique and original result of a discussion that shows the limits of a purely technological approach to innovation, whereas the above books use social innovation as their discussion's starting point. Our approach justifies why social innovation should be our primary concern, and our perspective is at the same time broader and more systematic. As it is based on an interdisciplinary approach, we hope it will engage readers from various disciplines in the discussion. In other words, our view is that this book's exploration of a key issue (social innovation) by gathering scholars from different disciplines and backgrounds constitutes its main quality. Its major contribution, therefore, is to present an original and truly interdisciplinary approach to innovation by some of the best specialists in the field, while offering a new and coherent vision of innovation based on both a broad overview and detailed case studies from diverse sectors and technologies. In doing so, we are providing an analysis based on the social sciences, not a manifesto for social innovation.

In the following section, we will expand on what we believe are the key contributions in this volume, namely, the importance of well-being as a criterion for directing research and assessing its quality, and the conditions of participatory sciences.

As discussed above, (human) well-being should be the ultimate criterion piloting the direction of science (Joly 2019; Oki 2019; Gaudillière 2019; Pestre 2019; Ruphy 2019; Hiroi 2019). One of the key ideas of this volume is that science has an increased responsibility and its social impact is not only felt at the end of the scientific process, when the social *consequences* of some discovery, development, or program become clear. People must be at the center of the process, not at its conclusion. What is called "societal" today is the simple recognition of the fact that the Earth is inhabited by humans and other living beings. This reveals what is so important about well-being: care, that is attention to the vulnerabilities of humans, necessarily means care for the world (Hiroi 2019; Laugier 2016), because these vulnerabilities are shared with others (animal species, environmental systems, etc.).

But, ultimately, what is well-being? How can it be defined or measured? The notion of well-being was specifically invented to take into consideration inequalities in well-being. In their work, Sen (1999, 2009) and Nussbaum (2011) set out to find a tool for comparing *well-being* between different countries and to contribute to a theory of justice. Their definition of the term "capability" refers to what an individual can do or be: a set of possibilities (most often interdependent) for choosing and acting. Sen (1999, 2009) sees the concept of capability as a diagnostic tool against what he calls "entrenched" inequalities: inequalities that are so rooted in a society that they are no longer experienced as unjust by those who are subject to them. Nussbaum proposes a list of "ten fundamental capabilities" that every just government must guarantee its citizens. For her, these ten capabilities form the crux of a good human life. Among them are: a normal life-span, enough to eat, good health, participation in political life, control of one's natural life environment. Nussbaum's list is a tool for contestation and also for discussion of the justice that a state can guarantee its citizens. But this list also suggests a core mission for science, which is to guarantee these capabilities, and not only for those living in Western countries.[7]

---

[7]It is worth noting here that globalization has not only expanded our knowledge, but also our concern for others, including those who are geographically or temporally far away. Networks currently play a key role, but they must reject their traditional roles. Some still want them to educate the public in order to encourage social acceptance of new technologies, or to simply measure the "impacts" of choices already made. They must instead develop with SSH research in order to inform public debate, nourish democratic discussion and analyze innovations that emerge from society. For example, the solutions found by people who have to monitor their electricity consumption in order to save money

1.6 Key Contribution(s) of the Book: Participatory and Citizen Sciences

The idea of participatory or citizen sciences—the second major contribution of this volume—is connected to the previous section's discussion on well-being, but approached from a different angle. It goes one step further, moving on from science *for* society to science *with* and *by* society.[8] This new approach to science is justified by the fact that citizens are directly affected by scientific progress in their daily life; it is therefore reasonable that they have a say in the process. Public decisions and deliberation must meet new criteria: the common good, inclusiveness, global solidarity, social and environmental utility and responsibility (Ruphy 2019; Laurent 2019; Hiroi 2019). Policy must accept multiple and competing mechanisms of consultation and must strive to include public authorities, scientific experts, and ordinary citizens in developing renewed, relevant criteria and indicators for data collection and mining.

Public participation in research and innovation is thus a way to foster responsible research and innovation. There are two options: citizen participation in defining science's agenda, and citizen participation in scientific research itself. The most common practices for the first option, in the present state of affairs, involve a *juxtaposition* of different actors: eminent scientists, elected representatives, spokespersons of the private sectors, sometimes other stakeholders of lay society (but the participation of lay citizens remains anecdotal) sit around a table and deliberate. As emphasized by Ruphy (2019), this is rarely satisfactory because it eventually leads to a power struggle between various groups defending their own interests. Thus, the discussion about the most adequate participatory processes has only just begun and the debate is extremely polarized between different possibilities, from the market to elected representation and/or to direct participation.

The second option is even more radical as it calls for citizens to participate in scientific research itself. By adding crowdsourcing, Big Data, community-based research, and open data into our research toolkit we can sketch the shape of a "participatory" science on the basis of the public's proven capacities for organizing and regulating the gathering and sharing of data and information, the role of citizens in scientific research, in a context where there is strong demand by the public to be included in handling matters that concern the quality of life of future generations.

Within this new paradigm of knowledge production, we can imagine science *with* society. The question then becomes in what ways good science emerges from citizen practices (Ruphy 2019; Laurent 2019; Ohya 2019; Hiroi 2019). An interesting example is biohacking, or do-it-yourself (DIY) biology, which can be placed within the broader open science movement. SSH researchers were the first to call attention to this phenomenon, which is more and more commonplace, attracting an increasing number of practitioners, academics, scientists, students, citizens, hackers, artists,

---

are of interest for current research on energy insecurity. This has nothing to do with behavior changes, but rather with immanent social innovation.

[8] In what follows, we put aside the epistemological discussion, which is well developed by Ruphy (2019), to focus on the political dimension.

and potential entrepreneurs. DIY biology is a continuation of this longer tradition of amateurs and professionals co-producing scientific knowledge and a successor to crowdsourcing methods. However, there is also a break with what came before. As the DIY biology community grows and spreads across the world, several crucial issues are raised about science and society. DIY biology is a sociopolitical movement that provides citizens a counter-power in the societal choices concerning the use of these technologies. To do this is not only to practice better science, science that is more attentive to the well-being of others, it is simply how to practice science in our shared vulnerable world.

DIY biology enables new partnerships between amateur and professional scientists and, hence, science with society. It is a good example of scientific progress through democratization. It represents both a conceptual and epistemological ambition as it aims to create a stronger form of self by providing ordinary people with access to scientific research, by helping them transform themselves into active producers of science.

1.7 Content of the Book

Part 1 of this book offers different critical views on innovation. Pierre-Benoît Joly (2019) explores our topic from the perspective of non-standard economics. He proposes to "reimagine" innovation by dispelling five myths and by looking in detail at three schools of thought that enrich the mainstream vision of innovation, namely "democratizing innovation", "responsible innovation", "transformative change". Sayaka Oki (2019) continues this reflection through the history of sciences and ideas, by looking at innovation both as an ideology and a historical concept. Oki's key argument is that "innovation" has gradually replaced "progress" as an instrument and as a value to be pursued by society. As a businessman, Shinichi Koizumi (2019) offers yet a different perspective. He gives a critical analysis of the so-called Fourth Industrial Revolution. This is the term usually used to describe the on-going technological transformations, based on how physical systems interconnect with digital Big Data, deriving from further development of disruptive and innovative technologies, such as artificial intelligence, robotics and IoT.

Parts 2 and 3 of the book use the above general reflections as a basis on which to analyze several cases studies in two major fields of application, the health and biotechnology sector and the environment, respectively, where innovation beyond technology is particularly meaningful. Robert Boyer (2019) shows that in order to understand the evolution of the healthcare sector, it is impossible to separate scientific breakthroughs from social innovation. Jean-Paul Gaudillière (2019) builds on the concept of alternative modernity by looking at the history of science and medicine outside Europe. Shintaro Sengoku (2019) undertakes a case study of a regional biotechnology industry, namely an experiment in consortium-based open innovation in Japan.

1 Innovation Beyond Technology—Introduction

Part 3, which focuses on environmental issues, is most obviously motivated by the Fukushima incident. Dominique Pestre (2019) gives a compelling argument that, contrary to a popular opinion, technology was never the solution to environmental issues. Takayoshi Kusago (2019) examines the United Nations' sustainable development goals (SDGs) and the way in which they fall short in the face of recovery from natural and man-made disasters, as exemplified by the Great East Japan Earthquake that occurred on 11 March 2011. Yuko Fujigaki (2019) focuses on the relationship between nuclear power plants (NPP) and society in Japan in the wake of the Fukushima Daiichi Nuclear Accidents in March 2011.

In Part 4 of this volume, we develop this last idea by asking another set of questions related to the relationship between innovation and society: innovation for whom and for what? This part starts with the contribution of Stéphanie Ruphy (2019), in which she discusses the conditions of public participation in science or "citizen science." Brice Laurent (2019) looks at city experiments in San Francisco. Such experiments are at the center of Takehiro Ohya's work (2019), where he conducts a legal discussion based on the famous "trolley" problem. This thought experiment is often used to illustrate the difficulty of choosing between two alternatives, and thus to show the danger of leaving such choices to non-human entities, such as AIs. Finally, Yoshinori Hiroi (2019) returns to our initial question about the legitimate goals of science in a post-growth context. By revisiting the two sectors that are examined in Parts 2 and 3 of this book (health and environment, analyzed from the perspective of renewable energy), he proposes a vision of "science as care" as a possible direction for science in post-growth society, based on a new relationship between technological innovation and social environments. In conclusion, the journey through this book has led us to believe in the possibility of a "sustainable welfare society".

References

Amable, B. (2003). *The diversity of modern capitalism*. Oxford: Oxford University Press.

Aoki, M., & Dore, R. (Eds.). (1994). *The Japanese firm: Sources of competitive strength*. Oxford: Oxford University Press.

Boyer, R. (2019). How scientific breakthroughs and social innovations shape the evolution of the healthcare sector. In S. Lechevalier (Ed.), *Innovation beyond technology* (pp. 89–119). Berlin: Springer.

Callon, M. (1981). Pour une sociologie des controverses socio-techniques. *Fundamenta Scientiae, 2*(3/4), 381–399.

Card, D., & DiNardo, J. E. (2002). Skill-biased technological change and rising wage inequality: Some problems and puzzles. *Journal of Labor Economics, 20*(4), 733–783.

Cohen, D. (2018). *The infinite desire for growth*. Princeton: Princeton University Press.

Collingridge, D. (1980). *The social construction of technology*. London: Frances Pinter.

Descola, P. (2005). *Par-delà nature et culture*. Paris: Gallimard.

Dewey, J. (1981). *The philosophy of John Dewey*. In J. J. McDermott (Ed.).

Franz, H.-W., Hochgerner, J., & Howaldt, J. (Eds.). (2012). *Challenge social innovation. Potentials for business, social entrepreneurship, welfare and civil society*. Berlin: Springer.

Freeman, C. (1974). *The economics of industrial innovation* (1st ed.). Harmondsworth: Penguin Books.

Freeman, C. (1995). The "National System of Innovation" in historical perspective. *Cambridge Journal of Economics, 1995*(19), 5–24.

Fujigaki, Y. (2019). Lessons from Fukushima for responsible innovation: How to construct a new relationship between science and society? In S. Lechevalier (Ed.), *Innovation beyond technology* (pp. 223–239). Berlin: Springer.

Gaudillière, J. P. (2019). From crisis to reformulation: Innovation in the global drug industry and the alternative modernization of Indian Ayurveda. In S. Lechevalier (Ed.), *Innovation beyond technology* (pp. 121–139). Berlin: Springer.

Godin, B. (2015). *Innovation contested—The idea of innovation over the centuries*. London: Routledge.

Haag, P., Lemieux, C., Remaud, O., Schaub, J.-F., Thireau, I., Désveaux, E., & de Fornel, M. (Eds.). (2012). *Faire des Sciences Sociales. Critiquer, comparer, généraliser*. Editions de l'Ecole des Hautes Etudes en Sciences Sociales.

Herman, R., & Avram, R. (2011). The contribution of the Neo-Schumpeterian approach to the development of the economic theory: Emphasis on the meso-economic level. *Theoretical and Applied Economics, XVIII*(7(560)), 111–132.

Hiroi, Y. (2019). Science as care: Science and innovation in post-growth society. In S. Lechevalier (Ed.), *Innovation beyond technology* (pp. 301–324). Berlin: Springer.

Howaldt, J., & Schwarz, M. (2010). Social innovation: Concepts, research fields and international trends. IMO international monitoring.

Joly, P. B. (2019). Reimagining innovation. In S. Lechevalier (Ed.), *Innovation beyond technology* (pp. 25–45). Berlin: Springer.

Joly, P. B. (2017). Beyond the competitiveness framework? Models of innovation revisited. *Journal of Economics and Management of Innovation, 1*(22), 79–96.

Joly, P. B., Rip, A., & Callon, M. (2010). Re-inventing innovation. In M. J. Arentsen, W. van Rossum, & A. E. Steenge (Eds.), *Governance of innovation*. Cheltenham: Edward Elgar.

Koizumi, S. (2019). The light and shadow of the fourth industrial revolution. In S. Lechevalier (Ed.), *Innovation beyond technology* (pp. 63–86). Berlin: Springer.

Kusago, T. (2019). Post-disaster community recovery and community-based collaborative action research—A case of process evaluation method for community life improvement. In S. Lechevalier (Ed.), *Innovation beyond technology* (pp. 195–221). Berlin: Springer.

Laugier, S. (2016). Politics of vulnerability and responsibility for ordinary others. *Critical Horizons, A Journal of Philosophy and Social Theory, 17.*

Laurent, B. (2019). Innovation for whom? City experiments and the redefinition of urban democracy. In S. Lechevalier (Ed.), *Innovation beyond technology* (pp. 265–283). Berlin: Springer.

Lazonick, W. (2013). The theory of innovative enterprise: Methodology, ideology, and institutions. In J. K. Moudud, C. Bina, & P. L. Mason (Eds.), *Alternative theories of competition: Challenges to the orthodoxy* (pp. 127–159). London: Routledge.

Lechevalier, S. (2006). Recent changes in the Japanese public research and innovation policies— Lessons for Europe. Research Project undertaken for European Union, Delegation of the European Commission to Japan.

Lechevalier, S. (2012). The Japanese firm: From the analysis of a model to the understanding of its increasing heterogeneity. In M. Dietrich & J. Krafft (Ed.), *Handbook on the economics and theory of the firm* (Chapter 16, pp. 194–208). Edward Elgar.

Lechevalier, S. (2014). *The great transformation of Japanese capitalism*. London: Routledge.

Lechevalier, S., Storz, C., & Nishimura, J. (2014). Diversity in patterns of industry evolution: How an "intrapreneurial" regime contributed to the emergence of the service robot industry in Japan. *Research Policy* (Special Section "The path-dependent dynamics of emergence and evolution of new industries"), *43*(10), 1716–1729.

Moulaert, F., MacCallum, D., Mehmood, A., & Hamdouch, A. (Eds.). (2014). *The international handbook on social innovation: Collective action, social learning and transdisciplinary research*. Edward Elgar Publishing Ltd.

Nature. (2010). «Asbestos scandal». 468, 868 (16 December 2010)

Nature. (2017). 542, 391.

Nicholls, A., Simon, J., Gabriel, M., & Whelan, C. (Eds.). (2015). *New frontiers in social innovation research*. Palgrave Macmillan.

Nussbaum, M. (2011). *Creating capabilities, the human development approach*. Cambridge: Harvard University Press.

OECD. (2005). *Innovation policy and performance. A cross country comparison*.

Ohya, T. (2019). Image of jurisprudence reconstructed to enhance innovation: Liability allocation for improved predictability. In S. Lechevalier (Ed.), *Innovation beyond technology* (pp. 285–299). Berlin: Springer.

Oki, S. (2019). 'Innovation' as an adaptation of 'Progress': Revisiting the epistemological and historical contexts of these terms. In S. Lechevalier (Ed.), *Innovation beyond technology* (pp. 47–62). Berlin: Springer.

Owen, R., Macnaghten, P., & Stilgoe, J. (2012). Responsible research and innovation: From science in society to science for society, with society. *Science and Public Policy, 39,* 751–760.

Pestre, D. (2019). Environment and social innovation: Why technology never was the solution. In S. Lechevalier (Ed.), *Innovation beyond technology* (pp. 175–194). Berlin: Springer.

Piketty, T. (2014). *Capital in the twenty-first century*. Cambridge: Harvard University Press.

Prahalad, C. K. (2005). *The fortune at the bottom of the pyramid: Eradicating poverty through profits*. Philadelphia: Wharton School Publishing.

Ruphy, S. (2019). Public participation in the setting of research and innovation agenda: Virtues and challenges from a philosophical perspective. In S. Lechevalier (Ed.), *Innovation beyond technology* (pp. 243–261). Berlin: Springer.

Schot, J., & Steinmueller, E. (2016). Framing innovation policy for transformative change: Innovation policy 3.0. Brighton: SPRU, Draft, 4/9/2016.

Schumpeter, J. A. (1943). *Capitalism, socialism and democracy*. London: Allen & Unwin.

Sen, A. (1999). *Development as freedom*. New York: Knopf.

Sen, A. (2009). *The idea of justice*. Harvard: Harvard University Press.

Sengoku, S. (2019). Consortium-based open innovation: Exploring a unique and optimal model for regional biotechnology industry. In S. Lechevalier (Ed.), *Innovation beyond technology* (pp. 141–171). Berlin: Springer.

Slade, G. (2009). *Made to break. Technology and obsolescence in America*. Cambridge, MA: Harvard University Press.

Soete, L. (2013). Is innovation always good? In J. Fagerberg, B. R. Martin, & E. S. Andersen (Eds.), *Innovation studies—Evolution and future challenges* (pp. 134–144). Oxford: Oxford University Press.

Thomas, O., & René, S. (Eds.). (2013). *Social innovation. Solutions for a sustainable future*. Berlin: Springer.

Veltz, P. (2017). La société hyper-industrielle, Le nouveau capitalisme productif, Seuil, coll. «La république des idées», 128 p.

von Hippel, E. (2004). *Democratizing innovation*. Cambridge, MA: MIT Press.

Part I
Critical Views on Innovation from Economics and History of Science, and Law

Chapter 2
Reimagining Innovation

Pierre-Benoit Joly

Abstract Innovation is presented as *the* solution to address grand societal challenges. Taking this new policy motto seriously requires to renew the dominant imaginary of innovation defined by a series of attributes—technology centeredness, market relatedness, competition, entrepreneurialism, diffusion, exclusivity and creative destruction—and above all by the belief that innovation is always good. To contribute to such an endeavour, this paper starts with the discussion of five innovation myths. This discussion of deep rooted beliefs that condition a narrow understanding of innovation and innovation policies is crucial for reimagining innovation. The presentation of three literature streams (Democratising innovation, Responsible innovation, Transformative change) that currently feed the innovation renewal allows consideration of explorations in academia as well as in public policy. A re-imagination and re-invention of innovation is underway, and this dynamic is constituted of different actors from different traditions but still has some limitations.

2.1 Introduction

In 1932, in the wake of the great depression, a New York real estate broker, Bernard London, published his essay *Ending the Depression Through Planned Obsolescence* which introduced the concept of 'planned obsolescence'.

> People generally, in a frightened and hysterical mood, are using everything that they own longer than was their custom before the depression. In the earlier period of prosperity, the American people did not wait until the last possible bit of use had been extracted from every commodity. They replaced old articles with new for reasons of fashion and up-to-datedness. They gave up old homes and old automobiles long before they were worn out, merely because they were obsolete. Perhaps, prior to the panic, people were too extravagant; if so, they have now gone to the other extreme and have become retrenchment-mad. People everywhere are today disobeying the law of obsolescence. They are using their old cars, their old tires, their old radios and their old clothing much longer than statisticians had expected.

P.-B. Joly (✉)
LISIS (CNRS, ESIEE Paris, INRA, UPEM), Marne-la-Vallée, France
e-mail: joly@inra-ifris.org

© Springer Nature Singapore Pte Ltd. 2019
S. Lechevalier (ed.), *Innovation Beyond Technology*, Creative Economy,
https://doi.org/10.1007/978-981-13-9053-1_2

As a solution to the economic crisis, London recommended that government should apply management and planning to undoing obsolete jobs from the past. Government should "assign a lease of life to shoes and homes and machines, to all products of manufacture (…) when they are first created." After their allotted time has expired, these things will legally be "dead" and would be controlled and destroyed in the case of widespread unemployment (Slade 2009). London's idea of planned obsolescence has become common practice. However, currently, government rules and controls are not needed; obsolescence is constructed technically through a set of practical elements that artificially reduce product lifetimes. The example of smartphones—with Apple taken to court accused of reducing the technical capacity of older versions of its star product, the iPhone—is a mere drop in the ocean. The practice of planned obsolescence has become widespread in the consumer society where innovation is considered as always good. However, the limitations of our planet are forcing us to consider seriously the damage wrought by an economic system based on planned obsolescence, and to challenge the underpinning socio-technical logic. Innovation does not systematically result in creative destruction. It can, contrary to Schumpeter's central thesis, be a destructive creation (Soete 2013).

Such reflections are crucial in an age when innovation is seen as *the* solution to major challenges such as climate change, world food security, natural resources depletion, an ageing society, etc. Hence, this paper's main objective is to reflect critically on the concept of innovation and to contribute to its reimagination.

This paper continues a research stream that originated many years earlier on the way innovation is understood, and on the shortcomings of current innovation policies. In a recent paper (Joly 2017), I argue that the 'master narrative' or innovation imaginary is defined by the attributes of technology centeredness, market relatedness, competition, entrepreneurialism, diffusion, exclusivity and creative destruction. I use the concepts of "models of innovation" to characterize different ways of innovating explored and experimented with by many actors. Models of innovation are conceptual frameworks that provide a stylised representation of how innovation is generated. These frameworks both describe the reality 'out there', and act as lenses to view and interpret this reality, and when shared widely they play a performative role (Joly et al. 2010). They guide how collectively, we see and order the world through its histories and its futures, and in this respect these models constitute a central part of what Sheila Jasanoff calls sociotechnical imaginaries (Jasanoff and Kim 2015). Models of innovation include not only economic impact and competitiveness but also the distribution of power and agency, collective learning, social relations, etc. They are value-laden and they embed a dimension of the social order; hence, they are also models of society. Finally, models of innovation involve not only discourses but also institutional devices, organisations, practices. The policies formulated follow these innovation models, although often unconsciously.

This paper deals with the same issues but in a different and complementary way. The aim is to explore why the understanding of innovation is associated so closely to this master narrative, and to highlight different initiatives and research streams that challenge this entrenched imaginary. First, I discuss five deeply-rooted innovation myths which are the pillars of the sociotechnical imaginaries of innovation. Critical reflection on these myths is an important step in the questioning of this imaginary and opening up innovation. In the second part of the paper, I adopt a different perspective focused on three streams of literature offering alternative visions of innovation and innovation policies.

The problem of values is the common thread running through this paper. The main idea is that there is a strong link between the way we value the outcomes of our actions, the way we know, and the way we act. Hence, raising the problem of values, valuing and valuation (Dewey 2013) is necessary for opening up innovation.

2.2 Challenging Some Deeply-Rooted Innovation Myths

In a long term research project "The idea of innovation," devoted to the intellectual and conceptual history of innovation, Benoit Godin poses three important questions:

> First, why has innovation acquired such a central place in our society or, put differently, where precisely does the idea of innovation come from? Second, why is innovation spontaneously understood as technological innovation? Third, why is the idea of innovation often restricted to commercialized innovation? (http://www.csiic.ca/en/the-idea-of-innovation/)

My discussion of the innovation myths is in line with his second and third questions. It is aimed at identifying and debating a set of strongly entrenched beliefs that constitute the pillars of the socio-technical imaginary of innovation. Of course, there are different ways to identify and present these myths. Here, I chose to be sufficiently comprehensive to take account of the different unquestioned beliefs that anchor the imaginary of innovation. The 1st and the 5th myths are the cornerstones of the mainstream master frame. Innovation policies aim at fostering innovation, assuming that it is always good (myth 5) and that, although considered in the competitiveness frame, innovation will increase available resources for dealing with the different challenges we face (myth 1). Myths 2, 3 and 4 are more closely related with disruptive innovation policies understood as the impact of research and innovation investments that allow to create new technologies.

"Myth 1—Trickle-down innovation" allows discussion of the strong association between innovation and the competitiveness frame, and the idea that the maximisation of economic value through innovation is the solution to all kinds of problems. Market mechanisms are of course important but if innovation is to be the solution to all challenges, we need to consider other values as well as economic value, and take the multi-dimensionality and directionality of innovation seriously.

"Myth 2—The linear model of innovation" which has been much discussed in the literature. It remains fixed, and discussion of it reveals the diversity among innovation models and sources of innovation.

"Myth 3—Innovation is driven by (new) technologies" is a central belief discussed in the various contributions in this book. We would include also the obsession with novelty, and suggest the need to shift from a culture of novelty and disruption to the heuristic of continuity, recycling and incremental improvement.

"Myth 4—The technology selected is always the best" which leads me to introduce the idea of path-dependency and lock-in effects that characterize socio-technical trajectories. Socio-technical transitions constitute a major problem barely considered by innovation policy, and especially when what is at stake is the discontinuation of a socio-technical system (what we call *out*-novation).

"Myth 5—Innovation as creative destruction" is the master myth alluded to in the introduction. If we consider that innovation is not always good, there is an urgent need to reflect on technical democracy as new power/knowledge configurations.

2.2.1 Myth 1—Trickle-Down Innovation

The myth of trickle-down innovation is borrowed from the myth of trickle-down economics, i.e. the idea that what the rich enjoy today will benefit the poor tomorrow (Bozeman and Sarewitz 2011). The core assumption is that reducing taxes on businesses and high income stimulates investment in the short term, and benefits society at large in the long term. The myth of trickle-down economics is challenged by empirical evidence which shows that since the 1980s (and the implementation of neo-liberal policies that led to tax cuts for high earners) the degree of inequality has increased sharply (Piketty 2013).

The myth of trickle-down innovation refers to the belief that the creation of wealth through innovation will not only benefit the impoverished but also will solve the major societal problems, including environmental. There is a widespread belief that investment in research and innovation is the best way to address grand challenges.

The European Commission is an emblematic example of this policy discourse. Since 2010, innovation has been seen as *the* solution to major societal challenges (climate change, depletion of fossil fuel resources, ageing societies, etc.), and is expected to boost competitiveness, maintain employment and protect our social models.

> As public deficits increase and as our labor force begins to shrink, what will be the basis for Europe's future competitiveness? How will we create new growth and jobs? How will we get Europe's economy back on track? How will we tackle growing societal challenges like climate change, energy supply, the scarcity of resources and the impact of demographic changes? How will we improve health and security and sustainably provide water and high-quality, affordable food? **The only answer is innovation**, which is at the core of the Europe 2020 Strategy. (Horizon 2020, Innovation Union, emphasis added)

The strength of the trickle-down innovation myth rests on several entrenched beliefs. First, technological fix, i.e. the idea that technology will provide the solutions to the problems confronting us, and that if these solutions bring new problems (damage related to use of the new technology), further technological progress will provide new solutions. Geoengineering is a representative example of the belief that technology can address any problem we might face.

The second belief is that resources are fungible, and hence, in some way unlimited. Economic growth and wealth will provide the resources needed to produce new knowledge and new technologies to address society's problems. The fact that

Malthus's prophecy of doom has not come true reinforces the belief that technology and innovative capacity continually push back the boundaries to the planet.

The strength of this myth lies also in the fact that it does not challenge our way of life or the current distribution of resources and social relations.[1] For instance, genetically modified organisms (GMOs) have been portrayed as the solution to the food security problem whereas foresight exercises demonstrate that a shift from animal to plant protein would allow us to 'feed the world' without increasing agricultural production (Paillard et al. 2014). Similarly, geoengineering is touted as the technical solution to climate change and does not necessitate a change to our way of life.

This myth can be challenged on different premises. Dominique Pestre (2019) shows that the green economy has not led to a significant reduction in the pressure exerted by human activity on natural resources. This may be explained—inter alia—by the rebound effect, i.e. the reduction (due to behavioral or other systemic responses) in the expected gains from new technologies that enable more efficient use of resources. Also, the scientific evidence is increasingly alarming; for instance, the Alliance of World Scientists[2] "warning to humanity" signed by more than 15,000 scientists.

> To prevent widespread misery and catastrophic biodiversity loss, humanity must practice a more environmentally sustainable alternative to business as usual. This prescription was well articulated by the world's leading scientists 25 years ago, but in most respects, we have not heeded their warning. Soon it will be too late to shift course away from our failing trajectory, and time is running out. We must recognize, in our day-to-day lives and in our governing institutions, that Earth with all its life is our only home. (Ripple et al. 2017)

If we are to challenge the myth of trickle-down innovation we must learn to consider that innovation involves more than competitiveness. Innovation defined as future society in the making, goes beyond this framing. Accordingly, the value of innovation is not limited to economic value. As Stirling (2009) suggests, we need to take account of the multi-dimensionality of innovation, and hence, both its directionality and distributional effects. New generations of approaches to measuring the impact of research beyond economic impact are crucial for opening up the valuation process and hopefully, providing new instruments for implementing directionality (Bozeman and Sarewitz 2011; Joly et al. 2015).

---

[1] Needless to quote the U.S. president George H. W. Bush: "The American way of life is not up for negotiation".

[2] http://scientistswarning.forestry.oregonstate.edu/.

2.2.2 Myth 2—The Linear Model of Innovation[3]

The so-called linear model postulates that innovation starts with basic research, and is followed by applied research and development, and finally production and diffusion.[4] It defines the roles of various actors and the division of labor, and offers a diagnosis of what is happening and what should be improved. The origin of this model can be attributed to Joseph Schumpeter and Vannevar Bush (Godin 2015).[5] Schumpeter made a clear distinction between invention and innovation, two processes that correspond to different motivations, competences and norms. Entrepreneurs are innovators; they have the ability to bring radical change by designing new products, and implementing new processes of production or new organisations. They are motivated by the potential economic benefits that are conditioned by the temporary monopoly associated to their advance in the diffusion of innovation. Bush's report *Science: the Endless Frontier* (1945) also is seen as a pillar of the linear model. By pursuing research in the "purest realms of science" scientists can build the foundations for new products and processes to deliver health, full employment and military security for the nation. Hence, public funding of basic research is vital for social progress and economic growth:

> "Advances in science when put to practical use mean more jobs, higher wages, shorter hours, more abundant crops, more leisure for recreation, for study, for learning how to live the deadening drudgery which has been the burden of the common man for past ages. Advances in science will also bring higher standards of living, will lead to the prevention or cure of diseases, will promote conservation of our limited resources, and will assure means of defense against aggression" (p. 10). "Without scientific progress no amount of achievement in other directions can insure our health, prosperity, and security as a nation in the modern world" (p. 11). (V. Bush, The Endless Frontier, quoted in Godin 2006: 644)

History of technology and innovation studies have for long challenged the model of innovation from various directions. Rosenberg (1982) argues convincingly that technology is not merely the application of scientific knowledge. It is itself a body of knowledge about certain classes of events and activities.[6] In the academic milieu, innovation generally is considered an interactive process. The chain-link model proposed by Kline and Rosenberg (1986) may be seen as a kind of consensual representation. Interactions are the crucial element in the process; knowledge is diverse (scientific knowledge, technological knowledge, action knowledge, etc.); scientific

---

[3] This section draws on Joly (2017).

[4] Such an imaginary draws on a strong link between innovation and progress. For an inspiring discussion of this link, see Oki (2019).

[5] For an interesting challenge of the myth of the linear model, see Edgerton (2004). Against this, Sarewitz (2016) demonstrates that the linear model is not only a contemporary invention but that it has had a central place in the imaginary of scientific institutions and innovation policies since WWII.

[6] Among the various examples he gives, the discovery of thermodynamics is probably among the most emblematic: "*Sadi Carnot's remarkable accomplishment in creating the science of thermodynamics was an attempt of the attempt, a half century or so after Watt's great innovation, to understand what determined the efficiency of steam engines*" (Rosenberg 1982: 142).

knowledge very often is produced as the answer to a practical problem; technological tools and infrastructure condition the agenda of research. This emphasis on the role of interactions has lead innovation studies to broaden the analytical scope and to take account of the innovation systems in which they are embedded (Fagerberg and Verspagen 2009).

However, despite a broadening of the notion of innovation in academia, institutions responsible for innovation policy continue to tend to adopt the definition of innovation proposed in the 1960s. To illustrate the lasting influence of the linear model, one could cite the European Union's Lisbon Agenda, the objective of 3% of GDP invested in research, and the shaping of the knowledge economy. This vision has led to implicit or explicit assertions that *"Science is the solution, society the problem"*. Society is expected to become more entrepreneurial, to become more accepting of and enthusiastic about new technology. It can be seen as the 21st century version of the Chicago World Exhibition's catchphrase that "society has to conform".

2.2.3 Myth 3—Innovation Is Driven by (New) Technologies

Although the definition of innovation often is broad and not limited to technological innovation (see for instance the definition in the Oslo Manual[7]), in the public arena, the term innovation generally is associated to technology. This is reflected in some of the most famous rankings of innovation, for instance Thomson Reuters which focuses on patents as a proxy for the capacity to innovate.[8] Some of these rankings have the ambition to implement a more comprehensive view, thus integrating a wide variety of sources of innovation including the human factor and entrepreneurship (see for instance, the Global Innovation Index[9]). However, the association with technology, and specifically new technologies remains very strong. It would be hard to imagine an Innovation Forum that would not stage nanotechnologies, digital technologies, big data in biology, etc.

The close association between innovation and technology is related to the technological fix discussed above. The technological solution avoids researching solutions that would imply societal changes. Also, there is a bias toward *new* technologies. The solutions will be found in new technology, not improvements to old ones. The historian of technology David Edgerton shows that this bias toward novelty is deep rooted. In *Shock of the Old* (Edgerton 2006), Edgerton demonstrates that historians of technology generally study technologies in their emergent stage and rarely look at technologies in use. Take for instance, the example of the Green Revolution. The

---

[7]Oslo Manual: "An innovation is the implementation of a new or significantly improved product (good or service). A product innovation is the introduction of a good or service. A process innovation is the implementation of a new or significantly improved production or delivery method." (OECD 2005).

[8]http://top100innovators.clarivate.com/content/methodology.

[9]https://www.globalinnovationindex.org/.

imaginary of the Green Revolution is associated to genetics and the diffusion of so-called high yielding varieties (HYV) which earned Norman Borlaugh his Nobel Peace Prize. However, recent research on the Green Revolution in India demonstrates that the increase in wheat production had little to do with HYV (Subramanian 2015). Rather, it was driven by rapid expansion of irrigation, facilitated not by Nehru's big dams but by small, privately-owned, traditional groundwater pumps. By highlighting the key role played by one of the oldest agricultural techniques (irrigation) in what was assumed to be a revolution based on new technologies, this research challenges the dominant view of innovation.[10]

Paying attention to technology in use, to incremental improvement and to maintenance calls for a Copernican revolution in innovation studies. It forces scholars to shift from the fascination with novelty to the heuristic of continuity (Joly 2015). Currently, a range of experiences run in this direction which materializes in the proliferation of new expressions such as: frugal innovation, grassroots innovation, reverse innovation or innovation from the bottom of the pyramid (Prahalad 2005). This goes along with a new geography (the "South" as a key source of innovation), and a new cosmology (the "users" at the core) of innovation. Hence, there is a need not only to acknowledge the non-technical sources of innovation but also to shift from a culture of novelty and disruption to a culture of incrementalism, recycling and maintenance.

2.2.4 Myth 4—The Technology Selected Is Always the Best[11]

The belief that technological competitions are, like sports competitions, processes that allow selection of "the best", is strongly anchored. Since the 1980s, the sociology of innovation, and the economics of technical change have been grounded on a very different assumption, namely that a technique is not used widely because it is intrinsically better but that it becomes the best because it is widely used.

For scholars who adopt a constructivist approach to technology (e.g. social construction of technology—SCOT, Bijker et al. 1987) the idea that technologies are not selected because they are most effective is obvious. The adoption of this idea by economists has been more difficult. Brian Arthur and Paul David, economists working at the Santa Fe Institute and Stanford University, helped to revise the myth of selection of best techniques by the market (Arthur 1989; David 1986). Studying technology competition, they show that increasing returns from adoption is a key explanation. If we assume that the efficiency of a technology is positively related to the number of users, then competition among technologies can produce surprising effects such as the exclusion of intrinsically superior techniques, or even lock-into technologies with lower intrinsic value. Under this hypothesis, competition models show that small events (Arthur) or historical accident (David) can give an initial

---

[10]Robert Boyer (2019) shows that innovation in healthcare is not merely determined by technological changes since it is conditioned by institutional arrangements.

[11]This section draws on Joly (2016).

advantage to one technology although it may not be intrinsically superior; cumulative effects do the rest.

Several examples are cited regularly. For instance, the QWERTY typewriter (and now computer) keyboard is a legacy of a design that took account of physical constraints (transmission by means of bars) to achieve greater efficiency which has proved impossible to displace although according to ergonomics other keyboard designs are more efficient (the CLIO keyboard seems to be the best). Another exemplar from the nuclear field is the diffusion of light water reactors despite the claim of many specialists that gas cooling would have proved more efficient if as many resources had been devoted to its development as were invested in light water reactors (Cowan 1990). The assumption of increasing returns to adoptions runs counter to the previous general assumption in economics. Increasing returns can be explained empirically by five complementary phenomena: (i) strong learning by doing; (ii) network externalities; (iii) economies of scale; (iv) informational increasing returns; and (v) technological complementarities. These features are applicable to most current and emerging technologies.

Taking account of the diversity of technological pathways is one of the important implications of this research stream. In the presence of high increasing returns, the exclusion of alternative techniques can be too rapid and too broad. It may be necessary to enact policy to incentivise the exploration of a wide range of options (Callon 1994; Stirling 2008). Also, in situations where technologies have high negative unintended effects, it may be necessary to imagine how to withdraw socio-technical elements (Goulet and Vinck 2012) which would require learning how to govern *out*novation processes.[12]

2.2.5 Myth 5—Innovation as Creative Destruction

Innovation as creative destruction can be considered the master myth. This myth is associated to Joseph Schumpeter who conceptualised innovation and the role of the entrepreneur as the drivers of economic development and stated forcefully that the destruction of existing elements is necessary for the creation of new ones.

> The fundamental impulse that sets and keeps the capitalist engine in motion comes from the new consumers' goods, the new methods of production or transportation, the new markets, the new forms of industrial organization that capitalist enterprise creates.
>
> [...] The opening up of new markets, foreign or domestic, and the organizational development from the craft shop and factory to such concerns as U.S. Steel illustrate the process of industrial mutation that incessantly revolutionizes the economic structure from within, incessantly destroying the old one, incessantly creating a new one. (Schumpeter 1942: 82–83).

That the birth of something new is conditioned by the destruction of something that exists is an old idea. Reinert and Reinert (2006) remind us that the Greeks inherited

---

[12]To learn more about outnovation, one can refer to the analysis of the governance of discontinuation of socio-technical systems. See the DiscGo project and the contribution of Stegmaier et al. (2014).

the myth of Phoenix from the bird Bennu in Egyptian mythology, symbolising the rising sun.

> Bennu or Phoenix was consumed to ashes, but out of the ashes grew a new Phoenix which, in time, repeated the 500 year cycle. In medieval Christian writings Phoenix was a symbol of the Resurrection of Christ, in itself a prime example of creative destruction.

The vision of creative destruction leads to a particular view of history in which the arrow of progress is associated to cyclicality. On the one hand, as with the Phoenix and its 500-year cycles, creative destruction leads to cyclical rather than linear historical patterns: take Schumpeter's 'clustering of innovations' as the basic cause of long economic (Kondratieff) cycles. On the other hand, new cycles are associated to new core technologies which are supposed to be better than the old ones. The steam engine and railroads were replaced by electricity, the internal combustion engine, oil and chemistry, which are being replaced by electronics and informatics, biotechnology, etc. New cycles bring economic and social progress (Perez 2002; Freeman and Louca 2001).

Hence, the myth of creative destruction is associated to the idea that innovation is always good. In this frame, actors who contest innovation are laggards. Against this, sociology and the history of technology show that controversies and contestations have played an important role in the innovation process (see inter alia Callon 1981; Rip 1986; Oki 2019; Pestre 2019; Fujigaki 2019). The concerns over the potential (economic, social and environmental) damage caused by new technologies led to the institutionalisation of technology assessment, first in the US with the establishment in 1972 of the Office of Technology Assessment, and then in most European countries in the 1980s and 1990s. However, de facto, technology assessment operates as a tool for improving and fostering technological change, not controlling it (Collingridge 1980; Joly 2015).

In a paper entitled "Is innovation always good?" Luc Soete, one of the leading economists of innovation, warned that contrary to mainstream beliefs, the creative part of innovation does not necessarily outweigh its destructive aspects (Soete 2013). Soete shows how innovations in consumer goods have led our societies to "a conspicuous consumption path of innovation-led 'destructive creation' growth" (Soete 2013:136).

> Easy and cheap ways in which existing usage value can be destroyed are, for example, through product design and restrictive aftermarket practices, and in the extreme case through so-called 'planned obsolescence' purposely limiting the life-span of particular consumer goods. (...) Probably the most extreme and widespread case would be new product design, for instance in fashion clothing or shoes, destroying existing output, but there are of course many other forms and sorts of restrictive aftermarket practices that can be found in many ICT-related sectors, such as software writers limiting backward compatibility, or electronic goods manufacturers ceasing to supply essential after-sales services or spare parts for older products, not to mention smart phones, mobiles, iPods, or iPads. It is actually surprising in how many areas processes of 'destructive creation' exist that hinder prolonged usage and induce customers to migrate continuously to newer models. (Soete 2013: 138)

As mentioned in the introduction to this chapter, the concept of planned obsolescence originated at the beginning of the XXth Century as a response to the economic crisis. Historians of technology have shown how planned obsolescence became a systematic pattern in the production and consumption of goods (Slade 2009). Heinz Wisman, a French philosopher, takes an extensive view of planned obsolescence and argues that it is the result of a desire-based economy invented in the late XIXth Century, a time when innovation was decoupled from progress, and novelty became the goal (Wisman 2015). Post WWII, the making of the consumer society and the invention of marketing considerably amplified this desire-based economy at the cost of depleted natural and also psychic and cognitive resources (Cohen and Todd 2018).

Contestation of planned obsolescence is growing in the public arena. Take France as an example. The French Law on Energy Transition (Law 2015-992) introduced the crime of planned obsolescence defined as "the set of techniques by which a manufacturer aims to deliberately shorten the lifetime of a product to increase its replacement rate". In 2017, the *Halte à l'Obsolescence Programmée*—HOP or Stop Planned Obsolescence program—filed a complaint against Apple after the company admitted to intentionally slowing the operation of its iPhones as they age. HOP had already filed a legal complaint against the printer manufacturers Canon, HP, Brother and Epson, claiming that their devices forced users to change their ink cartridges before they were empty.

If we take for granted that innovation is not always good—which is itself a strong stance, what are the implications of this position? This returns us to the problem of control of technology. David Collingridge referred to the dilemma of knowledge/control: the impacts of technologies which are still flexible are unknown whereas technologies whose impacts are well known have irreversible effects (Collingridge 1980). In this perspective, diversity is crucial for limiting irreversibility. This leads to consideration of how the balance of power and the related knowledge field, might increase the capacity to act.

2.2.6 Wrap Up 1. Challenging the Myths, Reimagining Innovation

As we have shown, master narratives that frame current innovation policies are based on two key beliefs. First, following Schumpeter's concept of creative destruction, innovation is considered as always good, and second, following the idea of trickle-down economic, improving economic competitiveness is supposed to create resources for solving any types of problems. Challenging these myths leads to reconsider innovation and innovation policies. This obviously raises difficult questions such as: how to define the good directions for innovation? How to assess the innovation according to these directions and their related values? How to govern or steer processes of innovation? Such questions are now addressed in the literature under the heading 'directionality of innovation'. Obviously, taking care of the diversity and flexibility of socio-technical systems is essential. However, as innovation is an uncertain journey (Van de Ven 2016), opening up the black box of directionality provides more questions than answers.

The discussion of innovation myths also allowed us to identify a set of complementary elements. First, we have to consider not only the results of innovation but also its process and to pay attention to the diversity of ways to innovate. This is not only a matter of efficiency but a matter of distribution of agency, dynamic of collective action, empowerment and social relations. Second, opening up innovation leads to challenge a culture of novelty and disruption. In many cases, we are confronted not to the challenge of introduction of a new idea, as traditionally meant by innovation, but to the need of discontinuing existing socio-technical systems, and hence to govern what we call *out*novation. Related to this, we have to balance the hype for novelty with a culture of maintenance, repair and recycling.

Challenging innovation myths is a good start on the reimagination path. However, the challenges are colossal. Fortunately, reimagination is under way and may be seen in the way actors reinvent new ways of innovation and scholars who explore transformations of innovation and innovation policies.

2.3 Re-inventing Innovation and Innovation Policies an Overview of Recent Re-openings

We now change perspective and consider literature streams that currently are feeding the renewal of innovation. Our analysis is centered mainly on academic works. However, this also concerns practices and public policies since strong coproduction processes are involved (Jasanoff 2004). The first strand of work "Democratizing innovation" owes much to the actors that explore and experiment with alternative ways to innovate from the centralized delegated model. It also owes much to academic research that has attracted public attention, and made local experiments transportable and generalizable to an extent.

The second and third streams involve the top down, and have close ties to European Commission initiatives, although both investigations are widespread. The "Responsible innovation" stream is related strongly to the perceived need to re-align science and society, triggered by strong contestation of new technologies. The European Commission Framework Programmes are important spaces for coproduction involving STS scholars among others. The third stream of work on "Transformative change" emerged from the strong convergence of academic research devoted to sustainable transitions, and the recasting of innovation policy around grand challenges. The appointment of Mariana Mazzucato as special advisor to Commissioner Moedas on mission driven science and innovation is an illustration of such convergence.[13]

---

[13]Professor of Economics at University College London, she is an advocate of the role of the State in innovation policy.

2.3.1 Democratising Innovation

The traditional view of innovation based on a strong division of labor between innovators and passive users (a centralized-delegated model of innovation) is increasingly being challenged. The literature on bottom up innovation, user centered innovation, distributed innovation, community-based innovation, etc. is burgeoning.

Eric Von Hippel, Professor of Management of Innovation at MIT, was one of the pioneers of this renewal. Working on innovation in very different areas, he demonstrated that the sources of innovation vary across situations, and that in sectors such as scientific instrumentation and semiconductors, users (usually companies rather than individuals) are the main source of innovation (Von Hippel 1988). Innovation is based on neither technology push nor demand pull; it is the result of interactions among actors with complementary knowledge. Users are no longer seen as only using; they learn by using, and in some situations they co-innovate. This means also that users learn from each other, and that innovators can learn from users. In his 1988 book, Von Hippel introduced the concept of distributed innovation. Innovation is distributed if the process is fed from various sources, for instance user-produced prototypes and experiments. Importantly, Von Hippel observed that the exploitation of this diversity is not natural but depends on the ability of firms to recognise these sources of innovation, and to develop forms of organisation and management tools to exploit them. He claimed that this has major implications for the management of innovation as well as for innovation policy (system level analysis and policy, property rights, support for users, etc.).

In his more recent *Democratizing Innovation*, Von Hippel (2004) goes beyond a firm-centric analysis to consider numerous actors, including creative communities. Distributed innovation challenges a structural feature of the social division of labour, the separation between users and consumers. Von Hippel identified two engines of distributed innovation. First, in the delegated model of innovation, standardised products are the rule. Large manufacturers design products to meet the needs of a large market segment to achieve wide diffusion and maximise turn-over and profits. Distributed innovation allows the customization of product design to respond to the diversity of user needs. Second, the contribution of users is growing as a result of continuing advances in computing and communications capabilities, and digitalisation of many areas.

The example of OSS (open source software)—and the wider development of open access information technology tools—is often used to illustrate the distributed model of innovation, and to show that one of the motives of its promoters is to redistribute agency, knowledge and power. In other words, a normative model of society is also being performed. A key feature is the invention of *collective property rights* through the creation of the general public licence (GPL or copyleft): the right to use the product at no cost, the right to modify it, and the right to distribute modified

---

https://marianamazzucato.com/uncategorized/mariana-mazzucato-appointed-as-special-advisor-for-mission-driven-science-and-innovation-to-eu-commissioner-for-research-carlos-moedas/.

or unmodified versions at no cost. Even when incorporated in commercial tools, software protected by a GPL is not proprietary.

There are other examples of the role of diverse actors in distributed innovation, ranging from the involvement of patient associations in medical research (Rabeharisoa and Callon 2004), the role of users in the design of software (Pollock et al. 2016), participatory plant breeding research experiments and exchanges of experience in French 'peasant networks' (Bonneuil et al. 2006), and bottom-up innovations in low-input agriculture (Wiskerke and Van der Ploeg 2004).[14] In addition, the recent cases of the OS models of 3D printer Reprap show how technical devices (information technologies coupled with new manufacturing devices) can reinforce the capacity of individuals to make (or hack) technology. Such technological transformations have some sociological drivers as illustrated by the burgeoning of communities of makers and the opening of new sites where the creation of technology is distributed (FabLabs, Living Labs, Hackers' Spaces, etc.). In a distributed network, everyone is supposed to contribute and to learn from each other. These peer-to-peer networks are commonplace in computing and information technology. They allow communities to share information and knowledge. The implications of peer-to-peer go well beyond computer systems, and some scholars predict that in the information age it becomes the basis for a new socio-political constitution (Benkler 2006).

We can sketch the set of values associated to the stream "democratising innovation". Of course, more research is needed to ground this on strong base. Democracy is indeed a central point. However, since it is an essentially contested concept (Gallie 1955), it needs to be qualified. Looking at the literature and previous experience, I suggest that the meaning intended is strong democracy (Barber 1984) in which communities are the main drivers. This stance towards democracy is developed in Callon et al. (2009) which focuses on concerned groups. It is accompanied by the values of empowerment and autonomy. Democratising innovation runs counter to the central/delegated model of innovation. This also is related to actors' curiosity, to valuing local experience, tinkering, making and hacking (well illustrated by the Do it Yourself (DiY) movement).

2.3.2 Responsible Innovation

The issue of research responsibility is not new. On the one hand, scientific responsibility has a long history of much debate within and around the scientific community, and institutionalised forms such as ethics committees, or guidelines and rules to prevent misconduct and misbehavior. On the other hand, the expression 'responsible innovation' (Guston 2004), or related expressions such as 'responsible development', date back to the late 1990s and appeared as a response to a series of crises (the GMO

---

[14]For a recent comprehensive analysis of the role of users and distributed innovation, cf. Hyysalo et al. (eds.) (2016).

2 Reimagining Innovation

crisis being the most memorable) (Owen et al. 2012). In contrast, the responsible research and innovation (RRI) frame, promoted by the European Commission since 2011 is more recent.

One of the most-cited definitions comes from René von Schomberg (2011: 9), a scientific officer at the DG Research, and one of the notable promoters of the concept:

> Responsible Research and Innovation is a transparent, interactive process by which societal actors and innovators become mutually responsive to each other with a view to the (ethical) acceptability, sustainability and societal desirability of the innovation process and its marketable products (in order to allow a proper embedding of scientific and technological advances in our society).

The definition of RRI adopted in official European Commission documents reads as follows.

> The grand societal challenges that lie before us will have a far better chance of being tackled if all societal actors are fully engaged in the co-construction of innovative solutions, products and services.

> Responsible Research and Innovation means that societal actors work together during the whole research and innovation process in order to better align both the process and its outcomes, with the values, needs and expectations of European society. RRI is an ambitious challenge for the creation of a Research and Innovation policy driven by the needs of society and engaging all societal actors via inclusive participatory approaches. (Directorate-General for Research and Innovation 2012: 2)

Textual analysis of the RRI literature demonstrates that RRI discourses are remarkably convergent and have three distinctive features (Tancoigne et al. forthcoming). First, they are about research and innovation outputs and goals, and take serious account of the desire to *steer* research and innovation towards solving societal problems, especially so-called 'grand challenges'. Second, RRI discourse refers to inclusive and participative forms of governance which clearly differentiates it from discourses premised on scientists' self-regulation of science. Third, the meaning of responsibility embedded in RRI is prospective rather than retrospective, moral rather than legal, and collective rather than individual.

Programmatic papers by influential scholars in the field of RRI elaborate on this. According to Owen et al. (2012) there are three main features of RRI that to an extent overlap the European Commission Framework:

- Democratic governance of the purposes of research and innovation and their orientation toward the "right impacts".
- Responsiveness, emphasising the integration and institutionalisation of established approaches of anticipation, reflection and deliberation in and around research and innovation, influencing the direction of these and associated policies.
- Framing of responsibility in the context of research and innovation as collective activities with uncertain and unpredictable consequences.

According to Stilgoe et al. (2013), RRI has four dimensions: (i) anticipation, (ii) reflexivity, (iii) inclusion, and (iv) responsiveness.

The future actual impact of RRI is much discussed. The possibility of responsible washing should not be excluded since the RRI frame is voluntary and highly flexible. It can be considered a strategic tool for maintaining corporate licenses to operate. Indeed, it needs not be taken at face value but seen as a discursive space that contributes to re-imagining innovation.

What is valued in the stream of responsible innovation is the alignment of science and society as a major lever for addressing grand challenges. This is related to the focus on new technologies and their contestation. This alignment is supposed to emerge through dialogue, anticipation and reflexivity. Responsibility is understood as care for the future which is framed as threats to be avoided. Openness is the core value.

2.3.3 Transformative Change

This third stream is also coproduced by public policy and academic research. On the policy side, the grand challenges discourse has become pervasive, both in Europe where it is a central political motto, and in other parts of the world. To address grand challenges such as climate change, world food security, natural resources depletion, ageing societies, etc. doing more of the same is no longer an option. It is necessary to do it differently, and hence, to promote deep transformations.

This echoes academic research which for more than 20 years has focused on socio-technical (sustainable) transitions (Rip and Kemp 1998; Geels 2002; Geels and Schot 2007). Drawing on the lessons from analyses that highlight the path-dependent character of technological trajectories (Cf. Myth 4—the technology selected is always the best), researchers have conceptualised transitions as dynamic processes that allow socio-technical systems to be unlocked and which re-open possibilities. Such dynamic processes are considered to be multilevel, involving a combination of transformation forces coming from the bottom (niche exploration), from the top (influence of the environment) but also from the socio-technical system itself (weakening of core technology, change in consumers' preferences, new incumbent strategies, changed expectations, etc.). This is a sketchy account of a complex and vibrant research stream but it suffices to demonstrate its core position: (i) due to strong environmental, social and economic limits, there is a need for sustainable transition; (ii) the changes are both technological and social (socio-technical); (iii) due to uncertainty, complexity and ambiguity, transitions cannot be governed by simple command and control processes.

As shown in a paper by Johan Schot and Ed Steinmueller from Science Policy Research Unit (SPRU), such a frame strongly shapes innovation and leads to the redesign of innovation policy (Schot and Steinmueller 2016). The core question is: "How to use science and technology policy for meeting social needs and addressing societal challenges?" (Schot and Steinmueller 2016: 5). In a transformative change perspective, this question leads to a focus on the way innovation policy can achieve system-wide transformation of the food, energy, material, mobility, healthcare and communication socio-technical systems. Deep transformations—not competitiveness or other targets—constitute the core objective of innovation policy. This requires

2 Reimagining Innovation

thinking far beyond the traditional innovation policy tools based on support for R&D and prioritisation of specific research avenues.

Innovation policy as a process within a transformative change perspective involves the opening up of the possibilities for system change through support from experimentations that go beyond—and often challenge—the incumbent frame.

> Innovation policy is not about setting priorities, but about improving the process of opening up to a wide range of choices (…). Innovation policy should allow for deep learning, challenges to dominant views, and nurturing a greater diversity of options. It should enable experimentation with options beyond those emerging within the narrow boundaries set by incumbent institutions (…). (Schot and Steinmueller 2016: 21)

In terms of governance, what is crucial is that transformative changes involve tensions and conflicts, and that it challenges the interests of incumbent groups often occupying dominant positions. Schot and Steinmueller consider that what are needed are new institutional arrangements and governance structures that bridge governments, markets and civil society. They suggest also, that public deliberation could shape collective expectations and strengthen commitment to the search for new solutions that might challenge current interests. In their view, transformative change involves democratising control over innovation production and diffusion.

Such a framework is tentative, and its ability to achieve its goals remains to be demonstrated. Concern over the diversity and directionality of innovation beyond the competitiveness framework—and the need to think of technical democracy as new power/knowledge configurations—are rightly pointed out. However, it probably overtrusts the ability of distributed governance systems to make such changes. Is it possible, for instance, to govern outnovation of major socio-technical trajectories such as pesticide use in agriculture? We would suggest that such changes require to consider very seriously strong asymmetries of power and resources. Hence, the weak part of the framework is the delegation to hybrid governance arrangement, which prevents consideration of the specific role of public authorities. Against this, Mazzucato (2015) suggests that it is necessary to consider this seriously, and to look at the broader implications for mission-oriented investments of not just fixing market or system failures but actively shaping and creating markets.

What is valued in the transformative change stream is the ability to govern and perform socio-technical transitions. The democratic values are important in so far that they contribute to successful unlocking of trajectories that are not sustainable. Since the emerging socio-technical systems are unknown, experimentation and technological diversity are both valued highly. Communities are not important per se but depending on whether they contribute to the needed transitions through local experimentation that potentially is generalised.

2.4 Conclusion

The dual approach developed in this paper is aimed at opening up the socio-technical imaginary in order to renew innovation. The discussion of the innovation myths is a first important step which makes visible the deep beliefs that condition this imaginary. The presentation of the three literature streams that currently feed the innovation renewal allows consideration of explorations in academia as well as in public policy. This shows that a re-imagination and re-invention of innovation is underway, and that the dynamic is constituted of different actors from different traditions.

These three streams share a need for diversity and directionality of innovation and they do take into consideration the strong uncertainty, complexity and ambiguity of innovation journeys. They share the need for system transformation, although with some important nuances on power and politic issues. The RRI stream is in strong continuation with the current system. Needed changes rest upon awareness, deliberation and reflexivity. These are indeed possible adaptations and a future world where powerful actors adopt a wider sense of responsibility may be imagined. However, this stream does not take into account asymmetries of power and the eventual role of incumbents in the limitation of strong changes. Climate change constitutes a real- and crucial-laboratory for testing this. So far, we can observe strong limitations of the effectiveness of changes mainly based on voluntary agreements. The meaning of democracy embedded in the 'Democratising innovation' stream is close to strong democracy (Barber 1984) and related to the dynamic of local communities. In a way, this is close to the experimentation part of the 'Deep transformation' stream and this is essential for opening up and exploration. This later stream also includes the need for upscaling local experimentation, a key step for deep transformations. As mentioned above, the trust on distributed governance to perform these changes may be challenged. We definitely need more research and discussion on the organisational and political capacities needed for governing socio-technical transformations (Borras and Edler 2014) and to pursue research on technical democracy (Callon et al. 2009). This discussion also implies that reimagining innovation not only requires to challenge the innovation myths but also the socio-technical agencements they are embedded in. Considering the difficulties, the knowledge produced may be qualified as uncomfortable (Rayner 2012) and there are good reasons for it to be ignored.

Although these streams share a need for diversity and directionality of innovation, they hardly challenge the fashion for novelty. This is not surprising if we consider that as suggested in Sect. 2.1, this would mean a Copernican revolution in innovation studies. However, the shift to—or to put it more gently the balance with—a heuristic of continuity, maintenance, repair and recycling will be necessary to reconcile innovation and progress (Wisman 2015).

Acknowledgements I am very grateful to the editors of this book and to my colleagues at LISIS, Evelyne Lhoste, Doug Robinson and Bruno Turnheim, for very helpful comments.

References

Arthur, B. (1989). Competing technologies, increasing returns, and lock-ins by historical events. *The Economic Journal, 99*(394), 116–131.

2 Reimagining Innovation

Barber, B. (1984). *Strong democracy: Participatory politics for a new age*. Oakland: University of California Press.

Benkler, Y. (2006). *The wealth of networks: How social production transforms markets and freedom*. New Haven, CT: Yale University Press.

Bijker, W., Hugh, T., & Pinch, T. (1987). *The social construction of technological systems: New directions in the sociology and history of technology* (p. 1987). Cambridge, MA; London: MIT press.

Bonneuil, C., Demeulenaere, E., Thomas, F., Joly, P. B., Allaire, G., & Goldringer, I. (2006). Innover autrement? La recherche agronomique face à l'avènement d'un nouveau régime de production et régulation des savoirs en génétique végétale. *Courrier de l'Environnement de l'INRA, 30*, pp. 29–52.

Borras, S., & Edler, J. (Eds.). (2014). *The governance of socio-technical systems* (pp. 111–131). Cheltenham: Edward Elgar.

Boyer, R. (2019). How scientific breakthroughs and social innovations shape the evolution of the healthcare sector. In S. Lechevalier (Ed.), *Innovation beyond technology* (pp. 89–119). Berlin: Springer.

Bozeman, B., & Sarewitz, D. (2011). Public value mapping and science policy evaluation. *Minerva, 49*, 1–23.

Callon, M. (1981). Pour une sociologie des controverses socio-techniques. *Fundamenta Scientiae, 2*(3/4), 381–399.

Callon, M. (1994). Is science a public good? *Science, Technology and Human Values, 19*(4), 395–424.

Callon, M., Lascoumes, P., & Barthe, Y. (2009). *Acting in an uncertain world: An essay on technical democracy*. Cambridge, MA, USA; London, UK: MIT Press.

Cohen, D., & Todd, J. M. (2018). *The infinite desire for growth*. Princeton: Princeton University Press.

Collingridge, D. (1980). *The social construction of technology*. London: Frances Pinter.

Cowan, R. (1990). Nuclear power reactors: A study in technological lock-in. *The Journal of Economic History, 50*(3), 541–567.

David, P. (1986). Understanding the economics of QWERTY: The necessity of history. In W. Parker (Ed.), *Economic history and the modern economist*. New York: Basil Blackwell.

Dewey, J. (2013). The problems of value. *Journal of Philosophy, Psychology and Scientific Methods, 10*(1913), 268–269.

Edgerton, D. (2004). 'The linear model' did not exist: Reflections on the history and historiography of science and research in industry in the twentieth century. In K. Grandin & N. Wormbs (Eds.), *The science-industry nexus: History, policy, implications*. New York: Watson.

Edgerton, D. (2006). *The shock of the Old: Technology and global history since 1900*. London: Profile Books.

Fagerberg, J., & Verspagen, B. (2009). Innovation studies—The emerging structure of a new scientific field. *Research Policy, 38*, 218–233.

Freeman, C., & Louca, F. (2001). *As times goes by. From the industrial revolutions to the information revolution*. Oxford: Oxford University Press.

Fujigaki, Y. (2019). Lessons from Fukushima for responsible innovation: How to construct a new relationship between science and society? In S. Lechevalier (Ed.), *Innovation beyond technology* (pp. 223–239). Berlin: Springer.

Gallie, W. B. (1955). Essentially contested concepts. In *Proceedings of the Aristotelian Society* (New Series, Vol. 56 (1955–1956), pp. 167–198).

Geels, F. W. (2002). Technological transitions as evolutionary reconfiguration processes: A multi-level perspective and a case-study. *Research Policy, 31*, 1257–1274.

Geels, F. W., & Schot, J. (2007). Typology of sociotechnical transition pathways. *Research Policy, 36*, 399–417.

Godin, B. (2006). The linear model of innovation: The historical construction of an analytical framework. *Science Technology & Human Values, 31*(6), 639–667.

Godin, B. (2015). Innovation: A conceptual history of an anonymous concept. WP available on www.csiic.ca.

Goulet, F., & Vinck, D. (2012). Innovation through withdrawal contribution to a sociology of detachment. *Revue française de sociologie (English Edition), 53*(2), 117–146.

Guston, D. (2004). Forget politicizing science: Let's democratize science! cspo.org/ourlibrary/articles/DemocratizeScience.htm.

Hyysalo, S., Jensen, T. E., & Oudshoorn, N. (Eds.). (2016). *The new production of users changing innovation collectives and involvement strategies.* New York: Routledge.

Jasanoff, S. (2004). *States of knowledge. The coproduction of science and social order.* New York: Routledge.

Jasanoff, S., & Kim, S. H. (2015). *Dreamscapes of modernity. Sociotechnical imaginaries and the fabrication of power.* Chicago: Chicago University Press.

Joly, P. B. (2015). Governing emerging technologies—The need to think outside the (black) box. In S. Hilgartner, C. Miller, & R. Hagendijk (Eds.), *Science and democracy: Knowledge as wealth and power in the biosciences and beyond.* New York: Routledge.

Joly, P. B. (2016). «Verrouillage socio-technique et transition écologique». In D. Bourg & D. Medda (Eds.), *Transitions écologiques.* Paris: Institut Veblen.

Joly, P. B. (2017). Beyond the competitiveness framework? Models of innovation revisited. *Journal of Economics and Management of Innovation, 1*(22), 79–96.

Joly, P. B., Matt, M., Gaunand, A., Colinet, L., Larédo, P., & Lemarié, S. (2015). ASIRPA: A comprehensive theory-based approach to assess societal impacts of a research organization. *Research Evaluation, 24*(4), 440–453.

Joly, P. B., Rip, A., & Callon, M. (2010). Re-inventing innovation. In M. J. Arentsen, W. van Rossum, & A. E. Steenge (Eds.), *Governance of innovation.* Cheltenham: Edward Elgar.

Kline, S. J., & Rosenberg, N. (1986). An overview of innovation. In R. Landau & N. Rosenberg (Eds.), *The positive sum strategy: Harnessing technology for economic growth* (pp. 275–305). Washington, D.C.: National Academy Press.

Mazzucato, M. (2015). From market fixing to market-creating: A new framework for economic policy. University of Sussex Working Paper Series. SWPS 2015-25 (September).

OECD. (2005). *Oslo manual. Guidelines for collecting and interpreting innovation data* (3rd ed.). OECD & Statistical Office of the European Communities.

Oki, S. (2019). 'Innovation' as an adaptation of 'Progress': Revisiting the epistemological and historical contexts of these terms. In S. Lechevalier (Ed.), *Innovation beyond technology* (pp. 47–62). Berlin: Springer.

Owen, R., Macnaghten, P., & Stilgoe, J. (2012). Responsible research and innovation: From science in society to science for society, with society. *Science and Public Policy, 39,* 751–760.

Paillard, S., Tréyer, S., & Dorin, B. (2014). Agrimonde: Scenarios and challenges for feeding the world in 2050 (p. 295). Versailles: Quae.

Perez, C. (2002). *Technological revolutions and financial capital.* Edward Elgar Publishing.

Pestre, D. (2019). Environment and social innovation: Why technology never was the solution. In S. Lechevalier (Ed.), *Innovation beyond technology* (pp. 175–194). Berlin: Springer.

Piketty, T. (2013). *Capital in the twenty-first century.* Harvard: Harvard University Press.

Pollock, N., Williams, R., & D'Adderio, L. (2016). Generification as a strategy: How software producers configure products, manage user communities and segment markets. In S. Hyysalo, T. E. Jensen, & N. Oudshoorn (Eds.), *The new production of users changing innovation collectives and involvement strategies* (pp. 287–334). New York: Routledge.

Prahalad, C. K. (2005). *Fortune at the bottom of the pyramid: Eradicating poverty through profits.* Philadelphia: Wharton School Publishing.

Rabeharisoa, V., & Callon, M. (2004). Patients and scientists in French muscular dystrophy research. In S. Jasanoff (Ed.), *States of knowledge. The co-production of science and social order* (pp. 142–160). New York: Routledge.

Rayner, S. (2012). Uncomfortable knowledge: The social construction of ignorance in science and environmental policy discourses. *Economy and Society, 41*(1), 107–125.

Reinert, H., & Reinert, E. (2006). Creative destruction in economics: Nietzsche, Sombart, Schumpeter. In J. Backhaus & W. Drechsler (Eds.), *Friedrich Nietzsche 1844–2000: economy and society*. Series *The European heritage in economics and the social sciences*. Kluwer: Boston.

Rip, A. (1986). Controversies as informal technology assessment. *Knowledge: Creation, Diffusion, Utilization, 8*(2), 349–371.

Rip, A., & Kemp, R. (1998). *Technological change*. Battelle Press.

Ripple, W. J., Wolf, C., Newsome, T. M., Galetti, M., Alamgir, M., Crist, E., et al. (2017). World scientists' warning to humanity: A second notice. *BioScience, 67*(12), 1026–1028.

Rosenberg, N. (1982). *Inside the black box. Technology and economics*. Cambridge MA: Cambridge University Press.

Sarewitz, D. (2016). Saving science. *The New Atlantis*, Spring-Summer, 5–30.

Schot, J., & Steinmueller, E. (2016). Framing innovation policy for transformative change: Innovation policy 3.0. Brighton: SPRU, Draft, 4/9/2016.

Schumpeter, J. (1942). *Capitalism, socialism and democracy*. New York: Harper and Brothers.

Slade, G. (2009). *Made to break. Technology and obsolescence in America*. Cambridge, MA: Harvard University Press.

Soete, L. (2013). Is innovation always good? In J. Fagerberg, B. R. Martin, & E. S. Andersen (Eds.), *Innovation studies—Evolution and future challenges* (pp. 134–144). Oxford: Oxford University Press.

Stilgoe, J., Owen, R., & Macnaghten, P. (2013). Developing a framework for responsible innovation. *Research Policy, 42,* 1568–1580.

Stegmaier, P., Kuhlmann, S., & Visser, V. R. (2014). The discontinuation of socio-technical systems as a governance proble. In S. Borras & J. Edler (Eds.), *The governance of socio-technical systems* (pp. 111–131). Cheltenham: Edward Elgar.

Stirling, A. (2008). 'Opening up' and 'closing down' power, participation, and pluralism in the social appraisal of technology. *Science, Technology and Human Values, 33*(2), 262–294.

Stirling, A. (2009). Direction, distribution, diversity! Pluralising Progress in Innovation, Sustainability and Development. STEPS Centre, University of Sussex, STEPS Working Paper 32.

Subramanian, K. (2015). *Revisiting the green revolution: Irrigation and food production in twentieth-century India* (Ph.D. dissertation). London: King' College, .

Tancoigne, E., Randles, S., & Joly, P. B. (forthcoming). RRI (Responsible Research and Innovation) as a new discursive space for science and society.

Van de Ven, A. H. (2016). The innovation journey: You can't control it, but you can learn to maneuver it. *Innovation*. https://doi.org/10.1080/14479338.2016.1256780.

von Hippel, E. (1988). *The sources of innovation*. Oxford: Oxford University Press.

von Hippel, E. (2004). *Democratizing innovation*. Cambridge (MA): MIT Press.

von Schomberg, R. (2011). Towards responsible research and innovation in the information and communication technologies and security technologies fields. In R. von Schomberg (Ed.), *Towards responsible research and innovation in the information and communication technologies and security technologies fields* (pp. 7–16). Luxembourg: Publications Office of the European Union.

Wiskerke, J. S. C., & van der Ploeg, J. D. (Eds.). (2004). *Seeds of transition. Essays on novelty production, niches and regimes in agriculture*. Assen: Royal Van Gorcum.

Wisman, H. (2015). Par delà le Progrès: les paradoxes de l'innovation. Paris: Conférence IHEST. https://www.ihest.fr/.

Chapter 3
'Innovation' as an Adaptation of 'Progress': Revisiting the Epistemological and Historical Contexts of These Terms

Sayaka Oki

Abstract In the 1990s, historians argued the necessity to rethink the word 'progress', as they thought that there was a breakdown of belief in the idea of progress. Twenty years later, many countries rely on the concept of 'innovation' both as an instrument and as a value to be pursued by society, while the use of 'progress' as a socio-political ideal has faded away in most public discourses. In this regard, this paper argues that the concept of innovation is an adaptation of the idea of progress to our age. First, it examines the exact meaning of progress in previous eras and its role, which is similar to today's concept of innovation for elite policymakers and intellectuals in the 19th and 20th centuries, with reference to European and non-European authors. Second, it examines how 'progress' was gradually replaced by the term 'innovation' to express socio-political value in socio-political discourses during the late 20th century. The concept of innovation differs from that of progress, particularly in that the former is based on discontinuity and diversity. On one hand, it obliges us to bet on abrupt and unpredictable changes as the only way to secure a better future. On the other hand, thanks to its principle of diversity, it is capable of liberating many non-Western societies from one-dimensional measures of civilisation, as West European countries and North America were once depicted as a model for everyone to follow. Despite these differences, innovation can be considered a legitimate heir of the social values from the Enlightenment, as was the case for progress in the past, especially after the decline of Marxist theory. Its remnants can be seen in some of today's expressions related to innovation, such as social inclusion and co-creation. However, innovation has inherited another troublesome aspect of the modern notion of progress, mostly derived from the 19th century: evolution through fierce competition. We need to find methods to integrate a more ethical and social perspective in the innovation process and develop a sense of social responsibility.

S. Oki (✉)
University of Nagoya, Nagoya, Japan
e-mail: okisayaka@gmail.com

© Springer Nature Singapore Pte Ltd. 2019
S. Lechevalier (ed.), *Innovation Beyond Technology*, Creative Economy,
https://doi.org/10.1007/978-981-13-9053-1_3

3.1 Introduction

Although there is no apparent 'crisis' concerning belief in innovation at least at the level of political discourse, this does not mean the notion has been without controversy. In the 1990s, the situation was clearer for the notion of progress. Faced with increasing scepticism about modernity, many historians and philosophers argued the necessity to rethink the word 'progress'. Bruce Mazlish, a historian, thought that 'a major crisis in our time is the breakdown of our belief in the idea of progress' (Burgen et al. 1997; Mazlish 1996, p. 28). About 20 years later, in an online discussion, Siva Vaidhyanathan, a researcher on cultural history, stated he regretted the situation where 'innovation' seems to have supplanted the idea of 'progress' in today's socio-political discourses (Vaidhyanathan 2015). While some theorists consider that too many countries and organizations now rely on innovation as if it offered 'magical' solutions to all sorts of social issues, others have tried to control it for the benefit of both society and research, coining a series of terms such as 'responsible innovation' and 'inclusive innovation' (Godin 2015; Niedzviecki 2015).[1] According to Vaidhyanathan, the overall situation seems problematic because 'innovation does not contain an implication of a grand path or a grand design of a knowable future'. Claiming that the ideology of progress appeared to have become obsolete and unpopular, he expressed his dissatisfaction, stating that 'States are now encouraged to innovate rather than solve big problems to correct for market failures. The ultimate goal of innovation seems to be more innovation' (Vaidhyanathan 2015).

In this discussion, I revisit the idea of 'progress', to rethink the word 'innovation', being inspired by debates occurring in several different fields in varying ways. My question is the following: has 'innovation' really replaced the idea of 'progress'? I contend that it has, and try to describe how it happened. From some recent studies on the intellectual history of the terms 'innovation' and 'progress', it is possible to understand the idea of innovation as playing a similar role to that of the concept of progress for European policymakers and intellectuals in the 19th century and for the rest of the world in the late 19th and 20th centuries. It is worth examining, from this perspective, what progress had meant previously, with specific reference to European and some Asian authors in the 18th and 19th centuries. Although the word 'innovation' gradually penetrated political discourse in the course of the 20th century, it seems that the most recent decisive moment of change occurred at the end of the Cold War. Around that period, 'innovation' became a value in itself, rather than a means to an end, while belief in the idea of progress underwent a terminal breakdown (Godin 2015, pp. 30–31; Mazlish 1996, pp. 28–29). Through investigating the similarities and differences between the socio-political ideals of the past and the current discourse on innovation, I hope to contribute to discussions on future directions for society.

---

[1] See also Koizumi (2019).

3.2 Progress Revisited

3.2.1 Progress in Socio-Political Discourse

To understand the position that 'progress' occupied in socio-political discourses in the past, it is worth looking at the following citation taken from the U.S. Constitution, which was inspired by 18th century Enlightenment thought.

> The Congress shall have power... To promote the progress of science and useful arts, by securing for limited times to authors and inventors the exclusive right to their respective writings and discoveries (U.S. Const., art. I, § 8, cl. 8).

This clause, which Vaidhyanathan also cites in his discussion, is famous for its role in empowering modern patent law.[2] The State protected intellectual property in the name of 'progress'. Today, the same is done in the name of 'innovation'.

Progress is a polysemic concept. Georg Henrik von Wright, a Finnish philosopher, distinguishes three kinds of progress within Enlightenment thought. The first involved the progress of knowledge in science and technology. The second concerned the improvement of the material well-being of individuals and societies, which was generally thought to be the result of the first kind of progress. The third comprised so-called 'moral perfection', expressed as two varying trends. One trend concerned an evaluation of modern (European) commercial civilisation as the source of politeness and 'civilized manners', a thesis defended especially by the Scottish Enlightenment thinkers, including Adam Smith and William Robertson. The other trend concerned the development of an intellectual capacity necessary to maintain a democratic society, typically expressed through Jean-Antoine-Nicolas de Condorcet's reasoning (Wright 1997, pp. 7–9; Mazlish 1996, pp. 1–8). As an approximation, it could be said that the former trend related to an economic vision of progress, while the latter trend related to a political vision of progress. It has often been claimed that these two trends became linked respectively to different socio-political ideals in the course of the 19th century, with the former inspiring economic liberalism and the latter socialism (Picon 2003, pp. 71–82), but these developments are not focused on here.

All these various kinds of progress shared a linear sense of time, derived from their cultural background in Judeo-Christianism. This time sense can be regarded as a secularised version of the Christian salvation story with its linear rather than cyclic sense of time that characterised most ancient civilisations such as the Babylonians, and the Greeks, as well as Hinduism and Buddhism. However, humans were now destined to advance into a better and more prosperous future on earth, instead of aiming for Heaven, in this modern European secular version of the salvation story.

---

[2]George Washington signed the bill that laid the foundation of the modern American patent system on 10 April 1790. Vaidhyanathan also cites this in his discussion.

3.2.2 Idea by Condorcet

An example of what the ultimate future vision of progress might involve was depicted by Condorcet in his posthumous works, *Fragment sur l'Atlantide* (*Fragment on the New Atlantis*) and the *Esquisse d'un tableau historique des progrès de l'esprit humain* (*Sketch for a Historical Picture of the Progress of the Human Mind*).[3] In this latter work, influential during post-revolutionary politics in France, he envisaged a future where the perfection of the human mind and morals had resulted in a democratic world-civilisation, composed of liberated human beings, guided only by their powers of reason, without prejudice:

> I find myself in a truly free country, where real equality reigns, where the simplicity of laws and administration makes it unnecessary to multiply the number of public officials and entrust them with functions that can excite greed and flatter ambition. Here, public positions are conferred for a very short time and distributed in such a way that each of them can be fulfilled by an individual of ordinary capacity, can become neither the object nor the exclusive occupation of a class of men who prepare for them by studies foreign to the rest of the citizens. Here finally, there no longer exist those institutions, those laws, uniquely contrived to offer the means of acquiring opulence and great wealth. (Condorcet 1988, pp. 303–304; English translation in Condorcet 1976, p. 287)

According to Condorcet, in such an ideal world, there would be no class distinctions, nor inequalities of wealth distribution, as society would have successfully designed laws and administrative institutions so that ordinary citizens could actively participate in socio-political activities. Even if differences in talents existed, this would never affect the equality shared among citizens, nor bring about any form of particular group isolation, as everyone would have the opportunity to obtain a systematic education enabling everyone to develop their own competencies fully. All citizens would love the pursuit of truth through science and the arts and would understand their value even if they did not excel particularly in any of these areas. They would not rely blindly on talented members nor become envious or sceptical concerning them. Condorcet went so far as to link democracy and science, stating that citizens would voluntarily come together to vote in choosing scientists (*savants*) who would develop a research plan for the 'progress' of science. Condorcet also imagined that these motivated citizens would be sufficiently numerous to support financially the research costs of projects they voted for (Condorcet 1988, pp. 275–276, 304–306, 340–344).

His image of democracy could be conceived as a kind of 'co-creative' and 'co-participative' society in relation to science and technology (known as 'arts' in his day). This interpretation is reinforced by the fact that he was one of the pioneers of the group decision-making (or social choice) theory. From a contemporary perspective, one of his contributions, jury theorem, is extremely important, as it opened a way to

---

[3]Precisely speaking, this 'Fragment' is one of the manuscripts prepared by Condorcet for his unfinished work *Tableau historique du progrès de l'Espreit humain*, of which the *Esquisse* is just a summary. From the first edition of the *Esquisse* in 1804, this manuscript continued to be published and well known. As to the details, see the explanation in Condorcet (2004).

investigate how to aggregate information by individuals to make the best decisions for a truly democratic society (Condorcet 1785).[4]

Condorcet's ideal future as an achievable vision of humanity had, however, a negative side. Its strong sense of linear time had difficulty in avoiding a conceptualisation of a linear order of development, involving a 'ladder of civilizations', which entailed a discriminatory view of non-Occidental countries and cultures. Although in a comparatively restrained manner, Condorcet described European people, especially Anglo-Americans and the French, as the 'most enlightened', and placed the 'barbarous' populations of the African continent at the opposite end of this scale (Condorcet 1988, p. 266).

This method of dividing societies into categories including 'savage' or 'barbarous' and 'civilized' classifications, had its roots in 17th-century Europe, but Condorcet had a more direct source of inspiration from the universal vision of history developed especially under the influence of the Scottish Enlightenment from the middle of 18th century. According to this understanding, all societies advanced through three or four stages, as they progressed from 'rudeness to refinement'. Adam Smith was one of the most well-known authors expressing views in this vein. In his *Lectures on Jurisprudence*, he divided history into the following ascending order, namely, hunter-gathering, pasturage, agriculture, and commerce. As was the case for his contemporaries, without sufficient reliable archaeological evidence, his arguments mainly relied on classical authors such as Homer and some rare contemporary witnesses of American indigenous societies (Smith 1978, p. 27; Brewer 2008; Pauchant 2016). However, this type of vision moulded a version of philosophical history that became very influential among a series of authors in the next generation, from William Robertson to James Mill, at the beginning of the 19th century.[5]

3.2.3 Effect by Social Darwinism

It appears that a fourth kind of progress was inspired with the emergence, from this tradition of philosophical history, of the evolutionary theory known as Social Darwinism. This understanding of progress eventually prevailed, as memorably encapsulated with the famous phrase of Herbert Spencer, 'survival of the fittest', and the word 'progress' came to be used almost interchangeably with 'evolution' in the course of the latter half of the 19th century (Nisbet 2009, p. 171). Although there remain many questions to explore further on the exact relationships between Enlightenment philosophical history, Spencer's own arguments, and the evolutionary theory of Charles Darwin,[6] it is at least certain that during the 19th century, the idea of 'progress'

---

[4]See also Mclean et al. (2012), pp. xxvi–xlviii. J. C. Borda preceded him in analyzing the paradox of voting of group. Condorcet examined it more systematically and expressed the theory named by Duncan Black as jury theorem.

[5]For example, see Rendall (1982), pp. 43–69.

[6]As Mark Francis puts it, Spencer has never accepted the idea that modern individuals and societies would continue to make progress through struggle for survival, contrary to popular belief prevailed

became completely secularised (Nisbet 2009, pp. 169–177),[7] and that some began to perceive it almost as a law of nature, as discussed below. In this context, Social Darwinism had a particular effect at the level of international politics, because it served directly as a justification of colonialism, both for the Western imperial powers and later for Japan as the first non-Western colonialising power.

Shigeru Nakayama and Masaki Miyake have contended that it was Social Darwinism that enabled non-Western countries to accept the idea of progress, as it offered them a seemingly 'scientific' version of the concept, omitting the elements strongly marked by a Christian cultural background, such as the idealised image of a promised future involving moral perfection. The notion that human beings and primates shared a common ancestry did not generate any major controversies in those regions lacking any Judeo-Christian cultural background concerning a strict separation of humanity from other animals.[8]

In Japan during its modernisation phase, social Darwinian theory came into vogue among intellectuals for two main reasons. First, under the pressure of understanding colonialization as undertaken by the Western countries, they perceived the idea of survival of the fittest as more realistic and more easily understandable than the philosophy of progress as derived from the Enlightenment. Second, Social Darwinism arrived in Japan at a politically crucial moment, namely, during a period of political crisis in the 1870s and 1880s (Nakayama 1997, pp. 65–76). In this context, the scholars close to the government eagerly adapted themselves to a social Darwinist vision to legitimate the government's authoritarian and nationalistic modernization policy, *Fukoku kyohei*. Hiroyuki Kato (加藤弘之), who would become president of Tokyo Imperial University in the 1890s, was a typical figure among these scholars. He tried to counter his political opponents, who were activists primarily inspired by English liberalism or French human rights theory, by insisting that their arguments were 'delusions', lacking any hard scientific foundation (Kato 1882, Chap. 1; Takeda 2003; Watanabe 1976, pp. 112–120).

By the 1890s, ideas such as 'progress through competition' also attracted political elites in China,[9] especially through those who had studied in Japan. A Chinese philosopher, K'ang Yu-wei (康有為), observed the effect of Social Darwinism on Asian people's perception of progress. Around the end of the 19th century, he expressed his disgust concerning the understanding of progress held by his contemporaries (Miyake 1999, p. 177).

---

even in historical discourses in the 20th century. The author suggests that Darwin himself is not free of historical culpability of Social Darwinism (Francis 2014, pp. 2–3).

[7]It is also to be noted that the 19th century used 'progress' and 'evolution' interchangeably (Nisbet 2009, p. 172).

[8]During the 1880s, social Darwinist discourses and the name of Spencer attracted more attention of Japanese intellectuals than Darwin's biological evolutionary theory itself; however, the trend was reversed at the beginning of the 20th century. In that period, biological Darwinism came to attract socialists and to be used for denying the divinity of the imperial family theory, a political invention in the 1890s, and then that kind of discourse was severely censored by the government (有田 2009, Chap. 1).

[9]For example, Yan Fu, who translated Huxley in China and studied in the UK.

3 'Innovation' as an Adaptation of 'Progress': Revisiting ...

> Nowadays the theory of natural selection is being proclaimed, and the idea of competition is being regarded as most rational [...] It is thought that talent and knowledge progress through competition, and that survival of the fittest is a Law of Nature [...]
>
> Those who discuss [these matters] nowadays hate the calm of unity, and exalt the hubbub of competition. They think that with competition there is progress; without strife there is retrogression. (K'ang 1958, pp. 50, 215–216)

While K'ang did not agree with the idea of Social Darwinism, he was prepared to compromise with this new philosophical trend by absorbing, as part of his historical vision, the idea of progress as a linear time process, and therefore abandoning the traditional Confucianist historical interpretation that presupposed antiquity as the exemplary Golden age of Chinese civilisation (Miyake 1999, pp. 178–179).

Soon after the First World War, the idea of progress was exposed to its first serious criticism in Europe. As part of the background, there occurred a spiritual crisis due to the involvement of Europe, long regarded as the source of 'civilisation', in a barbaric war. Nonetheless, the varying degrees of advance in the process of modernisation among countries seemed to have contributed to a suspension of doubts concerning an overall belief in progress around the world. For example, faith in progress in the popular mind never ceased. It was especially prevalent in the United States, in the midst of economic growth and of technological development after The First World War (Nisbet 2009, Chap. 8). The Soviet Union too began to develop, advocating straightforwardly for a 'progressive' revolution. The Second World War, with all its devastation and unprecedented slaughter, with two atomic bombs dropped, did not attenuate this tendency either, as many Western countries, including Japan, enjoyed significant improvements in material well-being during the Cold War period, due both to industrialization in the age of Fordism, and to protections offered through welfare state policies, which appeared to succeed in mediating capitalistic and social democratic policy expectations (Burgen et al. 1997, pp. 65–76; Amin 1994, Chap. 3).

Serious disillusionment with progress arrived in the period from the 1970s to the 1990s. One of its major causes resulted from environmental problems due to the development of science and technology, and industrialization. Additionally, the decline of Marxism had exposed as an illusion the idea of a 'progressive' revolution of society controlled through rationality and science. Furthermore, the concept of progress, involving universal claims, began to be condemned as Western-centric and male-centric, with a rising tide of criticism against colonialism, and from mobilising feminist campaigns (Mazlish 1996, pp. 1–8; Pestre 2010, p. 125).[10] All these elements provide the context for Mazlish's statement cited at the beginning of this discussion.

3.3 Innovation as a Historical Concept

Given this background, it is time to consider the similarities and differences between the two notions of progress and innovation. More specifically, to what extent is

---

[10]See also the discussion of Laugier and Lechevalier (2019).

innovation an heir of progress? To elucidate a response, it is worth verifying the meaning of innovation, in terms of how it has been understood in the past and the present.

3.3.1 Innovation in 19th Century and in First-Half of 20th Century

As Benoît Godin highlighted in his recent studies on the history of this concept, the term was initially not connected with either creativity or originality. It simply meant 'introducing change in the established order', mostly at the level of thought or concept, and appeared in various contexts, including philosophy, politics, and history. During the early modern period, the word innovation was principally used with negative connotations for polemical purposes, as introducing newness in societal or moral issues itself often had negative value for the majority of people at that time. For example, as Godin showed, French theologian Jacques–Bénigne Bossuet was an ardent opponent of innovation, particularly the Reformation, and he accused the Protestant churches of having a 'spirit of innovation'.[11] Interestingly, those who wanted to introduce new things usually did not call themselves innovators; rather, their opponents primarily used the word. As Jean le Rond D'Alembert, a French mathematician and philosopher, remarked, *'C'est une innovation'* ('it is an innovation') appeared as a cry of reproach against a proposal that presented something new and might disturb the established order (d'Alembert 1787, p. 293; cf. Godin 2015, p. 259).

Thus, it is not surprising that the term innovation was absent from the minds of political elites in the Enlightenment period, as is suggested in the American Constitution, cited above. However, the first noteworthy shift to a positive connotation began gradually in the late 18th century. Driven by the socio-political context of that time, people started talking about innovation in relation to words representing the central values of modernity, such as rationality, usefulness, originality, and progress. Innovation also came to be associated with the quest for freedom, always in various fields involving religious and political matters. It came to include thought as well as action, within its broad scope. For example, the word 'social innovator' served as a label for the social reformer or socialist in the first decades of the 19th century (Godin 2015, Chaps. 6 and 8).

Discussions on innovation became associated with industry only at the beginning of the 20th century, and creativity was recognised as a basic element of innovation only in the first half of the 20th century. Further, it was only after The Second World War, especially with Rupert William Maclaurin, an economic historian, that

---

[11] Bossuet forgets the controversy on innovation in the England of his age, where the bishops accused the Protestant church of innovations in discipline and doctrine because they believed that the innovations brought it towards the superstitious and 'innovating' Catholic Church (Godin 2015, p. 246).

the phrase 'technological innovation' prevailed for the first time, and eventually became the dominant representation of innovation during the latter half of the 20th century (Godin 2015, pp. 384–386). This trend is clearly visible even in crude surveys conducted using Google Ngram, with the number of occurrences of the phrase 'technological innovation' increasing significantly in the 1950s (Google 2019). It appears that 'technological innovation' was typically mentioned in the following two ways during the 1950s. First, in debates concerning the dramatic technological changes of the time, represented by automation and nuclear power technology, and second, in discussions on the possibility of economic growth within developing countries.[12] Moreover, many authors, especially in the fields of management and economics, tried to analyse and define innovation during that period, and some authors even proposed abandoning the term because of its ambiguity (Godin 2015, p. 360, n. 96). It should be noted that in this context, technological innovation was still considered to be instrumental towards attaining a future end, such as growth, not an end to pursue therefore, but rather as purely a means to attain promised future economic growth, perceived as 'progress'.

3.3.2 Innovation Studies in 1970s–1990s

The most important shift in the epistemic status of the word innovation occurred during the period towards the end of the Cold War, from the 1970s to the 1990s, which was also the very period when the idea of progress began to be seriously questioned. The major proponents of the shift were writers from within the neo-Schumpeterian school, especially Christopher Freeman and Richard Nelson, both pioneers of innovation studies in the 1970s, and later several authors such as Bengt-Åke Lundvall, Luc Soete, and Giovanni Dosi. These writers essentially rewrote the definition of the word 'innovation' and changed it into a core concept of science and technology policy as well as of economic policy. In their new theory of innovation, technological innovation became firmly connected with the market, and innovations that were highly oriented towards consumer needs came to be privileged (Freeman 1974; Bengt-Åke 1992, pp. 325–328). This new trend implied a shift from the techno-expert-centric attitude of the 1950s to technological innovation as comprising a more social nature, involving the wider public and its collective creativity. At the same time, it also fostered an industrial/market-centeredness in relation to innovation policy, with a social vision that tended to view citizens as consumers (Jiang 2008, pp. 267–287).

Their emphasis on the innovative and creativity-based market economy was derived from the idea of 'evolutionary' economics that the neo-Schumpeterian school embraced, originally inspired by Joseph Schumpeter. In its framework, the capitalist

---

[12]The Google Ngram database has incomplete information on publications in the 1950 s, which include the phrase 'technological innovation'. Many errors were noted in the publication years. The number of publications was insufficient to draw a generalised conclusion. Nevertheless, we were able to observe that both the *Bulletin of the Atomic Scientists* and Japan, a developing country, have presence among miscellaneous titles.

system was perceived as a growing and living organism within a process of 'evolution'. It was thought to be constantly evolving and to be driven by 'new consumers' goods, the new methods of production or transportation, the new markets, the new forms of industrial organization' (Schumpeter 1943, p. 83), namely innovations of all kinds, in today's terminology. According to these authors, in this process, the so-called 'creative destruction' occurred with the displacement of older with newer technologies, goods, or firms (Freeman 1974, Chap. 1; Herman and Avram 2011, pp. 111–132; Dupont 2017, pp. 197–198).

Their theory was also based on assessments of a series of historical case studies that OECD reports had accumulated in the latter half of the 20th century. According to Freeman, through their investigation of these reports, 'two contrasting experiences made a very powerful impression in the 1980s both on policy-makers and on researchers: on the one hand the extraordinary success of first Japan and then South Korea in technological and economic catch-up; and on the other hand, the collapse of the Socialist economies of Eastern Europe' (Freeman 1995, p. 11). Apparently, for him and his colleagues, those two experiences provided evidence for extremely opposing models. One model involved a totally decentralized firm-centred innovative approach without any prior overall planning, while the other model involved a rationally calculated centralized approach, with virtually no interaction between consumers and suppliers. The performance of high performing Asian countries, especially Japan in the 1980s, was explained in terms of R&D intensity, 'as Japanese R&D was highly concentrated in the fastest growing civil industries, such as electronics' (Freeman 1995, p. 11). In contrast, the examples of the Soviet Union and other East European countries showed that investment of huge resources into R&D 'did not in itself guarantee successful innovation, diffusion and productivity gains' (Freeman 1995, pp. 11–12).

Thus, the 'innovation studies' school no longer accepted the role of private enterprises as being mere recipients of inventions, but rather as entities actively involved in discoveries alongside other actors such as scientists and engineers in universities. Its insights led to proposals for developed countries to design national R&D structures, or a 'national system of innovation'. The aim was to take into consideration the role of private companies and to increase interactivity between R&D and the market economy.

This trend of innovation policy was diffused via international organisations, especially by OECD, which had already employed Freeman as a consultant in the 1960s and had created a unified framework for collecting and publishing statistics on R&D activities on an international scale. These institutions also produced key notions and normative criteria for implementing this new approach in economic policy as well as in science and technology policy within most developed countries in Western Europe and in the United States, where experts had already raised questions concerning the efficiency of increasing investment in basic research, and in the military-industrial complex from the Cold War period (Fagerberg et al. 2013, p. 13; Pestre 2009, pp. 243–260).

The 'Budapest Declaration', adopted at the World Science Conference in 1999, provides an insightful example of what occurs in political discourses when the new orthodoxy of innovation theory confronts the decreasing hegemonic idea of progress. The declaration, famous for its phrase 'science in society and science for society', mentions both the importance of constructing a 'National Innovation System' (WCS 1999, § 37)[13] and the importance of progress in the sense of the development of scientific knowledge ('Science for knowledge: knowledge for progress'). At the same time, it also stated that 'the applications of scientific advances and the development and expansion of human activity have also led to environmental degradation and technological disasters, and have contributed to social imbalance or exclusion'. From these statements, it can be understood that, by this time, international communities had abandoned any blind enthusiasm for the progress of science, at least within international agenda formation. What was considered as now being required was 'a need for a vigorous and informed democratic debate on the production and use of scientific knowledge'.[14]

Following these developments, the uses of the word innovation have further expanded from the turn of the century, to include organisational and marketing innovations, as clearly stated in the *Oslo Manual* of the OECD (2005).[15] Not only the globalization of the market economy but also a recognition of environmental issues as part of a serious political agenda appeared to have contributed to this expanded use. The expression 'social innovation', generally used to mean structural change within the organization of society, began to be evoked more often in discussions on environmental issues, such as global warming (Vermeulen et al. 2002). Nowadays, innovation is a value-laden word, meaning almost anything good, new, and useful, and innovation is expected to play a major role in the 'urgent challenges society faces' (European Commission 2011, p. 2), for example, from helping to address environmental issues to dealing with social inequalities.

A Japanese case study has shown this most recent shift in meaning regarding the use of the word innovation very clearly through a close examination of the translation of the word innovation in a *White Paper on Science and Technology* for Japan from 1958 to the present. Initially, in 1958, the word innovation was translated into the Japanese phrase 'gijutsu-kakushin' (技術革新), which literally means technological (=gijitsu, technology) innovation (=kakushin, reform). However, since the beginning of the 2000s, its transliterated form 'inobêshon' has appeared and gradually gained status as the official translation of innovation, in place of 'gijitsu-kakushin'. In 2002, the *White Paper* stated that innovation could no longer refer solely to technological innovation, and it described innovation, 'inobêshon' (イノベーション), as something almost equal to 'social reform' (Ministry of Education 1958; 有賀・

---

[13]For the contents of the Budapest Declaration, Tateo Arimoto and Satoru Ohtake gave me advice.

[14]Declaration on Science and the Use of Scientific Knowledge.

[15]The *Oslo Manual* states that 'the definition of innovation is expanded to include two additional types of innovations: organisational innovation and marketing innovation. [...] The definitions of these types of innovations are still under development and are less well established than the definitions of product and process innovation' (OECD 2005, pp. 11–12).

亀井 2014, pp. 24–41).[16] This version of innovation appears to have also attracted the attention of political leaders from many other countries. For example, in China, Hu Jintao announced an objective to make China an innovative nation, at the 17th National Congress of the Communist Party of China. It is noteworthy that the Chinese language does not have issues with translating the word innovation, as it uses the term 'chuàngxīn' (創新) for innovations of all kinds, including technological and socio-political innovations (People's Daily Online 2007).

3.4 Conclusion

The term innovation seems to be an adaptation of the idea of progress to our age. It has inherited or absorbed social values from the Enlightenment project, incorporating a range of modern values such as originality, utility, rationality, and progress. With Marxist theory becoming less influential in development thinking, it has become a very useful concept for persuading political leaders to invest further into science and technology. In particular, the key notions of today's understanding of innovation, such as social inclusion and co-creation, can be regarded as part of its Enlightenment heritage, as their direct linkage to Condorcet's question on information aggregation suggests.

On the other hand, innovation differs considerably from progress, particularly in that it is based on concepts such as discontinuity and diversity. As discussed, the essential components in the term 'innovation' involve a sense of abrupt change, and emotions caused by such change, despite its dramatic shift in connotation from negative to positive associations. Nowadays, the concept of innovation has been adapted to the post-modern, globalised, and market-centred society that emerged after the Cold War. Innovation now means almost anything good and new. It is represented as an indispensable element in dealing with societal problems. In other words, innovation is no longer viewed as challenging the established political order, but rather as an integral part of the socio-political order itself.

This new political order is less Eurocentric than the order that had incorporated the idea of progress. It is more open to diversity, with one-dimensional measures or approaches quickly abandoned (Shigeru Nakayama 1997, p. 72). The resulting change also means that the concept of innovation does not foster a linear sense of progressive order, because innovation entails very abrupt change. Many non-Western countries, China and Japan for example, have embraced without hesitation the slogan of innovation as part of their own national strategy of socio-economic policy, without sharing any specific common future goal.

Despite these differences, however, innovation appears to involve another inherited and disruptive aspect from the modern notion of progress, namely, evolution

---

[16]Notably, they did not try to replace 'kakushin' (reform) with 'gijutsu-kakushin'. At this point, I am unaware of the exact reason, but I believe it is noteworthy that 'kakushin' is mostly used to refer to political or social reform rather than being associated with economic issues or business.

through fierce competition. The neo-Schumpeterian school embraced the idea of 'evolutionary' economics and described the innovative and creativity-based economy as a source of growth. The thinking of this school helped to effectively open the minds of political decision-makers to see the economy as an organism within a process of 'evolution', which, due to its original Darwinian connotation, involved no sense of a determined goal, except accumulation of capital through competition. As a result, various innovations have been accelerated through policy guidance promoting more creativity, and disjointed changes have increasingly occurred, without accompanying mature considerations on their social, ethical, and environmental impacts (Block and Lemmens 2015, p. 29; Girel 2015).

Concerns about the global use of innovation have recently been expressed from the heart of the innovation studies group. Soete has raised an alarm concerning the existence not only of 'creative destruction' but also of 'destructive creation'. He has claimed that destructive creation can bring about the destruction of socially-shared values and a non-sustainable consumption pattern. He has also pointed out that the encouragement of innovation has systematically created 'outdated products' and excessive consumption trends, typically in the Information and Communication Technology sector and in most manufacturing industries selling goods using image strategy marketing (Fagerberg et al. 2013, Chap. 6).[17] Some authors have also pointed out the 'Faustian' aspect of innovation, giving society an unexpected negative output (Block and Lemmens 2015, p. 30).

I think it is time to reconsider how innovation is perceived. I am not nostalgic regarding the concept of progress, as it purported to provide not only a grand design of a knowable future but also helped to inculcate feelings of prejudice towards non-European countries as well as an excessive optimism that science and technology could resolve all the problems. The new tide of innovation policy in the 2010s, symbolized both by European Horizon 2020 and by the implementation of the Sustainable Development Goals in each country (Schot and Steinmuller 2016),[18] seem to favour my intention. What seems more indispensable now is to seek a way to attenuate the disruptive or 'Faustian' nature of innovation, while retaining the other positive values involved with the term, such as co-creation and diversity. As S. Laugier, and S. Lechevalier claim in the introduction of this volume, 'human factor' should be involved from the outset in designing science and technology.[19] We need to find methods to further democratize the innovation process and develop a sense of social responsibility, to avoid any 'destructive creation'.

---

[17]I am grateful to Pierre-Benoît Joly for suggesting this title.

[18]See the argument by Joly (2019).

[19]Some other chapters give the case studies of the application of this principle. See Pestre (2019), Kusago (2019), Fujigaki (2019), Ruphy (2019), Hiroi (2019).

References

Amin, A. (Ed.). (1994). *Post-fordism*. Oxford and Massachusetts: Blackwell Publishers Ltd.

Ariga, N., & Kamei, S. [有賀暢迪・亀井修].(2014). 「科学技術白書に見る『技術革新』の意味合いの変遷」. *Bulletin of the National Museum of Nature and Science*, Series E (Physical Sciences & Engineering), (Vol. 37, pp. 25–41).

Bengt-Åke, L. (Ed.). (1992). *National systems of innovation: Toward a theory of innovation and interactive learning*. London: Pinter Publishers.

Block, V., & Lemmens, P. (2015). The emerging concept of responsible innovation. Three reasons why it is questionable and calls for a radical transformation of the concept of innovation. In B.-J. Koops, I. Oosterlaken, H. Romijn, T. Swierstra, & J. van den Hoven (Eds.) *Responsible innovation 2, concepts, approaches, and applications*, Ch. 2. Heidelberg, New York, Dordrecht, London: Springer.

Brewer, A. (2008, March). *Adam Smith's stages of history*. Bristol Economics Discussion Papers No. 08/601, Department of Economics, University of Bristol, UK.

Burgen, A., McLaughlin, P., & Mittelstraß, J. (Eds.) (1997). *The idea of progress*. Berlin, New York: Walter de Gruyter.

Condorcet. (1976). *Selected Writings* (K. M. Baker, Ed.). Indianapolis: The Bobbs-Merrill Company, Inc.

Condorcet. (1785). *Essai sur l'application de l'analyse à la probabilité des décisions rendues à la pluralité des voix*. Paris.

Condorcet. (1988). *Esquisse d'un tableau historique des progrès de l'esprit humain. Fragment sur l'Atlantide*. Paris: GF-Flammarion.

Condorcet. (2004). *Tableau historique du progrès de l'Espreit humain* (J.-P. Schandeler & P. Crépel, Eds.). Paris: INED.

d'Alembert, J. L. R. (1787). Eloge de l'Abbé François Régnier Desmarais. *Histoire des membres de l'Académie Française, morts depuis 1700 jusqu'en 1771, pour servir de suite aux éloges imprimés et lus dans les séances publiques de cette Compagnie*. Paris, t. III Democratic Societies: An Introduction. *Minerva, 47*, 243–260. https://doi.org/10.1007/s11024-009-9126-2.

Dupont, B. (2017). *The history of economic ideas: economic thought in contemporary context*. London, New York.

European Commission. (2011). *Communication from the Commission to the European Parliament, the Council, the European Economic and Social Committee and the Committee of the Regions: Horizon 2020—The Framework Programme for Research and Innovation*. Retrieved April 4, 2019 from http://eur-lex.europa.eu/legal-content/EN/TXT/PDF/?uri=CELEX:52011DC0808&from=EN.

Fagerberg, J., Martin, B. R., & Andersen, E. S. (Eds.). (2013). *Innovation studies: Evolution & future challenges*. Oxford: Oxford University Press.

Francis, M. (2014). *Herbert spencer and the invention of modern life*. London, New York: Routledge.

Freeman, C. (1974). *The economics of industrial innovation* (1st edn.). Penguin Books.

Freeman, C. (1995). The "National System of Innovation" in historical perspective. *Cambridge Journal of Economics, 1995*(19), 5–24.

Fujigaki, Y. (2019). Lessons from Fukushima for responsible innovation: How to construct a new relationship between science and society? In S. Lechevalier (Ed.), *Innovation beyond technology* (pp. 223–239). Berlin: Springer.

Girel, M. (2015). Innovation, Progress and Acceleration, talk given in Engaging Society in Innovation and Creativity, International Workshop organized by the CNRS, the Foundation France-Japon de l'EHESS and the JST/RISTEX, 2 June 2015, Paris.

Godin, B. (2015). *Innovation contested—The idea of innovation over the centuries*. London: Routledge.

Google. (2019). Google Books Ngram Viewer. [Search result]. Retrieved April 5, 2019 from https://books.google.com/ngrams/interactive_chart?content=Technological+innovation&

year_start=1900&year_end=2000&corpus=15&smoothing=1&share=&direct_url=t1%3B%2CTechnological%20innovation%3B%2Cc0.

Herman, R., Avram, R. (2011). The contribution of the Neo-Schumpeterian approach to the development of the economic theory: Emphasis on the meso-economic level. *Theoretical and Applied Economics, XVIII*, 7(560), 111–132.

Hiroi, Y. (2019). Science as care: Science and innovation in post-growth society. In S. Lechevalier (Ed.), *Innovation beyond technology* (pp. 301–324). Berlin: Springer.

Jiang, J. [姜 娟].(2008).「『イノベーション政策』の概念変化に関する考.察—OECDの政策議論を中心とする—」『研究 技術 計画』Vol. 23(3), 267–287.

Joly, P. B. (2019). Reimagining innovation. In S. Lechevalier (Ed.), *Innovation beyond technology* (pp. 25–45). Berlin: Springer.

Kato, H. [加藤弘之].(1882).『人権新説』谷山楼.

K'ang, Y. (1958). *Ta t'ung shu: The one-world philosophy* (L. G. Thompson, Trans.). London: Allen & Unwin.

Koizumi, S. (2019). The light and shadow of the fourth industrial revolution. In S. Lechevalier (Ed.), *Innovation beyond technology* (pp. 63–86). Berlin: Springer.

Kusago, T. (2019). Post-disaster community recovery and community-based collaborative action research—A case of process evaluation method for community life improvement. In S. Lechevalier (Ed.), *Innovation beyond technology* (pp. 195–221). Berlin: Springer.

Lechevalier, S., Laugier, S. (2019). Innovation Beyond Technology—Introduction. In S. Lechevalier (Ed.), *Innovation beyond technology* (pp. 1–21). Berlin: Springer.

Mazlish, B. (1996). Progress: A historical and critical perspective. In L. Marx & B. Mazlish (Eds.) *Progress: Fact or illusion?* Michigan: University of Michigan Press.

Mclean, I. S., McMillan, A., & Monroe, B. L. (Eds.). (2012). *The theory of committees and elections by Duncan Black and committee decisions with contemporary valuation by Duncan Black and R. A. Newing* (2nd ed.). New York: Springer Science+Business Media.

Migita, H. [右田裕規]. (2009).『天皇制と進化論』青弓社.

Ministry of Education. (1958). *White paper on science and technology*. Retrieved April 4, 2019 from http://www.mext.go.jp/b_menu/hakusho/html/hpaa195801/index.html.

Miyake, M. [三宅正樹]. (1999).「ヨーロッパとアジアにおける進歩の理念の比較文明論的考察」『明治大学社会科学研究所紀要』第37号.

Niedzviecki, H. (2015). *Trees on mars: Our obsession with the future*. Seven Stories Press.

Nisbet, R. (2009). *History of the idea of progress* (Fourth edn.). New Brunswish, London.

OECD. (2005). *Oslo manual: Guidelines for collecting and interpreting innovation Data* (3rd Edn.).

Pauchant, T. C. (2016). Adam Smith's four-stages theory of socio-cultural evolution. *The Adam Smith Review, 9*, 49–74.

People's Daily Online. (2007). *Full text of Hu Jintao's report at 17th Party Congress* [News report]. Press center of the 17th National Congress of the Communist Party of China. Retrieved May 29, 2015 from http://english.cpc.people.com.cn/66102/6290205.html.

Pestre, D. (2009). Understanding the forms of government in today's liberal and democratic societies: An introduction. *Minerva, 47*(3), 243–260.

Pestre, D. (2010). Des sciences et des productions techniques depuis trente ans. Chronique d'une mutation. *Le Débat, 3*(160), 115–131. https://doi.org/10.3917/deba.160.0115.

Pestre, D. (2019). Environment and social innovation: Why technology never was the solution. In S. Lechevalier (Ed.), *Innovation beyond technology* (pp. 175–194). Berlin: Springer.

Picon, A., (2003). Utopian socialism and social science. *Cambridge history of science* (Vol. 7, pp. 71–82). *The Modern Social Sciences* (Th. M. Porter & D. Ross, Eds.). Cambridge, Cambridge University Press.

Rendall, J. (1982). Scottish orientalism: From Robertson to James Mill. *The Historical Journal, 25*(1), 43–69. https://doi.org/10.1017/s0018246x00009857.

Ruphy, S. (2019). Public participation in the setting of research and innovation agenda: Virtues and challenges from a philosophical perspective. In S. Lechevalier (Ed.), *Innovation beyond technology* (pp. 243–261). Berlin: Springer.

Schot, J., & Steinmuller, E. (2016). *Framing innovation policy for transformative change: Innovation policy 3.0*. Brighton: SPRU, Draft, 4/9/2016.

Schumpeter, J. A. (1943). *Capitalism, socialism and democracy*. London: Allen & Unwin.

Shigeru Nakayama, S. (1997). Chinese 'cyclic' view of history vs Japanese 'progress'. *The Idea of Progress*, 65–76.

Smith, A. (1978). *Lectures on jurisprudence* (R. Meek, D. Raphael, & P. Stein, Eds.). Oxford: Clarendon Press.

Takeda, T. [武田時昌]. (2003). 「加藤弘之の新科学事始」『変異するダーウィニズム』阪上孝編、京都大学学術出版会 U.S. Constitution, art. I, § 8, cl. 8.

Vaidhyanathan, S. (2015). Why has innovation supplanted the idea of progress. [Discussion board post]. Retrieved December 12, 2017 from https://aeon.co/conversations/why-has-innovation-supplanted-the-idea-of-progress.

Von Wright, G. H. (1997). Progress: Fact and fiction. *The Idea of Progress*, 1–18.

Walter Vermeulen, W., Kok, M. et al. (2002). *Global warming and social innovation: The challenge of a climate-neutral society*. Routledge.

Watanabe, M. [渡部正雄]. (1976). 『日本人と近代科学——西洋への対応と課題——』岩波新書.

World Conference on Science. (1999). *Declaration on science and the use of scientific knowledge*. Text adopted by the World Conference on Science. Definitive version in 1999. Retrieved April, 5 2019 from http://www.unesco.org/science/wcs/eng/declaration_e.htm.

Chapter 4
The Light and Shadow of the Fourth Industrial Revolution

Shinichi Koizumi

Abstract GDP growth of OECD member countries has gradually declined during the past 20 years, and advanced economies are expected to see relatively flat growth in the coming years. Among GDP growth factors, total factor productivity (TFP) is also declining in the 21st Century. Meanwhile, distribution of outcome from economic growth seems to be unfair and impartial. For example, in the U.S., the share of all income held by the top one percent wealthy class has been steadily growing since the mid-1970s, on the other hand, ordinary middle-class people feel that they can't expect a prosperous life for their children. Under such circumstances, many people believe that the Fourth Industrial Revolution should lead economic growth by creating new value and industry through interconnections between physical systems and digital Big Data, deriving from further development of disruptive and innovative technologies such as artificial intelligence, robotics and IoT. The Fourth Industrial Revolution is expected to reshape the economic, social and cultural context in which we live, and we might expect dazzling results. In a world where people, goods, information and money can freely travel back and forth, we have to establish an orderly system based upon international common rules and regulations. However, in the context of rising income disparity and continued decline of middle-class status, people feel strong distrust of existing politics and political leaders. As a consequence, anti-globalism, nationalism and unilateralism are emerging, and credence to common values such as liberalism, democracy and market economy is weakening. Today, technical innovation is progressing at a dizzying speed, and industry, government and academia across the globe should cooperatively and sincerely explore necessary action programs to govern new disruptive technologies in advance so that we can establish stable, sustainable and inclusive development of our society. Unless many hurdles are overcome through real global collaboration, many innovative ideas will be swept away, or implemented with serious negative side effects. We must tackle the truly challenging tasks in order to change the mindset of the middle class towards the expectation of a positive future for their children.

S. Koizumi (✉)
DeNA Co., Ltd., Tokyo, Japan
e-mail: shinichi.koizumi@dena.com

© Springer Nature Singapore Pte Ltd. 2019
S. Lechevalier (ed.), *Innovation Beyond Technology*, Creative Economy,
https://doi.org/10.1007/978-981-13-9053-1_4

4.1 Introduction

In recent years, various forms of information media such as newspapers, magazines, TV, Internet media, etc., are featuring articles on the situation concerning the drastic industry structural reforms being made, centering on Digital Technology Innovation (Big Data, AI—Artificial Intelligence, Robotics and IoT—Internet of Things), on the future image of industry value chain which is expected to arise, and on considerable changes which will be brought to the social structure and daily lifestyle. They publish examples of various actions taken in an industry or across various industrial fields. Books and papers themed on these issues have been published one after another worldwide, and workshops, symposiums and lecture meetings are being held every week by experts in their respective fields.

Currently, this trend is collectively called the Fourth Industrial Revolution. Most of these reports are packed with optimistic views: promotion of the Fourth Industrial Revolution will make it much easier to address many serious problems that we face now, such as climate change, food and water shortage that is expected to become more serious in the future and declining birthrate and a growing proportion of elderly people that are common problems in developed countries, and it will realize a sustainable Smart Society, the achievement of which will benefit all humans.

However, I myself am not able to envision the future so optimistically, as the Fourth Industrial Revolution is usually an initiative to create a new innovative value chain from a global point of view. A situation can be assumed where a portion of major countries prioritize the advantages of their own countries, completely ignoring their roles of proactive contributions to the world, which should be played as a world leader—for example, the U.S. President Trump's abrupt declaration of secession from the Paris Climate Accord, which scandalized the world. As a result, global collaborations among countries will become extremely hard to realize. It is therefore easy to imagine that the Fourth Industrial Revolution cannot be achieved in a simple manner as an initiative that creates true values.

If we cannot accomplish global collaborations, no matter what advanced disruptive technology innovation occurs and ideas of innovative business models are created, it is expected that, in most cases, they will end up being left uncompleted or being applied only in limited fields and areas if they were realized. On the contrary, if they were to be launched prematurely while global collaborations haven't been realized, as a result of seeking immediate outcomes even without bad intentions, we must be ready for a very high frequency of substantial risk occurring, causing a series of serious side effects throughout the world.

4.2 A Widening Gap in the Growth Process and Distrust in Politics

4.2.1 Economic Growth Slowdown, and Stagnation of Productivity Improvement

As soon as the world thought it had overcome the Year 2000 (Y2K) Problem without any serious issues—which is remembered as an event that symbolized the arrival of the full-scale information society in the last year of the 20th century, the so-called Dot-com Bubble burst due to a world-scale inventory and stock price adjustment mainly in the computer and internet-related industries. After that turbulence, the world economy gradually returned to a recovery path. In order to give it robust support, all major countries adopted continuous easy monetary policies.

However, since 2004, U.S. Federal Reserve Board (FRB) has retightened the monetary policy, and the real estate market in the United States started to show a rapid downturn. In the aftermath of this policy change, the world faced what is known as the Global Financial Crisis triggered by the Bankruptcy of Lehman Brothers (Lehman Collapse).

The Lehman Collapse could also have been the natural consequence of the distortion within the financial capitalism that had been led by the U.S. The entire world economy slumped considerably after the Lehman Collapse. Since then, the world economy gradually recovered. However, what led the recovery was the economic growth of emerging countries such as China, India and the ASEAN countries, and the proportion of emerging and developing countries in the world economy rapidly expanded, with an increased size to over 41% at present from around 21% in 2000 (IMF 2015). On the other hand, the Real GDP Growth Rate of OECD countries dropped from 3.8% in the 1970s to 3.0% in the 1980s and 2.6% in the 1990s. The average annual growth rate between 2000 and 2015 decreased to 1.8% (World Bank and OECD Data). It is expected that the annual growth rate will continue to remain just under 2%.

The three factors comprising economic growth rate are defined to be (1) Growth Rate of Capital Input, (2) Growth Rate of Labor Input and (3) TFP: Total Factor Productivity. In the case of developed countries, the Growth Rate of Labor Input will continue to be on a downturn trend given that the low birthrate and aging population are accelerating in the medium to long term.

The state finances in most developed countries are generally not favorable (Total Government Debt Balance in Japan is more than 200% of GDP) (OECD Data 2018), and it is extremely difficult to take large-scale fiscal actions. The private sector is also being discreet in their approach to large capital investment for the purpose of simply expanding the size of their existing business (OECD Data 2018), due to volatility in the future business environment. It means that it is difficult to expect the increase of the Growth Rate of Capital Input by the private sector. Consequently, in order to achieve sustainable and high economic growth in most developed countries, it is a

4.2.2 Issues Concerning Distribution System of Economic Growth

Economic growth in developed countries has steadily increased the size of the pie to be sliced up. For example, in the U.S., the real GDP increased 1.82 times in the past 25 years. GDP per capita also increased 1.43 times in the same period (Sekai Keizai no Neta chou 2018). This shows that the size of a slice per person is steadily improving on a simple average basis.

However, the percentage of the middle-class (which falls in an income group between two-thirds and two times the median value of the total income) that was once the majority of population (over 60% in early 1970s) has already dropped below half of the population, and the number of people in the low-income class increased (Pew Research Center 2015). I was repeatedly told by my reliable friends in the USA that the great majority of the middle-class complains that they don't feel affluent with their everyday life in comparison with their parents' generation and has an extremely pessimistic outlook about their children being more affluent in the future than themselves.

Certainly, middle-class people must actually feel that their real salaries hardly increased if taxes and social security payments are deducted from the earnings they receive. Moreover, education costs for receiving a leading university degree are skyrocketing. While average life expectancy is rising, the social security benefits after retirement seem to be insufficient. Many people think that the current payment-by-results system is extremely unfair as the results from economic growth only benefit partial and certain people in the high-class. I believe that they feel that the abilities to reform the current situation and to execute appropriate policies as well as political ethical values of policymakers, who haven't dealt with the problem, are highly problematic.

The percentage of the income of the top 1% of the highest income group in the U.S., which only accounted for about 10% of the total from the 1950s to 1970s (Piketty and Saez 2003), currently stands at around 25% in 2012 (Saez 2014) and another source (Saez and Zucman 2016; Kobayashi 2017), shows the comparison of assets, which reveals a larger difference between classes. The percentage of net assets owned by the bottom 90% to the total continued to decrease after having peaked in 1986 at 36.4%, and fell to 22.8% in 2012. This is only as much as 22.0%, the percentage of net assets owned by the top 0.1%.

Comparing the median value of household incomes, the nominal household income increased 2.4 times from $ 22,000/year to $ 54,000/year in the past 30 years (1984–2014). Comparing real household net incomes excluding inflation, the median value of household incomes converted with the present price levels only increased by 10% in 30 years (U.S. Bureau of the Census).

In the United States, it seems to be necessary for the middle and low-income classes to send their children to leading educational institutions for a high-quality education in order for them to be able to enter into an elite class of the society. In that case, the financial burden of parents is considerably large even if students hold a scholarship, as their income does not increase as aforementioned. For the middle-class, therefore, the hurdle to sending their children to renowned universities is extremely high.

This situation is apt to immobilize the middle and low-income classes: it is likely that a structure will take root where winners continue to win over generations and losers will never be rewarded no matter how much effort they put in.

4.2.3 Skepticism Towards Liberal Democracy and the Fourth Industrial Revolution

At present, we share a number of problems in the world for which we cannot easily find solutions. In addition to the various problems caused by gaps in incomes and assets as mentioned in the previous section, these include frequently occurring natural disasters in recent years, which can be considered to be caused partially by global warming and climate change; food and water shortage, which is a medium to long term critical issue; threats of indiscriminate terrorism attacks conducted by people who are unable to have hope in the future, including young people who are infected with religious extremism like the Islamic State; territorial disputes over the Crimea and the South China Sea; massive inflow of refugees and immigrants caused by regional political instabilities; and other national security issues, such as the threat of nuclear weapons from North Korea.

Although many of the problems listed here have been repeatedly pointed out in the past, some of them have been generated or further exacerbated through the following situations. As a consequence of the end of the monopolization by the U.S. great power, multi polarization of the world emerged and nations and groups with various values unilaterally ignored the world's common rules led by the liberal democracy nations, and pushed through their own principles and opinions with the support of dogmatism and violence. The position of the Global Commons such as the freedom of navigation, the free trade system, international order and peace, and the United Nations, which have been considered stable, is now at serious risk. As the international society is becoming unstable, many people feel that measures for these issues taken by their national government are inappropriate and inadequate. They have growing doubts and frustrations with the political ruling power of the government and leaders who cannot respond to these issues in an appropriate and timely manner.

A liberal democratic country requires a process in which it discusses with all stakeholders with patience according to the rules of democracy and tries to find a compromise by gaining understanding and agreement with their policies. However, a majority of policymakers who regularly receive lessons of elections have an unstable political foundation, and it is not so easy for them to realize a policy that requires voters to suffer by facing issues. As a result, discussions over radical reforms to tackle difficult issues will usually be postponed. The general public always has to blame rulers unilaterally for their lack of abilities to produce a result.

Under these circumstances, the skepticism about liberal democracy and the expansion of the global market economic zone is spreading like basso continuo. In response to this, the U.S. President, who must have been appointed as the advocate of liberal democracy, proudly talks about the "Our Country First" slogan, the skepticism about free trade and the secession from the multilateral trade and economic partnership agreement, which are completely out of the basic philosophy of "contributing to the world by respecting the rule of law and basic human rights and protecting free-market economies" that liberal democratic nations have previously adopted. In Europe, far-right powers that uphold an anti-immigration policy, protected trade and nationalism are emerging. In response to people's anxiety and dissatisfaction, some politicians known as populists and demagogues draw the enthusiastic support of some voters by curbing people's irritations through the continuous advocating of "simple but wrong and easy solution" to individual important issues of the country, which is apt to sound nice to people.

As mentioned earlier, OECD countries have extremely serious and complex common problems such as complaints about the distribution of the fruits of growth that a large number of people have accumulated in the transition of the countries to the low-growth era, and the skepticism toward liberal democracy and the Global Commons, which have been recognized and shared as common human values. However, none of these countries have been able to make a definite prescription. I am going to express my opinion about points such as whether or not the Fourth Industrial Revolution, which has been transforming the world at an amazing speed with disruptive digital innovation technologies, will prove to be a true cure for these circumstances, and what kinds of effort will be needed to achieve that. However, before expressing my opinion, let me touch upon a path to the Fourth Industrial Revolution in the next section.

4.3 A Path to the Fourth Industrial Revolution

The First Industrial Revolution went into full swing from the late 18th century after the arrival of the steam engine, and the production of various types of power engines started. The Second Industrial Revolution began between the late 19th century and the early 20th century, and it featured a revolution of the manufacturing industry—a mass production method for the same quality and same standard products that were made possible by the invention of electricity and automation known as Ford Production Method. During the Third Industrial Revolution, semiconductor-integrated circuits and personal computers appeared in the late 20th century and became widely used in a relatively short period. These led to the introduction of industrial robots, sophisticated machine tools, etc., in production sites and accelerated mechanization and automatization. However, the period of Third Industrial Revolution is now rapidly getting swallowed by a wave of the Fourth Industrial Revolution. Of course, the wave of the Fourth Industrial Revolution did not occur spontaneously as a result of the Third Industrial Revolution. Various prerequisites need to be fulfilled to launch the Fourth Industrial Revolution, and it should be considered that the ideas of existing advanced digital innovation projects could finally be realized by gradually satisfying these conditions.

The primary requirement was fulfilled when a number of sensors became overwhelmingly affordable as sensor related technologies had advanced in an astonishing speed. The development of information communication infrastructure was also an indispensable condition so that innumerable information derived from these sensors could become interactive in safety and security. Moreover, we had to wait until these information communication infrastructure technologies became deepened and lowered communication cost to make information derived in this way interactive, and processed and stored securely in a fine balance with economic viability. It should not be forgotten that major countries have worked patiently without having the idea of "Our Country First" in order to normalize the standards and specifications necessary to promote the results of various disruptive technology development and innovative business models across borders using these information communication infrastructures.

I would also like to explain the historical background to encouraging these rapid technological evolutions and deepening thereof. From the late 20th century, major companies of developed countries such as Western countries and Japan set a goal of establishing an optimal global supply chain by dividing industrial structure by region as a core strategy to strengthen competitiveness in quality and cost. They proactively established production as well as marketing and sales bases in East Asia, Southeast Asia and Latin America to gradually expand and deepen the global production networks. The automobile industry, for example, first started relocating sites for the knockdown production process overseas, which does not require a huge amount of capital investment and is relatively easy to learn parts assembling skills. Next, they gradually expanded the production network overseas from auto body parts production and final assembly process to the production of engine, transmission and other essential core parts, and production of basic materials to be used for such key elements production.

As a result, overseas countries (emerging countries) were able to achieve their own industrial development through the acquisition of key technologies and management know-how that were brought from developed countries while they play a major role in the supply chain of these global companies. These countries have by degrees established a position as a base for developed countries to produce electric appliances and electronic parts, and commodity materials such as synthetic fibers and general-purpose plastics. In particular, the production network has expanded in Hong Kong,

South Korea, Taiwan and Singapore (Four Asian Tigers), followed by the major powers in Southeast Asia—Thailand, Indonesia and Malaysia between the 1960s and 1980s. In the 1990s, China revealed its shift to a route of economic reform and partial market liberalization after the famous "Southern Tour Lectures" of Deng Xiaoping. It invited foreign capital mainly in the special economic zones established in the Pearl River Delta Metropolitan Region and the Shanghai Pu Dong East Region in order to develop a large production base. In this way, China has started its unique economic reform to become the so-called World's Factory.

Against this backdrop, developed countries in the West could procure various products and parts from emerging countries at very competitive prices. On the other hand, the widespread use of personal computers and the development of information revolution started in the 1980s through the deepening of technologies related to integrated circuits and personal computers. In the context of this situation, the manufacturing sector used and applied information network proactively and tried to promote the shift to higher value-added products, strengthening of basic research and technology development capability and the enhancement of strategy for securing their intellectual property rights. The service industry strived for productivity improvement using information revolution and the structural innovation and global development of financial businesses (shift to Financial Capitalism) in an effort to promote a significant transition of the industrial structure.

In particular, the financial industry in the U.S. has created various kinds of complicated financial institutions using advanced Information and Communication Technology (ICT) since the 1980s. As a result, high-frequency trading using the algorithm trading system was created. Today, in heyday of hedge funds, 75% of all stock trading is now algorithm based dealings (Corkery and Zornada 2012). Mathematicians and AI scientists have taken profits in a frenzy in a complex and huge financial market and have developed a system where only a wealthy class can benefit through their political donations, consequently contributing significantly to the uneven distribution of wealth. Although this can be considered a financialization of the economy, many people in management positions in financial institutions are losing awareness as service providers to depositors, businesses, the economy and the society and seek the growth of their own benefits: the term "fiducial duty" seems to be forgotten. In addition, thousands of brokers exist between depositors and fund operators, and the expansion in their activities has driven up GDP. In 2014, 4.4% of the total employed population in the U.S., 7.0% of GDP and 19.2% of corporate profits were generated in the finance and insurance sector (Kobayashi 2017).

4.4 Measures in Each Country and Typical Example of Application

4.4.1 Efforts of Germany and the United States

In Germany, people were becoming clearly aware that the productivity improvement in the manufacturing sector, which has led German industries for a long time, had gradually peaked out. However, they couldn't transform them into the industrial structure based on financial capitalism like the one in the U.S., and the creation of emerging new industries such as the ones led by ICT ventures based in the West Coast, including Silicon Valley, was as slow as a snail. Under these circumstances, creation of a new driving force for economic growth became the urgent task. In response to this sense of crisis, under the leadership of Chancellor Merkel, industry, government and academia jointly summarized an innovation program as a national project—Industry 4.0 to drastically strengthen competitiveness in the manufacturing sector. This applies IoT in the production process, and analyzes Big Data acquired from countless sensors attached to facilities using AI, etc., and provides feedback on the results for the optimization of the production process. This develops the "Cyber Physical System" that connects cyber space and the real physical world and realizes "Smart Factory" in the near future.

This project is primarily led by SAP, a world-leading business software developer, global manufacturers representing Germany such as Siemens, Bosch, and Volkswagen, RWTH Aachen University, Technical University of Munich, Fraunhofer Society, and other machinery, electricity and information industry groups, and they started discussions around 2011. The results of the discussions were published as the "Recommendations for implementing the strategic initiatives INDUSTRIE 4.0, Final report of the Industries 4.0 Working group, April 2013" (BMBF 2013).

In response to these, IG Metal (metalworkers' labor union) and the Chamber of Commerce and Industry became members, and at present they evaluate various impacts of these industrial innovations on the society. At the same time, the government is conducting various considerations, including ways to encourage SMEs' (small and medium-sized enterprises) participation from the viewpoint of inclusivity. It also intends to share the acquired results with other EU countries in the future.

On the other hand, the U.S. is taking accelerating measures towards the Fourth Industrial Revolution from a different angle. As the country made an early start in relocating manufacturing industry overseas and the procurement of overseas products and parts, industries that lead economic growth changed from the manufacturing sector, which dropped to around 10% of GDP (Germany and Japan maintain around 20%) (DBJ 2015), to highly advanced financial sector and ICT industries. As a result, the government put emphasis to provide common platforms to exchange information to many participants who would develop new business models one after another using Big Data that accumulates in such platforms. Big Data is leading the accelerating trend of the Fourth Industrial Revolution. Here, Big Data exists in cyber space including (1) an enormous amount of data accumulated and owned by administrative organizations as various kinds of public databases, (2) data on the operational conditions of machinery, which is acquired through various sensors and owned by private companies, as well as (3) huge amount of information acquired from the users of Blog or Social Networking Services (SNS) such as Facebook, Twitter and Instagram. Various kinds of entrepreneurial ventures try to obtain a huge amount of data from websites legally and create various new business models using such data as invaluable information sources by analyzing them with the state-of-the-art data-mining algorithm.

In other words, the trend in the U.S. is considered in a completely different way from measures taken in Germany: evolving manufacturing sites to smart factories to rapidly increase global competitiveness in the manufacturing industry. The Fourth Industrial Revolution in the U.S. is centered on countless efforts towards the drastic innovation of business models—to design new values by themselves which are potentially considered necessary by people and the society by using open markets and legally obtainable Big Data, and realize them across industrial borders by connecting cyber space and physical space. These are promoted by various enterprising bodies from big global firms to small and medium sized enterprises, start-ups, and venture enterprises before operation. These efforts in industry in particular are collectively called the Industrial Internet on an occasional basis.

A leading example of the Industrial Internet is the business model innovation in jet engine business operated by GE. GE is originally the world's top maker of jet engines, and incorporates countless sensors in a jet engine in order to collect data related to various operations from aircrafts mounted with their jet engines. Big Data obtained here is analyzed using AI in their data center and is used to predict necessary maintenance times and potential unplanned troubles in order to decrease repair costs significantly, creating new values from operation data and providing analytical findings to client airline companies. GE is expanding this new business model into other businesses such as gas turbine business for power generation.

If a typical example of B to B is the jet engine business of GE, an example of C to C is the car and driver dispatch business of Uber Technologies. Uber provides a basic service in which it matches people who would like to use a car with drivers who would like to use their unoperated cars and free time. It also adjusts prices at an appropriate level according to the current supply and demand status of cars in the city using an algorithm called surge (dynamic) pricing. This is a business model evolving every day from a viewpoint of finding a balance that satisfies both users and drivers.

In parallel with these efforts of individual companies, various consortiums in view of future standardization have been established as cross-industrial measures to accelerate these movements. Examples include the "Industrial Internet Consortium" participated by GE, IBM, Cisco Systems, INTEL, Bosch, SAP, etc., the "All Seen Alliance/Open Connectivity Foundation" by QUALCOMM, Microsoft, Electrolux, etc., and the "Open Interconnect Consortium" by INTEL, QUALCOMM and Cisco Systems (Nagashima 2015). These organizations cooperate with each other to promote various measures.

4.4.2 Efforts of Japan

From the early 1990s, Japan suffered a long-term deflation and low economic growth. This period is called the "Lost 20 Years". In December 2012, the second Abe administration was inaugurated and established the "Abenomics" policies which incorporate economic and financial policies in one package for Japan's economic recovery. In addition to the two core policies—the bold monetary policy and the flexible fiscal policy, the primary target was set on the third core policy—the growth strategy to encourage private investment in order to overcome the deflation and slow growth.

Japan, where measures for the Fourth Industrial Revolution have been considerably delayed, now needs to overcome the current situation of extremely slow economic growth compared with other OECD countries and to put the economy back on the track of growth. The important key to realize this agenda is that the corporate side should conduct a fundamental revision of their business models and promote a structural innovation by building new business models using the most-advanced innovation technologies and in particular the latest information communication technologies such as Big Data, AI, Robotics and IoT, and invest in them in a proactive manner. This has become a common awareness among the public, private and academia sectors. Japan Business Federation (KEIDANREN) summarized the "Toward realization of the new economy and society—Reform of the economy and society by the deepening of *Society 5.0*" as a policy proposal in 2016 (Keidanren 2016), and in response, the government raised the "Actions for the Realization of the Society 5.0 (super-smart society)" as the most important project to improve productivity in the "Basic Policy on Economic and Fiscal Management and Reform 2016" (Cabinet Office 2016). In June 2017, based on the outcomes of discussions made with the industry sectors, more concrete measures were formulated as the "Future Investment Strategy 2017—Reform toward the Realization of Society 5.0." (Cabinet Office 2017).

The elderly population in Japan reached 34.59 million as of October 2016, and the percentage of the elderly (age 65 and above) to total population (aging rate) has already reached 27.3%. However, the population aging rate is projected to reach 33.3% in 2036 and 38.4% in 2065 respectively (National Institute of Population and Social Security Research 2017).

In addition to essential issues, including the decrease in the productive-age population caused by the low birthrate and aging population and the way the society where a number of elderly people and a small number of young people coexist, Japan has various critical issues, including resource and energy related challenges, crafting a new approach to global warming, response to large-scale natural disasters such as earthquakes and tsunami, overcoming of demand shortage and deflation, deterioration of infrastructure, etc. The above-mentioned Society 5.0 incorporates the intention to use the Fourth Industrial Revolution as a tow to achieve recovery in Japan, which is known as an "Advanced Country in Tackling Issues".

Companies in the Japanese manufacturing sector have applied the so-called Just-in-time Delivery system in the production processes of their factories and the surrounding supply chains through the years, including affiliated enterprises in the group including those known as Tier 1 and Tier 2, which drastically reduced unnecessary stock. They also promote efforts for productivity increase on a daily basis through KAIZEN activities in small groups—thoroughly reviewing quality specification for all processes, raw materials and products. Through these efforts, they have persistently reduced costs and promoted structural reforms to survive in global market. With this base, the concept of Smart Factory using information and communication technologies, one of the representative examples of the Fourth Industrial Revolution, was accepted comfortably with comparative ease. As a result of aging population and a lower birthrate coming earlier than other developed countries, which is coupled with the recent economic upturn, the shortage of working force is becoming more serious day by day. Increasing productivity by cutting the number of working force in operation processes is an urgent issue to tackle labor shortage. These conditions also support the trend of Smart Factory.

4.4.3 Typical Examples of the Fourth Industrial Revolution

As the outcomes of the Fourth Industrial Revolution, I would like to explain some of the representative examples of various efforts that have already been realized or are soon expected to be made.

First, I would like to mention the arrival of the next-generation manufacturing system as an advanced version of Smart Factory. Many factories in the world have already taken action to dramatically improve production efficiency of the manufacturing process using advanced ICT in specific production lines of the company or in a factory. In addition to this, companies now make a link between their own factories and even with working processes in other partner companies which comprise a value chain to dramatically extend connectivity. Through this connectivity, Big Data is collected from production equipment, devices allocated in each production process and control devices of operation conditions, etc. through entire supply chain including upstream/downstream partners. Based on the results of the Big Data analysis, simulated optimization conditions are derived for the function in each process, which is used in the real physical space to check against the simulation results and achieve continuous further optimization. In other words, this is a deepened form of digital simulation conducted in a cyber space using the real physical production activities, AI and computers, interconnected and entered on-line. It is considered to be a matter of time before this next-generation manufacturing system will be widely applied.

Next, I should talk about the implementation of the fully autonomous driving system. Autonomous driving is expected to contribute greatly to the social life of people through the realization of significant decrease in car accidents, response to traffic jams, and the use of ultra-efficient vehicles in future society, which will be mentioned later. Many companies, including manufacturers of automobiles, automobile parts, electric parts and semiconductors, ICT enterprises, logistics and carriers, vehicle operators, etc., throughout the world, participate in and focus on the development of this system in various forms. If the autonomous driving system is realized, it is considered that the system will also greatly contribute to the ultimate measure against the shortage of drivers which is the largest problem in progressing the structural reform of global logistics networks led by Amazon, etc.

The definition of autonomous driving is divided into 5 levels in the international standards defined by the U.S. National Highway Traffic Safety Administration (NHTSA): Level 1: Driver Assistance for brake and accelerator, Level 2: Level 1 + Partial Driving Automation such as semi-automatic handle operation, Level 3: Conditioned Driving Automation under good conditions, Level 4: High Driving Automation, and Level 5: Full Driving Automation (unmanned). Levels 1 and 2 have already been used at a commercial level and companies are engaging in fierce competition toward the development of Levels 3 and 4.

There are some points to note here. Vehicles which operate driving and the surrounding autonomous driving system are both essential items to be developed at the same time. The development target seems to be limited to Level 4 for the time being, where the autonomous driving system operates on the condition that the equivalent of a driver exists outside the vehicle (remote) and it is operated under his/her monitoring (within the designed driving area including geography, roads, environment, traffic conditions, speed, and temporary limits under specific conditions). It also became clear that the system operator takes responsibility in case of an accident, not the driver in Levels 3 and 4. We need to be fully aware of the fact that related people all over the world have held various discussions over a long period of time based on the accident case of Tesla, Inc. The feasibility of Level 5, fully autonomous driving under any condition, is much more difficult compared with that of Level 4. Therefore, the path to an agreement among major stakeholders in the world is long and complicated, and the possibility of many unexpected problems need be assumed during reviewing processes.

The market of the aforementioned car dispatch service through smart phones which was set out by Uber is expanding with other newcomers that follow similar business models as Uber, and it has become common to use these car dispatch services in many countries. In China, Didi Chuxing is rapidly expanding its business network and trying to enter the Japanese market, while the Singaporean company Grab is rapidly growing in Southeast Asia. It should be noted that it is necessary to come to terms with the taxi industry, which is a vested interest, about the distribution of the service in one way or another. The complex web of this and the agenda of policymakers in each country can sometimes be the invisible hurdle to entering the market. For example, Japan has extremely strict regulations on commercial driving, as there are different driver's licenses: for individual use (regular driver's license) and for paid driving for customers (commercial driver's license). Therefore, existing taxi companies are bundled as a group in each region, and the dispatch service is provided in the form of a one-stop taxi dispatch service using smart phones. This is aimed at developing a new business model that gains understanding of vested interests within a framework of existing regulations. Various services related to mobility like these are provided with a view to further deepen the business model in combination with the above-mentioned autonomous driving in the future. In that case, the occupation of driver will completely be replaced by AI and robots.

Furthermore, a bicycle rental matching business (Mobike) with a similar concept is rapidly expanding in China. The company is working on full-scale overseas business development. As a similar business model other than the mobility area, the "vacation rental room" business that offers private vacant rooms and houses for rent is expanding its market around the world. A representative company is the U.S. Airbnb.

These projects are, in any cases, the basic business models that match people in need with those who want to use their own products and free time for remuneration in a shared information platform. In addition to this, they can continue to improve service quality by collecting and analyzing a huge amount of data acquired from the actual transport of people and vehicles. At present, this project style is generally known as Sharing Economy.

In the healthcare area, intensive management and various analysis on Big Data, such as information on health or other attributions of individuals or groups acquired from periodical health checkup and clinic visits, information available on-line through wearable healthcare devices, and genome information of individuals, is expected to contribute to the improvement of medical quality through individuals' awareness raising, preventive care of diseases through the improvement to appropriate lifestyle, prescription of personalized medicine according to individuals' characteristics, combination and optimization of home care and home-visit medical care. Various trials to realize extremely early diagnosis of intractable diseases such as cancer are being implemented throughout the world using AI and super computers based on systematic integrated understanding with Big Data on individual characteristics as a base.

"*Virtual Singapore*" is a larger-scale project which is carried out by the Singaporean government (NRF 2018). This project intends to build the whole land and space in Singapore in a 3-dimensional model and collects all kinds of information from buildings, civil engineering infrastructure to people's daily life patterns as Big Data, and to design and create the next-generation city by simulating major functions in a cyber space that are considered necessary in urban areas in developed countries, and is an extremely challenging plan. These functions include the allocation of buildings and parking space with optimum usage of space, development of optimum means of transportation, optimization of energy infrastructure such as electricity, and most suitable places to install security cameras with due considerations to environmental issues such as ventilation in the entire city, control of rainfall and water levels, and greenhouse gas emissions.

Originally, the application of ICT was already widespread in the infrastructure area in Singapore and the submission of BIM (Building Information Modeling) is compulsory for the application of a new building certification. This might be a project only Singapore can carry out at this moment as the land area is relatively compact and other necessary conditions would be relatively easily fulfilled. The National Research Foundation symbolically calls this "Twin Singapore." Moreover, people related to the project claim that, when this project is completed, Big Data can be collected and

4 The Light and Shadow of the Fourth Industrial Revolution

analyzed by attaching a sensor to people, cars and buildings, which can be used in countless ways, including provision of necessary guidance on facilities and services using various applications in smart phones in any place, clearing up traffic, and the use of relief simulation to make evacuation more efficient in case of disasters.

In this way, waves of the Fourth Industrial Revolution are incited. This movement is spreading not only in OECD countries but in emerging countries in a steady manner. In emerging countries, the power of vested interests to resist disruptive innovation using regulations to maintain the interests is weaker than that in developed countries. Therefore, it is relatively easy to catch up with new technology innovations and business platforms at once in a Leap Frog style if conditions allow. Governments in many countries and regions strongly promote the movement to catch up with developed countries with the Fourth Industrial Revolution as the indispensable driving force.

According to a report by the World Economic Forum, which holds the Annual Meeting of World Economic Forum in Davos, and the outcome of Trillion Sensors Summit 2015 held in Orlando, FL, USA, it is estimated that a trillion of sensors will be installed throughout the world and 80% of the world population will be interconnected on-line in information network by 2025 (World Economic Forum 2015). It is expected that goods and data will be interconnected in physical space and cyber space and the existing industrial structure will change dramatically. According to the results of a provisional calculation by McKinsey & Company, it is estimated that an economic effect equivalent to 4 to 11 trillion dollars (current global GDP is about 75 trillion dollars) will be generated by 2025 through a radical innovation of the industrial structure caused by the Fourth Industrial Revolution (Manyika and Chui 2015).

Will the Fourth Industrial Revolution really become a driving force of sustainable global economic growth in the future? From the next section, we will consider issues to realize it, and new problems and threats that will be brought by it.

4.5 The Negative Side of the Fourth Industrial Revolution

As mentioned in the previous sections, a major transformation of the industrial structure, mainly in digital technology innovation known as the Fourth Industrial Revolution, is strongly promoted by industry, government and academia in both developed countries and emerging countries. The Fourth Industrial Revolution could be a Savior in realizing our sustainable future. However, at the same time, we must face the negative aspects of the Fourth Industrial Revolution in a calm and objective manner.

For example, the creation of innovative business models and new value chains supported by disruptive technology innovation might smash existing business models to smithereens and completely replace them in various industrial fields. In the long term, human resources needed by these new value chains might be replenished from older generations who have worked in the traditional industry through improvement in education and vocational training. However, during the transition period, the gap between the haves and have-nots might further expand, and the society will become un-stable as an extreme mismatch of supply and demand appears in the labor market, generated by the radical change of the industrial structure, unless truly workable policy responses are made.

As the supply chain and the value chain have been connected globally now, it is also necessary to establish fair and rational international common standards and regulations among major countries that are related to the value chain during the process of forming a new global industrial value chain.

The core of the new global industrial value chain is obviously information (Big Data). An enormous amount of information, which can be obtained from various thought and behavior patterns of humans as well as vast operation records of machines and plants, is certainly the source of various values, and can also be regarded as a new industrial fuel that will overwhelmingly surpass positions of oil and semiconductors. However, various questions remain, such as, who owns the rights to data, whether or not the transparency of rules and regulations for use of such data is guaranteed, whether or not such data is preferentially captured by global dominant players, whether or not any intentional access and/or control for data is imposed by the government from the viewpoint of giving priority to the home country, how the allocation of the profits obtained from the businesses derived from various data should be fairly calculated, and how privacy of individuals should be properly protected in the acquisition and utilization of personal information. In addition, from the perspective of cyber security, due to the nature of information networks, in which the whole system will face a threat if a marginal part of the global industrial value chain has any vulnerability. Therefore, the formation of a global value chain in industrial fields that are directly connected to the lives, security and/or safety of people, such as mobility, healthcare and power generation might be limited to the countries or regions where cyber security can be reliably guaranteed. As a result, the economic disparities between developing countries, which have achieved industrial development based on low wages, and developed countries, may be further widened. Furthermore, critical issues surrounding AI, which include AI ethics and elimination of any threat to humans, liability sharing for accidents caused by AI/robots, and ownership of intellectual properties developed by AI, are also pressing issues that should be solved.

To cope with these various issues, major countries in the world have hastily started their unique efforts while considering their countries' individual specific circumstances. However, if these countries or regions randomly establish their own original rules in order to prioritize their own interests, it will be extremely difficult to build a global industrial value chain that crosses national borders. In order to make the Fourth Industrial Revolution truly fruitful, industrial, governmental and academic leaders in each country will be required to make a firm determination and untiring efforts to establish a universal competition rule that is fair and consistent for the sake of the international community so that we can achieve a good balance between regulations and innovations, standing in the position of consumers from a medium- to long-term perspective rather than pursuing only short-term benefits for their own countries or companies.

4 The Light and Shadow of the Fourth Industrial Revolution

However, we can't deny the possibility that the major transformation in the industrial structure might have adverse effects on social customs, culture, morality, religious ethics, etc., that are inherent to each country and region. Given that the populism and the idea of "Our Country First" are emerging in various places of the world, negotiations are expected to be rather difficult and the path to a constructive agreement is likely to be significantly long.

It is also necessary to consider and respond fully to various specific risks assumed from the nature of the leading digital technology innovation. The primary issue to be considered is measures for cyber security as threats are increasing year by year. As the number of cyberattacks and the complexity of methods are increasing every year, measures that can be taken beforehand by estimating assumed attacks are limited, and many challenges are expected when implementing after-action measures. In general, cyberattacks can be divided into three categories: (1) Cyber Crime mainly for the robbery of money, (2) Cyber Espionage for the acquisition of national confidential and subtle information, and (3) Cyber Sabotage for self-fulfillment by realizing advanced cyber-attacks. The threat of (3) Cyber Sabotage has been increasing in recent years.

The actual purpose of most Cyber Sabotage cases is to show off the criminal's own abilities as a hacker to the world. The targets of attack are all advanced core systems throughout the world, such as infrastructure systems that widely support people's daily lives. Therefore, it is extremely difficult to anticipate and identify the target and purpose of criminals (or criminal groups) in advance. In the future, if the autonomous driving system and various public infrastructure, including power plants, railway network and communication network, are connected in cyber space and physical space through IoT across national borders, target areas of attacks can exist all over the world. Although protecting core infrastructure from cyberattacks is an urgent issue, it is my strong belief that we need to take as many measures as possible with a cool-headed awareness of the hard facts that the current situation of measures is extremely vulnerable and it is not feasible to immediately achieve this in the short term since human resources who can address these issues are tremendously lacking both in quantity and quality.

There are various problems in acquiring and using Big Data on individuals for public purposes, and a variety of discussions have been made. Most information of Big Data is on the characteristics and behaviors of individuals, and inappropriate acquisition and use of personal information must be avoided by balancing it from the viewpoint of effective utilization for the realization of privacy protection and common interest of the society. In return for the privilege that individuals can receive free services to use search engines and SNS, operators of information exchanging common infrastructure (collectively called super platformers) such as Google and Facebook can obtain data on personal behaviors through cyber segments. It has long been pointed out in many articles of newspapers including Financial Times and Japanese NIKKEI that the current situation of creating new businesses using such personal information can involve unfair trading. Under these circumstances, as exemplified by GDPR (General Data Protection Regulation), which was enforced in May 2018 at EU, movements toward building a mechanism in which fairness of data collection and utilization is achieved and various businesses can effectively utilize data through control of abuse of exclusive positions by super platformers, and realization of digital portability, are becoming visibly active.

Although currently representing a minority opinion, intellectuals are gradually transmitting more information on the risk of humans losing control of AI, which is rapidly evolving through deep learning, etc. AI is evolving not only to the Narrow Artificial Intelligence designed for specific purposes such as autonomous driving, which is a vast majority of current development, but also to the Artificial General Intelligence which, like humans, gains its own multiple problem-solving abilities in various areas and solve problems, and to the Artificial Super Intelligence through the exponential development of the evolving speed. Some scientists predict a disastrous future for humans in which AI is linked to robots, etc., through IoT and dominates both cyber and physical spaces like in SF (Science Fiction). Government-related national defense organizations (military-industrial-academia complex) and their supportive military industry invest the largest amounts of human resources and capital in AI research. From this nature, it should be noted that there are other risk factors such as the fact that the transparency of information on research details is hardly ensured.

4.6 For the Successful Fourth Industrial Revolution

Negative events expected to occur in association with the Fourth Industrial Revolution have been mentioned in the previous chapter. Our challenge is to realize a more advanced value chain and the value of diverse people inclusively through the exponential improvement of productivity and increase of social common interests by appropriately controlling such various risk factors. Below is a brief explanation of points to note from this point of view, although they are rather superficial.

First, I will point out some requirements for the smooth promotion of the Fourth Industrial Revolution. It is primarily important for all the industry, government and academia to eliminate their invisible boundaries and work on environmental development to lead the Fourth Industrial Revolution to a success. In relation to this, critical issues include the strict review of numerous regulations and legal frameworks designed based on the present industrial structure and the development of new regulations and legal frameworks that respond to the newly generated and forthcoming various business models and value chain. Policymakers in all countries and regions must be fully aware that they should not nip new challenging venture projects in the bud by protecting specific industries or stakeholders from the viewpoint of short term profits, and that this action could eventually become a factor that could hugely affect the nation's sustainable development in the future. In the meantime, each of us is required to recognize various fundamental issues, such as how we should view the shared direction of the future society and the symbiosis between humans and AI, how we should govern innovative technologies by predicting social structure changes derived from such technologies, and what kinds of education programs should be provided to adapt to new social structure changes, as our own agenda, and proactively

4 The Light and Shadow of the Fourth Industrial Revolution

participate in the decision making process through our own independent thinking and by expressing opinions on various occasions, instead of leaving it to policymakers.

In addition, the role of the mass media in the Internet age is extremely important. Younger generations tend to use information media such as Google and Facebook to quickly access various kinds of information available in cyber space, and don't spend much time intensively reading articles provided by traditional mass media such as newspapers, information publications and TV. On the other hand, it is also necessary to fully recognize the fact that it has become possible to manipulate public opinions as biased opinions spread to ordinary citizens in an extremely artful manner through the Internet, as exemplified by the alleged intervention of the Russian government in the U.S. presidency election using an SNS (Facebook).

The existing media must not see the backgrounds of such facts simply as the natural flow of the Internet age. Media personnel of conscience must recognize the fact that the behavior of media in general in the Internet age, such as competing for click counts serving as the source of ad revenue with importance attached to article delivery speed, not scrutinizing the contents of complex issues concerning politics, economy and society, and not giving suggestions to their readers by pursuing the essence of things, could gradually dampen the learning ability, insight or judgment of readers, leading to a crisis with the liberal democracy as a result.

Policymakers should greatly respect the enhancement of entrepreneurial spirit and proactively support the trend of the Fourth Industrial Revolution, by developing a system to provide financial support for entrepreneurs who would lead new industries, and considering a framework of incubation which encourages experimental initiatives of temporarily abandon existing regulations such as the Regulatory Sand-box system. There is an extremely high hurdle for individual enterprises to obtain and use various information attributing to individuals with their consent. For example, they should consider developing an environment in which they develop and operate a common platform of individual Big Data while ensuring security as the government's responsibility in terms of privacy protection by designating specific areas as advanced examples.

The roles of SMEs (small and medium-sized enterprises) as promoters of new industries are extremely important as the industrial structure goes through significant changes as a result of the Fourth Industrial Revolution. Many SMEs do not hold sufficient human resources and capitals that can be invested in terms of quality and quantity even if they would like to focus on research and technology development in an effort to shift the business structure from existing business to new business using digital technologies. The central government and local governments should closely work together to develop a systematic framework to provide various support for companies motivated to carry out these activities, and large-scale companies should allocate part of development outcomes obtained through their own projects by establishing a mechanism for personnel and technical exchanges. It is necessary for the industry and policymakers in the central and local governments to work together to support SMEs. If they fail to do this, the Fourth Industrial Revolution might remain a superficial movement only among the central government and large companies with global business opportunities.

Moreover, it is strongly required to develop international common rules and regulations in a varied and timely manner by sharing various changes in politics, economy and society as common preconditions, which can occur as a result of the outcomes of innovative digital technology development—the Fourth Industrial Revolution. We require the earnest determination of all policymakers, including political leaders in major countries, to steadily solve each issue of concern through proactive involvement and fair, constructive and mutual dialogues between parties concerned, based on the mutual trust that has been accumulated during the process of various strict international negotiations conducted among multiple countries. As often seen in the Doha Round negotiations of WTO, in multilateral negotiations where essential interest coordination can be diverse, negotiations would not progress without honest and patient exchange of opinions and interest coordination between negotiation teams of each country. It should be kept in mind that, even if it reaches an agreement of an overall framework, negotiations to summarize the final agreement will be required for a rather long period of time after that.

In addition, it is necessary to hold down-to-earth discussions across industry, government and academia fields to find answers as to what credentials and skills people in each country should hold during the period of the Fourth Industrial Revolution, given each country's present situation. Each country then must consider the type of educational system to realize this, introduce various systems to enhance effectiveness of education, try to input necessary human resources proactively and secure financial resources for it. For example, it is considered necessary to review the type of primary and secondary education. For skills, focus should be on balance allocation between EQ (Emotional Quotient), CQ (Creative Quotient) and AQ (Adversity Quotient) rather than IQ (Intelligence Quotient) emphasis tendency, and for abilities, those to understand and use ICT and lead innovation to solve various problems in the society should be gained.

Finally, I would like to mention basic direction of measures toward the mitigation of risks that may be caused by the Fourth Industrial Revolution. As repeated in the previous sections, the Fourth Industrial Revolution is caused by the rapid advancement of digital technology (nature of revolution), and outcomes of the revolution will be transmitted to the world at a tremendous speed and bring drastic changes in the basic structure of the industry and the society. Given these hard facts, the risk that should be considered primarily is the destruction of the basic social infrastructure that is related to all people's daily lives such as electric power generation and supply, mobility field such as railway networks, and financial systems. Concerning electric power generation and supply, the adaption of innovative digital technologies is rapidly expanding in order to accelerate the further improvement of energy efficiency and the shift toward renewable energy by integrally controlling various power generating/storing functions according to the supply and demand situation for electric power generation and supply systems, as exemplified by the virtual power plant concept. Concerning autonomous driving technologies, as the first step, commercialization of various efforts utilizing AI technology in the field of public transportation systems such as trucks, buses and taxis is just around the corner. In the meantime, in the financial field, Internet payments with smartphones such as *Alipay* and *WeChat-*

4 The Light and Shadow of the Fourth Industrial Revolution

Pay in China are rapidly spreading, and the future picture of the financial industry will be significantly different from what it is today, with the development of various virtual currencies supported by the rapid progress of the blockchain technologies being just one example.

In these fundamental social infrastructure fields, the streamlining of business operations is rapidly progressing. On the other hand, the damage suffered in the event of a system failure caused by a slight system design bug or a malicious cyber-attack would be extremely extensive, and there is only a limited number of expert personnel available across the globe. Accordingly, the recovery from a system failure would require considerable time. Therefore, it is expected that such an incident will result in an extremely major catastrophe.

We need to understand the contradiction that, no matter how much productive efficiency improves and excellent infrastructure eco system is developed, which is stable from the viewpoint of protection of the earth and the environment, the more advanced the system is and the more useful it is for people, the more likely it is to become an ideal target of Cyber Sabotage. We should consider risks that we are likely to face when we are actually attacked and prepare means of response before and after the risk occurrence from various points of view. Major countries should bear in mind that the most urgent tasks for them are to establish a workable global network to secure cyber security and to share information with each other on a steady basis.

Although it is not limited to the Fourth Industrial Revolution, in the process of determining various (domestic or international) policy frameworks, it is extremely important to evaluate their effectiveness in a fair and transparent manner with consideration for the whole diversity in the society from the viewpoints of humanity, ethical and safety and security, not only focusing on short-term economic effects and the selection of electorates. For policymakers, this is no doubt a thorny issue that needs to be addressed with discipline and patience as the procedure is extremely complicated. However, if people know that policymakers are not working on issues with good faith, various disputes over the Fourth Industrial Revolution will erupt and the political confusion will make it extremely difficult to pave the way for the realization of sustainable and inclusive development of the society.

The Fourth Industrial Revolution will certainly contribute to the continuous growth of future world economy by leading the upward trend of the entire world economy. However, as repeatedly mentioned in the previous, it is extremely important that the expected outcomes of economic growth will be allocated in a fair manner without any arbitrariness, and as a result, sustainable inclusive growth will become feasible. I myself consider that it is not too much to say that the success or failure of the Fourth Industrial Revolution depends on whether the low and middle-income class, who now feel that they are oppressed, will see a brighter future than present.

It is also necessary to fully consider the fact that the advancement of the Sharing Economy will diversify people's working styles, offering various working ways that haven't been assumed in the existing policy frameworks. In the U.S., a flexible lifestyle in which people work part time in various industry sectors according to their vocational skills and life-style rather than working full time in a specific company is favored by more and more people (*Gig-Workers*). Policymakers need to fully consider ways of social security systems for such diverse working styles and the safety net of a new society such as a kind of minimum wage system (Basic Income) with a view to the possibility of demand for radical reforms.

As mentioned in the previous section, although there are various views on the future of AI, most advanced science technologies have been misused in various ways far from the inventors' intentions. I believe that, as for how people engaged in the research and technical development of AI should act for humans' happiness, international "shared ethics" need to be developed with a comprehensive consideration to the effects on the society, including views from social science and humanity science, rather than being discussed only among AI experts who are also scientists. Not to be funny but I think an international rule is necessary for measures such as incorporating a common program in the process of future AI development for in-advance self-control from an ethical perspective in order not to head down a path toward annihilation.

In the period of radical changes caused by the Fourth Industrial Revolution, a large majority of developed countries run their countries based on the rules of liberal democracy, which still remains the basic common philosophy of the present society. And, haven't a majority of people seen the collapse of the Berlin Wall and the end of the Cold War as a victory of liberal democracy, and haven't they led their lives in the climate of leaving the running of their countries up to their policymakers, and taking political apathy for granted, while benefiting from peace and some degree of economic growth in the framework of the global market economy, which has since rapidly expanded? Haven't they pushed forward with the expansion of their own incomes and assets in the given framework, rather than building a society to aim for on their own will, and fulfilling the proper duties and observing the rules to follow in such a society? Aren't they simply bewildered by the waves of huge changes of the times, namely the Fourth Industrial Revolution, and don't they intend to cling to vested interests without even thinking of future generations?

However, as mentioned in the previous section, some people who are not satisfied with the response of present policymakers are attracted by populism policies which claim easy solutions lacking consistency and effectiveness. As the world becomes multi-polarized and diverse in values, it is becoming increasingly difficult to form an international consensus led by liberal democratic countries which shares the same values as in the existing way. Given this situation, we need to not only advocate liberal democracy on the pretext of Winston Churchill's quote "Democracy is the worst form of government except for all those other forms that have been tried from time to time" but also contemplate a better way of running a nation that professes the philosophy of liberal democracy and fundamental philosophy of the liberal democracy itself in a calm and open-minded manner.

For example, the political regime of democracy gives justice to the decision of the majority. If misused, this can become a means to eliminate or suppress the minority's opinions to achieve the majority's purposes. In this case, there may be a risk that some people who feel ignored or suppressed can easily accept opinions of populism. It is a historical fact that some politicians have made promises that sound attractive

4 The Light and Shadow of the Fourth Industrial Revolution

to voters but are difficult to carry out to collect votes during the election in order to form a majority and only actually carried out policies that were convenient for them.

In order for us to realize a sustainable and balanced society beyond national borders, when entering into a completely new era of the Fourth Industrial Revolution, thorough discussions on fundamental subjects are necessary: for example, how the necessary frameworks of regulations and legal systems should be created, how we can develop comprehensive policies to realize a balance between haves and have-nots while maintaining people's motivation to work hard, how much the freedom of individuals should be restricted in terms of the balance between individuals' freedom and social justice or social common interests, and whether positive and negative common values that are now considered the same for all humans will remain universal in the future.

In recent years, we often encounter limitation in activities among various Global Commons that have been developed by many nations professing liberal democracy over a long period of time and among multiple countries, and our frustration is considered to be one of the factors that nurtured a culture of successful populists and demagogues in many countries. Their statements will only make difficult issues more complicated and they will provide no contribution to an ultimate solution. What is worse, these demagogues will avert people's eyes from the essence of problems we face, which could prevent serious discussions on fundamental issues, and this is an extremely serious problem. Now is the time we have to redefine liberal democracy after having thorough discussions on its nature and how it should be.

References

AllSeen Alliance/Open Connectivity Foundation, https://openconnectivity.org/announcements/allseen-alliance-merges-open-connectivity-foundation-accelerate-internet-things.

Aspen Institute Future of Work Initiative, "What is a gig worker?" Gig Economy Data Hub https://www.gigeconomydata.org/basics/what-gig-worker. Accessed on October 26, 2018. (for instance).

Cabinet Office. (2016, June 2). Basic policy on economic and fiscal management and reform 2016. http://www5.cao.go.jp/keizai-shimon/kaigi/cabinet/2016/decision0602.html.

Cabinet Office. (2017, June 9). Investments for the future strategy 2017—Reforms to achieve Society 5.0. (Summary). https://www.kantei.go.jp/jp/singi/keizaisaisei/pdf/miraitousi2017_summary.pdf; (Initiatives and Programs) https://www.kantei.go.jp/jp/singi/keizaisaisei/pdf/miraitousi2017_inttv_prgrm.pdf.

Communication Promoters Group of the Industry-Science Research Alliance, German National Academy of Science and Engineering. (2013, April). Recommendations for implementing the strategic initiative INDUSTRIE 4.0. Final report of the Industrie 4.0 Working Group.

Corkery, J., & Zornada, K. (2012). High-frequency trading and a financial transactions tax. *Revenue Law Journal, 22*(1), Article 3.

Development Bank of Japan Inc. (2015, September). *DBJ monthly overview* (pp. 62–70).

Fukuyama, F. (1992). *The end of history and the last man.* Free Press. ISBN 0-02-910975-2.

Industrial Internet Consortium, https://www.iiconsortium.org/.

IMF World Economic Outlook. (2015). https://www.imf.org/external/pubs/ft/weo/2015/02/weodata/index.aspx. Accessed on October 26, 2018.

Keidanren (2016, April 19). Toward realization of the new economy and society. http://www.keidanren.or.jp/en/policy/2016/029_outline.pdf, Policy & Action.

Kobayashi, Y. (2017). *Chou Ikkyoku Shuuchuu Shakai Amerika no Bousou* 超一極集中社会アメリカの暴走, Shinchosha. ISBN 978-4103508717.

Manyika, J., Chui, M. (2015, July 22). By 2025, Internet of things applications could have $11 trillion impact. *Global Institute*; repurposed in FORTUNE http://fortune.com/2015/07/22/mckinsey-internet-of-things/. Accessed on October 26, 2018.

Nagashima, S. (2015). *Japanese Model Industrie 4.0* 日本型インダストリー*4.0*. Nikkei Publishing Inc. ISBN 978-4532320355.

National Institute of Population and Social Security Research. (2017). *Population Research Series*; No. 336, p. 81. ISSN 1347-5428.

OECD. (2018). General government debt (indicator). https://doi.org/10.1787/a0528cc2-en, https://data.oecd.org/gga/general-government-debt.htm; GDP and spending - Investment (GFCF) (indicator). https://doi.org/10.1787/b6793677-en, https://data.oecd.org/gdp/investment-gfcf.htm. Accessed on October 26, 2018.

Pew Research Center. (2015). Social & demographic trends. http://www.pewsocialtrends.org/2015/12/09/the-american-middle-class-is-losing-ground/. Accessed on October 26, 2018.

Piketty, T., & Saez, E. (2003). Income inequality in the United States 1913–1998. *The Quarterly Journal of Economics, CXVIII*(1), 7–14.

Saez, E. (2014, October). Income and wealth inequality: Evidence and policy implications. UC Berkeley, Neubauer Collegium Lecture, University of Chicago. https://eml.berkeley.edu/~saez/lecture_saez_chicago14.pdf. Accessed October 26, 2018.

Saez, E., & Zucman, G. (2016). Wealth inequality in the United States since 1913: Evidence from capitalized income tax data. *The Quarterly Journal of Economics, 131*(2), 519–578.

Sekai Keizai no Neta Chou 世界経済のネタ帳 "United States GDP". http://ecodb.net/country/US/imf_gdp.html. Accessed on October 26, 2018.

Singapore National Research Foundation. (2018). *Virtual Singapore*. https://www.nrf.gov.sg/programmes/virtual-singapore. Accessed on October 26, 2018.

U.S. Bureau of the Census, Median Household Income in the United States [MEHOINUSA646N], retrieved from FRED, Federal Reserve Bank of St. Louis; https://fred.stlouisfed.org/series/MEHOINUSA646N. Accessed on October 26, 2018.

U.S. Bureau of the Census, Real Median Household Income in the United States [MEHOINUSA672N], retrieved from FRED, Federal Reserve Bank of St. Louis. https://fred.stlouisfed.org/series/MEHOINUSA672N. Accessed October 26, 2018.

World Bank National Accounts Data, and OECD National Accounts Data Files. (2018). https://data.worldbank.org/indicator/NY.GDP.MKTP.KD.ZG. Accessed on October 26, 2018.

World Economic Forum. (2015). *Deep shift: Technology tipping points and societal Impact* (p. 16). Global Agenda Council on the Future of Software & Society.

Part II
Case Studies 1: Health and Medicine

Chapter 5
How Scientific Breakthroughs and Social Innovations Shape the Evolution of the Healthcare Sector

Robert Boyer

Abstract The chapter argues that the conventional scientific determinism does not explain the long term evolution of health care systems. First the illness and the medical knowledge and techniques are socially constructed and historically determined. Second the methods for financing and organizing care shape the intensity and direction of medical breakthroughs. Third scientific advances generally do not reduce the medical costs because the new therapies diffuse and more complex diseases challenge medical expertise. It is thus important to replace a static equilibrium-based approach with an evolutionary and institutionalized vision that takes into account the two sided causalities between social innovations and the invention and diffusion of new therapies. The performance of the health care sector cannot be measured by usual productivity indexes since so many factors determine the life expectancy in good health of the population. A large diffusion of education exerts positive spill overs upon the prevention of diseases and the preservation of health. This calls for a society wide approach to health as a component of a genuine to, "anthropogenic" mode of development. Clear social innovations are required for this mode to prosper and not only purely medical breakthroughs.

5.1 Introduction

The health care system is an especially dynamic sector moved by multifaceted and intense medical breakthroughs and a major concern for governments' policies. The analyses of technical change define a very active field for economists and experts in science, technology and innovation (STI). Nevertheless, innovations in health care challenge most of the traditional approaches to technical change.

In the 1970s the leading conception has been developing a sequential and linear model of technical change: first scientific advances in the academic world, then research and development tries to convert them into products and/or techniques to be sold on the market by entrepreneurs in search for profit (Godin 2006). This approach has encountered many critiques that are pointed out by Joly (2019). Generally the full

---

R. Boyer (✉)
Institute of the Americas, Vanves, France
e-mail: r.boyer2@orange.fr

© Springer Nature Singapore Pte Ltd. 2019
S. Lechevalier (ed.), *Innovation Beyond Technology*, Creative Economy,
https://doi.org/10.1007/978-981-13-9053-1_5

efficiency of the related innovations calls for specific private organizations and public infrastructures. Basically techniques shape economic and social configurations. This linear model of technical change is closely associated with a quite general conception of progress (Oki 2019). When this sequence is operating, the initial rents associated with innovation are progressively eroded by the process of imitation, under the pressure of competition. The general pattern is thus a decline of prices along with the maturing of the industry created by the scientific breakthrough. This linear model implies a technological determinism of private organizations and public policies by scientific advances (Fig. 5.1a). It fits with the key role of medical science in the transformation of doctors' practices but in the health care, the diffusion of modern techniques and new medicines does not generate a cumulative decrease of costs and relative prices. This is a paradox addressed by the health care system to conventional STI theory.

Since the 1980s the rise of information and communication technologies (ICT) has promoted a new approach based upon closer interactions between innovators and users because both of them have to cooperate in order to design successful products. This theme had already been explored concerning the users of scientific instruments (Von Hippel 1976) but it is now extended to the learning by using by final consumers. This aggiornamento opens an avenue for democratizing innovation (Koizumi 2019).

Anticipating and inventing new mass markets has become crucial and it has challenged the vertically integrated firm that had been emerging out of the post WWII productive paradigm. Actually an acute competition has driven a fast reduction of price along with spectacular improvements in the performance and quality of ICT products (Fig. 5.1b). This second conception only partially captures the specificity of medical innovation. For instance, in the fight against AID, patients themselves have been actors and they exerted a pressure on research and public authorities. Nevertheless, patients are the final buyers of new medicines and users of hospitals but indirectly only: public welfare and private insurers are the central actors in price formation and more generally the direction of medical innovations. The endogeneity of financing drastically impacts the dynamics of cost that do not follow the decline observed for electronic goods. Health sector dynamics is not easily captured by this second theory.

The concept of National System of Innovation (NSI) is a step towards such and understanding because it is built upon the hypothesis that the Science-Technology-Innovation triad is inserted into a society wide web of relations governing education, labor, State and finance (Lundvall 1992). The related social relations can be powerful enough to redefine the precise objectives pursued by STI actors. Conversely some generic innovations have the potential to transform the whole society (Koizumi 2019). Furthermore, these innovations can bear on coordinating mechanisms, organizations and even economy wide institutions and their diffusion may shape the inner functioning of quite any sector. This feature is now widely recognized as stated by a recent OECD report on STI:

> Innovation goes beyond science and technology, and involves investments in a wide range of knowledge based-assets that extend beyond research and development (R&D). Social and

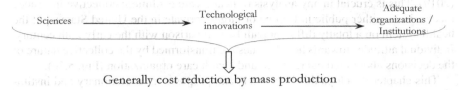

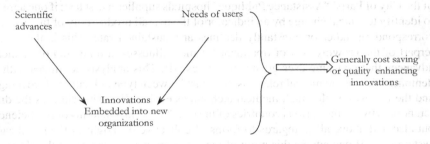

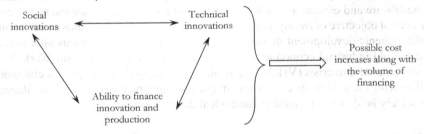

Fig. 5.1 Three conceptions of technical change

organizational innovations, including new business models, are increasingly important to complement innovation.

The post WWII growth regime is an example of the complementarity between the mass production paradigm and the invention of collective agreements between capital and labor. Similarly the constitution of welfare systems have had a definite impact upon the coverage of individual risks in terms of unemployment, industrial injuries, illness but also support to families and retired workers. By contrast, during the interwar, social innovation was the solution, fast technological advances the problem. For instance, the potential impressive rise in productivity generated by the assembly line could only be mobilized when the invention and diffusion of collective agreements synchronized mass production with mass consumption (Boyer and

Saillard 2000). This is an argument convergent with the developments of Koizumi (2019). This is crucial in any analysis of health care evolution: collective insurance mechanisms, either public in Europe or largely private in the United States, put the health system on a totally different path by comparison with the early 20th century. Individual attitudes towards health issues are transformed by the collective nature of the decisions about medical research and health care organization (Fig. 5.1c).

This chapter develops this hypothesis and proposes an evolutionary and institutionalist approach based on the coevolution of illness, medical techniques and the organization of healthcare systems and the manner in which they are financed: the corresponding configurations vary across space and time (I). A retrospective analysis of the City of Paris' "Assistance Publique" hospitals supplies a first test: if one agrees to identify technical change by an indicator of the overall productivity of factors, the corresponding indicator constantly declines at a sustained rate. This is the counterpart of the growing cost of treatment for most illnesses, a reflection of medical advances that consume ever greater resources (II). This analysis continues with a demonstration of the mutual relations that exist between type of health risk coverage and the intensity with which medical techniques evolve (III). This clarifies the differences between the various countries of the OECD, not just in terms of inefficiency but also and above all in regards to forms of collective oversight of the healthcare system (IV). If one adopts this point of view, the irresistible growth of the share of resources devoted to healthcare no longer seems anomalous but rather the consequence of the emergence of a new mode of development in which the improvement of healthcare and education and the promotion of culture are at once the means and the central objective of twenty-first century societies (V). One may thus examine this anthropogenic development model from the perspective of the various alternatives that the old industrial economies have explored since the post-Second World War model entered into crisis (VI). In conclusion introducing the concept of social innovation brings new insights concerning major contemporary issues and it challenges the widely held view of a hard technological determinism.

5.2 The Coevolution of Illness, Medical Techniques and Healthcare Systems

Contemporary economic theories are for the most part built upon the hypothesis of nomenclature—that is, the existence of a complete list of goods and services of generally recognized quality. On the basis of this nomenclature, agents create a series of supplies and demands that result in an equilibrium price system. Theories inspired by Joseph Schumpeter are a happy exception since they take into account the fact that innovation is among the strategies employed by entrepreneurs to free themselves from the tyranny of static equilibria, marked by the nullity of net profit. The extent of advances in medical techniques argues for enlarging this analytical framework beyond innovation in products, productive processes and organizational forms to the healthcare sector.

5.2.1 An Evolutionary and Institutionalist Approach

Historians have extensively shown that the recognition of illnesses results from conceptual and social processes of construction and is thus evolutionary by nature: "In the past, a major difficulty for the quantitative study of pathocenosis stemmed from the fact that perpetual change took place, not only in regards to the illnesses themselves and their frequency, but also in the manner in which doctors conceived of them. The conceptual foundations of medical diagnosis are far from unchanging" (Grmek 1969).

This characterization of what was necessary for the emergence of modern medicine is particularly relevant at a time when the mission of university hospitals and research laboratories is to advance medical knowledge and treatments.

When the corresponding accumulation of knowledge allows effective treatment procedures to be discovered and developed, their practical implementation and diffusion thus brings into play the capacity of individuals to pay and, by extension, that of the society in which they live. This presupposes that the economy is sufficiently productive to allow surplus wealth to be allocated to medical care and possesses the forms of organization and financing needed to provide for access to care. For, in contrast to traditional practices, the cost of treatment can exceed individuals' capacity to pay. This calls for risk to be mutualized within the family, the social group or via subscription to private insurance and ultimately for the creation of an integrated healthcare system at the level of the collectivity. These forms of organization and financing in turn have a retroactive effect on the direction of medical research via the overall volume of resources allocated to healthcare and as a consequence of each of the entities that make up the healthcare system pursuing its specific objectives (Fig. 5.2).

An already old literature review underscored this interdependence:

> As legitimate as it may be, the view that the definition of health is endogenous to the economic and political system within which health insurance is defined has important implications. If, as was the case, insurance is to cover new techniques independently of their cost and implement an ever-broader concept of health [...] the research and development sector will continue to respond to incentives that encourage costly new developments rather than cost-cutting innovations. (Weisbrod 1991)

Since then, the public authorities have continually reformed the organization and financing of healthcare but each of the configurations thereby explored continues to possess a common characteristic: the forms of health risk coverage and the direction of medical innovation are interdependent.

5.2.2 The Diversity of Medical Techniques: A Taxonomy

Given the proliferation of medical advances, constructing a taxonomy that would allow them to be correlated with the evolution of costs is not straightforward. Here resides the interest of the taxonomy implemented by Burton Weisbrod (cited above), who himself borrowed it from Lewis Thomas (1975).

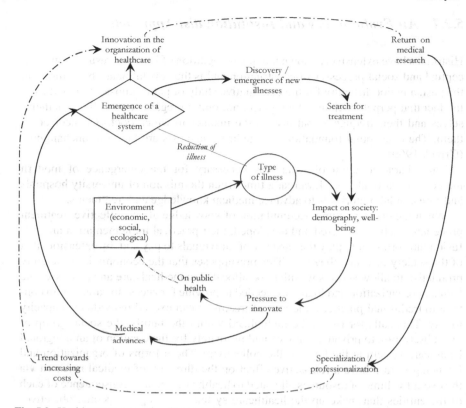

Fig. 5.2 Healthcare as a social and historical construction: a dynamic and evolutionary conception of "health"

(i) The first group concerns poorly understood illnesses for which *the absence of treatment* leads to mere support without hope of recovery. As a consequence, cost is limited by the fact that sophisticated technical resources have not been mobilized.

(ii) The second is that of the *intermediary technologies* that allow one to compensate for the incapacities associated with an illness over which medicine can do little to control the course. The cost may be high as this category covers transplants, artificial organs and most cancers.

(iii) The third set draws upon *advanced treatments* that result from an understanding of the mechanisms of an illness and may lend themselves to what are in some cases inexpensive procedures such as vaccines and antibiotics.

Intuitively, the first configuration corresponds to traditional doctors and it is the development of intermediary and advanced technologies that leads to increased healthcare costs. The public health consequences, however, are much different for each group: where the former is incapable of eradicating the illness, the latter raises the prospect of its total disappearance, *provided that* society succeeds in mobilizing the corresponding resources, something that is not the case in the poorest of contemporary societies. This underscores the interdependence between the mode of development and the possibilities available to the healthcare system. The case study on Indian drug industry provides a suggestive example of this interdependence between tradition and the development of a specific style in the drug industry (Gaudillière 2019).

5.2.3 Microeconomic Theory Confuses the Dispersion of Costs with the Factors of Their Growth

Statistical and econometric analyses of panel data—for hospitals, for example—have repeatedly shown that most establishments are far removed from the cutting edge of technological innovation: this is the case for private hospitals in the United States (Chansky et al. 2013) as well as for the National Health Service in the United Kingdom (Department of Health 2010). The corresponding additional costs draw the attention of managers, who are tempted to see them as evidence of mismanagement that can and should be corrected. In the foreword to the 2010 World Health Organization (WHO) report on the *State of Global Health*, one thus finds the following diagnosis:

> […] 20 to 40% of all healthcare expenditures were wasted due to inefficiency and it [the report] indicates 10 specific domains in which best practices and policies might increase the impact of expenditures, sometimes in a spectacular fashion. Investing these resources in a more judicious way can help countries get closer to universal coverage without increasing expenditures.

It is thus said that there is a hidden treasure that will allow health coverage to be extended without significantly increasing budgets.

The present article contests the notion that this is the alpha and omega for controlling healthcare costs (Table 5.1). One reason for this stems from the fact that all industrial surveys show that the heterogeneity of firms' performance is a permanent and universal characteristic of all sectors and is in no way exclusive to healthcare. Yet, in a very general way, most industrial sectors exhibit growth in productivity indicators thanks to improved production techniques and the entry and exit movement of firms. A second, even more fundamental reason has to do with the confusion between reasoning in terms of equilibria in a static environment and taking into consideration innovation and the economic dynamic it entails. A convergence of all firms towards the technological frontier has never been observed, if only because innovation permanently transforms the distribution of firms. This argument particularly applies to the healthcare sector, which is driven by the interaction between medical innovation and the manner in which care is financed.

Table 5.1 Two conceptions of health

	Microeconomic theory	Evolutionist/institutionalist theories
Central hypothesis	Atypical good (moral hazard, adverse selection, externality, asymmetric information)	Historicity of healthcare as a social construction in response to environmental change
Mechanisms driving growing costs	Growing static inefficiencies relative to a static optimum	Interaction between the mode of financing, healthcare system organization and the direction of medical advances
Recommendations	Public intervention restoring the efficiency of market competition	Collective (political) choices concerning the orientation of medical progress

5.3 Medical Advances as the Source of Growing Costs: A Case Study

Research regarding the evolution of a particular hospital, Paris' Assistance Publique, long ago cast light on this hypothesis (Boyer 1971). To the degree that this hospital had been at the forefront of exploring new medical practices in the areas of diagnosis and treatment, it confirmed the inadequacy of a static approach that exclusively applied to a stationary world.

5.3.1 The Paradox of a Cumulative Reduction in the Overall Productivity of Factors

It is customary to measure technical change as the gap between the evolution of an output indicator and one measuring all of the factors and inputs that contributed to production. In industrial branches, statistical data generally show a tendency towards improvement in the total productivity of factors (TPF) from one period to the next. Other analysts instead see this as possibly a measure of ignorance or a mere technical artefact.

This is in striking contrast with the healthcare sector. At the Assistance publique de Paris, TPF thus decreased at an average annual rate of 6% between 1950 and 1965. Even more remarkably, there was not a single year during which this indicator improved. It must be concluded that, at the hospital, technical change is reflected in an increased volume of resources for a given number of days (Table 5.2). Other, more sophisticated indicators (number of admissions, cost of illness and so on) yield the same result. Taken literally, this would imply a cumulative reduction in economic efficiency.

It was claimed that this was an erroneous conclusion on the grounds that many other indices suggest that the hospital is the site where medical knowledge and the therapies resulting from it advance. Managerial accounting for this same establishment shows that the stability of this activity's traditional measurements is associated

5 How Scientific Breakthroughs and Social Innovations Shape … 97

Table 5.2 A marked, cumulative reduction in the total factor productivity on the basis of a traditional indicator of hospital activity (Assistance publique de Paris)

Years	Index of the volume of days	Index of the volume of factors	Index of overall productivity
1950	100	100	100
1951	117.5	110.2	106.5
1952	119.7	120.9	99.1
1953	117.3	130.5	90.1
1954	114.6	135.2	84.8
1955	114.1	141.7	80.7
1956	115.6	168.6	68.7
1957	118.6	164.9	72.1
1958	124.1	177.7	70.0
1959	120.0	198.8	60.4
1960	119.4	219.4	54.4
1961	120.8	246.7	49.0
1962	124.7	271.9	45.9
1963	120.2	289.6	44.7
1964	135.6	317.3	42.8
1965	141.8	349.1	40.6
Average annual rate	+2.4%	+8.6%	−6.0%

Source Boyer (1971)

with explosive growth in the number of technical procedures performed. While hospital admissions increased by 3% between 1962 and 1969, over the same period the number of surgical procedures increased by 37%, radiological tests by 60% and biological analyses by 113%. The technical content of the average visit experienced a qualitative change reflected in the apparent deterioration of efficiency indicators. In a way, technical change was expressed in improved quality of care rather than a reduction in inputs. These technical procedures were intended to clarify diagnoses and make it easier to find therapies for a large variety of ailments, thereby achieving healing—a rare phenomenon in the medieval hospice, ancestor of the Assistance publique de Paris, and a more appropriate measurement of a healthcare system's output.

5.3.2 Medical Advances Consume Ever Greater Resources Without Affecting Morbidity

By comparing two studies, respectively conducted in 1954 and 1968, it is possible to evaluate at first glance the evolving cost of treating a number of precisely defined

Table 5.3 Costs for treating all illnesses increase, though unevenly

Illness	Survey FNOS 1951–1954		Survey CAMPRP 1968 Average cost of hospital (old francs)	Index of cost (basis 100, 1954)	
	% of hospital expenditures in total cost	Average cost of treatment		At current prices	At constant prices
Appendicitis	70.3	35.284	182.300	517	271
Abdominal hernia	70.2	17.456	234.100	1341	702
Congenital malformations	86.5	63.407	382.457	603	316
Tuberculosis	87.9	182.504	591.800	324	170
Malignant neoplasms	72.6	104.632	545.500	521	273
Diabetic sugar	56.4	34.347	344.700	1004	527
Alcoholism	92.7	66.241	307.100	464	243
Epilepsy	56.1	23.143	178.300	779	403
Heart disease	61.1	17.817	351.857	1975	1034
Average cost index for medical services (basis 100, 1954)					191

Source Boyer (1971)

illnesses. Doing so shows that none of them exhibited a reduction in estimated expenditure at constant prices. A rare example of reduced costs concerns the treatment of tuberculosis (Table 5.3).

Faced with this evolution of hospital costs, both the micro-economist and the manager are tempted to attribute such an exceptional situation to a loss of efficiency and mismanagement, respectively. It was thus proposed to reduce the length of hospital stays, rationalize the spatial distribution of establishments in order to maximize occupancy rates and increase patient contributions to reduce demand and limit the overall cost of healthcare. In fact, the hospital does not operate at the frontier of efficiency postulated by standard microeconomic theory any more so than do many other organizations, even those subject to market competition. One must turn to the concept of X efficiency (Leibenstein 1966) and examine the factors that allow one to get closer to this frontier: the quality of coordination; competitive pressure; the nature of the payment system; and the productive configuration. When one uses the rich data of the Assistance Publique de Paris to estimate the impact of the three variables mentioned above, one notes to one's surprise that, in the period 1950–1968, their union explains less than 5% of the overall cost increase. Once again, these everyday management parameters, which determine short-term production costs, play only a secondary role in the long-term dynamic.

5.3.3 The Need for a Dynamic Approach Focusing on Changing Medical Techniques and an Understanding of the Driving Forces

Analysis of the healthcare sector thus foregrounds a methodological difficulty that is at the heart of standard theories: the economist first formulates a static model in which a stable equilibrium prevails and then considers the factors that shift that equilibrium, a role often played by exogenous technical progress. Lacking a truly dynamic theory, however, the economist only emphasizes the conclusions of his static model in making political-economic recommendations. In the case of healthcare, this strategy leads one to over-estimate the role of factors that explain the heterogeneity of costs between entities falling more or less short of best practices and to neglect those in which medical research has the effect of shifting these best practices. It is thus above all worth studying the factors that affect organizational structures and medical technologies over the long run (Fig. 5.3).

One thus measures the scale of diagnosis error that result from using a static analysis to understand a historical evolution. This dramatically neglects the role of innovation in terms of health insurance coverage, the consequence of mixing medical care, research and teaching in some large hospitals and the evolution of work organization and everyday practices.

5.4 Intensity and Direction of Medical Techniques in Contemporary Systems

The above results concern a very particular period marked by fast-paced economic growth that allowed for the resources necessary for extending social coverage—and health coverage, in particular—to be levied. In this context, the insurance system was based on reimbursing care in keeping with the actually incurred cost. The various conditions thus came together to allow for the search and subsequent diffusion of medical practices drawing upon the latest scientific advances. From that time on, the postwar growth regime was in crisis and the financial imbalances of social coverage gave rise to a series of reforms.

5.4.1 Forms of Insurance and the Organization of Care More Than Individual Behavior: Institutions Matter

For typical market goods of easily identifiable value, consumer preferences and choices contribute to orienting the supply structure. The market mechanism is faulty when imperfect or asymmetric information dominates. The goods that contribute to health belong to a third category: not only do the suppliers have a mastery of medical procedure but the expenditures incurred are covered by insurance or by a system of social coverage. It is the latter, in fact, that is responsible for seeing to the quality/cost relationship by means of contracts or public rules. The individual choices of patients take place within a system characterized by the interdependence of modes of health risk coverage, the organization of the distribution of care and the orientation of medical research (Fig. 5.4).

As medical advances become established, the number of organizations and institutions responsible for overseeing the supply of care increases in such a way that the system's overall dynamic very broadly escapes the preferences and choices that patients might formulate. In this sense, changing medical techniques are endogenous because largely conditioned by the socio-economic context. As soon as the

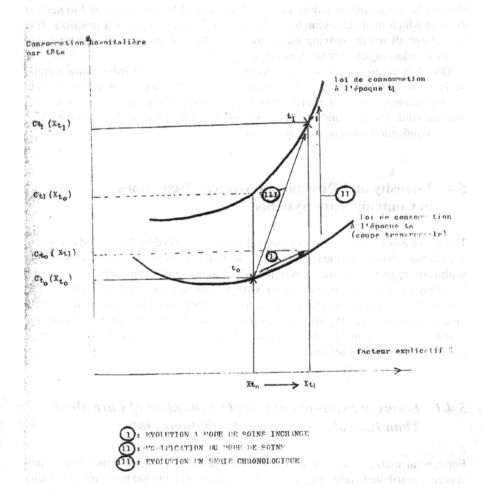

Fig. 5.3 Confusing static analysis with historical evolution

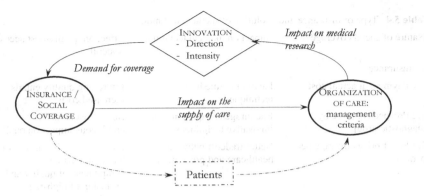

Fig. 5.4 The interdependence of insurance and medical progress. *Source* Inspired by Weisbrod (1991)

latter evolves, the objectives and modes of research are in the medium/long term redefined.

5.4.2 The Consequences of Changing Modes of Health Risk Coverage

Between 1960 and 1980, the extension of illness risk coverage went hand in hand with a growing share of healthcare expenditure as part of Gross Domestic Product (GDP). Since then, pressure on public finances has led to a broad array of reforms seeking to limit the cost of healthcare (see Sect. 5.6 below). It might be said that institutional innovations are the daughter of the dynamism of advances in medical practices and, conversely, that the redefinition of institutions, organizations and financial criteria over time entails their reorientation. This two sided causality is the core of the present analysis (Table 5.4).

Thus, when one moves from payment at actual cost to payment at a price forecast by diagnostic group, the management of healthcare units must take the necessary oversight of costs into account and restrict the introduction of techniques that do not efficiently contribute to treating the ailments in question. In this way, one seeks to use the reality of healthcare activity as the measure of production rather than, as in the past, the volume of resources that are mobilized. We still do not possess sufficient retrospective data to test this theoretical hypothesis. In the United States, Health Maintenance Organizations (HMO) have explored another form of coverage that consists in a contract guaranteeing fixed-price coverage to each contracting party. One effect of this is to reintroduce prevention and lifestyle assessment expenditures as possible substitutes for care expenditures but it appears that the expected savings have not materialized (Shin and Moon 2007). This is perhaps not so surprising given that HMO only represent a limited fraction of the American healthcare system, where

Table 5.4 Type of insurance and evolution of medical techniques

Nature of social coverage	Impact on medical techniques	Effect on quality/cost/access tradeoff
1. Insurance		
1.1 Payment at actual cost	Favors intermediary techniques	Improving quality entails increased costs
1.2 Prospective price by diagnostic group	Encourages adapted and/or innovative techniques	Better cost control, ambiguous impact on quality
1.3 Fixed-price coverage per person	Better tradeoff between healthcare and prevention	Possible negative impact on the least apparent components of quality and exclusion of high-risk populations
2. Public system for organizing healthcare		
2.1 Fixing an annual norm for growth of overall expenditures	Limitation of costly intermediary techniques	Possible moderation of costs but risk of rationing access
2.2 National healthcare system	Authorizes collective oversight of medical advances by direct action on supply	In general moderation of costs but tension on quality (waiting list) and possible rationing of patients

Source Extension of y Weisbrod (1991)

the mode of operation remains largely unchanged in what concerns the orientation of medical techniques and thus increasing costs.

Other systems, particularly in Europe, are characterized by a desire on the part of governments to control healthcare expenditures in two major ways. The first seeks to establish an annual norm for the growth of overall expenditures in the expectation that this will limit the spread of particularly costly intermediary techniques at the risk of limiting access to care for some and/or reducing the quality of care as it is perceived by the patients. The problem is, care entities continue to pursue objectives that do not necessarily coincide with those of the government, including recurrent tensions between the imperatives of macro-economic management and those of public health. This is not the case in the National Health System (NHS), for which the supply of care is exclusively public. In principle, this allows for overall optimization in line with a political choice concerning the ultimate aim of the healthcare system. Better oversight of costs by reference to decentralized systems is associated with a limitation of quality that in its turn gives rise to demands on the part of citizens for the financial resources allocated to healthcare to be increased (Department of Health 2010). Such demands are all the more likely to be satisfied when the macro-economic prospects for growth are favorable. This implies crucial interdependence between healthcare systems and modes of development.

5.4.3 The Uneven Spread of New Techniques, Their Impact on Reducing Mortality

The treatment of cardiac ailments is a good example of the trends at work in contemporary healthcare systems. As a technique, bypass surgery has been gradually replaced by angioplasty, allowing unit costs to be reduced by more than half (OECD 2013: 94). However, this technological breakthrough has been accompanied by a growing number of procedures, resulting in higher overall cost. This is one of the central mechanisms behind growing healthcare costs: when a new practice radically reduces costs, its use spreads to such a point that costs swell (Cutler and McClellan 2001). It does not spread in uniform fashion, however, for it depends on the volume of available financial resources and practices that may significantly differ among the various national healthcare systems (OCDE 2013: 95).

Yet no clear relationship with the organization of the system of coverage is to be found since, at the level of each diagnostic category, many national idiosyncrasies prevail, to say nothing of differences of nomenclature and in the manner in which statistics are collected. In this respect, it is easier to evaluate the effects of care at the level of an ailment than at that of the healthcare system taken as a whole, if only because exhaustive statistics on patient outcomes are not generally available. For example, a remarkable, two-decade reduction in the rate of heart attack mortality may be observed in nearly all countries but as of 2011 considerable disparities persisted (OCDE 2013: 98).

Yet the value of medical change varies considerably: it largely exceeds the cost of treating heart attacks and premature births, is limited for depression and entails quality improvement in the case of cataracts but the cost-benefit appraisal is merely balanced for breast cancer, at least in the years around 2000 (Cutler and McClellan 2001). Since then, the terms of this assessment will have likely changed, once again underscoring the significant historicity that characterizes healthcare analyses.

5.5 Understanding the Contemporary Dynamics of Health Care

It is now possible to derive two major lessons from the previous developments that both explicit the endogeneity of medical advances with respect to the methods for financing research and the supply of medical care.

5.5.1 The More Advanced the Country in Medical Research, the Higher the Health Care Costs

The United States is not just the most advanced country from the point of view of productive, organizational and, more recently, financial innovation; it is also at the cutting edge of medical innovation, a response to the needs of a rich population for whom a healthy life is a legitimate objective once more essential needs have been met and the constantly replenished desires produced by the consumer society have been satisfied. From 1961 to 2012, North American healthcare expenditures have increased at a rate that is more than twice that of GDP (Blumenthal et al. 2013): Is it not a luxury good as that is understood within systems of demand? It is to be noted that, during the crisis periods of the 1970s and, later, the subprime crisis, the volume of healthcare expenditures slowed more rapidly than national production. Yet despite such episodes, which may also be observed in the second half of the 1990s, health costs grow faster than those of the economy taken as a whole. What other goods and services exhibit the same divergence? At the scale of the past half-century, it would seem that none do, especially if one reasons in terms of value rather than of volume. One should thus not exclusively focus on the genesis of the individual demand for healthcare but also and above all on what determines its supply and evolution over time. In passing, it is worth noting that this sectoral disproportionality discredits the foundational models of the standard theory of growth.

5.5.2 Contrasting National Trajectories

If one adopts the hypotheses of neo-Schumpeterian theory and holds that advances in lifestyle and medical practice are diffused at the global level, one should expect that most economies would converge towards the same ratio of healthcare expenditures relative to GDP. Over the course of the 2000s, however, this was not the case : the ratio significantly increased in the United States while remaining much lower and only slightly growing in Japan, with Canada occupying an intermediary position. Two English-speaking capitalist economies seen as market-coordinated (the United States and Canada) thus occupied opposite positions, a fact that indicates the distinctive position of healthcare vis-à-vis other sectors. The diversity of healthcare sector development only becomes more obvious when one turns to consider the European countries that are presently catching up. This dispersion suggests two hypotheses. First, national modes of healthcare system organization (together with demographic factors, of course) create significant disparities in long-term development profiles. Second, different economies explore different growth regimes (export-driven in Northern Europe, consumption-driven in the South) and their rates of healthcare expenditure vary accordingly.

The diversity of healthcare systems is also reflected in the manner in which care is distributed among patient categories. Whatever the period or country, statistics regularly show strong growth in medical care for the elderly (White 2007). The result is a single profile for the distribution of care by age, with care significantly increasing from age 65 and stabilizing or only slightly diminishing after 75. Yet the latter group exhibits much greater heterogeneity than do other stages in life. This likely reflects variations in social preferences, modes of financing and healthcare system priorities from one society to the next. In the institutionalized approach adopted here, the intrinsic complexity of the medical care provision system allows for a significant variety in the manner in which relations between the various entities contributing to healthcare are organized. This is again another evidence about the need to mix technological advances with a wide range of social innovation.

5.6 The Future of the Anthropogenic Development Model: A Matter of Social Innovation

Let us push a step further the analysis of social innovations in contemporary modes of development. The embeddedness of science and technology advances in society calls for taking into account the formation of human competences and the role of culture.

5.6.1 Healthcare, Education and Culture All Shape the Very Conditions of Human Activity

The healthcare sector contributes to quality of life by reducing morbidity and extending healthy life expectancy, thereby allowing the economic agent to exercise choice as well as his or her political rights. It aims to produce a fundamental good, the premise of man's activities in society. The educational sector also supplies the foundations of socialization and the ability to decipher and understand the social and natural world, a role it shares with the transmission of culture. All three thus shape what Pierre Bourdieu called the agent's "habitus", or what the standard theory refers to as "preferences".

They thus occupy a hierarchical position, something that also holds true for economies in which education, culture and healthcare have been commodified. This is one reason why they should be considered foundational to the process of socialization specific to mankind. The fact that their benefits express themselves over the course of the life cycle rather than in the repetition of economic exchanges is a second shared factor. This makes it difficult to evaluate their contribution to well-being for the duration of a life is largely unpredictable, rendering any assessment in terms of human capital difficult.

Healthcare and education share a third characteristic: far from supplying an elementary (that is, narrowly defined) product or service, they offer a composite service, an assemblage of extremely diversified procedures and goods. A healthcare trajectory is to be analyzed as the implementation of a series of routines, which are themselves the result of a given state of knowledge and medical technology. The education system offers a series of degree courses distributed over time that nurtures a very diverse array of skills. The corresponding programs are a collective construction based upon a conception of the learning and knowledge considered necessary at each period.

Like healthcare, the objectives and content of education are characterized by significant historicity. Finally, all three sectors are labor intensive and employ a broad array of skills. There is no obvious way to readily substitute equipment for skilled labor in what concerns their central activities. The culture sector is of particular importance in this respect due to the extreme difficulty of achieving productivity gains that characterizes it, a fact that inspired an original theory of price formation known as the Baumol-Bowen effect (1966): if wages evolve in tandem with the economy as a whole then one consequence of the quasi-stagnation of productivity will be the permanent growth of relative prices. To date, the education sector for its part does not seem to have found a way to reduce costs via increased productivity, a concept that is difficult to define in the area of education (Hallak 1968), even though the share of education expenditures has not grown at the same pace as that of healthcare (OECD 2013b). In their broad outlines, healthcare, education and culture are exceptions to the conception of innovation that sees it as combining technical progress, increased productivity and lower costs. This calls for an updating of the theorizing of STI and its reinsertion into a wider social science approach.

5.6.2 The Complementarity of Education and Healthcare

This homology is not the only argument in favor of grouping these three sectors together. For in a sense their activities are complementary, particularly in the case of education and healthcare (Cutler and Lleras-Muney 2006). From a theoretical point of view, various mechanisms link these two sectors: better education generally ensures a higher income, which allows access to healthcare, in particular, to be financed at the individual and collective levels; the skills acquired at school allow one to better appreciate risks and more accurately assess the possibilities offered by the healthcare system; in principle, education encourages one to take the long-term into account, something that entails giving greater attention to health issues; inversely, the lengthening of life expectancy makes it more attractive to invest in education and training (Fig. 5.5).

These same authors survey various statistical analyses concerning the United States: they confirm that there is a positive relationship between state of health, rates of survival for a series of serious illnesses (though there are exceptions, such as cancer) and finally, life expectancy and education level. The gain associated with education seems to increase over time, one consequence of which is to simultaneously increase inequality in the areas of healthcare and education. In the aggregate, international comparisons suggest a systematic discrepancy in life expectancy in favor

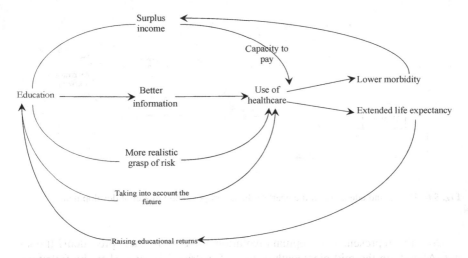

Fig. 5.5 How education influences health. *Source* Inspired by Cutler and Lleras-Muney (2006)

of the most educated, with notable differences existing between men and women (OCDE 2013: 27).

5.6.3 A New Conception of Development

In the past, analysts tended to consider that improved quality of life and longer life expectancy were the result of society's enrichment, something that allowed it to devote more resources to the healthcare sector. Today, theorists and practitioners also insist on the impact of education and healthcare on the development process. On the one hand, they improve skills, including those involved in the healthcare provided within families by women (Esping-Andersen 2008). On the other hand, lower infant mortality and the victory over major epidemics has changed the demographic regime, allowing for a demographic dividend via, for example the rejuvenation of the population. At the same time, investment in general education and training yield additional benefits thanks to the extension of the life cycle which carries over into professional life and increases the return on education policies (Fig. 5.6).

Successful development thus results from a circular process and, in this case of cumulative success, it runs from business investment, which creates productive capital, to educational expenditures, which contributes to social capital. The latter then enter into synergy with government-created infrastructure. On this view of things, a proactive strategy in the area of healthcare can in some cases help accelerate growth. This holds even more so for education since it also shapes access to healthcare and generates interest in efforts to promote the well-being of children and the family.

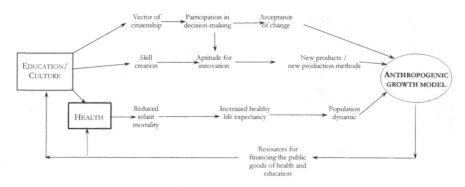

Fig. 5.6 Health and education at the heart of the anthropogenetic model of development

Does this represent a conceptual revolution without historical precedent? It does not. Already in the mid-nineteenth century, Friedrich List had taken the following stance:

> Those who raise pigs and those who manufacture bagpipes or pills are indeed productive but the instructors of youth and of manhood, musicians, virtuosos, physicians, judges and statesmen are productive in a much higher degree. The former produce exchangeable values; the latter, productive power: of the latter, some prepare future generations for production [...] others restore the productive power of the sick or disabled; others acts as legal guardians; others maintain social order. (List 1856: 221)

What is new in the past two decades is that this conception of development has been joined with more orthodox analyses in terms of human capital and (more fundamentally) capacity development by way of the fundamental goods that are access to education and healthcare (Sen 1999). The human development indicators regularly published by international organizations (UNDP 2014), among them the World Bank, testify to this modernization. They are no longer merely results of success in accelerating growth; they can be the conditions of a better quality of development. This change of paradigm does not only hold for emergent countries; above all, it applies—perhaps especially—to the most advanced countries, where the search for prosperity might gradually be substituted for that of growth (Cassiers 2011). This is the central argument of the present article.

Once again, we here encounter a theme that has already been developed in historical research inspired by the regulation school: healthcare, education and retirement expenditures have indeed been decisive in the post-1945 growth regime and the stabilization of productive relations. As such, they represent so many contributions to the development of men (Fontvieille and Michel 2002; Michel and Vallade 2007), a concept that ultimately has much in common with the anthropogenic model.

This conception has the advantage of moving beyond the exclusive emphasis placed on healthcare costs by making explicit the direct and indirect benefits of improved healthcare. On the one hand, the gains in terms of well-being and life expectancy point to what is in fact the true result of the healthcare sector's activity.

On the other hand, the corresponding improvements create favorable conditions for economic activity by promoting education, making innovation acceptable and extending skills—in short, healthcare and education are at the source of the dynamic efficiency that drives economic development. In a sense, these are the principles that supply the foundation for the social-democratic type models that insist on the contribution of social coverage systems to creating a collective capital that is then mobilized in the search for competitiveness (Visser and Hemerijck 1997; Madsen 2008; Campbell et al. 2008). Hiroi (2019) develops a similar argument when it proposes a "Sustainable Welfare Society". Furthermore, social sustainability has to be completed by environmental viability and again economic innovations (institution of norms, carbon tax, market for polluting rights...) are as important as purely technical breakthroughs (Pestre 2019).

This conception is of interest for yet another reason: instead of exclusively focusing attention on the efficiency of resource allocation relative to traditional indicators of healthcare system activity, it allows one to consider a cost/benefit type approach at the level of the economy and society as a whole. Authors who have attempted such an exercise in general reach surprising conclusions: in the United States, for example, it is claimed that gains in health and life expectancy between 1970 and 2000 each year added nearly 32% of GDP while healthcare expenditures constituted only 15% of GDP in 2000 (Murphy and Topel 2006). It is thus argued that long-term effects on well-being and growth generously compensate for the range of possible static inefficiencies. Can one trust such findings and therefore propose increasing healthcare expenditures in light of their remarkable return? Some methodological caution is called for here.

5.6.4 Costs Easy to Measure and Increasing, Effects More Difficult to Quantify

It is time to summarize the present article's central argument. Growing healthcare costs only seem anomalous if one adopts the hypotheses of the old microeconomic theory in the context of a stationary environment. As soon as one recognizes that the medical sector is a site of rapid progress in techniques, treatments and their subsequent diffusion, the continuous decline in the usual indicators of total factor productivity merely serves as recognition of this decisive characteristic. The second step of the argument consists in explaining the discrepancy between management indicators at the level of healthcare suppliers and those that seek to identify the impact in terms of health level, for example by means of the notion of healthy life expectancy. It is at this second level that the considerable benefits associated with medical progress appear but no trace of them is to be found in the simplest, microeconomic-type methods for evaluating the effects of public policies.

At the price of greatly simplifying, one might attribute the "mystery" of growing healthcare costs to the failure to recognize the complementarity between apparent

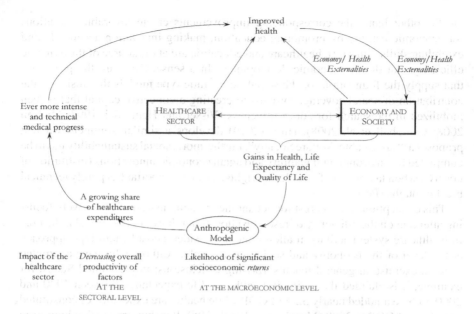

Fig. 5.7 A synoptic view of the healthcare sector and its relations with the anthropogenic model

managerial inefficiency at the microeconomic level—mainly a reflection of the evolution of treatments for a given ailment—and what seem to be significant gains in terms of the population's well-being, which can only be measured very incompletely by way of the contribution to reducing morbidity and mortality in promoting investment in education and training (Fig. 5.7).

5.7 Putting Matters in Theoretical, Historical and Comparative Perspective

If one adopts this analytical framework, a model of emergent development based on the production of man by human labor deserves to be taken into account. However, its significance for economic theory must be defined, it must be set in long-term historical context and its relevance must be verified by way of international comparisons concerning the contemporary period.

5 How Scientific Breakthroughs and Social Innovations Shape …

Table 5.5 The place of healthcare in major economic theories

Theory	Central mechanism	Status of healthcare	Consequence for healthcare
Classical (Sraffa after Ricardo)	Production of commodities by commodities	Implicitly included in the reproduction of wage earners	No specific role for healthcare
Development (List)	Productive forces result from the accumulation of discoveries and inventions	Conservation and extension of productive forces	A direct contribution to development, like education
Marxist (Marx)	Production by and for capital	Healthcare as commodity	Governed by the logic of profit
Neoclassical, human capitalism theory (Becker)	Individual consumption strategy/investment in human capital	Means for increasing human capital and therefore life expectancy	Healthcare as an individual choice
Endogenous growth (Romer)	Production of ideas on the basis of ideas	A question of medical innovation	Organization of system of innovation, including medical innovation

5.7.1 The Major Conceptions of Political Economy

In the classical tradition stretching from David Ricardo to Piero Sraffa, healthcare is merely one sector among others. For, at the time, this activity was in an embryonic state and constituted a very small component of labor force reproduction. More helpful, in this connection, is Malthusian theory, which presents mortality and demographic evolution as the adjustment variables of economic activity in societies dominated by recurrent shortages. The Marxist tradition, for its part, replaces the classical authors' production of commodities by commodities with production according to the profit principle and the accumulation of capital. This problematic is of particular relevance in the present context, marked as it is by a trend towards healthcare sector commodification, with the pharmacy sector having long exhibited many typically capitalist tendencies (Table 5.5).

Interestingly such a commodification can also take place by mobilizing set of alternative knowledge built by a long domestic tradition, when modern research enters the zone of deceasing returns. This reconfiguration of Ayurvedic medicine seems to confirm this typical Marxist intuition (Gaudillière 2019).

List's theory of development is built on the decisive role played by productive forces. These are seen as resulting, not just from the accumulation of private capital, but also from education, improved health and the role of the legal system. Contemporary development analysts have rediscovered this old and long-marginalized contribution. The notion of an anthropogenic model is in keeping with this tradition while at the same time underscoring that health and education are at once factors of development and the realization of one of its objectives, something that contemporary literature describes as the prosperity economy.

Originally, neoclassical theory showed little interest in healthcare and implicitly supposed that its theory of supply and demand applied to it. In the contemporary period, two conceptual breakthroughs have taken place. First, the microeconomics of imperfect and asymmetrical information has permitted better understanding of the healthcare sector. Second, human capital theory implied that healthcare and educational expenditures are not just part of consumption but also represent a capital investment—on the one hand, by extending skills (education) and, on the other, by improving healthy life expectancy. Alas, the addition of the hypothesis of rational expectation implies that individuals completely grasp the repercussions of their choices for their health. Indeed, some Chicago School models went so far as to present the individual as deterministically choosing the date of his death, which corresponded to the dissolution of his human capital (Grossman 1972). It is a good example of confusion as to the direction of causality and the consequences of a hypothesis of reversibility.

Finally, the theory of endogenous growth can be called upon in analyzing the dynamic of healthcare costs because techniques of care are the object of research leading to innovations that are subsequently spread nearly throughout the healthcare system. Medical innovation should be recognized as an important component of social systems of innovation. But one cannot content oneself with transposing models concerning differentiation by quality since "medical technical progress" is of an entirely different kind: it results from the interaction among various actors shown in Fig. 5.3 and not just from companies in search of oligopolistic rents relating to innovation resulting in a purely private good. The present article initially adopts the hypothesis of medical innovation shaped by the institutional context and subsequently sketches the overlapping relations between healthcare and the macroeconomic dynamic.

5.7.2 Successors of Fordism Among Potential Modes of Development

If one leaves behind the short-term framework of the conjuncture and project them over the scale of several decades, the preceding analyses reveal the characteristics of a development model that is rarely recognized as such. Contemporary discussions most often concern the opportunities for and obstacles to the emergence of a regime that would overcome ecological problems. Other analysts continue to bet on the fallout of an information and then knowledge economy at a time when growing inequality threatens the governmentality of contemporary societies. Perhaps one must also consider the possibility of a form of development centered on education, healthcare and culture. This theory was early developed in connection with the impact of social

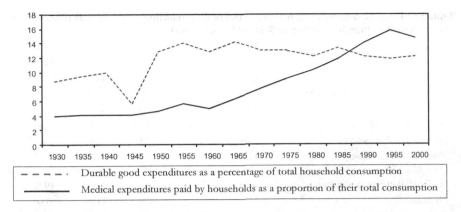

Fig. 5.8 The United States: the anthropogenic model in action *Source* Boyer (2002)

coverage systems (Théret 1997) and has been revisited in the context of discussions regarding successors to the Fordist regime (Boyer 2002).

What evidence supports such a theory? It is important in this connection to first revisit American history over the long-term for the United States continues to be at the forefront of exploring the technological frontier, not just in the area of goods and services, including financial ones, but also in that of medical innovation. Is it not remarkable that the share of durable goods in total household consumption should be more or less constant since the advent of mass consumption while medical expenditures have over the long term continuously grown, a few phases of stabilization notwithstanding? Indeed, the healthcare sector has already supplanted that of durable goods (Fig. 5.8).

The evolution of employment by large sectors over the course of the past four decades confirms this diagnosis and allows for an initial evaluation of the relevance of the various models of development that are said to have succeeded Fordism (Table 5.6). It is not surprising to observe that agriculture and extraction represent no more than a minimal part of total employment. During the 1970s and 80s, the manufacturing industry was still the most important sector, not just in terms of volume of employment but also from the point of view of the creation and distribution of productivity gains. In the two decades that followed, the sectors of healthcare, education and leisure collectively became the principal employer at the level of the United States, a development that the crisis that began in 2008 does not seem to have curbed. By contrast, the latter marked a halt to the growth of employment in the financial and business services sectors.

This result is interesting relative to the chronology put forward for regimes of accumulation by research inspired by the theory of regulation. On the one hand, it is true that tertiarization is a long-term evolution, gradually eroding the impetus supplied by the model of mass production and consumption (Petit 1985). On the other hand, however, it is essential to distinguish between the various dynamics

Table 5.6 From the domination of industry to that of the production of man by man (Distribution of employment by branch of activity in % in the United States)

Sector	1970	1980	1990	2000	2010
(1) Agriculture	3.46	3.36	3.22	3.75	3.42
(2) Mines	0.68	1.08	0.77	0.6	0.75
(3) Relating to nature (1) + (2)	4.14	4.44	3.99	4.35	4.17
(4) Construction	**3.65**	**4.45**	**5.26**	**6.75**	**5.52**
(5) Durable goods	**10.7**	**11.68**	**10.74**	**10.88**	**7.06**
(6) Non-durable goods	**7.09**	**7.05**	**6.96**	**6.39**	**4.46**
Manufacturing industry (7) = (5) + (6)	17.85	18.73	17.70	17.27	11.52
(8) Education and healthcare	4.58	7.07	10.98	15.11	19.53
(9) Leisure	4.79	6.72	9.29	11.86	13.05
Anthropogenic sector (10) = (8) + (9)	9.37	13.79	20.27	26.97	32.58
(11) Finance	3.53	5.03	6.61	7.69	7.65
(12) Business services	5.27	7.54	10.85	16.67	16.73
(13) Financial sector	8.80	12.57	17.46	24.36	24.38
Other services distribution, transport	56.19	45.7	35.32	20.26	21.83
Total	100	100	100	100	100
Key		1st sector in terms of employment			
		2nd sector in terms of employment			

Sources Employment, hours, earnings calculations from the Bureau of Labor Statistics http://data.bis.gov/cgi-bin/survey.most?

that tertiarization brings into play: it would seem that a capitalism dominated by financialization (Aglietta and Rebérioux 2004; Boyer 2011) is silently giving way to an anthropogenic form of capitalism. It would doubtless be wrong to characterize them as jointly falling under the aegis of cognitive capitalism, for example (Moulier Boutang 2007), for they have much different consequences for the economic dynamic and the reconfiguration of social relations. It is remarkable in this connection that the two great reforms of Barack Obama's presidency respectively consisted in an effort to regulate finance—hampered by the power of Wall Street pressure groups—and a reorganization of health insurance to ensure better coverage for the population as a whole. In both cases, the question arose as to the relationship between the government's responsibility towards citizens and difficult compromises with the dominant economic powers.

5.7.3 Japan: The Muted Emergence of an Anthropogenic Model

It is nevertheless difficult for the American configuration to gain widespread acceptance: it is costly and unequal for various ideological and political obstacles prevent a system rationally organized under the aegis of the state from fully developing. President Obama's healthcare reform made a start on correcting the trajectory but its long-term impact remains problematic, if only because of the extreme polarization of public opinion and political parties regarding the question of what mechanisms should govern the healthcare system.

Another country has long explored the possibility of implementing the anthropogenic model. It is generally known for having invented an alternate system of production to that of Fordism. Following a financial crisis provoked by financial liberalization, it later suffered a long period of stagnation. More recently, it has gained attention for its efforts to implement a "heterodox" economic theory to move beyond the crisis. We are of course referring to Japan here. A term-by-term comparison with the United States is instructive (Table 5.7).

Mean life expectancy among the Japanese is significantly higher than that for Americans, with healthcare expenditures 40% lower than in the United States even though the elderly share of the population is much greater. The share of expenditures for public education is lower in Japan but access to higher education better than in the United States. To judge by the frequency of crimes and homicides, Japanese society is much more peaceful than that of the United States. Finally, there is much less inequality. The only cloud on the horizon—albeit an important one—is the low Japanese fertility rate, which has resulted in an aging and shrinking population. On the one hand, this development significantly reflects the unequal economic status of men and women in Japanese society and is thus one weakness of this version of an anthropogenic model. On the other hand, however, it provides the point of departure for a reconfiguration of the Japanese economy and society taken as a whole (Matsutani 2006). Since it seems unlikely that there will be a return to rapid growth, why not create an economy of prosperity centered on the search for an improved quality of life? It is possible that such a strategy corresponds to the present of the old continent—and perhaps also its future.

5.8 Conclusion

1. In analyzing healthcare, the vast majority of economists fall victim to a methodological bias when they suppose that the growth of costs over the middle-term is only the consequence of exogenous shocks affecting a succession of short-term static equilibria of unchanging structure. They thus often confuse the observation that health care costs increase with age during a given period with the fact that medical innovation allows one to better treat diseases related to aging. Similarly,

Table 5.7 Misunderstood Japan: exploring the paths of an anthropogenic model

	United States	Japan
1. Life expectancy		
– Men	75.4	79.3
– Women	80.5	86.1
2. Rate of higher education		
– Men	48.7	58.8
– Women	60.6	56.4
3. Healthcare expenditures		
– /per capita PPP 2010	3967	2443
– Healthcare expenditures	2.3	2.9
4. Inequality		
– GINI of income (2009)	0.471	0.357
5. Fertility		
– 2005–2010	2.07	1.32
6. Urban population (%)		
– 2011	84.7	91.3
7. Population > 65		22.7
– 2010	13.1	22.7
8. Public education expenditures		
– % GDP (2009)	5.4	3.4
– Defense/GDP	4.7	1.0
9. Crimaes, homicides		
– (100,000)	5.0	0.9

Source Developed on the basis of Keizai Koho Center data (2013)

it is absurd to interpret the trend towards falling total factor productivity—as measured by traditional indicators of activity—as the expression of repeated mistakes in managing the healthcare sector. Hospitals, for example, are the site, not just of the delivery of care for a given state of medical practices, but also of medical research and thus the transformation of care. The evolution of medical technique is endogenous and is the major explanatory factor of long-term growth in the relative cost of healthcare.

2. An evolutionist and institutionalist approach is thus called for to understand the temporal and spatial variability of the healthcare sector's dynamic of production. Medical advances allow one to treat formerly incurable ailments but at the price of increased costs, requiring that mechanisms of collective insurance and coverage be established. In turn, the organization of financing and the production of care act retroactively upon the nature of advances in medical diagnosis and techniques of treatment. The system created after the Second World War thus favored improved quality at the price of increased cost and various reforms have subsequently been enacted to allow another healthcare cost-quality tradeoff. In this way, one may

also explain the diversity of national evolutions that resulted from the interaction between an insurance regime, an organization of healthcare production and an orientation of medical advances within a given socio-economic regime.

3. The conception according to which growing healthcare costs are the only consequence of economic development provoked by the technical and organizational innovations of the productive sector should thus be put into perspective. On the one hand, medical innovation plays such a decisive role in the growth of healthcare costs that it is useful to consider its determinants as well as its benefits in what concerns healthy life expectancy while recognizing that many other factors also contribute to its evolution (lifestyle, diet, environmental risks, impact of education on recourse to the healthcare system…). It is thus particularly difficult to draw up a cost/benefit appraisal that fully takes the impact of healthcare sector activity into account. On the other hand, healthcare and education can play the role of catalyzer and factor of development, both in countries that are seeking to catch up vis-à-vis their long-industrialized counterparts and in those that are exploring alternatives to the growth models of the post-Second World War years.

4. Indeed, analysts and political leaders wonder about the modes of development that might over time replace most of those that are today in crisis. In contrast to earlier industrial revolutions, communication and information technologies do not seem to have raised prospects for productivity growth in lasting fashion. Public policies, business strategies and even life styles are already partly shaped by the recognition of ecological constraints but radical uncertainty prevails as to the emergence and diffusion of regimes powered by some set of green technologies. The observation that expenditures linked to education, training, healthcare and culture tend to supplant the acquisition of standard goods and services seems somewhat neglected. Many indices already suggest that late twenty-first century development might be anthropogenic in nature—that is, centered on the production of man by man.

5. This article advances a general interpretation but only offers a few partial and preliminary tests of the main hypotheses upon which it is based. It underscores the convergence of diverse problematics and contributes various indices but is far from supplying a fully confident response. It is an argument for pursuing a research program that brings an evolutionary and institutionalist method to bear on the matter. In particular, it does not address a central question: what are the institutional forms that would allow the anthropogenic model to fully develop? Is the trend to commodification capable of supplying a viable socioeconomic configuration or do new forms of collective intervention need to be conceived? Will North America explore the first option under the transhumanist project and can the European Union defend a more equal and democratic variant of the anthropogenic model? What might be the consequences of free exchange treaties for the geography of healthcare and education activities?

References

Aglietta, M., & Rebérioux, A. (2004). *Les dérives de la finance*. Paris: Albin Michel.

Baumol, W., & Bowen, W. (1966). *Performing arts, the economic dilemma: A study of problems common to theater, opera, music and dance*. New York: Twentieth Century Fund.

Blumenthal, D., Stremikis, K., & Cutler, D. (2013). Health care spending—A giant slain or sleeping? *The New England Journal of Medicine, 369*, 2551–2557.

Boyer, R. (1971). *Essai d'analyse de la dynamique des coûts hospitaliers* (Mémoire de DEA). Université Paris 1, n° 24/21-1-71.

Boyer, R. (2002). *La croissance, début de siècle. De l'octet au gène*. Paris: Albin Michel.

Boyer, R. (2011). *Les financiers détruiront-ils le capitalisme?* Paris: Economica.

Boyer, R., & Saillard, Y. (2000). *Regulation theory: The state of the art*. London: Routledge.

Campbell, J., Hall, J., & Pedersen, O. K. (2008). *National identity and the varieties of capitalism. The Danish experience*. Copenhagen: DJOF Publishing.

Cassiers, I. (Ed.). (2011). *Redéfinir la prospérité. Jalons pour un débat public*. Editions de l'Aube.

Chansky, B., Garner, C., & Raichoudhary, R. (2013). *Measuring output and productivity in private hospitals*. U.S. Bureau of Labor Statistics.

Cutler, D. M., & Lleras-Muney, A. (2006). *Education and health: Evaluating theories and evidence*. Working Paper NBER 12352, http://www.nber.org/papers/w12352.

Cutler, D. M., & McClellan, M. (2001). Is technological change in medicine worth it? *Health Affairs, 20*(5), 11–29.

Department of Health. (2010). *Management of NHS hospital productivity*. Report by the Comptroller and Auditor General, HC 491, Session 2010–2011, 17 December.

Esping-Andersen, G. (2008). Childhood investments and skill formation. *International Tax and Public Finance, 15*, 14–49.

Fontvieille, L., & Michel, S. (2002). Analysis of the transition between two successive social orders—Application to the relation between education and growth. *Review, 25*(1), 23–46. New York: Fernand Braudel Centre.

Gaudillière, J. P. (2019). From crisis to reformulation: Innovation in the global drug industry and the alternative modernization of Indian ayurveda. In S. Lechevalier (Ed.), *Innovation beyond technology* (pp. 121–139). Berlin: Springer.

Godin, B. (2006). The Linear model of innovation, the historical construction of an analytical framework. *Science, Technology, & Human Values, 31*(6), 639–667. https://doi.org/10.1177/0162243906291865.

Grmek, M. D. (1969). Préliminaires d'une étude historique des maladies. *Annales. Économies, Sociétés, Civilisations*. 24e année, *6*, 1473–1483.

Grossman, M. (1972). On the concept of health capital and the demand for health. *Journal of Political Economy, 80*(2), 223–255.

Hallak, J. (1968). La productivité, le rendement et l'analyse des systèmes. *Institut international de planification de l'éducation*. Paris: UNESCO.

Hiroi, Y. (2019). Science as care: Science and innovation in post-growth society. In S. Lechevalier (Ed.), *Innovation beyond technology* (pp. 301–324). Berlin: Springer.

Joly, P. B. (2019). Reimagining innovation. In S. Lechevalier (Ed.), *Innovation beyond technology* (pp. 25–45). Berlin: Springer.

Koizumi, S. (2019). The light and shadow of the fourth industrial revolution. In S. Lechevalier (Ed.), *Innovation beyond technology* (pp. 63–86). Berlin: Springer.

Leibenstein, H. (1966). Allocative efficiency vs. "X-Efficiency". *The American Economic Review, 56*(3).

List, F. (1856). *National system of political economy* (p. 221) (G. A. Matile, Trans.). Philadelphia: J.B. Lippincott & co.

Lundvall, B. A. (Ed.). (1992). *National systems of innovation: Toward a theory of innovation and interactive learning*. London: Pinter.

Madsen, K. (2008). How can it fly? The paradox of a dynamic labour market in a Scandinavian Welfare State. In J. Campbell, J. Hall, & O. K. Pedersen (Eds.), *National identity and the varieties of capitalism. The Danish experience* (pp. 321–355). Copenhagen: DJOF Publishing.

Matsutani, A. (2006). *Shrinking population economics*. Tokyo: I House Press.

Michel, S., & Vallade, D. (2007). Une analyse de long terme des dépenses sociales: vers un indicateur synthétique de développement des hommes. *Revue de la Régulation*. http://regulation.revues.org/1507.

Moulier Boutang, Y. (2007). *Le capitalisme cognitif, la nouvelle grande transformation*. Paris: Amsterdam.

Murphy, K., & Topel, R. (2006). The value of health and longevity. *Journal of Political Economy, 114*(5), 871–904.

OCDE. (2013). *Regards sur l'éducation*. Paris: les indicateurs de l'OCDE.

Oki, S. (2019). 'Innovation' as an adaptation of 'Progress': Revisiting the epistemological and historical contexts of these terms. In S. Lechevalier (Ed.), *Innovation beyond technology* (pp. 47–62). Berlin: Springer.

Pestre, D. (2019). Environment and social innovation: Why technology never was the solution. In S. Lechevalier (Ed.), *Innovation beyond technology* (pp. 175–194). Berlin: Springer.

Petit, P. (1985). *Slow growth and the service economy*. London: Pinter.

Sen, A. (1999). *Development as freedom*. Oxford: Oxford University Press.

Shin, J., & Moon, S. (2007). Do HMO plans reduce expenditure in the private sector? *Economic Inquiry, 45*(1), 82–99.

Théret, B. (1997). Méthodologie des comparaisons internationales, approches de l'effet sociétal et de la régulation: fondements pour une lecture structuraliste des systèmes nationaux de protection sociale. *L'Année de la régulation, 1*, 163–228.

Thomas, L. (1975). *The lives of a cell*. NY: Bantam Books.

UNDP. (2014). *Human development report 2014. Sustaining human progress: Reducing vulnerabilities and building resilience*. New York: UN publication.

Visser, J., & Hemerijck, A. (1997). *'A Dutch Miracle'—Job growth, welfare reform and corporatism in the Netherlands*. Amsterdam: University Press.

Von Hippel, E. A. (1976). The dominant role of users in the scientific instrument innovation process. *Research Policy, 5*(3), 212–239. https://doi.org/10.1016/0048-7333(76)90028.

Weisbrod, B. A. (1991). The health care quadrilemma: An essay on technological change, insurance, quality of care and cost containment. *Journal of Economic Literature, XXIX*(2), 523–552.

White, C. (2007). Health care spending growth: How different is the United States from the rest of the OECD? *Health Affairs, 26*(1), 154–161.

Chapter 6
From Crisis to Reformulation: Innovation in the Global Drug Industry and the Alternative Modernization of Indian Ayurveda

Jean-Paul Gaudillière

Abstract Alternative modernity has become a key notion in the history of science and medicine outside Europe. The aim of the following chapter is to illustrate the fecundity of this concept for addressing the role of non-technological factors in innovation, beyond the "time of empires". "Modern without being Western" remains a central feature of our present and global fascination for innovation as a driving force of economic and social development. To this purpose this chapter links two issues which have generally been discussed as two unrelated developments in the very recent history of health, pharmacy and industry. First, it discusses the putative crisis of innovation that is presently considered to be a major feature of this critical sector in global capitalism. While the origins of this crisis are often located in non-technological factors, beginning with the changes in the administrative regulation of markets, the articulation of their technological and non-technological aspects warrants closer consideration. Building on an epistemic and social interpretation of the crisis, the chapter then looks at the alternatives that are emerging outside the prevailing Western economy of pharmacy, following the form of alternative modernity associated with the industrialization and globalization of the "traditional" medical systems of Asia. Taking Ayurveda as example, it shows how Indian companies are now reformulating traditional medical knowledge to produce industrial, standardized and simplified poly-herbal remedies targeting biomedically defined disorders, especially the complex chronic disorders that global health now puts high on its agenda. Placing these developments in relation one to the other not only reveal a strong case of innovation beyond technology, but also sheds light on the more general juxtaposition of heterogeneous political economies within what is superficially perceived as a single hegemonic logic of global pharmaceutical capitalism.

J.-P. Gaudillière (✉)
Cermes3, Inserm-EHESS, Paris, France
e-mail: gaudilli@vjf.cnrs.fr

© Springer Nature Singapore Pte Ltd. 2019
S. Lechevalier (ed.), *Innovation Beyond Technology*, Creative Economy,
https://doi.org/10.1007/978-981-13-9053-1_6

6.1 Introduction

In his recent book on the political debates and political reforms of Meiji Japan, the historian Pierre-François Souyri insists on the idea that modernity has historically taken various forms and should not be reduced to the paths followed in Europe. He thus sees the late 19th-century and early 20th-century transformations of Japanese society as processes of "modernization without westernization" (Souyri 2016). This perspective echoes that which many historians of Asian societies confronted with the challenges of industrialization, imperial expansion, nation-state building and claims for civil and political rights have proposed in order to account for both the convergences and the sharp differences between these societies' responses, on the one hand, and European forms of modernization, on the other.

In *The Nation and its Fragments*, the Indian historian and political scientist Partha Chatterjee, for instance, analyzed the fundamental tension of modernization as the Indian nationalist elite envisioned it, namely as an opposition between the outside world of materiality and the inside world of culture, the latter being the locus of a decidedly non-Western modernism: "By my reading anti-colonial nationalism creates its own domain of sovereignty within colonial society well before it begins its political battle with the imperial power. It does this by dividing the world of social institutions and practices into two domains—the material and the spiritual. The material is the domain of the 'outside', of the economy and of statecraft, of science and technology, a domain where the West has proved its superiority and the East has succumbed. In this domain then Western superiority has to be acknowledged and its accomplishment carefully studied and replicated. The spiritual, on the other hand, is an 'inner' domain bearing the 'essential' marks of cultural identity. The greater is one's success in imitating Western skills in the material domain therefore the greater the need to preserve the distinctiveness of one's spiritual culture. (…) The colonial state, in other words, is kept out of the 'inner' domain of national culture, but it is not as though this so-called spiritual domain is left unchanged. In fact, here nationalism launches its most powerful, creative, and historically significant project: to fashion a 'modern' national culture that is nevertheless not Western" (Chatterjee 1993: 6).

Chatterjee and his colleagues from the Subaltern Studies Collective thus considered the material domain of industry, science and innovation as the most obvious realm of derivative discourses and alignment on Western standards. A rich historiography of science and medicine in colonial India has however demonstrated that the two realms were separated but not isolated, that modernizing the medical systems of India without losing their roots in (re-invented) traditions became a central motive in the 20th-century practices of Indian scientists and physicians (Arnold 1993; Mukharji 2011, 2016).

Alternative modernity has thus become a key notion in the history of science and medicine outside of Europe. The aim of the following chapter is to illustrate its fecundity for addressing the role of non-technological factors in innovation beyond the "time of empires", i.e. the 1850–1950 period. "Modern without being Western" remains a central feature of our present and global fascination for innovation as a driving force of economic and social development.

To this purpose the chapter links two issues which have generally been discussed as two unrelated developments in the very recent history of health, pharmacy and industry. First, it discusses the putative crisis of innovation that is presently considered to be a major feature of this critical sector in global capitalism. While the origins of this crisis are often located in non-technological factors, beginning with the changes of the administrative regulation of markets, the articulation of the technological and non-technological aspects warrants closer consideration. Building on an epistemic and social interpretation of the crisis, the chapter then looks at the alternatives emerging outside of the prevailing Western economy of pharmacy, following the form of alternative modernity associated with the industrialization and globalization of the "traditional" medical systems of Asia. Taking Ayurveda as an example, it places these developments in relation to one another. In so doing, it not only reveals a strong case of innovation beyond technology, but also sheds light on the more general juxtaposition of heterogeneous political economies within what is superficially perceived as a single hegemonic logic of global pharmaceutical capitalism.

6.2 The Crisis of Pharmaceutical Innovation: From Overload of Regulation to an Epistemic Dead-End

The idea that, after a thirty-year "therapeutic revolution", pharmacy is facing a lack of new molecules has been a matter of public concern for more than a decade. It was actually around the year 2000 that a first wave of papers, most of them written by health economists or industry managers, started to discuss the declining productivity of pharmaceutical research and development. This in itself was not entirely new. Papers with analogous concerns had been published in the 1980s, even in the late 1970s, although with more limited scope since they often dealt with one type of therapeutic agents, primarily antibiotics. Today the literature on the crisis of innovation has not only expanded but has gained in generality with a new richness of data and interpretations.

6.2.1 The Crisis Discourse in Contemporary Pharmacy: A Political Rather Than Technological Problem

Within the pharmaceutical literature, the idea of a crisis is associated with three types of indicators: the number of New Molecular Entity (NME) approvals, the costs of drug research and development (R&D), and the rates of attrition.

Approval data are almost exclusively those of the US Food and Drug Administration, the only agency for which we have data dating back far enough, on the numbers of applications filed and the substances or indications authorized. This has however created a kind of bias due to the administrative reorganization of the agency in the 1990s. The widely circulated figures showing a sharp decline in the number of authorized NME entities in the late 1990s is thus a consequence of the accelerated treatment of a backlog of applications filed in the late 1980s and early 1990s (Cohen 2005). Even if the data regarding the number of applications filed each year at the FDA are more significant, data regarding "new molecules" have been contested with claims that the crisis of innovation is a kind of myth invented by the industry to legitimize high costs of its products and changes in the legal context. NMEs are actually very rough indicators, which for instance say nothing about the intensity of the research effort or the nature of these innovations. Other parameters have therefore been introduced.

The most significant are related to R&D investments and costs. Authors like Booth have for instance computed productivity indicators (in that case the ratio of NMEs authorized to the money invested in research), notwithstanding the difficulty of estimating the costs of development (Booth and Zemmel 2004). All results then converge to point to a decade of slow decline of productivity, resulting in a startling 300–500% increase in the costs associated with the launch of one molecule. This has strongly reinforced the idea of the "end of the therapeutic revolution", which links the crisis of innovation to a historical scenario characterized by the highly successful period from 1945 to 1975 when most of the therapeutic classes that we presently know were renewed or invented: antibiotics, psychotropic drugs, anti-inflammatory and corticoids, etc. One impressive study in this respect is that of Basil Achilladelis and Nicholas Antonakis, published in 2001 (Achilladelis and Antonakis 2001). Taking into account more than 1700 widely-used products, they examined the time of their discovery, their commercial success and their technological similarities. On this basis they identified breakthrough and cumulative innovations, with five waves of major product introductions, the three most important of which took place between 1930 and 1980. The study did not point to the decreasing pace after 1990, but, as the authors suggest, it did reveal that the postwar waves of innovation, in contrast to previous ones, were associated with a few giant companies, all of which sustained large in-house research infrastructures.

One last type of more refined indicators are attrition rates. These have been computed only for recent periods since they require comprehensive data about the research projects and about the clinical trials and their outcomes. A recent paper by Fabio Pammolli amply illustrates a trend that matches the cost figures (Pammolli et al. 2011): attrition rates have been growing since the 1990s. The phenomenon stems however not so much from preclinical studies as from the human trials, especially those corresponding to phase III when efficacy is the issue and larger groups of patients are surveyed. In contrast, attrition rates at the level of registration remain relatively stable and low.

This leads to the question of the interpretative framework. The discussion has brought in many possible culprits for the crisis of productivity, some more temporary than others, some cognitive, others organizational. Focusing on the particularities of the 1990s, authors like Booth have insisted on the nature of the research. Building on the current idea that—for reasons that warrant more in-depth analysis—, the industry refocused its investments on biological macromolecules and biotechnologies, they emphasize the fact that these technologies were non-validated targets, meaning they were of unproven clinical utility and therefore much more risky. On the other hand, authors like Kneller who are interested in institutional and organizational models have pointed to the wave of mergers and reorganizations in the 1980s and 1990s. They have suggested that these changes were both a reflection of and a contribution to the fact that the big companies involved had become very big, increasingly complex if not bureaucratic structures (Kneller 2010). In short, pharmaceutical firms are now just "too big to innovate".[1]

A widely shared idea is however of a different kind. Building on the supposed links between market incentives and innovation, it looks for the changes in the administrative regulatory framework as the main source of difficulties. The idea is supported by data on R&D investments (for instance in DiMasi et al. 2003 or Cohen 2005), as well as the disaggregated attrition rates. It is that the introduction, growth, and increasingly complex requirements of clinical trials mandated to obtain a marketing authorization have caused the booming costs and rising attrition rates. Accordingly, the crisis of innovation is a result of regulatory rather than market failure.

Given the diversity of interpretations, it is hardly surprising that the discussion has also pointed to a variety of "responses" experimented with in the industry. Hughes tried to list them in a temporal-complexity order, beginning with the simplest one, then those with bigger financial investments, followed by attempts to diversify the knowledge (and target) basis with biotech acquisition, and finally more fundamental changes in the organizational and economical model, with tendencies to externalize R&D or exploration of an open-source model that would limit the domination of patents as a mode of appropriation (Hughes 2007).

6.2.2 Screening and the Historical Roots of the Crisis: An Epistemic and Systemic View

As an alternative to this narrow political interpretation, one needs to mention another type of consideration, which is both more historical and more troubling. It may be illustrated with a widely discussed paper published by Munos in 2009 on "60 years of pharmaceutical innovation" (Munos 2009). The first thing its authors did was to belie the assumption on the number of NMEs authorized, stressing that the long-term trends at the FDA show remarkably stable numbers, apart from occasional blips like the 1996 administrative peak. Should one conclude that the very notion of crisis should therefore be given up? Munos and his colleagues clearly say no, pointing to the escalating costs. The novelty of their analysis is however to argue, on the basis of fragmentary but very compelling industrial data, that this is also a long-

---

[1]This line of interpretation is actually consistent with a set of studies that have looked at the innovation potential of biotech firms and start ups, albeit with mixed results.

term phenomenon and not a by-product of the last twenty years. If one accepts their comparison, costs started to rise as early as the beginning of the therapeutic revolution in the 1950s. Since then they have never declined and, more importantly, their growth has remained exponential. The dynamics has not been affected by any discontinuity, including major regulatory changes like the 1962 law making controlled clinical trials of efficacy mandatory. In other words, the declining productivity is not only old, it seems to have remained the "same" since the present organization of drug R&D stabilized in the first two decades after WW2.

In the eyes of the historian, this is a problematic, almost a-historical, pattern. One could therefore dismiss Munos' results as being too partial, preliminary, etc. Yet, as discussed elsewhere, it is possible to make sense of them on the basis of the recent historiography of pharmacy, especially the historiography of what may be called the "screening model" of drug invention, which became dominant in the 1960s and 1970s (Gaudillière, in review). The core hypothesis is that the nature of the problem, its recurrence and its longevity, are not merely the consequence of "external" circumstances like the changes of regulation; they are an effect of screening operations *per se*, and the internal contradictions—both epistemic and economic—which plagued screening from its early days and were aggravated by its generalization in the 1960s–1980s.

Within this context, screening should not be taken in its narrow sense, i.e. the strong coupling of chemical synthesis and pharmacological testing within the premises of the industry, which emerged in the German industry in the interwar period. Instead, it should be considered as a broader regime of innovation performed by pharmaceutical drug companies in the global North, and which integrates research, production, promotion and sales in a linear pipe-line including clinical trials, scientific marketing, sales and regulation beyond the mere practices of laboratory-centered innovation (Gaudillière 2015). That this regime—like modern biomedicine in general—places molecules at its very center goes without saying. One of its more specific and recent features is however the strong articulation that screening has created between three elements: (a) the growth of in-house R&D with the mounting and now dominant role of large drug companies in the planning, monitoring and diffusion of clinical trials; (b) the generalization of pre-marketing evaluation of efficacy by national drug agencies mandating the organization of controlled (usually randomized) trials as standard methodology; and (c) the rapid expansion of "scientific marketing" in the form of publications, meetings, visits of representatives or financial incentives targeting general practitioners as well as specialists in order to boost prescriptions.

One can actually find in the literature of the 1960s–1980s, when enlarged screening became the norm, a few discussions of why the pipeline structure, its commitment to chemistry and the coupling between research and marketing may finally hinder innovation. They all revolve around the idea that screening has made the relationship between the selection of valuable molecules and clinical knowledge problematic. Three layers of argumentation can be distinguished:

(1) The epistemic problem: screening enables investigations centered on biomolecular properties and modeling, thus relegating clinical knowledge and the care experience to a secondary role.
(2) The organizational problem: the screening pipeline is a linear "lab to hospital" organization that does not facilitate "feedback", while standardized protocols marginalize clinical bricolage and routine practices.
(3) The economic problem: scientific marketing is an integral part of screening and enhances the selection of "incremental" molecular innovation and enlarged indications rather than breakthrough innovations.

How can this further our understanding of the contemporary discourses on the crisis of innovation? In terms of change and temporality, one first remark is that the history of the screening model fits the chronology of the crisis economic studies propose. Geigy (now part of Novartis) is for instance typical of the majority of postwar rapidly growing firms, which—in contrast to Bayer—did not organize their research on the basis of full-fledged screening before the early 1970s (Gaudillière and Thoms 2015). Geigy had a strong chemical research infrastructure and little biological modeling, and operated the selection of its promising substances through a loosely organized network of trusted and regularly reporting clinicians. This radically changed during the decade 1965–1975 when the company increased its chemical workforce, established a clinical department monitoring dozens of standardized trials, massively hired prep-representatives, and set up committees gathering research and marketing personnel to plan both R&D and scientific promotion.

A second remark is that the limitations of screening may account for several phenomena to which the discussion on the crisis of innovation has pointed, beginning with the high rates of attrition at the clinical stage or the so-called "efficacy-effectiveness" gap. The latter is the way in which regulatory agencies like the FDA or EMA target the major differences between the efficacy of a given drug as it is objectified in controlled trials, and the effectiveness of the same compound when it is used in routine practices under normal—meaning average—conditions of prescription and in association with basic care rather than the exceptional means available in frontier research hospitals.

A third remark is that the screening hypothesis sheds interesting light on the chronology of recent changes in the R&D practices of the industry. For instance, analysts like Jeremy Greene, Robert Aronowitz or Jospeh Dumit have documented the mounting importance of the pharmaceutical management of health-related cardiovascular and psychiatric risks (Aronowitz 1999; Greene 2007; Dumit 2012). This form of intervention largely fuelled the drug market's growth in the 1980s and 1990s through massive investments in the redefinition of disease boundaries and the correlative transformation of risks into entities that must be handled as if they were already pathologies. In terms of research, this dynamics has increasingly relied on the "me-too strategy", namely the development of a vast palette of molecular variants from a few and already old "head of series". Me-too show relatively similar clinical properties to the substances used as references, but allow a regular renewal of patents and other property rights.

At a more theoretical level, the screening hypothesis suggests a new reading of the drug industry's place within the "knowledge economy" on the one hand, and in the speculative economy, on the other. Sociologists and economists of innovation often define the creation of a knowledge economy, i.e. the "commodification" of research, as a conjunction of three elements: (1) the emergence of new forms of knowledge; (2) the creation of startups that transfer research results in a more less straightforward way through patenting; and (3) the financing of these startups through venture capital and innovation markets. It is well known that this transformation would not have taken place without major political and institutional changes. In the US context, the 1980s witnessed the conjunction of three initiatives originating in the neoliberal agenda: (1) the transformation of the Nasdaq into a speculative market for financing innovative firms not (yet) involved in the production of goods or services; (2) the passing of the Bayh-Dole Act to foster technology transfers from academia; and (3) the extended practices of patent approval at United States Patent and Trademark Office, which culminated in the normalization of property rights on genes, cells and entire organisms.

When global industry investments are concerned, however, making new wine out of old grapes is not the preferred response. Since the mid-1980s, biotech has been the most favored target to restore the declining productivity of in-house R&D. This pattern powerfully testifies of the dialectics of use value and exchange value. Its massiveness (in comparison with other forms of responses to the crisis of productivity) may be understood as the conjunction of two powerful incentives respectively linked, on the one hand to "use" as defined in the screening model—i.e. identifying radically new molecular targets and controlling the clinical aspects through biological rather than chemical lenses—, and to "exchange" on the other hand—i.e. securing financial returns by participating in the highly promising juncture between the knowledge economy and the speculative economy out of which biotech—as a frontier market—emerged.

It is one of the most salient evidence in favor of an analytics trying to integrate the epistemic and the economical that the pay-offs of these investments are still rather limited. The conjuncture of speculation and knowledge transfer has thus created situations of major disjunctions between speculative value and product sales, resulting in the same sort of "bubbles" that characterize other sectors of the financial economy. A paramount case was the creation in the second half of the 1990s of hundreds of gene therapy start-ups and their subsequent collapse in the mid-2000s when, confronted with recurrent difficulties in translating laboratory promises—often based on the use of genetically modified animal models—into human clinical trials results, the investors' faith in an ADN "blockbuster" vanished (Martin 1999). Changing the targets from chemical to biological molecules did not alter the linear and reductionist logic inherited from screening, or the difficulty of integrating clinical work and care. The crisis in the construction of clinical utility resulted all the more quickly in a collapse of these companies' exchange value, given that the overall promise of biotech remained unfulfilled. Of course, the number of products (or services) and the value attached to them are far from nil but—after 30 years of investments—biotech-based health goods are still not matching (or even replacing) classical pharmaceuticals and their markets. In the US in 2012 the total value of sales was 63 billion for biotech, compared to 326 billion for the classical pharmaceutical market.[2]

6.3 Alternative Responses: The Globalization and Industrialization of Indian Ayurveda

Anthropologists and Science and Technology Studies scholars have documented the radical transformation of Indian Ayurvedic medicine over the past twenty years. This reinvention of one of the most widely used non-Western forms of medical care originated in a complex process of industrialization and unequal but significant integration within the world of global pharmacy.

Ayurveda is one of the multiple "traditional" medicines currently recognized by the state of India as an autonomous system of knowledge and practice, regulated as such and officially integrated into the country's health infrastructure. Half the population regularly seeks care from the practitioners of this form of humoral and holistic medicine, whose basic corpus of texts is more than a thousand years old. Very often they do so in parallel with the use of the biomedical system. Analysts have shown that alternative modernization has gone through several waves since the early 20th century: professionalization before independence; institutionalization after 1947 with the gradual creation of an infrastructure (diplomas, medical schools, hospitals and dispensaries) juxtaposed to the dominant biomedical health system; and attempts at integration in the primary health care when the latter was officially prioritized in the 1980s (Attewell 2007; Banerjee 2009; Bode 2008). Since the neo-liberal turn of international health in the 1990s, the modernization of Ayurveda has meant industrialization. It has gone hand in hand with the rise of a pharmaceutical sector mass-producing ready-made therapeutic combinations of plants, which are "reformulated" (often radically simplified) versions of recipes from the official corpus of Ayurveda treaties (Pordié and Gaudillière 2014). The firms trading in these remedies range from small local ventures originating in one family to global players with thousands of employees, which market products throughout Asia using "scientific marketing" tools exactly like those of any large capitalistic Western drug company. Their preparations are mostly purchased by consumers in the new urban middle-class as part of a self-management of health, risks and bodies that largely resembles what Western users critical of biomedicine do when looking for alternative forms of care rooted in "traditional" medical systems.

The reformulation of classical combinations of medicinal plants described in centuries-old reference texts used by Ayurvedic practitioners lies at the heart of this process. Reformulation means simultaneously simplifying and standardizing polyherbal combinations in order to (1) adapt them to mass and mechanized industrial processing; (2) draw on elements of biomedical experimentation in the laboratory and clinical medicine to provide evidence of medical value, and (3) combine Ayurvedic

---

[2]US Pharmaceutical Industry Statistics. www.statista.com.

130 J.-P. Gaudillière

and biomedical categories in order to address the health needs of cosmopolitan consumers.

The political economy underlying this transformation and the Indian path to biocapital that it reveals are especially visible in two domains worth discussing in the context of this chapter: (1) the creation of intellectual property rights over the new preparations; (2) the creation of markets through the coupling of Ayurvedic formulas and biomedical disorders. Both suggest that reformulation is a "Southern" alternative response to the crisis of innovation—but an alternative that is more decisively targeting the epistemic (bio) than the economic (capital) dimensions of the crisis.

6.3.1 The Traditional Knowledge Digital Library: An Alternative to Global Patents

Intellectual property rights play a peculiar role in the reformulation strategy since Ayurvedic formulas are viewed on the one hand (when they more or less replicate the classical combinations described in Ayurvedic treatises) as collective resources that must be protected from private ownership to ensure further mining of classical texts, and on the other hand (when they significantly differ in ingredients or proportions from the classical—meaning included in classical texts—preparations) as innovative products that can be appropriated through trademarks and patents. The status and operations of the Traditional Knowledge Digital Library established by the Indian government in order to oppose the patenting of poly-herbal therapeutic preparations, which originate in Indian traditional knowledge, powerfully illustrates this conundrum. The TKDL was set up in 2000 as a national resource to oppose both "biopiracy" and, more specifically, the globalization of patents on traditional remedies that the crisis of innovation, the Trips agreement and the shift toward biotech conjured to render more attractive than ever (Gaudillière 2014).

Unlike many databases in biological and medical research, the TKDL premises not only host computers, software, and connecting cables run by highly qualified information technology experts, but also house a library in the conventional sense of the term: a place filled with ancient books and manuscripts, handwritten notes, and darkened photocopies that are carefully examined by teams made up of young, mostly female, practitioners of Ayurveda, Unani, Siddha, or Yoga, the main traditional medical systems officially recognized in India. The translations they craft suppose a set of scarcely obvious equivalences between the vernacular denominations of medical materials and the "modern" botanical denominations, or between the etiological and nosological categories of biomedicine and those of the Indian medical system under consideration. A typical formulation sheet thus needs to provide the following information: the name of the formula, the list and quantities of plants included, with their botanical identities, a broad description of the preparation mode (basically a Galenic equivalent of Ayurvedic groups of drugs), its indications for use, and the sources documenting the formulation, in other words, its traditional nature.

6 From Crisis to Reformulation: Innovation in the Global Drug ...

Yet the final format of TKDL documents does more than simply provide an English inventory of tens of thousands of recorded recipes, which in practice correspond to a much smaller number of clinically different formulations. By arranging the knowledge according to composition, production process, and usage, the new format closely follows the structure of patents, focusing on the combination of matter rather than on the medical context and the clinical meaning of the original texts. This alignment with the structure of patents can be read as mandatory to ensure the usability of the database. As a resource in intellectual property disputes, the TKDL formulas are targeted at patent examiners. They need to be easy to grasp, and the whole corpus must be searchable on the basis of legal intellectual property categories. It is therefore not surprising that at the TKDL, Indian medical traditional knowledge is reformulated according to the chemical ontology of patents, that is, in terms of composition and preparation process. The major adjustment to this framework, however, is the fact that TKDL information also strongly revolves around plants and botanical categories.

By borrowing the patent-derived notion of "composition of matter", the digital library is not only a means in intellectual property disputes but also a powerful instrument in the "pharmaceuticalization" of Ayurveda. It provides a tacit understanding of therapeutic efficacy as originating in the self-contained assemblage of plant extracts, in the *materia medica* rather than in a clinical process that—in Ayurveda—assesses the humoral status of the body, takes into account the patient's entire way of life, and designs ad hoc preparations rather than standard compositions.

Given the TKDL's official aim of resisting "biopiracy", contractual access agreements have been signed only with national partners, i.e. the intellectual property agencies of the "North". The European Patent Office has been authorized to consult the TKDL since February 2009. An access agreement with the USPTO was reached a year later, in 2010. The impact of this access on intellectual property practices seems to be significant, at least in the European context. Since 2009, dozens of patent applications have been denied on the basis of "prior art" information provided by the TKDL and its lawyers.

The opposition documents thus drawn up reiterate a general and critical policy regarding the boundaries of traditional knowledge and the nature of legitimate innovation through reformulation. Two notions pertaining to the specificity of the formulas originating in the Indian Systems of Medicine, as inventoried in the TKDL, play a critical role: (1) formulations are not recipes but medical protocols participating in a holistic and individualized approach to diseases, and therefore are references to be adapted and varied according to available plants, diagnosis, and clinical practice; and (2) the translation of traditional books into TKDL English standard files is bound to give rise to uncertainties regarding the naming of both ingredients and diseases. Consequently, the operators of the database consider that a whole series of "innovations" should not qualify for patent recognition, especially those based on changes of a few ingredients, their specific proportions in the combination, or the dosages, since such variations are deemed normal practice in Indian traditional medicine.

However, not all contested patents are canceled. The tensions between the logic the TKDL seeks to enforce and an emerging EPO regime of patentability focusing on the innovative value of reformulation is best illustrated with the instances of patents for which the claims have been modified following examiners' demands. The EPO is recognizing not only the prior art status of traditional knowledge but also its status as a resource to be mined. Legitimate innovation with medicinal plants is no longer addressed in terms of isolation and characterization of active ingredients but, rather, takes up the logic of invention through reformulation: newly defined poly-herbals are also deemed patentable, at least when associated with standardization and biological evaluation of the effects. EPO examiners thus use and help reinforce the translation of Ayurvedic medicine in terms of *materia medica* already embedded in the TKDL documents. In other words, the price paid by TKDL managers for their success at the international level is the juxtaposition of two contradictory results: a reinforced protection of the compendia of classical formulas turned into national inventory, and a reinforced industrial appropriation of reformulated compositions. On the one hand, tradition is being stabilized through the reference corpus and its translation; on the other, the path is open for its "pharmaceuticalization" and inscription into the drug knowledge economy.

This contradiction in the global roles of the TKDL is not devoid of internal resonance in India. The claimed function of the TKDL is to preserve the status of "common" knowledge associated with the classical formulas. "Common" in this context is synonymous with "national." The classical formulas are viewed as an Indian heritage, and the TKDL's first official goal is to avoid foreign (meaning Western) appropriation. With this national dimension it is all the more important that the existence of the TKDL does not preclude the possibility of patenting *new* formulations, in addition to their mandatory registration as "Ayurvedic proprietary medicines." The Indian Patent Office has accordingly granted hundreds of patents in the past ten years, most of them with no international status. This brings in a second, less visible dimension of the TKDL. In practice, it has created a vast unified corpus which, because of its digital nature (and in spite of its heterogeneity), can easily be mined, that is, for specific plants, for specific diseases or symptoms, and for correlations between the botanical and the medical.

From the knowledge transfer perspective advocated by Indian officials, the TKDL was therefore a means to foster reformulation. Despite the separation of its operations according to the different systems included in the institutional package of Indian traditional medicine, the digital library technically makes thorough mining possible, abolishing the practical and epistemic differences between these systems. The standardization of categories, the dominant focus on plants, and digitalization all combined to create what Indian Systems of Medicine administrators welcomed as a new stage in a modernization-based integration of the various Indian medical systems. That such mining should target not only the public academic world but also the industry was not a matter of debate. The main provision envisioned in the mid-2000s for granting TKDL access to third parties was, accordingly, a joint ownership and licensing of IPR [intellectual property rights] on the products to be created on the basis of TKDL information. This joint ownership "may include a lump sum initial payment and payment of periodic royalties on a mutually agreed basis, such as agreed percentage of gross turnover of the product(s) concerned." To whom such payment should go was, and remains, unclear since collaborative (industrial) mining of the database has barely taken place, for reasons pertaining to the manufacturing dynamics of reformulation discussed below.

6.3.2 Reformulation and the Production of Alternative Remedies for Global Diseases

Although widespread among social scientists, the viewpoint of Indian traditional medicines, that "traditional" Ayurveda and "modern" biomedicine are two mutually incompatible medical systems, and that the former is gradually disappearing through its alignment with the latter, is unable to render the complexities of the contemporary re-invention and globalization of these medicines. Such a dichotomous perspective misses the ways in which the reformulation practices involved in the industrialization of Ayurvedic formulations borrow from heterogeneous medical knowledge, combine bits and pieces from various bodies of practices (more than two) and invent previously unknown preparations, thus providing for modes of (pharmaceutical) intervention irreducible to biomedicine (Pordié and Gaudillière 2014). The invention of industrialized Ayurvedic remedies not only relies on technological work, such as turning compounded powders or oily extracts into ready-made pills, but also mobilizes a complex set of experimental, clinical, economic, and legal practices that are deemed indispensable in building markets and granting the new products a twofold legitimacy, both traditional and modern.

An essential dimension of reformulation is its industrial nature. Industrialization means that the core actors are Indian Ayurvedic drug-producing companies, some of them large enough to operate as global players. It also relates to the manufacturing process, that is, the search for productivity and large-scale output through the use of mechanized processing, automated machinery, standardization, and possibly laboratory-based quality control. The reformulation regime thus produces new compositions of medicinal plants based on unique knowledge-prospecting mechanisms, borrowing from sometimes very distant medical resources, such as modern galenics, biomedicine, or the various Indian traditional medical systems. Reformulation thus feeds the emergence of an autonomous "pharmacy" (in the sense of a social world exclusively devoted to therapeutic substances) that breaks with Ayurvedic clinical practice both from a sociological point of view (preparations are no longer made by doctors but by persons specializing in medicinal plants and their manipulation) and an epistemic point of view (formulations are ready-to-use mixes for specific indications, no longer ad hoc mixes that are part of an individualized treatment regimen).

Like pharmaceutical capitalism in the North, the Indian Ayurvedic industry engages in processes of market construction that mingle experimentation, sales and prescriptions. However, the work of reformulation entails specific contradictions stemming from its original way of combining (epistemic) tradition and (capitalistic) modernity. This may be illustrated with the development of a neo-traditional polyherbal remedy to treat symptoms of menopause. Menopause is a peculiar category in

Western medicine. Although its trajectory is as ancient as that of reproductive physiology, and took on a decidedly hormonal meaning in the early 20th century, it remained a marginal medical category until WW2. The main reason for this marginality is the fact that menopause was primarily associated with normal changes in women's reproductive life: it could cause undesirable symptoms but these had no pathological dimensions and were deemed to be transitory.

As recounted by historians of medicine like Elisabeth Watkins, the medicalization of menopause is deeply rooted in a process which took place during the therapeutic revolution, namely the transformation of women's sex hormones—estrogens and progesterone—into pharmaceuticals, that is, chemicals purified and produced in bulk—a process which, by the late 1950s, resulted in the invention of a vast palette of molecules bearing common structural features with natural hormones but acting either as analogs or as antagonists. This provided the material infrastructure for enlarged uses, including the management of menopausal symptoms, which started to be a mainstream rather than peripheral activity of gynecologists and general practitioners in the 1960s (Siegel Watkins 2007).

By the early 2000s, however, biomedical hormonal replacement therapy (HRT) faced a dramatic crisis. In the mid-1990s the US women health movement successfully lobbied the National Institutes of Health. They obtained the funding of a very large epidemiological study of HRT significantly called the Women Health Initiative study. In 2002 when the first results were made public they clearly opposed the claims (and previous studies) made by the promoters of HRT, showing that women under medication showed an increasing risk not only of breast cancer but also of cardiovascular disorders. The WHI triggered a major crisis of confidence, which resulted in many women choosing to go off the treatment. By 2004 prescriptions had dropped by 30–50% not only in the US but also in most European countries. The problem was compounded when epidemiologists started to correlate this change in drug consumption with a drop in the incidence of breast cancer—a premiere in the recent history of the disease. Given that a majority of women in Europe and the US were not as keen as their grandmothers to simply wait for the end of the menopausal transition and the disappearance of undesirable symptoms, the HRT crisis opened a vast potential market for alternative treatments.

This opportunity was not missed by the Indian Ayurvedic industry, as the case of Menosan, a preparation invented at the premises of The Himalaya Drug Company in Bangalore, shows. Himalaya started to market Menosan in 2002 as a safe and natural response to the problems recently identified with biomedical HRT, namely increased risks of cancer and cardiovascular disorders. Like the promoters of HRT, Himalaya promotes pharmaceutical intervention in order to remedy the hormonal "deficiency" defining a medical entity that is considered as a quasi pathology.

Himalaya thus presents Menosan as typically suited to fulfill the demands for more natural therapies for menopause since it is a plant-derived "natural" product. In other words, it is an industrial poly-herbal, whose complex composition is defined in terms of wholesome plant ingredients and is claimed as an asset since the combination provides for critical synergies between the qualities and effects of individual plants.

In order to understand the origins of Menosan and its "multiple ontology" one must however look beyond Himalaya's public discourse stressing the botanical and pharmacological rendering of the composition. When discussing the reformulation practices involved in the invention of the new preparation, the Ayurvedic practitioners (*vaidyas*) at The Himalaya Drug Company actually reveal another world, a world strongly committed to the mining of Ayurvedic classical texts.

The firm's mining of Ayurveda actually rests on a feedback loop between the texts and the laboratory, which obey two different logics. The first is a logic of translation and *materia medica*, focusing on the supposedly stable composition of plants and a series of equivalences between botanical denominations on the one hand, and vernacular and Sanskrit names on the other, that were worked out over two centuries of interactions between pharmacists, botanists and *vaidyas*. This logic serves to examine the classical *shastric* formulations, looking for combinations containing plants whose ingredients have been linked by biomedical as well as Ayurvedic pharmacology to processes responsible for menopausal symptoms (for instance neurological regulation of the vascular system). The second logic is one of commonalities and clinical knowledge. It focuses on the supposedly stable symptoms of "real" pathologies, bringing into play another series of equivalences, this time between the concepts used in clinical descriptions. This logic makes it possible to look for classical formulations targeting the components of the menopausal syndrome. Given the flexibility of equivalencies and combinations, it is not surprising that Himalaya scientists explored the properties of more than 40 formulations in the early stages of Menosan research, and that this poly-herbal was actually made through the testing of many putative Menosan, which appeared or disappeared through the contingencies of reformulation.

Note that what is at stake in the trajectory of this neo-traditional remedy is not only the making and commercialization of a new product for a known pathology, but also the making of a new medical problem since there was "no menopause in India" for which Menosan could be presented as a solution.[3] This is a decisive component of Himalaya's market construction. The company actively works to make it acceptable by Indian physicians and Indian women, borrowing many practices from multinational firms, scientific marketing included. Scientific marketing at Himalaya is a mode of promotion targeting physicians rather than patients. It relies on a palette of tools among which the system of medical representatives predominates. The collaboration with clinicians is as intimate as it is in the screening model. It is not only the design of clinical trials that is negotiated with hospital practitioners; as in the case of biomedical firms, trials are chosen and organized by both the clinical and business departments of the firm.

The scientific marketing of Menosan is nonetheless particular in one major respect. Given the "no menopause in India" situation, it is the promotion not only of a product

---

[3] Himalaya Ayurveda specialists thus consider that the need for a preparation like Menosan is therefore not the recognition of a previously invisible, unrecognized disorder, but the emergence of a new problem whose roots are in the changing structure of families, in processes of individualization and urbanization. In other words, menopause is a disease of modernity.

for a well-defined indication, but also simultaneously of menopause and its associated risks. One important partner in this work to increase the visibility and recognition of a new indication is therefore the Indian Menopause Society, founded in 1995. Himalaya regularly supports IMS events. It also collaborates with the society in the production of flyers and posters on menopause, without any mention of Menosan, to be posted in physicians' waiting rooms.

The limitations of the enterprise are however undeniable. They are rooted in the problematic relations that the dialectics of bio-capital maintains with the dialectics of modernity and tradition. After fifteen years of marketing, the sales of Menosan are significant but limited. Mimicking "big pharma" in order to shift the practices of Himalaya's main target, i.e. biomedical practitioners, toward neo-traditional remedies also faces resistance from the biomedical world in India. This is evidenced in the recommendations of the Indian Menopause Society, which—up to now—has not endorsed treatments other than HRT. Following the early 2000s crisis, Indian specialists followed the same path as their Euro-American colleagues, namely rewriting guidelines for shorter hormonal treatment to alleviate symptoms and reduce the risk of osteoporosis, and excluding patients with cardiovascular risks. The IMS official literature barely mentions herbal preparations in its guidelines (which make no mention of Ayurveda), and insists that the clinical value of (all) alternative treatment is unproven (in spite of Himalaya's trials) and that safety might be a problem.

Rather than a straightforward alignment on "Northern" pharmaceutical practices, the reformulation of Indian Ayurveda thus consists in attempts to invent alternative products and alternative rules for their commercialization, both nationally and globally. The trajectories of the TKDL as well as that of Menosan reveal the strong hierarchies shaping this Indian path toward a form of drug capitalism departing from the screening model. Unsurprisingly, these constraints operate at epistemic (the targeting of biomedical disorders), economic (the adoption of scientific marketing) and regulatory levels (the reliance on patents and minimal clinical trials prior to registration). These signs of hegemony do not imply that the construction of markets for neo-traditional herbal preparations erases the particularity of Indian responses to the crisis of innovation. The commodification of Indian poly-herbal drugs is actually predicated upon a dialectics between (re-invented) tradition and biomedical modernity. The consequence is that the cognitive, productive and speculative economies of global pharmacy are shifted significantly, creating a new space of innovation with both epistemic and economic dimensions.

The emergence of such neo-traditional and to some extent alternative capitalism should not be viewed simply as the outcome of industrialization, that is, of the existence, growth and operations of Ayurvedic drug companies. Since the late 1990s, the Indian state has played a central role in creating institutions and regulations fostering the reformulation and growth of the Ayurvedic market. The case of the TKDL is just one example in a palette of initiatives, including the creation of a National Medicinal Plant Board to address the problems of medicinal plant supplies, the establishment of regional and state-based schemes for helping small companies develop "good manufacturing practices" and quality control, or the enactment of a new registration law for Ayurvedic proprietary medicines. In this respect, the development of the Ayurvedic industry is no exception to the "neo-liberal" turn that, from the early 1990s onward, put an end to the state-based development strategy of the Indian federal government.

6.4 Conclusion

The so-called "therapeutic revolution" of the 1940s–1970s, that is the invention of a set of new pharmaceutical classes ranging from antibiotics and steroids to psychotropic drugs and statins, is usually interpreted as a major technological change stemming from chemical research and mounting investments in organic synthesis within drug companies (Gaudillière 2015). The contemporary debate about the crisis of innovation in pharmacy runs counter to this reading, as it often singles out the putative role of regulation and drug policies.

As argued in this chapter, although it points to "social determinants" of innovation, this interpretation is short-sighted. We need a more articulated view of the technological and non-technological in order to grasp the complexity of the crisis in general, as well as its roots in what has been, for fifty years now, the dominant model of drug innovation, that is, the screening system. The crisis of innovation should accordingly be viewed as the crisis of a peculiar capitalistic regime of innovation in the health sector (Boyer 2019) with its highly integrated epistemic, organizational and economic dimensions.

The present situation of drug innovation thus illustrates the reasons why careful historicization is needed to understand "innovation beyond technology". The crisis is not reducible to the declining number of new, clinically useful, therapeutic agents that large drug companies manage to introduce on the market; it has also facilitated—if not opened—new paths for non-Western socio-epistemic alternatives.

The reformulation regime of the Indian Ayurveda industry is one of these alternative responses at both the epistemic and the economic levels. But it is not the only one. Generalizing the case of the Ayurvedic industry, one may consider that the "Southern" political economies of drugs, whether they focus on the production of generics (Brazil and China), the making of herbal preparations (India and China), or the informal circulation of products (India and Nigeria), challenge the hegemonic regime of post-World War II pharmacy in two ways. Firstly, they challenge the domination of patents and their logic of monopolistic appropriation. Secondly, they challenge the domination of molecular and chemical knowledge as the most important factor in the invention of valuable therapeutic intervention.

"Southern" political economies of health thus materialize original and differentiated links between alternative modes of capitalization and alternative modes of care, even though they are constrained by hegemonic formations of capital and governance that are not of their own making. Investigating these configurations is therefore an entry point into projects that both resonate with the post-war state-based "development" agendas and challenge them, providing for alternative forms of modernity with their singular dialectics of the metropolis and the periphery, the scientific and the cultural, the "outer" and the "inner".

References

Achilladelis, B., & Antonakis, N. (2001). The dynamics of technological innovation: The case of the pharmaceutical industry. *Research Policy, 30,* 535–588.

Arnold, D. (1993). *Colonizing the body. State medicine and epidemic disease in 19th century India.* University of California Press.

Aronowitz, R. (1999). *Making sense of illness. Science, society and diseases.* Cambridge: Cambridge University Press.

Attewell, G. (2007). *Refiguring Unani Tibb. Plural healing in late colonial India.* Hyderabad: Orient Longman.

Banerjee, M. (2009). *Power, knowledge, medicine. Ayurvedic pharmaceuticals at home and in the world.* Hyderabad: Orient Blackswan.

Bode, M. (2008). *Taking traditional knowledge to the market.* Hyderabad: Orient Longman.

Booth, B., & Zemmel, R. (2004). Prospects for productivity. *Nature Reviews Drug Discovery, 3,* 451–456.

Boyer, R. (2019). How scientific breakthroughs and social innovations shape the evolution of the healthcare sector. In S. Lechevalier (Ed.), *Innovation beyond technology* (pp. 89–119). Berlin: Springer.

Chatterjee, P. (1993). *The nation and its fragments. Colonial and postcolonial histories.* Princeton: Princeton University Press.

Cohen, F. J. (2005). Macro trends in pharmaceutical innovation. *Nature Reviews Drug Discovery, 4,* 78–84.

DiMasi, J. A., Hansen, R. W., & Grabowski, H. G. (2003). The price of innovation: New estimates of drug development costs. *Journal of Health Economics, 22,* 151–185.

Dumit, J. (2012). *Drugs for life: How pharmaceutical companies define our health.* Durham: Duke University Press.

Gaudillière, J.-P. (2014). An Indian path to biocapital? The Traditional Knowledge Digital Library (TKDL), drug patents and the reformulation regime of contemporary Ayurveda. *East Asian Science Technology and Society, 8,* 391–415.

Gaudillière, J.-P. (2015). Une manière industrielle de savoir. In C. Bonneuil & D. Pestre (Eds.), *Histoire des sciences et des savoirs—3. Le siècle des technosciences,* pp. 85–106. Paris: Le Seuil.

Gaudillière, J.-P. (in review). Innovation and its others: Pharmaceutical development, global capitalism and the dialectics of value. *Biosocieties.*

Gaudillière, J.-P., & Thoms, U. (Eds.). (2015). *The development of scientific marketing in the twentieth century.* New York: Pickering & Chatto.

Greene, J. (2007). *Prescribing by numbers: Drugs and the definition of disease.* Baltimore: The Johns Hopkins University Press.

Hughes, R. (2007). *The innovation gap in pharmaceutical drug discovery and new models of R&D success.* Kellogg School of Management. Accessible at http://www.kellogg.northwestern.edu/biotech/faculty/articles/newrdmodel.pdf.

Kneller, R. (2010). The importance of new companies for drug discovery: The origins of a decade of new drugs. *Nature Reviews Drug Discovery, 9,* 867–882.

Martin, P. (1999). Gene as drugs: The social shaping of gene therapy and the reconstruction of genetic disease. *Sociology of Health & Illness, 21*(5), 517–538.

Mukharji, P. (2011). *Nationalizing the body. The medical market, print and daktari medicine.* London: Anthem Press.

Mukharji, P. (2016). *Doctoring traditions. Ayurveda, small technologies and braided sciences.* Chicago: University of Chicago Press.

Munos, B. (2009). Lessons of 60 years of pharmaceutical innovation. *Nature Reviews Drug Discovery, 8,* 959–968.

Pammolli, F., Magazzini, L., & Riccaboni, M. (2011). The productivity crisis in pharmaceutical R&D. *Nature Reviews Drug Discovery, 10,* 428–438.

Pordié, L., & Gaudillière, J.-P. (2014). The reformulation regime in drug discovery: Revisiting poly-herbals and property rights in the Ayurvedic industry. *East Asian Science Technology and Society, 8,* 57–79.

Siegel Watkins, E. (2007). *The estrogen elixir. A history of hormone replacement therapy in America.* Baltimore: The Johns Hopkins University Press.

Souyri, P.-F. (2016). *Moderne sans être occidental. Aux origines du Japon d'aujourd'hui.* Paris: Gallimard.

Chapter 7
Consortium-Based Open Innovation: Exploring a Unique and Optimal Model for Regional Biotechnology Industry

Shintaro Sengoku

Abstract Developing high-tech start-ups has been embedded into political efforts that require a large, long-term investment whereas the uncertainty of research and development and the business risks are high. In the biotechnology and health-care field, the emergence of new modalities such as cell and gene therapy and nanomedicine need to be implemented complying multidimensional societal requirements that covers ethics, regulations and adoption by the citizens. Considering these issues, the present chapter aims to explore a unique and optimal innovation model for regional biotech industry in Japan—the research and development consortium from the viewpoints of the theories of organisation on inter-firm collaboration, regional innovation system and intellectual property management. Next, cases of entrepreneurial and innovative activities around drug discovery firms in Japan to date are provided, focusing on the fields of advanced science and technology and the way to develop entrepreneurs and start-up firms from the perspective of sectorial and regional innovation systems. In the third section, in order to specifically examine the challenges and measures for developing drug discovery firms in Japan, a case of newly developed biotech cluster is examined. Conclusively, a view on the direction for boosting biotech innovation suitable to the environment is proposed, with particular foci on two non-technological elements—the design of implementation ecosystem with an R&D consortium and entrepreneurs, and the significance of socioeconomic forms of organisation in order to develop technologies properly with high ethical, regulatory and scientific linkages.

7.1 Introduction

Developing high-tech start-ups, which is key to Japan's national strategy, has been embedded into political efforts for a long time. However, it requires a large, long-term investment and moreover, in the pharmaceutical industry where the uncertainty of research and development (R&D) and the business risks are high, adequate results

---

S. Sengoku (✉)
Tokyo Institute of Technology, Tokyo, Japan
e-mail: sengoku@mot.titech.ac.jp

© Springer Nature Singapore Pte Ltd. 2019
S. Lechevalier (ed.), *Innovation Beyond Technology*, Creative Economy,
https://doi.org/10.1007/978-981-13-9053-1_7

have not been obtained to compensate this effort. In addition to technological considerations, the emergence of new modalities such as cell and gene therapy and nanomedicine need to be implemented complying multidimensional societal requirements that covers ethics, regulations and adoption by the citizens. Considering these issues, the present chapter aims to explore a unique and optimal innovation model for regional biotech industry particularly in Japan.

The present chapter consists of mainly three parts. The first section provides theoretical and practical background for key concept herein, begun with an introduction of the R&D consortium from the viewpoints of the theories of organisation on inter-firm collaboration, regional innovation system and intellectual property management. It then deals with a general overview of entrepreneurship and small-and-medium entities (SMEs) in relation to the consortium.

The second section provides the background information of entrepreneurial and innovative activities around drug discovery firms (DDFs) in Japan to date. Consequently, we will focus on the fields of advanced science and technology, which are the common ground between biotechnology and drug discovery, and discuss the way the development of entrepreneurs and start-up firms should be from the perspective of sectorial and regional innovation systems. As precedent studies we created a database of Japanese biotech firms by using publicly-available information and commercially-available databases. We subsequently focus on early-stage DDFs and analyse the relationships between business origin and patent acquisition, as well as the ones amongst business representatives, partnership history, and development pipeline to understand the course from founding a business to creating value and the role of entrepreneurs.

In the third, in order to specifically examine the challenges and measures for developing DDFs in Japan, a case of such trials in the Kawasaki Innovation Gateway at Skyfront (or KING Skyfront), a newly developed biotech cluster located in the City of Kawasaki in the Tokyo metropolitan area, is examined. Specifically, the Center of Open Innovation Network for Smart Health (COINS), a project of the COI STREAM programme funded by the Ministry of Education, Culture, Sports, Science and Technology (MEXT) and partnered with the Institute of Industrial Promotion Kawasaki, as a case of these trials. In particular, the COI STREAM and COINS have strived to identify research themes based on so called 'backcasting' and enabling open innovation through interdisciplinary research and fusion scientific approaches. Subsequently, we discuss the way development of DDFs in Japan should be and propose a new approach in that respect.

The final section concludes the discussions to provide a view on the direction for boosting biotech innovation suitable to the environment, with particular foci on two non-technological elements—the design of implementation ecosystem with an R&D consortium and entrepreneurs, and the significance of socioeconomic forms of organisation in order to develop technologies properly with high ethical, regulatory and scientific linkages.

7.2 Introducing the Key Concepts of the Paper

This section provides the theoretical and practical background for the key concepts within this paper, beginning with the introduction of the R&D consortium from the viewpoints of the theories of organisation on inter-firm collaboration, regional innovation systems, and intellectual property management. It then deals with a general overview of entrepreneurship and SMEs in relation to the key topics.

7.2.1 Industrial Cluster

The importance of the formation of industrial clusters is recognised today as an indispensable tool for the technical development of firms in the region, promotion of growth through collaboration and competition, and establishment of competitive advantage with other regions. Many theoretical studies have been done on this point in the streams of competitive strategies, regional capabilities and regional innovation systems.

A series of studies based on Porter's competitive strategy theory (e.g. Porter 1998, 2000) formed a basal theory for industry clusters. These studies describe industrial clusters as a group of firms and related organisations that are mutually coupled by commonality and complementarity within a specific geographical range. On the other hand, the concept of regional innovation system has been proposed by Cooke (2002) through research focusing on the progress of innovation as a source of competitive advantage and mutual aiming for knowledge transfer. The concept of regional innovation system adds explanation to the unified functions of various stakeholders with different specificities and purpose consciousness by region, especially in the latter point close to the concept of industrial clusters (Cooke 2002).

It does not wait for the fact that innovation is the source of the acquisition of competitiveness—innovation is interpreted as a change based on an improvement and a new combination (Schumpeter 1927), but this change is accelerated by the realisation of knowledge-based economics (Etzkowitz and Leydesdorff 1995; Malmberg and Maskell 2002) that is, the accumulation of intellectual assets and the chain of learning on a global scale (Lundvall and Johnson 1994; Foray and Lundvall 1998). This implies that innovation is inseparable from the application process of new knowledge, that knowledge accumulation and innovation are cooperative (Nonaka and Takeuchi 1995). In other words, areas that satisfy various conditions such as excellent workforce, competent enterprises or research institutes, fulfilling capital and infrastructure can enjoy the growth and prosperity of the regional economy through the knowledge accumulation (Malmberg et al. 1996).

As a result of such a dissertation, the concept of regional innovation systems has attracted interest from policy parties globally to the present day. In particular, it has been said that Cooke (2002) came to be widely recognised after associating the definition of this term with organisational learning or institutional learning. Also, the background of the rapid development of related measures in OECD countries since 1990 would have been a strong incentive to complement the shortcomings of the European traditional regional development model (Okamoto 2011). There, the regional innovation system is not necessarily defined as a geographic area, was rather focuses on the relationships and interactions in the resource exchange between firms and research institutions that exist in the region, the local milieu (Camagni 1991) has been adopted as an idea. Lawson and Lorenz (1999) subsequently proposed the concept of regional innovation capability by seeing this ability as active development object.

After that, several researchers have been exploring what kind of regional resources promote regional innovation capability and corporates to acquire their competitiveness. For example, Doloreux and Parto (2005) point out that the interaction amongst heterogeneous actors in the innovation process, the role of firms and research institutes, and the situation of utilisation for policy making are important explanatory factors for regional innovation and system formation. It is also proposed open innovation (Chesbrough 2003) that enhances regional technical diversity, which can promote the entry of new firms. Zahra and George (2002) present an opinion that open innovation diversifies the technical composition of products, resulting in a wider selection of product designs and contributing to the promotion of innovation.

However, with the implementation in policy in mind, consideration from a more microscopic perspective, that is, what is the subject of absorptive capacity for local firms and institutions (Cohen and Levinthal 1990; Lane and Lubatkin 1998), what kind of ability, knowledge, or insight is needed to contribute to assimilation and utilisation and contribute to improvement of performance and competitiveness. According to Zahra and George (2002) mentioned earlier, this is explained in the process of acquisition, assimilation, transformation and exploitation of knowledge, and this skill is found in the area as a regulatory factor of the absorbing capacity of the enterprise.

Regional innovation capability implies that firms located there can utilize appropriate knowledge, experience, skills in their own innovation and competition. To realize that, it is an important requirement to form a high-quality network (Wakabayashi 2009). The importance of such network formation was raised in the National Innovation System (NIS) theory (Freeman 1987; Nelson and Rosenberg 1993). NIS theory focuses on linkages and interaction networks in the innovation system, because this is the main way for firms to absorb and assimilate knowledge. In other words, networks are positioned as a means of accessing important knowledge, skills and competencies (Nonaka and Takeuchi 1995; Gertler and Wolfe 2006).

If we consider industrial clusters as the mother of innovation system, we can observe various network formation. As an example, Malmberg and Maskell (2002) examined the significance of these arrangements and visualisation through actual measurement of information exchange between actors and firms. Amongst them, they found that these networks are formed by transferring resources or learning processes, and transferring human resources between firms (Tsai 2001). Meanwhile, in the field of organisation theory, network formation is described as the result of external factors such as spread of technology (Gulati and Gargiulo 1999). In any case, a good quality network is essential to promote partnerships with partners that

7 Consortium-Based Open Innovation: Exploring a Unique … 145

are trustworthy and capable, and thus to maintain continuous relationships amongst actors within an industrial cluster.

Amongst the obstacles to cooperation amongst actors are uncertainty and physical distance (Porter 2000; Boschma 2005). Uncertainty can prescribe trust amongst actors and limit cooperation between individuals and organisations (Gulati 1995). Also, the distance between actors is inversely proportional to the degree of fulfilment of collaborative relationships (Breschi and Lissoni 2001; Morgan 2004). For example, there are opportunities for collaboration amongst firms located in a specific area, as compared with the case where these firms are located across national borders. This is because the existence of the borders makes it difficult to form alliances mainly due to imperfections of information. In particular, with regard to the Japanese pharmaceutical and biotechnology industry, developing liaison organization to take advantage of overseas cluster has been pointed out as a crucial issue (Nakamura and Asakawa 2006).

7.2.2 R&D Consortium

With respect to the R&D consortium, various studies have provided perspectives on the theory of organisation management, with a focus on R&D activities (Hawkins 1999). Aldrich and Sasaki (1995) conducted a large scale-comparative study centred on a survey of 39 and 54 R&D consortia in the US and Japan, respectively. This study confirmed that cases in Japan tend to cover a narrower scope than those in the US, that the government's support and subsidies are more extensive, and the basic research that is conducted at universities and public research institutes tends to be excluded. Also, as a characteristic feature of the cases in Japan, public support and subsidies provide an incentive for firms to participate.

Sakakibara (1997) discussed the relationship between the scope of the R&D consortium and the gain of industrial competitiveness, as demonstrated in over 237 cases in Japan over the course of 34 years until 1991. Regarding SMEs, the primary motivations to participate are the ability to access complementary knowledge, as well as to find a cue to enter into new businesses or technologies, which yield competitive advantages across the industry.

In addition to the mainstream perspectives generated by previous studies on the R&D consortium, some research trends outline the concept from a variety of different viewpoints: the theories of organisation on inter-firm collaboration, regional innovation system, and intellectual property management.

7.2.2.1 Organisation of Inter-firm Collaboration

The promotion of innovation through cooperation across firm boundaries is a concept that has been cultivated in both theoretical and practical perspectives. Hannan and Freeman (1987) focused on the significance and utility of an R&D consortium as a potential origin of Japan's industrial competitiveness in the era of observation. Belderbos et al. (2004) conducted an empirical study in accordance with the CIS Survey in the Netherlands and clarified the relationship between the attributes of partners in R&D and the outcomes of collaboration. The findings yielded that collaboration with suppliers and competitors tends to contribute to incremental innovation, collaboration with universities and competitors leads to new product creation, and collaboration with universities and clients produces radical innovation.

The concept of open innovation as advocated by Chesbrough (2003) has spread widely. Particularly in the field of life sciences, as it relates to innovative pharmaceuticals and medical products, the outcomes of universities and public research institutes are quite significant when they collaborate with private firms. Furthermore, the pharmaceutical industry itself has been leading biotechnology and recognised to be a type of industry that requires strong scientific knowledge; a concept which generates a network advantage for pharmaceutical firms, as demonstrated by their performance.

In recent years, a trend of previous research in Japan has been re-evaluated in order to consider the viewpoint of project management. Based on the case observation of R&D projects accompanied with a consortium, Kobayashi (2001) proposed various requirements to be carried out according to the implementation of the project. Another case study conveyed the relationship between organisations in an R&D consortium with a strategic alliance. Lechevalier et al. (2010) examined the effect of participation in government-sponsored R&D consortia on the R&D productivity of firms in the case of robot technology in Japan and argued the significance of government involvement as a coordinator of R&D collaboration. Watanabe (2010) conducted a survey across a set of firms participating in an R&D consortium in order to evaluate their motivations and expectations. In addition, the study highlighted the role of technology research associations, intermediary organisations for the management of technological development and inter-firm collaboration, in order to understand their perspectives relative to technology management. The viewpoints spanned across the following subject matter: the management of intellectual properties, strategic alliances, and organisational relationships.

7.2.2.2 Regional Innovation System

Innovative regions are fortunate to have conditions such as excellent workforces, competitive firms, universities and public research institutes, as well as fulfilling capital and infrastructure. As a result, they enjoy the growth and prosperity of regional economies through the accumulation of knowledge capital. Cooke et al. (1997) proposed the concept of regional innovation systems in the early 1990s; a concept which implies that actors that are located in the regional community and oriented towards innovation can be superior in utilising their technological experience and the expertise of others through mutual collaboration and knowledge transfer. The realisation of this concept is an important requirement in forming a high-quality network. High-quality networks also promote partnerships between actors that are trustworthy and competent, thus maintaining a continuous relationship amongst actors within an industrial cluster. Conversely, the obstacles to cooperation amongst actors include the uncertainty of R&D projects and physical distance.

It is widely supported that such network formations do not necessarily occur autogenously; rather, they are coupled with proactive and institutional efforts. A regional comparative study across Europe, the United States, and Japan led by Nakamura and Asakawa (2006) revealed that the external conditions of Japanese pharmaceutical and biotech firms has yet to be well matured. In order to overcome geographical and cultural difficulties with respect to international collaboration in R&D, the study outlines that well-designed liaison structures are necessary in the regional cluster where these firms are located. Such liaison functionality is not only critical for international collaboration, but also for local development of relationships. An observatory study by Munisi et al. (2013) found a distinction in historical and cultural environments amongst sub-regions focusing on the Kansai Biocluster, which is the second largest industrial cluster for pharmaceutical and biotech businesses next to the Tokyo metropolitan area, and a hindrance to uniformity as a single cluster body. Furthermore, the study pointed out through a multiregional observation of clusters in Kansai, Medicon Valley in Scandinavia and Lyon Biopôle in France, that the absence of the cluster hub functionality in Kansai is a crucial issue for both inter- and intra-regional network formation. These arguments support a notion that an R&D consortium that consists of universities, public research institutions, and private firms is expected to be a realistic solution in Japan. It would enable the formation of a regional hub in early phases of business development through facilitating university-industry collaboration with internal and external partners, resulting in a core focus on the regional innovation system.

7.2.2.3 Intellectual Property Management

Appropriate management of intellectual property is essential to promoting R&D across the industry, as well as across universities and public research institutions. Moreover, several studies have formed a stream of research in response to practical demands of the management and operation of intellectual properties.

As a remarkable example, a survey on the R&D consortium was conducted in 2009 led by Japanese Patent Office. According to the results, three elements were highlighted as factors in improving collaborative performance relative to the creation of intellectual properties: the clarity of the objective, the completeness of a contract at initial agreement within the consortium, and the flexibility to respond to changes in collaborative conditions.

Regarding the management of intellectual properties, Samejima and Shibuya (2010) proposed concrete suggestions from a practical viewpoint on the necessity of forming licencing agreements through an R&D consortium. In particular, they centred on the concepts of accepting public funding, including an agreement amongst the participants on the background of intellectual properties related to patents filed before the formation of consortium, as well as foreground intellectual properties that consist of patents after their establishment.

Furthermore, the study proposed the assignment of an 'intellectual property producer' as a key component of overall intellectual property management in society. The importance of this functionality was also detailed in a publication by Miki (2012) that proposed a methodology for centralised management of intellectual properties through describing stocks, flows and a process cycle for their conversion.

7.2.3 Entrepreneurship

Entrepreneurship is a human activity where a person leads a business opportunity to realisation. It is complementary to business development, which can be regarded as the process that guides business opportunities to realisation. Both are common not only to the start-up of businesses, but also to all corporate activities oriented towards innovation, such as scientific research or technology development. Under this premise, this section deals with the significance and utility of entrepreneurship and the elements required for innovation.

Looking at entrepreneurship in the context of economics, Schumpeter (1927) first advocated the concept of innovation, where an entrepreneur was a founder of the initiative and the driving force of the innovation. In contrast, Kirzner (1979, 1997) focused on the agility of entrepreneurs as agents that contributed to faster realisation of business opportunities through trial-and-error improvement efforts, especially at the founding stage.

From the viewpoint of business administration, Penrose (2002) identified an entrepreneur as a talent who discovered and grew a new business opportunity within a firm, presenting a way of corporate growth, i.e. a diversification of its business scope, not fully relying upon scale. Stevenson and Jarillo (2007) defined entrepreneurship as the pursuit of opportunities beyond controllable resources, which covers transcending resource limitations by developing truly innovative products, creating new business models, improving cost-efficiency, and marketing to new customers. To conceptualise entrepreneurial models, Timmons et al. (1994) abstracted three elements: entrepreneurship as a business opportunity, management resources, and a management team, with three modulators for their dynamic relationship: creativity, communication, and leadership.

Why is entrepreneurship indispensable to realise innovation? Entrepreneurship can be an effective response to the dilemma of innovation (Christensen 2013). Entrepreneurs can be the driving force to exploit destructive innovation, for customers to accept products, and to lead small turning organisations tailored to a market size. This is not necessarily exclusive to start-up cases, and can include existing firms and consortium organisations of multiple firms (Munisi et al. 2013). Such an entrepreneurial initiative can be effectively demonstrated by establishing a semi-independent unit with values, management policies, systems, and operations distinguished from the majority of the firm.

7.2.4 Small and Medium Enterprise (SME)

As it relates to particular SMEs, Grindley et al. (1994) point out through case studies, that both a close link to participants from the private sector and a sustainable operation of a consortium are key elements of success in technological development and transformation for member firms. Furthermore, in advanced technological fields, a flexible management system, the participation of experienced managers, and the facilitation of mutual communication are key factors for performing R&D consortia.

There are over 3.8 million SMEs in Japan, which is essential to the creation of new industries and the revitalization of regional economies (Cabinet Office of Japan 2016). A significant number of these SMEs that hold an international competitiveness with their technological bases and competences form a basis in manufacturing for a wide range of industries. However, according to a survey on the performance side of so-called start-up firms that are a growth core of SMEs, approximately half of them do not achieve a successful level of evaluation. This confirms that the capabilities of new business development are still inferior. In particular, for advanced industries based on state-of-the-art science and technology, opportunities for SMEs to enter a new market are significantly limited to large firms due to the uncertainty of science and technology, reasons of limited expertise or capacity for absorption of the newness, the lack of knowledge base, etc. (Cabinet Office of Japan 2016).

Such discussions on the management of SMEs and innovation have been active in both the academic and practical forums, but have not fully addressed the issue of SMEs' business development for new market entry and the effect of micro- or macro-level business environments. In other words, it is a remaining issue in terms of how to formulate an approach for new business development and market entry based on collaboration with universities and public research institutions, as well as firms in other industrial fields. In this context, forming an R&D consortium that focuses on value creation through university-industry and multi-sectorial collaboration aims to provide a practical solution with a specific fit relative to its regional context.

To date, indeed, various consortia are formed and are under operation as part of cooperation across industries, academia, and governments. Furthermore, as its characteristic, clear goals are set, such as technological and market development, it is common to operate solely for that purpose. Although not all consortia are intended for entering different industries or new business development, the promotion of innovation is implied as a means for firms to acquire managerial resources, skills, expertise and credibility, especially in advanced scientific and technological arenas (Sengoku 2013). Compared with large enterprises, SMEs lack strategic freedom and management resources, as well as the significance of cross-border partnerships in market entry and business development. This phenomenon has existed for an extensive period of time (Sengoku 2013).

Okamuro (2001, 2003) analysed the impact of a variety of joint projects that have SMEs in Japan. Utilising aggregated data of government statistics, it was found that only R&D-oriented projects have a significant positive effect on their economic impact. In addition, regarding the factors of technological and commercial success, an analysis on differences between successful firms and others suggested that the success or failure of SMEs' joint projects depends on an organisational structure and a contractual formation. Motohashi (2003) investigated differences in style of university-industry collaboration between SMEs and large firms, highlighting that a difference in expected length of time to achieve goals is one of the primary factors, in addition to firm history in which SMEs with younger entrepreneurial age have higher aggressiveness and commitment to university-university collaboration.

Okamuro (2006) added several in-depth findings in his analysis using large-scale panel data in Japan that consists of 1,547 SMEs and 294 large firms. SMEs, like large firms, had multiple collaborations, both outside the prefecture or municipalities, and showed a higher level of learning effects from external technologies. However, SMEs were relatively passive in collaborating with national universities and tend to collaborate with universities inside the same prefectures or municipalities.

As per the regional nature of SMEs' business activities, there are studies that discuss the significance of inter-firm and university-industry networks within a region. Through a network analysis, Morioka (2007) discusses the utility of collaborative platforms in his observation of inter-firm networks in Kyoto.

7.3 Innovation and Interfirm Relationship: A Case of Drug Discovery Firms in Japan

This section provides the background information of entrepreneurial and innovative activities around DDFs in Japan to date. Specifically, early-stage DDFs were analysed on their relationships between business origin and patent acquisition, as well as the ones amongst business representatives, partnership history, and development pipeline to understand the course from founding a business to creating value and the role of entrepreneurs.

7.3.1 Characteristics of Pharmaceutical Industry

The R&D activities of pharmaceutical firms are characterised by high levels of volatility compared to those of firms in other industries. For example, even long-term R&D projects that span a decade have a very low probability of resulting in a marketable product; however, these projects could lead to the creation of a product that is a blockbuster hit, with annual sales of US$1 billion (Pisano 2006). As per regulations, development processes are categorised as preclinical if they involve cells or animals, and clinical trials are classified from phase 1 through phase 3 (Federsel 2010). All processes must be carried out as per the guidelines of national governments. In most countries, pricing is based on a product's novelty and is governed by official government decisions. Patents protect the uniqueness of a product's formula, manufacturing methods, dosage form, and indications, providing the creator/inventor with exclusive sales rights until the patent expires. In addition, skilful life-cycle management can have a major impact on a product's profitability, as patent periods may be extended through changes in dosage forms or the development of new combinations (Yamanaka and Kano 2016; Sandner and Ziegelbauer 2008; Dubey and Dubey 2009).

Strategies in the pharmaceutical industry take on unique forms and involve licensing and other active inter-corporate transactions. As was mentioned earlier, the probability of R&D success is low in this industry, and approval for sales is needed in each country where a product is to be sold. Therefore, in addition to selling their own products, pharmaceutical firms often consider other strategies, including buying-in or licensing products, establishing joint ventures (a combination of part or all of a business with other firms; Koller et al. 2010), or engaging in co-promotions. In fact, licensed-in or licensed-out products account for 30% of the major product volume in this industry (DiMasi et al. 2010). With this regard, DDFs are key providers of product candidates and platform technologies for pharmaceutical firms. Furthermore, in accordance to the diversification of modalities and technological means, DDFs are also recognised as a source of state-of-the-art technologies and a leading role of pharmaceutical innovation.

Whilst the probability of R&D success has never been high in the pharmaceutical industry, productivity has fallen further in recent years according to several studies (Booth and Zemmel 2004; Paul et al. 2010; Khanna 2012; Scannell et al. 2012). The reasons for this trend include shrinking needs and the completeness of product offerings in existing therapeutic areas, more intense competition in new disease areas, the diversification of seed chemical compounds, increased complexity and difficulty in R&D technologies in antibody drugs and nucleic acid drugs, and high costs (Pharmaceutical Research and Manufacturers of America 2013; Booth and Zemmel 2004). Additionally, changes have been made recently to the authorities' examination and approval processes. The procedures of the U.S. Food & Drug Administration and those for new drug applications have become stricter. Priority is now given to disease areas with strong unmet medical needs, and a clear advantage over existing products is becoming a necessary condition for the approval of new drugs (Reichert 2003).

7.3.2 Environment for Founding Drug Discovery Firms

In a study on Japanese dedicated biotech firms (DBFs), Motohashi (2007) and Eyo (2011) present a quantitative comparative study between Japan and the United States by using firm-level data for 443 Japanese firms, 12 of which are listed, and 1,446 U.S. firms, 431 of which are listed. Honjo et al. (2010, 2012, 2013) also report on Japan-based DBFs' growth process since their launch, R&D financing, changes in the core technology, the state of alliance and patent system, representatives, and scientific sources based on the trend statistics and surveys by the Japan Bioindustry Association (JBA). DBFs covered in these previous studies are engaged in a wide variety of business activities, including medical and healthcare, agriculture, forestry and fisheries, environment and energy, research support, contracted production, and other services.

Whilst these research studies present basic information and key beliefs, there are issues to be considered. One of them is the breadth of subjects. The pharmaceutical industry is unique even amongst bio-related industries, as nine to 17 years and over 50 billion yen of R&D funds are required in order to release one new drug in the market. There is also a large risk since only one drug is created out of more than 30,000 chemical compounds. Therefore, previous studies that analysed biotech firms do not necessarily explain the reality and issues of the pharmaceutical industry, drug discovery biotech firms in particular, with these characteristics. Another point is that the roles entrepreneurs should play have not been fully discussed. Whilst Honjo et al. (2010, 2012, 2013) examine how replacing the representative is related to R&D funds and licensing, they do not show a statistically significant difference between having and not having the representative replaced.

As for previous studies in areas other than Japan, Patzelt et al. (2008) analysed 99 DBFs in Germany and examine the relationship between the experience of management teams and the growth of their firms. They observed a statistically significant correlation between the management team's tenure at pharmaceutical firms and the growth of the firm amongst 49 out of the 99 DBFs studied. However, they do not explain the impact of the management team's experience on the creation of corporate value, since they measure the growth of the firm by the increase in the number of employees. Additionally, considering the difference between Germany and Japan in terms of the environment of drug discovery R&D and starting a business, it would be inadequate to apply these results to Japan without any examination.

7.3.3 The Firm Type and Patents

Sakurai et al. (2014) analysed the relationship between business origination (joint venture, academia source, license source, and individual or unidentified) and patent acquisition amongst unlisted DDFs based on a defined framework (Valentin et al. 2008, Table 7.1). The results show that the average number of patent allowance notices amongst joint venture (JV) firms (15.0 for domestic patents, 18.6 for foreign patents) was significantly higher than the average amongst other types of firms i.e. academia source firms (5.7 for domestic patents and 3.6 for foreign patents), license source firms (3.5 for national patents and 2.6 for foreign ones), individual or unidentified firm types (2.8 for national patents and 0.8 for foreign ones).

In terms of the rate of receiving notices of patent allowance, licence source firms had the highest average rate of notice of the national patent allowance (40.2%; the notice rate for foreign patent allowance was 23.0%), whilst JV firms had the highest average notice rate for foreign patent allowance (48.6%; the notice rate for national patent allowance was 24.4%). Academia source firms ranked second in terms of the notice rate for both national and foreign patent allowance (31.0% for national

7 Consortium-Based Open Innovation: Exploring a Unique …

Table 7.1 The patenting status of unlisted DDFs by the type of firms

Firm category	No. of firms	Percent	Domestic granted patents		Foreign granted patents	
			Av no. of patents	Mean granted rate (%)	Av no. of patents	Mean granted rate (%)
Academia	25	56.8	5.7	31.0	3.6[¶]	29.8
Joint venture	2	4.5	15.0*	24.4	18.0[¶†‡]	48.6
License	8	18.2	3.5	40.2	2.6[†]	23.0
Individual or unidentified	9	20.5	2.8*	21.5	0.8[‡]	17.6
Total	44	100	5.1	30.4	3.5	26.9

Note Significant differences were shown at $p < 0.05$ (* and †) and $p < 0.01$ (¶ and ‡)

patents and 29.8% for foreign ones) and individual or unidentified firm types ranked last (21.5% for national patents and 17.6% for foreign ones).

These results can be summarised as follows:

- A relatively high percentage of academia source firms have patentable research results, both in Japan and overseas.
- JV firms have advanced research results as well and the industrial perspective for commercialisation. Consequently, they have numerous patented assets.
- Whilst license source firms have a high rate of receiving notices of national patent allowance from the perspective of protecting commercialisation within Japan, they do not have significant research results that could potentially be patented.
- Individual or unidentified firm types do not have numerous research results that are patentable either in Japan or overseas.

7.3.4 The Firm Type and Representative Directors

We also focused on a relation between the type and performance of firms and the career background of the firm's representative directors. Table 7.2 exhibits the allocation of unlisted DDFs by the background of the representative director in terms of (i) the number of unlisted DDFs, (ii) the percentage of unlisted DDFs with a partnership programme, and (iii) the percentage of unlisted DDFs with a product in clinical development. Although the percentage is high amongst firms with a representative director from the pharmaceutical industry, it was the highest amongst firms with a representative director from the financial industry. Since their main partners are pharmaceutical firms, it is understandable that those who come from a pharmaceutical firm or academia with a network of pharmaceutical firms would have an advantage. On the other hand, the superior capability of the representative directors who came

Table 7.2 Track record of unlisted DDFs by the career background of the top management

Career path category	No. of firms	Percent	Firms with alliance		Firms with clinical programmes	
			No. of firms	Percent	No. of firms	Percent
Academia	9	20.5	4	44.4	2	22.2
Pharmaceutical firm	17	38.6	10	58.8	10	58.8
Other firm	9	20.5	2	22.2	2	22.2
Financial sector	5	11.4	4	80.0	2	40.0
n.a.	4	9.1	2	50.0	3	75.0
Total	44	100.0	22	50.0	19	86.4

from the financial industry in establishing partnerships is probably attributed to their view on the return on investment, as well as to not allowing the firm to take on more than what is necessary since they have limited experience in pharmaceutical business.

As per the background of the representative director, as expected, there were many firms with a representative director who came from the pharmaceutical industry. Since knowledge and experience for decision-making and handling pharmaceutical regulations related to drug development are required, it is logical to rely on the leadership of representative directors from the pharmaceutical industry.

From the present results it was confirmed that academia source firms and JV-business source firms perform well in terms of obtaining patents. Patents from these groups of firms are more likely to be dependent on academic research results. Conversely, DDFs play an important role in commercialising academic research results; therefore, developing and supporting DDFs should lead to further innovations.

7.3.5 Biotech Clusters and Drug Discovery Firms

Today's biotechnology, which is a source of innovative products of DDFs, tends to be produced through interdisciplinary research and fusion-scientific approaches (Gibbons et al. 1994; Bozeman and Boardman 2003; Klein 2004). That is, researchers from related disciplines work together to solve common issues by combining various technologies whilst using bioscience as the core (Rafols and Meyer 2007; Anzai et al. 2012). In terms of medical-engineering cooperation in the medical field, for example, universities are expected to extract more social and economic implications out of their research results by promoting cooperation between departments and researchers and matching clinical needs with technology (Anzai et al. 2012; Lauto and Sengoku 2015; Anzai and Sengoku 2016).

The importance of open innovation in R&D (Chesbrough 2003; Perkmann and Walsh 2007) has also been pointed out by the government of Japan. Defined as 'for a firm to utilise external ideas in its own business more than ever whilst allowing unused ideas to be utilised by other firms more than ever', open innovation can be understood as a concept that includes both (i) utilising external knowledge and (ii) releasing knowledge to the outside. Therefore, universities are increasingly launching proactive initiatives to create social value, such as inter-university collaboration, international collaboration, shared use of research resources, by encouraging cooperation between departments, universities, and university-industry, and even founding start-ups, in addition to university-industry collaboration (Kodama et al. 2013; Avila-Robinson and Sengoku 2017a, b).

7.4 Trials for Open Innovation Initiatives: A Case of COINS

In order to examine the specific challenges and measures for developing DDFs in Japan, this section introduces and examines a case study of trials in the Kawasaki Innovation Gateway at Skyfront (or KING Skyfront), a newly developed biotech cluster located in the City of Kawasaki in the Tokyo metropolitan area. Specifically, the Center of Open Innovation Network for Smart Health (COINS), a project of the COI STREAM programme funded by MEXT and partnered with the Kawasaki Institute of Industrial Promotion, is analysed as an example of these trials. In particular, the COI STREAM and COINS have strived to identify research themes based on so-called 'backcasting' and enabling open innovation through interdisciplinary research and the fusion of scientific approaches. Subsequently, we discuss the optimal development of DDFs in Japan, and propose a new approach in that respect.

7.4.1 The Overview of KING Skyfront

Nowadays, Kawasaki City is one of the independent government-designated cities in the Tokyo metropolitan area and has a population of 1.47 million people. Having played a central role in the development of the Keihin Coastal Industrial Zone after World War II through the high economic growth period, the city has a wealth of experience in forming industrial clusters. Based on their experience, they are currently developing a biotech cluster named 'KING Skyfront' in the Tonomachi District, adjacent to the Tokyo Bay, and have been successful in attracting a large number of public research institutions, including COINS and other innovative institutions or firms (Fig. 7.1).

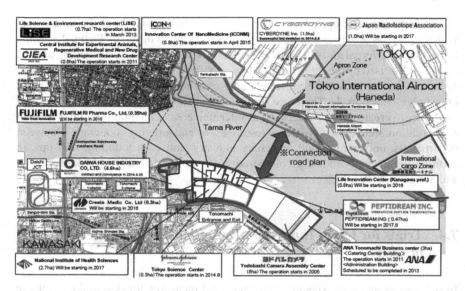

Fig. 7.1 The geographical overview of the KING Skyfront and major facilities (As of March 2016)

7.4.2 The Profile and History of COINS

Presenting new methodologies for determining research themes and managing R&D, COI STREAM is a programme launched in FY2013 and led by MEXT. The programme defines the ideal society and living standards derived from the potential needs of the future society and, based on that vision, identifies innovative R&D challenges for the next ten years. It also removes existing barriers between disciplines and organisations and conducts a 'backcasting' type of R&D (Brandes and Brooks 2007) that enables, through university-industry collaboration, the kind of innovation that firms cannot realise on their own.

With respect to R&D management for interdisciplinary research, by studying at interdisciplinary research institutes through case studies on university-industry collaboration where multiple firms participate, it is strongly suggested that these consortium-style approaches have noteworthy characteristics from the perspective of developing high-tech start-ups. In other words, a better way of developing high-tech start-ups, including DDFs, is created by institutionally designing and creating an innovation platform rooted in interdisciplinary research and fusion-scientific approaches within a biotech cluster.

The profile of COINS as of March 2016 was as follows:

- Core agency: Institute of Industrial Promotion Kawasaki,
- Project leader: Dr. Hiromichi Kimura,
- Research leader: Dr. Kazunori Kataoka,

- Participating organisations at the time of the proposal: 22 organisations that consist of 5 universities, 6 research institutes, 11 firms, and 2 corporations, together with 2 municipalities.

The COINS, one of the COI STREAM designated projects, has the following characteristics which are not necessarily seen in other designated projects.

One is the fact that the COINS is based on massive experience in past: in particular, the development of management tools and frameworks for interdisciplinary research originated from the Center for NanoBio Integration (CNBI) of the University of Tokyo funded by the MEXT (Anzai et al. 2012; Lauto and Sengoku 2015; Anzai and Sengoku 2016), from Nanobio First of the University of Tokyo funded by the FIRST Program of the Cabinet Office. Although these institutes had different goals and implementation periods, they can be regarded as a continuous R&D project, since they not only place nano/biotechnology as the core underlying technology, but also have the same research leader.

Another characteristic is that the COINS is operated by the local government of Kawasaki City, since all core agencies for the COI institutes except for the COINS have been proposed by universities or jointly proposed by universities and firms. Moreover, the COINS is operated by a foundation controlled by the City of Kawasaki.

Finally, the COINS established the Innovation Center of NanoMedicine (iCONM) in Kawasaki City, Kanagawa, in order to embody the idea of practising open innovation under one roof. The iCONM functions as the core facility where researchers from different universities and firms conduct research and has the following profile:

- Construction cost: around 3.5 million yen
- Shared laboratory equipment: around 1 million yen
- Site area: 7,999.99 m^2
- Total floor area: 9,444.04 m^2
- Number of floors: 4 stories
- Main facilities: microfabrication, synthesis laboratory, biochemical laboratory, human disease model laboratory.

7.4.3 Backcasting: An Approach for Setting Research Themes

The COINS discussed future social issues not only with participating researchers, but also with researchers in the field of sociology and business people by requesting their participation. Through workshop-style brainstorming sessions on social issues of the year 2030 and the COINS general conference sessions on research themes, they promote common understanding regarding setting research themes by backcasting (Brandes and Brooks 2007), as well as methodologies in an effort to develop a sense of unity as an institute.

As a result, the COINS holds 'ensuring sustainability as an aging developed country' as a future vision and aims for a society where all citizens can enjoy their health, or 'a society with smart life care' where everyone is free of illness and treatment and able to obtain health autonomously in everyday life without being conscious of the trouble, costs, and distance to receive medical care. The concept derived by backcasting to achieve this vision is the 'in-body hospital'. Based on an innovative idea to create a virus-size nano-machine with an ultra-fine, high-density integration of high-tech medical functions by auto-associating functional molecules with pre-installed navigation, sensor, and operation functions, they aim to develop an internal hospital that performs 'necessary medical examination and treatment at the necessary places within the human body when it is necessary'.

Subsequently, in order for the nano-machine to have the function of internal hospital, five challenges i.e., shoot, overcome, prevent, examine, and treat, need to be researched and developed in creating a nano-machine and have been identified as their focus, based on further backcasting thinking. Additionally, they are identifying possible bottlenecks and hurdles when introducing products and services from R&D in the market, and resolving these issues at the same time to accelerate social implementation (Fig. 7.2). As such, they aim to establish infrastructure such as developing regulatory and policy frameworks, environment, etc. and ecosystems for aspects such as investment and human resource development, create start-ups that do not stagnate, and develop local and social foundations to do so.

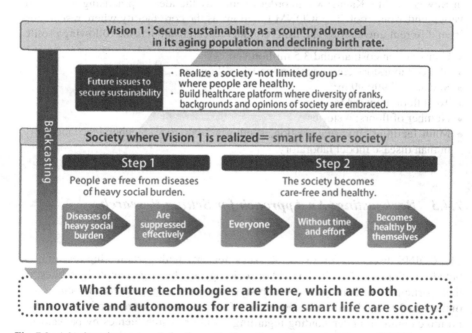

Fig. 7.2 A backcasting approach for the realisation of smart life care society at COINS

7.4.4 The Measures of Open Innovation

In this section, we look at the open innovation measures taken by the COINS and examine them from the organisation management perspective.

7.4.4.1 Operating Structure and Governance of the Research Institute

As previously mentioned, there are 22 organisations from the industry, academia, and government participating in the COINS (Fig. 7.3). Since multiple firms and universities work on open innovation, sophisticated operation of the institute is required. At the COINS, they established a management system for the institute by referencing the idea of corporate governance under corporate management.

The above-mentioned CNBI and Nanobio First have been mainly undertaking projects related to supporting and managing research by placing a secretariat within the university. On the other hand, the COINS coordinates the stakeholders, which becomes an issue in promoting open innovation, by placing a research promotion agency as the centre of the institute's management to establish a governance that is neutral to the interest of specific universities, firms, and local government. As such, the agency has been given proactive functionalities, such as planning the R&D strategy through industry-university-government partnerships, proposing a new research theme based on research seeds and future needs, providing research support, and practising social implementation, that would have been difficult for a traditional university-industry collaboration agency in academia to execute.

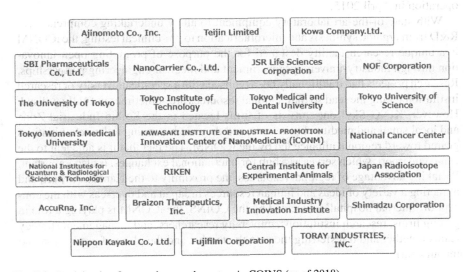

Fig. 7.3 Participating firms and research centres in COINS (as of 2018)

In order to promote open innovation, where various universities and firms bring competitive technology and product series, as well as the capabilities of researchers, it is necessary to design a completely new framework to allow many participating agencies and firms to fully utilise their intellectual capacities whilst providing incentives to participate in the institute. Consequently, the COINS executes an agreement listing the philosophy of the institute and a bylaw for research implementation based on the agreement of all participating agencies.

As previously described, the COINS referenced the idea of corporate governance and established systems for managerial decision-making, such as hiring people, installing large research equipment, obtaining external funds, executing licensing agreement, making commercialisation decisions, etc., in the same manner as corporations. They regularly hold an operation committee meeting equivalent to the board meeting of a corporation in order to govern the institute, whilst placing a research promotion committee equivalent to the steering committee at a corporation as a decision-making organism to make rapid decisions on R&D. They also appoint external advisors for third-party opinions regarding the operation of the institute.

7.4.4.2 Constructing an Open Innovation Platform

To realise the 'in-body hospital', it is necessary to gather all possible research resources such as equipment, human resources, funds, information and technology, etc., across different research fields and develop a community to provide a forum to innovate. Therefore, the iCONM was developed, which is independent of universities and firms, in the KING Skyfront, located close to Haneda Airport and began its operation in April 2015.

With state-of-the-art laboratory equipment to allow undertaking comprehensive R&D from organic synthesis and microfabrication to pre-clinical testing, the iCONM is a unique research facility designed for the purpose of promoting open innovation through industry-university-government and medical-engineering partnerships. Research projects had traditionally been realised with a specific university or research institution taking the lead so that regional resources are sometimes not fully utilised. However, KING Skyfront consists of firms located in the Keihin Industrial Zone and local small and medium businesses, and they are beginning to launch initiatives geared toward regional alliance led by the iCONM. The fact that it is adjacent to the Haneda Airport, which serves as a hub for international exchanges, is also important. By taking advantage of regional resources, the proximity to the Haneda Airport, and attracting a variety of ideas and human resources in Japan and overseas with the concept of 'internal hospital' advocated by the COINS, the iCONM is playing a role in getting firms, research institutions, university researchers, and management strategy teams together and transferring those to the market and the place of production and manufacturing.

7.4.4.3 Organisational Efforts for Innovation

To make continuous innovation possible, forums and systems for promoting different ideas to cross-pollinate and create dynamic relationships in the organisation become necessary. As such, the COINS implements mechanisms for firms, research institutions, and university researchers to gather under one roof and continuously innovate. New research themes for the COINS and visions for the iCONM are generated through workshop-style discussions for backcasting and group discussions at the two-night, three-day retreat where approximately 80 people from COINS participating organisations (i.e., universities, research institutions, businesses, and local government members) participate. Valuing innovation through dialogue with participating organisations, the COINS, including all committees, plans to keep holding this type of forum on a regular basis in the future. In addition, they are working on holding a symposium for local businesses, medical associations, and citizens, and to establish partnerships with overseas institutes, aiming for regional and international cooperation.

7.5 Discussion

This section concludes the discussions and provides a direction for boosting environmentally suitable biotech innovation, with a particular focus on two non-technological elements—the design of the implementation ecosystem with an R&D consortium and entrepreneurs, and the significance of socioeconomic forms of organisation—in order to develop technologies properly, with high ethical, regulatory, and scientific linkages.

7.5.1 Review of the Case of COINS

Based on the above examination, the COINS is supposed to be creating a unique ecosystem geared toward establishing high-tech start-ups. First, founding start-up firms is positioned as one of the missions of the COINS. Looking at previous R&D programmes led by the government, their primary objective was to generate results in innovation or scientific technology (i.e., papers and patents). There is the tendency that creating start-up firms has not necessarily been the main goal of participants, even if listed in proposals and plans. On the other hand, as described previously, this goal is shared amongst COINS participating members; founding start-up firms is clearly stated as one of the required project goals and a management structure has been put in place since establishment to pursue this goal strategically. The fact the project leader of the COINS manages an independent venture capital and is committed to developing start-ups is also notable.

Second, as mentioned in Sect. 7.4.2, the local government is committed to founding start-ups as well. Previously, core agencies for projects like the COI STREAM had customarily been particular universities and firms. As indicated by past track records, initiatives by universities tend to reducing scale without being able to procure sufficient management resources, particularly management personnel and funding support, on their own. Meanwhile, initiatives by firms tend to directly reflect the business strategy of the firm and be affected by the business conditions. In the case of large firms, in particular, they were prone to fall into the trap of so-called 'innovator's dilemma'. Learning from these negative effects, the COINS placed a government-affiliated organisation as their core agency. Consequently, it is possible to involve various regional firms and management resources without limiting member organisations of the COINS or COI STREAM. In other words, this ecosystem is being promoted as a regional innovation system.

Finally, they can provide management resources such as skills and staff to start-ups originated from the COINS through university-industry collaboration, as described in Sect. 7.4.3. Regardless of being affiliated with businesses or universities, many of the participating members have been involved in the project since the time of its predecessor, CNBI and Nanobio First. As such, they are familiar with the nature of the project leader. Furthermore, a total of 11 leading firms in their fields participate in the COINS, which is capable of generously providing various management resources. In fact, two start-ups have been founded through the COINS already at the time of writing this paper and both were launched under the above-described network and support.

7.5.2 Benefits of the Consortium-Based Approach

The cases described above are consortia composed of industry, academia, and government rooted in the activities of all of the players. As noted in previous studies in the field of stem cell technology (Watatani et al. 2013; Munisi et al. 2014), a consortium of collaborative players is of significant value.

7.5.2.1 Intellectual Property Management

One of the most important aspects of R&D is the systematic creation of intellectual property (Bergman and Graff 2007; Mills and Tereskerz 2010). In publicly funded R&D projects, intellectual property is often considered to the most valuable component. Regarding patents, the intellectual property of background patents is also considered important because intellectual property is shared amongst multiple players before starting the project; thus, a mechanism for managing intellectual property within the consortium is necessary. Intellectual property is not limited to patents; it also includes physical assets, e.g. a stem cell bank, expertise, skills, designs, and brand (Taylor et al. 2005; Rao and Auerbach 2006; Crook et al. 2010; Ilic and

Stephenson 2013). This type of systematic patent strategy leads to the acquisition of intellectual property by individual players and the formation of an overall patent pool, which directly confers a competitive advantage.

7.5.2.2 Technology Standardisation

The development of technology standards has become increasingly important in recent years (Swann 2000; Sengoku et al. 2011). The standards formed through cooperation amongst multiple consortium members are called 'consensus' or 'forum' standards (Weiss and Cargill 1992). Technology standardisation has become common, particularly in fields with remarkable technological innovation. Naturally, these standards gain more traction as de facto standards, if the relevant standards are market leading. Furthermore, standards may eventually become official, or de jure, standards through the intervention of regulatory authorities and standardisation entities, such as the International Organization for Standardization (ISO), which has given particularly important implications in the medical and pharmaceutical industries.

7.5.2.3 Product and Service Development

Products and services are created based on intellectual properties and standards. These are not necessarily limited to final products and services but also include parts based on elemental technologies, i.e., components, and parts with combined functionality, i.e., modules. One of the expectations of product and service development by a consortium, especially those comprised of different industries, is the creation of more complex and complete products and services than those produced by a firm working alone. Another expectation is the opportunity for so-called 'collective intelligence' to be exerted (Brown and Lauder 2001; Boder 2006). Although collective intelligence initially referred to 'the accumulation and utilisation of knowledge to solve problems to reach common goals' (Brown and Lauder 2001), the recent expansion of open innovation has led to an additional understanding of collective intelligence as 'knowledge for problem solving using collective creativity' (Boder 2006). The consortium-based approach discussed here seems consistent with this 'collective creativity', as it facilitates collaboration that exceeds the boundaries imposed by the prescribed rules and arrangements of individual firms.

7.5.2.4 Funding

The consortium-based approach also works favourably for fund raising, which benefits research and development that requires more extensive funding (Mason 2008; Rao 2011; Thomas 2012). Specifically, the financing process includes the implementation of a programme that matches public and private sector funds, securing the commitment of operating firms by involving them in the early phases, and entering into partnerships with corporate ventures. These actions are particularly useful in Japan, where obtaining funds through equity financing is sometimes difficult (Sipp 2012).

7.5.2.5 Human Resource Development

Finally, consortium members participating in a research and development project acquire skills and abilities that they would not have acquired at their affiliated firms. Recently, an academic medical fellowship-training program was revised to encompass newer and more diverse forms of advanced therapies (Knoepfler 2013). In addition, consortium activities may enhance expertise, knowledge, and problem solving abilities.

7.5.3 Key Challenges to the Consortium-Based Approach

The consortium-based approach has various advantages; however, its greatest challenge is its complicated organisation. Therefore, to continue to steadily produce expected results, satisfying the following organisational management requirements may be necessary. The following elements are particularly essential for a consortium that spans industry, academia, and government, although these are comparably applicable to organisational theory in general.

7.5.3.1 Leadership

Research and development projects require a unifying force to manage multiple participants: whilst these individuals share the same purpose, they typically have slightly different backgrounds, intentions, and agendas. Although nominating a well-known researcher from the primary research institution as a leader is common, the leadership qualities and abilities required for a consortium composed of industry, academia, and government are different from those required in one's own research group. Because it is extremely difficult to replace the leader once appointed, personnel selection should be thoroughly considered when a consortium is launched.

7.5.3.2 Entrepreneurship

As previously indicated, each case discussed in this paper had a start-up firm at the centre of the consortium. These start-up firms contribute to the risk-taking aspect of R&D activities; liaise with universities for IP licensing; proactively network with key stakeholders; provide financial incentives to participants through equity investment; and obtain capital from investors, such as venture capitalists (VCs). By contrast, these consortiums might provide start-up firms with a biotope that becomes sustainable through substantial relationships with other participants. The effective formation of an R&D consortium should be investigated in accordance with a policy for the development of biotech start-up firms.

7.5.3.3 Organisational Management Capabilities

Although it is possible to advance the consortium within a committee-meeting structure, whereby agreements and contracts are established amongst voluntary organisations and participants, incorporation may be essential for the proper management of intellectual property, funds, and physical assets. The establishment of business structures, such as limited liability partnerships (LLP) and research associations, should also be proactively considered. In contrast, the changes to organisational management that may follow incorporation often carry the risk of enhancing the 'inner circle' in a manner that prevents new firms from entering the business or allows such expansive development of the organisational management that the means outweigh the objectives. Therefore, an organisational design that fully ensures flexibility for participation and promptness of decision-making is essential.

7.5.3.4 Process/System Design

A process system design that ensures operation is as essential as the development of organisational management. In particular, a consensus amongst participants and concerned parties regarding policy and the means of organisational management is mandatory when the consortium is established or when the research and development project is launched. It is crucial that the goals and structure of the consortium are clearly specified and unexpected situations are considered. Further, in addition to the appointment of a leader, a dedicated project manager with the authority and responsibility to facilitate the R&D project should be designated to promote compliance in day-to-day activities. Similarly, the establishment of specialised internal and external units responsible for intellectual property, public relations support, legal affairs, and accounting is desirable.

7.5.3.5 Culture and Style

Finally, although the importance of a sound culture and style within a consortium is often unstated, we believe it warrants discussion. It is not an exaggeration to say that the success of the consortium-based approach depends on a spirit of equal partnership that exceeds the boundaries of industry, academia, and government. The leader/management should strive to maintain an environment where firms feel comfortable expressing opinions to well-known research institutions. One should also be mindful that regular project meetings often become the only opportunity for communicatin. This issue is best addressed by holding 'soft' meetings to disseminate general knowledge and 'hard' meetings geared towards project updates and decision-making. Such efforts will promote smooth information sharing and the exchange of honest opinions, which will encourage creative thinking and maximise the previously described 'collective intelligence'.

7.6 Conclusions and Future Prospects

In this Chapter we tried to explore the formation and growth requirements of biotech industrial cluster through case observation. As a result, these can be consolidated into three factors. The first point is the formation of regional innovation capabilities rooted in the capacity of local firms and institutions. The second point is the ability to fund the private sector as well as the public sector and pharmaceutical firms, and it is indispensable in the capital-intensive biotech industry. The third point is the existence of industrial clusters and hub organizations that help the participating firms collaborate and are closely related to cluster management.

The present Chapter also reviewed the situation of domestic DDF cases in section 7.3 and examined the issues in the course of founding a firm and reaching the early stage from the perspective of intellectual property and human resources. As a result, it is efficient to use and apply the results of academia or an existing firm in the form of patent licenses to develop a core technology whilst founding a firm. Moreover, the presence of individuals who came from a pharmaceutical firm is significant in R&D after the early stage.

The subsequent Sect. 7.4 studied the cases of forming open innovation institutes and pointed out that the key to success in effectively establishing high-tech start-ups included the project-wide commitment to found start-ups, implications of the regional innovation system and development of consortium-style start-ups.

Through discussion in Sect. 7.5, we believe that these findings provide practical ideas for exploratory research results in academia, overcome the 'valley of death' in the drug discovery business, and establish innovation. Furthermore, whilst studies in the past have emphasised the importance of R&D collaborations for the sake of productivity and innovation, especially in the pharmaceutical sector, the case of COINS demonstrates that the concrete organisation of present R&D collaborations matters, in particular regarding the emergence of topics that solicit long term values to society. This discussion corresponds to the handles of innovation—democratising, responsible, and transformative—detailed by Koizumi (2019). Furthermore, the utilisation of the consortium-based approach is expected to contribute to forming the intellectual and conceptual basis of an evolutionary and institutionalised vision, and the contours of a new mode in the healthcare sector, as explored by Boyer (2019).

As a limitation, the present argument only covers the pharmaceutical sector and Japan as a region of interest. More exploration of cases to identify commonalities and specificities in the sector needs to be conducted, in comparison to case studies in other sectors across regions, in order to generalise the contributions to theory and practice. Secondly, the case observation, COINS as a part of COI-STREAM, deals with a single ongoing trial. The aim and approach taken in COINS is worth investigating; however, its innovative performance needs to be proven in an empirical study.

To overcome various problems in the 21st century and maintain and develop a global presence, it is essential to nurture new industries rooted in each region and to expand employment, 'restoration of the region'. Industrial clusters are the core of regional innovation and system construction, and effective formation of bio industry clusters is directly linked to the success of the government's life-innovation policy.

Acknowledgements The author thanks all the members of COINS for their cooperation to the surveillance and interviews. Several parts of the contents and discussion refer related studies in past thus the author is thankful for the contributions by all the authors herein, and the editors and reviewers for their helpful comments. The studies mentioned in this chapter were financially supported by the Japan Society for the Promotion of Science (JSPS)/MEXT Grant-in-Aid for Scientific Research and Japan Science (grant no. 26285084 and 26301022).

References

Aldrich, H. E., & Sasaki, T. (1995). R&D consortia in the United States and Japan. *Research Policy, 24*(2), 301–316.

Anzai, T., Kusama, R., Kodama, H., & Sengoku, S. (2012). Holistic observation and monitoring of the impact of interdisciplinary academic research projects: An empirical assessment in Japan. *Technovation, 32*(6), 345–357.

Anzai, T., & Sengoku, S. (2016). Managing academic interdisciplinary research towards innovation: A resource and communication-based approach. *Technology Transfer and Entrepreneurship, 3*(2), 70–81.

Avila-Robinson, A., & Sengoku, S. (2017a). Multilevel exploration of the realities of interdisciplinary research centers for the management of knowledge integration. *Technovation, 62*(63), 22–41.

Avila-Robinson, A., & Sengoku, S. (2017b). Tracing the knowledge-building dynamics in new stem cell technologies through techno-scientific networks. *Scientometrics, 112*(3), 1691–1720.

Belderbos, R., Carree, M., & Lokshin, B. (2004). Cooperative R&D and firm performance. *Research Policy, 33*(10), 1477–1492.

Bergman, K., & Graff, G. D. (2007). The global stem cell patent landscape: Implications for efficient technology transfer and commercial development. *Nature Biotechnology, 25*(4), 419–424.

Boder, A. (2006). Collective intelligence: a keystone in knowledge management. *Journal of Knowledge Management, 10*(1), 81–93.

Booth, B., & Zemmel, R. (2004). Opinion: Prospects for productivity. *Nature Reviews Drug Discovery, 3*(5), 451.

Boschma, R. (2005). Proximity and innovation: A critical assessment. *Regional Studies, 39*(1), 61–74.

Boyer, R. (2019). How scientific breakthroughs and social innovations shape the evolution of the healthcare sector. In S. Lechevalier (Ed.), *Innovation beyond technology* (pp. 89–119). Berlin: Springer.

Bozeman, B., & Boardman, P. C. (2003). *Managing the new multipurpose, multidiscipline university research*. IBM Center for the Business of Government.

Brandes, O. M., & Brooks, D. B. (2007). *The soft path for water in a nutshell*. Friends of the Earth Canada & POLIS Project on Ecological Governance, University of Victoria.

Breschi, S., & Lissoni, F. (2001). Knowledge spillovers and local innovation systems: A critical survey. *Industrial and Corporate Change, 10*(4), 975–1005.

Brown, P., & Lauder, H. (2001). Human capital, social capital and collective intelligence. In S. Baron, J. Field, & T. Schuller (Eds.), *Social capital: Critical perspectives* (pp. 226–242). Oxford: Oxford University Press.

Cabinet Office of Japan. (2016). *Japan is back*. Available at: http://www.kantei.go.jp/jp/singi/keizaisaisei/pdf/2016_zentaihombun.pdf (reviewed on 1 Apr 2019, in Japanese).

Camagni, R. (1991). Local 'milieu', uncertainty and innovation networks: towards a new dynamic theory of economic space. *Innovation Networks: Spatial Perspectives*, 121–144.

Chesbrough, H. (2003). *Open innovation: The new imperative for creating and profiting from technology*. Harvard Business School press.

Christensen, C. (2013). *The innovator's dilemma: When new technologies cause great firms to fail*. Harvard Business Review Press.

Cohen, W. M., & Levinthal, D. A. (1990). Absorptive capacity: A new perspective on learning and innovation. *Administrative Science Quarterly*, 128–152.

Cooke, P. (2002). *Knowledge economies: Clusters, learning and cooperative advantage*. Routledge.

Cooke, P., Uranga, M. G., & Etxebarria, G. (1997). Regional innovation systems: Institutional and organisational dimensions. *Research Policy, 26*(4), 475–491.

Crook, J. M., Hei, D., & Stacey, G. (2010). The international stem cell banking initiative (ISCBI): Raising standards to bank on. *Vitro Cellular & Developmental Biology-Animal, 46*(3–4), 169–172.

DiMasi, J. A., Feldman, L., Seckler, A., & Wilson, A. (2010). Trends in risks associated with new drug development: Success rates for investigational drugs. *Clinical Pharmacology and Therapeutics, 87*(3), 272–277.

Doloreux, D., & Parto, S. (2005). Regional innovation systems: Current discourse and unresolved issues. *Technology in Society, 27*(2), 133–153.

Dubey, R., & Dubey, J. (2009). Pharmaceutical product differentiation: A strategy for strengthening product pipeline and life cycle management. *Journal of Medical Marketing., 9*(2), 104–118.

Etzkowitz, H., & Leydesdorff, L. (1995). *The triple helix–University-industry-government relations: A laboratory for knowledge based economic development.*

Eyo, S. J. (2011). A comparison of biotechnology industry in Japan and other developed countries. *Hitotsubashi University Working Paper Series*, July 2011.

Federsel, H. J. (2010). Process R&D under the magnifying glass: Organization, business model, challenges, and scientific context. *Bioorganic & Medicinal Chemistry, 18*(16), 5775–5794.

Foray, D., & Lundvall, B. (1998). The knowledge-based economy: From the economics of knowledge to the learning economy. *The Economic Impact of Knowledge*, 115–121.

Freeman, C. (1987). Technical innovation, diffusion, and long cycles of economic development. In *The long-wave debate* (pp. 295–309). Berlin, Heidelberg: Springer.

Gertler, M. S., & Wolfe, D. A. (2006). Spaces of knowledge flows: Clusters in a global context. *Clusters and regional development: Critical reflections and explorations*, 218–235.

Gibbons, M., Limoges, C., Nowotny, H., Schwartzman, S., Scott, P., & Trow, M. (1994). *The new production of knowledge: The dynamics of science and research in contemporary societies*. Sage.

Grindley, P., Mowery, D. C., & Silverman, B. (1994). SEMATECH and collaborative research: Lessons in the design of high-technology consortia. *Journal of Policy Analysis and Management, 13*(4), 723–758.

Gulati, R. (1995). Does familiarity breed trust? The implications of repeated ties for contractual choice in alliances. *Academy of Management Journal, 38*(1), 85–112.

Gulati, R., & Gargiulo, M. (1999). Where do interorganizational networks come from? *American Journal of Sociology, 104*(5), 1439–1493.

Hannan, M. T., & Freeman, J. (1987). Structural inertia and organizational change. *American Sociological Review, 49*(2), 149–164.

Hawkins, R. (1999). The rise of consortia in the information and communication technology industries: emerging implications for policy. *Telecommunications Policy, 23*, 159–173.

Honjo, Y., Nagaoka, S., Nakamura, K., & Shimizu, Y. (2010). *Challenges in biotech firms' growth—Survey mainly on funding, core technology, alliance and patent system.* IIR Working Paper, WP#10-03, Institute of Innovation Research, Hitotsubashi University, July 2010.

Honjo, Y., Nagaoka, S., Nakamura, K., & Shimizu, Y. (2012). *Challenges in biotech firms' growth - Survey mainly on alliances and changes in company representatives.* IIR Working Paper, WP#12-01, Institute of Innovation Research, Hitotsubashi University, January 2012.

Honjo, Y., Nagaoka, S., Nakamura, K., & Shimizu, Y. (2013). *Challenges in biotech firms' growth—Attention to scientific sources.* IIR Working Paper, WP#13-03, Institute of Innovation Research, Hitotsubashi University, January 2013.

Ilic, D., & Stephenson, E. (2013). Promises and challenges of the first clinical-grade induced pluripotent stem cell bank. *Regenerative Medicine, 8*(2), 101–102.

Khanna, I. (2012). Drug discovery in pharmaceutical industry: Productivity challenges and trends. *Drug Discovery Today, 17*(19–20), 1088–1102.

Kirzner, I. M. (1979). *Perception, opportunity, and profit.* University.

Kirzner, I. M. (1997). Entrepreneurial discovery and the competitive market process: An Austrian approach. *Journal of economic Literature, 35*(1), 60–85.

Klein, J. T. (2004). Prospects for transdisciplinarity. *Futures, 36*(4), 515–526.

Knoepfler, P. S. (2013). Call for fellowship programs in stem cell-based regenerative and cellular medicine: New stem cell training is essential for physicians. *Regenerative Medicine, 8*(2), 223–225.

Kobayashi, K. (2001). *Journal of the Society of Project Management, 3*(3), 21–26 (in Japanese).

Kodama, H., Watatani, K., & Sengoku, S. (2013). Competency-based assessment of academic interdisciplinary research and implication to university management. *Research Evaluation, 22,* 93–104.

Koizumi, S. (2019). The light and shadow of the fourth industrial revolution. In S. Lechevalier (Ed.), *Innovation beyond technology* (pp. 63–86). Berlin: Springer.

Koller, T., Goedhart, M., & Wessels, D. (2010). *Valuation: Measuring and managing the value of companies* (Vol. 499). Wiley.

Lane, P. J., & Lubatkin, M. (1998). Relative absorptive capacity and interorganizational learning. *Strategic Management Journal,* 461–477.

Lauto, G., & Sengoku, S. (2015). Perceived incentives to transdisciplinarity in a Japanese university research center. *Futures, 65,* 136–149.

Lawson, C., & Lorenz, E. (1999). Collective learning, tacit knowledge and regional innovative capacity. *Regional Studies, 33*(4), 305–317.

Lechevalier, S., Ikeda, Y., & Nishimura, J. (2010). The effect of participation in government consortia on the R&D productivity of firms: a case study of robot technology in Japan. *Economics of Innovation and New Technology, 19*(8), 669–692.

Lundvall, B. Ä., & Johnson, B. (1994). The learning economy. *Journal of Industry Studies, 1*(2), 23–42.

Malmberg, A., Sölvell, Ö., & Zander, I. (1996). Spatial clustering, local accumulation of knowledge and firm competitiveness. *Geografiska Annaler. Series B. Human Geography,* 85–97.

Malmberg, A., & Maskell, P. (2002). The elusive concept of localization economies: towards a knowledge-based theory of spatial clustering. *Environment and Planning A, 34*(3), 429–449.

Mason, C. (2008). Regenerative medicine 2.0. *Regenerative Medicine, 2*(1), 11–8.

Miki, T. (2012). *Japio Yearbook 2012* (pp. 58–63) (in Japanese).

Mills, A. E., & Tereskerz, P. M. (2010). Empirical analysis of major stem cell patent cases: The role of universities. *Nature Biotechnology, 28*(4), 325–328.

Morgan, K. (2004). The exaggerated death of geography: Learning, proximity and territorial innovation systems. *Journal of Economic Geography, 4*(1), 3–21.

Morioka, T. (2007). A study of local small business enterprises alliance from the network perspective. *Proceedings of Research Institute for Industry and Economics, Chubu University, 17,* 103–117.

Motohashi, K. (2003). *RIETI Discussion Paper Series* 03-J-015 (in Japanese).

Motohashi, K. (2007). International comparison of biotech firms between Japan and the United States. *Iryo To Shakai, 17*, 55–70.

Munisi, H. I., Le, T. K. Y., Jolivet, E., & Sengoku, S. (2013). Formation and management of biotech industrial clusters: Reviewing the Medicon Valley and Lyon in order to draw lessons for Kansai. *The Kyoto Economic Review, 189*(4), 1–18. (in Japanese).

Munisi, H. I., Xie, Z., & Sengoku, S. (2014). Exploring the innovation of stem cells and regenerative medicine in Japan: The power of consortium-based approach. *Regenerative Medicine, 9*(4), 467–477.

Nakamura, H., & Asakawa, K. (2006). *RIETI Discussion Paper Series* 06-J-019 (in Japanese).

Nelson, R. R., & Rosenberg, N. (1993). Technical innovation and national systems. *National Innovation Systems: A Comparative Analysis, 1*, 3–21.

Nonaka, I., & Takeuchi, H. (1995). *The knowledge-creating company: How Japanese companies create the dynamics of innovation.* Oxford university press.

Okamoto, Y. (2011). *Stem cells as a driver of the knowledge economy: Progress and challenges facing scotland* (No. 189). SPRU-Science and Technology Policy Research, University of Sussex.

Okamuro, H. (2001). The normative evaluation and social choice of contemporary economic systems. *COE/RES Discussion Paper Series*, No. 66. (in Japanese).

Okamuro, H. (2003). Inter-firm co-operation of the Japanese SMEs in the manufacturing sector: An empirical analysis on the organizational and contractual structure of co-operation. *Shoko Kinyu, 53*(1), 21–31. (in Japanese).

Okamuro, H. (2006). *Shoko Kinyu, 56*(6), 35–51. (in Japanese).

Patzelt, H., Zu Knyphausen-Aufseß, D., & Niko, P. (2008). Top Management teams, business models, and performance of biotechnology ventures: An upper echelon perspective. *British Journal of Management, 19*(3), 205–221.

Paul, S. M., Mytelka, D. S., Dunwiddie, C. T., Persinger, C. C., Munos, B. H., Lindborg, S. R., et al. (2010). How to improve R&D productivity: The pharmaceutical industry's grand challenge. *Nature Reviews Drug Discovery, 9*(3), 203.

Penrose, E. T. (2002). *The growth of the firm: The legacy of Edith Penrose.* Oxford University Press on Demand.

Perkmann, M., & Walsh, K. (2007). University–industry relationships and open innovation: Towards a research agenda. *International Journal of Management Reviews, 9*(4), 259–280.

Pharmaceutical Research and Manufacturers of America. (2013). *Biopharmaceutical research industry profile.*

Pisano, G. P. (2006). *Science business: The promise, the reality, and the future of biotech.* Harvard Business Press.

Porter, M. E. (1998). Clusters and the new economics of competition. *Harvard Business Review, 76*(6), 77–90.

Porter, M. E. (2000). Location, competition, and economic development: Local clusters in a global economy. *Economic development quarterly, 14*(1), 15–34.

Rafols, I., & Meyer, M. (2007). How cross-disciplinary is bionanotechnology? Explorations in the specialty of molecular motors. *Scientometrics, 70*(3), 633–650.

Rao, M. S., & Auerbach, J. M. (2006). Estimating human embryonic stem-cell numbers. *Lancet, 367*(9511), 650.

Rao, M. S. (2011). Funding translational work in cell-based therapy. *Cell Stem Cell, 9*(1), 7–10.

Reichert, J. M. (2003). A guide to drug discovery: Trends in development and approval times for new therapeutics in the United States. *Nature Reviews Drug Discovery, 2*(9), 695.

Sakakibara, M. (1997). Evaluating government-sponsored R&D consortia in Japan: who benefits and how? *Research Policy, 26*, 447–473.

Scannell, J. W., Blanckley, A., Boldon, H., & Warrington, B. (2012). Diagnosing the decline in pharmaceutical R&D efficiency. *Nature Reviews Drug Discovery, 11*(3), 191.

Sakurai, M., Munisi, H. I., Kakihara, H., & Sengoku, S. (2014, July). The current status and value creation of unlisted biotech drug discovery/development firms (biotech DDFs) in Japan: A holistic approach. In *Management of Engineering & Technology (PICMET), 2014 Portland International Conference* on (pp. 3612–3620). IEEE.

Samejima, M., & Shibuya, Y. (2010). The issues of the R&D consortium project funded by the government, and the need of "IP Producer". *Patent Studies, 49,* 44–54. (in Japanese).

Sandner, P., & Ziegelbauer, K. (2008). Product-related research: how research can contribute to successful life-cycle management. *Drug Discovery Today, 13*(9–10), 457–463.

Schumpeter, J. (1927). The explanation of the business cycle. *Economica, 21,* 286–311.

Sipp, D. (2012). Pay-to-participate funding schemes in human cell and tissue clinical studies. *Regenerative Medicine, 7*(6 Suppl), 105–111.

Sengoku, S., Sumikura, K., Oki, T., & Nakatsuji, N. (2011). Redefining the concept of standardization for pluripotent stem cells. *Stem Cell Review, 7*(2), 221–226.

Sengoku, S. (2013). A consortium-based approach for open innovation: Exploring a unique and optimal model for Japan and stem cell technology. *Hitotsubashi Business Review, 61*(3), 68–84. (in Japanese).

Stevenson, H. H., & Jarillo, J. C. (2007). A paradigm of entrepreneurship: Entrepreneurial management. In: *Entrepreneurship* (pp. 155–170). Berlin, Heidelberg: Springer.

Swann, G. M. P. (2000). *The economics of standardization: Final report for standards and technical regulations directorate.* Manchester: University of Manchester Press.

Taylor, C. J., Bolton, E. M., Pocock, S., Sharples, L. D., Pedersen, R. A., & Bradley, J. A. (2005). Banking on human embryonic stem cells: Estimating the number of donor cell lines needed for HLA matching. *Lancet, 366*(9502), 2019–2025.

Thomas, J. (2012). Collaborations in stem cell science. *Regenerative Medicine, 7*(6 Suppl), 71–72.

Timmons, J. A., Spinelli, S., & Tan, Y. (1994). *New venture creation: Entrepreneurship for the 21st century* (Vol. 4). Burr Ridge, IL: Irwin.

Tsai, W. (2001). Knowledge transfer in intraorganizational networks: Effects of network position and absorptive capacity on business unit innovation and performance. *Academy of Management Journal, 44*(5), 996–1004.

Valentin, F., Jensen, R. L., & Dahlgren, H. (2008). How venture capital shapes emerging bio-clusters—A cross-country comparison. *European Planning Studies, 16*(3), 441–463.

Wakabayashi, N. (2009). *The network organization: New insights of organization from social network theories.* Tokyo, Japan: Yuhikaku. (in Japanese).

Watanabe, T. (2010). Interorganizational relation in research and development consortium as a strategic alliance. *Journal of Intellectual Property Association of Japan, 7*(2), 35–44. (in Japanese).

Watatani, K., Xie, Z., Nakatsuji, N., & Sengoku, S. (2013). Global competencies from regional stem cell research: Bibliometrics for investigating and forecasting research trends. *Regenerative Medicine, 8*(5), 659–668.

Weiss, M., & Cargill, C. (1992). Consortia in the standards development process. *Journal of American Society of Information Science, 43*(8), 559–565.

Yamanaka, T., & Kano, S. (2016). Patent term extension systems differentiate Japanese and US drug lifecycle management. *Drug Discovery Today, 21*(1), 111–117.

Zahra, S. A., & George, G. (2002). Absorptive capacity: A review, reconceptualization, and extension. *Academy of Management Review, 27*(2), 185–203.

Part III
Case Studies 2: Environment

Chapter 8
Environment and Social Innovation: Why Technology Never Was *the* Solution

Dominique Pestre

Abstract For environmental protection, innovation in products and processes is often seen as the ideal solution. Contributing to economic activity while being 'environmentally friendly', it tends to have the favour of all, notably industry and governments. This paper takes the question of environmental protection from another angle and claims that it mainly relies on other kinds of tools than technical innovation—namely compensation schemes, norms, spatial zoning, Environmental Impact Assessments, economic instruments, management techniques, audits, lifecycle analysis, labels, etc. These tools are political, economic and legal in nature and they aim at controlling technical progress and its unwanted, negative side effects. Considering day-to-day usages of these tools, how they are concretely deployed, the compromises that define them, and the actors who mobilize them, it leads to an image that is less optimistic than the one often associated with innovation and green technologies. What it shows is the gap between claims and results, and the fact that these tools do not lead to serious reductions of environmental problems—the key reason being the unwillingness to alter growth and development, to transform our modes of production and our ways of life.

8.1 Introduction

8.1.1 *The Dream of the Perfect Technology*

For environmental protection, as in most domains, innovation in products and processes is often taken as *the* solution: technical innovations—solar panels or wind mills for energy production for example—are seen as the ideal solutions since they allow for reductions in pollutions and adverse sanitary effects without stopping or slowing down economic development. Contributing to economic activity while being 'envi-

---

D. Pestre (✉)
Ecole des Hautes Etudes en Sciences Sociales, Paris, France
e-mail: pestre.dominique@gmail.com

© Springer Nature Singapore Pte Ltd. 2019
S. Lechevalier (ed.), *Innovation Beyond Technology*, Creative Economy,
https://doi.org/10.1007/978-981-13-9053-1_8

ronmentally friendly', clean technologies tend to have the favour of all—industry, governments, and some environmental movements.

I do not want, in this text, to deny the importance of technological development as a solution to environmental problems—it is definitely a strong answer, an answer that has to be followed with all seriousness. But the argument often carries with it implicit and simplistic promises: the dream of a technology that could be perfect and without default; the dream of a growth that could be without negative consequences—the dream of a good without evil, something that does not exist. We know that technological development has its own hidden costs and is never free from unanticipated consequences; that production and consumption are never without environmental effects—even the greenest production confronts the material limits of the Spaceship Earth for example; and people may favour alternative values than full and constant growth, precautionary attitudes or more frugal ways of developing for example (for more comprehensive analyses of innovation, see Joly (2019) and Oki (2019)).

In fact, when looking at the last two centuries, and the last 50 years in particular, it appears that the tools mobilised to confront environmental crises are not essentially material or technical in nature. In the vast majority of cases, in face of a problem, other means than technical solutions are devised. When a disaster occurs, when spill outs or pollutions are there, technologies are rarely specific enough to face the quite varied set of negative and lasting consequences thus created. Since answers have to take care of the great variety of 'victims' (people, landscape, biosphere); since they have to consider immediate and long term effects; since they have to take into account problems that are technical but also social and political, economic and legal—the solutions that are proposed cannot be first of a technological kind.

Very early on, for example, industrialists financially compensated people for destroying their environments; environmental norms of all kinds were established to control air or water quality; the production and use of particular molecules were monitored by ad hoc bodies comprising industrialists, professionals, medical doctors and civil servants; spatial zoning was devised to protect specific areas; international treaties were written to protect oceans and fauna. Over the last 50 years, Environmental Impact Assessments were made mandatory; and economists proposed solutions to protect the environment: the Polluter Pays Principle, the fee on pollutions, and markets of pollution rights. More recently, environmental voluntary commitments were put forward by corporations; environmental audits were performed to check these commitments; lifecycle analysis of products and processes became a tool to help produce in a more friendly way to environments; Total Quality Management was adapted to include environmental preoccupations; environmental marketing exploded in the 1990s and labels of all kinds spread; companies met with environmental NGOs and local governments in the global South to decide on sustainable norms for products, and so on and so forth.

So, over the last two centuries—and with far more systematicity since the 1960s—environmental destruction has led to the deployment of a great number of answers, of a large set of social, political, economic and legal tools. The aim of this paper is to understand them—to characterise this ensemble of solutions and show how it worked. It is also to understand why things changed over time, which situations led to the emergence of new tools—what was at stake, which actors were central and how they succeeded having these tools accepted. As importantly it is to try and comment on the strength and limits of the various tools, their advantages and intrinsic weaknesses, and on what were the benefits, if any, for the commonwealth.

Before analysing them, however, some preliminary remarks are in order. We must first realize that there is rarely one obvious target in environmental matters; there are rather different problems asking for different solutions. Then we must understand that a common assumption often grounds these solutions: the fact that environmental protection should not unduly affect growth and economic development. Finally a historical move is clearly visible, from a more state-centred, Keynesian moment to a more business-dominated globalization process. Let me give some precisions on these points.

8.1.2 *Environmental Damages Is the Other Side of Production and Consumption*

The first, most important remark is that environmental destructions largely *derive from* technology, production and consumption; from our modes of life; and that reducing the former might lead to seriously affecting the latter. For that reason, environmental damages have rarely been taken in themselves and for themselves. Over the last two centuries, it has been common practice for all influential actors in economic and political spheres to devise forms of protection of environments that do not affect economic activity too much. What is behind the idea of not affecting industrial progress too much when protecting environment are the importance of economic development—for populations, industry and political leaders; the seduction of what an affluent society could offer; but also the necessity not to weaken, in global contexts of war and economic competition, the economic strength of the Nation.

So any answer to environmental damages has always taken into account what other countries were doing; and weighed benefits for health, nature and environment against costs for employment, national strength and industrial competitiveness. That was often done empirically, through political and social negotiations, but it was also done, since WWII, through more formal tools like cost-benefit analysis. And in times of economic crisis, means deployed for environmental protection tend to be reduced and make subservient to the need of economic development. That does not mean that nothing changed over time, far from it, but this global constraining frame is structural, and it is still central today.

8.1.3 There Is Not One Environment and No Unique Solution

The second key warning is that it is preferable not to start with the idea that there is one environmental problem, one objective—and even less one technology to answer them. In environmental matters there are different preoccupations defined differently by people. Not everybody aims at a common thing and the problems anchor in quite varied sets of human and social experiences. The word could be absent or replaced by other expressions—nature or sustainability for example—that induce other orientations of the mind. And if one were to focus and consider only *one* dimension and only *one* metrics (the quantity of CO_2 in the atmosphere as indicator of climate change defined as *the* environmental question *par excellence*), the approach would be far too limited; it would erase preoccupations that are for most people as important, and it would not lead to adequate solutions.

Just to give an example, the under-developed countries experts gathered in Founex (Switzerland) in 1971 to prepare the Stockholm UN Conference on Human Environment refused the privilege given to pollutions that characterised European, Japanese and North American experts. They declared that 'environmental problems [first] reflect [in their countries] the poverty and very lack of development [...]; life itself is endangered by poor water, housing, sanitation and nutrition' they claimed—and they added: 'these are problems, no less than those of industrial pollution, that clamour for attention' (Development and Environment 1972: 6–7). In other words, environmental protection never was an entity to which a coherent field of research questions and technological developments could be dedicated.

For some people, what matters is to save whales, pandas and elephants, to recover and restore an original nature, to create sanctuaries and parks—from which local populations could be excluded, by the way, as was not uncommon in Africa in the colonial tradition of hunting preserves (Blanc 2015). The protection of environments could imply the reduction of noise in town, the control of pesticides and their use, the mastery of industrial wastes. It could mean a choice for other agricultural practices (and they have become quite numerous over the last decades), certified wood production (with also a large variety of labels), measures to protect marine resources on the long run (fish stocks for example). It could suppose industrial ecology, recycling or the mastering of environmental damages via industrial management. It could aim at protecting regional biodiversity, rescuing wetlands, attenuating climate change. And at Founex, five categories of problems were identified: the deterioration of resources, notably soils and forests; biological pollution (pathogens for humans, animals and plants); chemical pollution; physical disruptions—but also 'social disruption, of which congestion [in towns] and loss of a sense of community are examples' (Development and Environment 1972; see also Manulak 2017).

On the other side, for most economists of the period, the key question was the tension between growth (or development) and the destruction of the environment—a problem that had, according to theory, one best solution: a fee imposed on polluters to compensate for the negative externalities their activity generated. But for other, less mainstream economists, that was not to be an efficient solution since the limits of the spaceship Earth were *the* main long-term problem; and it asked for a larger range of economic but also material solutions. Anticipating the Club of Rome report of 1972, Kenneth E. Boulding wrote in 1966, for example, that the question of the Earth physical limits had to be put center stage in economic theory, and that it should lead to its renewal (Boulding 1966).

And for some, let's be clear, investing in environmental protection might only be a slogan, an opportunity for business, or a way to escape a regulation.

8.2 The Legal, Political and Scientific Measures

Let me now present the main solutions that were proposed and put into place to face environmental degradation over the last two centuries, and in particular the last 50 years. They were extremely numerous, they heavily depended on contexts and actors—and I have put the most important of them, to simplify my work, in six sets. I present them chronologically, roughly in the order in which they appeared over time; but I also tried to keep some form of intellectual coherence for each set. Which means that there is some arbitrariness in this presentation, as in all classification.

8.2.1 Compensation: The Liberal Tenet

Compensation is the oldest way to 'deal' with environmental destruction—even if still quite topical. It dates from the turn of the 19th Century and consists in financially compensating victims for damages—at least for the time being, the industrialist expecting better technical solutions in the future. Compensation is not specific to environmental protection; it is rather a general principle that is part and parcel of any liberal order: when damages have been inflicted to someone's health or property, reparation is due. In the case of a chemical plant destroying olive trees through fumes in early 19th Century around Marseille, compensation was given to the owner of the trees—for her to plant new ones, if so she wished (Jarrige and Le Roux 2017; Fressoz 2012; Le Roux 2011).

The compensation scheme could derive from direct an arrangement between polluters and victims—and industrialists were so much accustomed to it in 19th Century France that they often included these compensation fees in the overheads of the company. After a judicial battle of experts around responsibilities, compensation could be imposed by a legal decision of justice, with a fine that applies up to the moment the pollution problem is solved. But the risk of damage could also be taken over by insurance companies—in mid-19th Century England for example, the obligation to be covered by insurance was for example used by state to force companies to become more precautious with their equipment and avoid accidents (Fressoz 2012).

Compensating is the oldest way to include environmental and sanitary damages into production costs; for polluters the advantage is that it allows anticipation in terms of costs for the company—and it is an easy way to absolve oneself (Fressoz talks of disinhibition), maintain social peace (with neighbours) and go on unhindered with production (the key advantage of compensation). One might consider that these solutions are not directly targeting environmental *protection*—which is true. But since damages are sometime considered unavoidable by certain people (industrialists for example), caring about their consequences cannot but be negative; and since compensating adds a cost for the polluter, it might be a way to induce changes in her/his behaviours and help protect environments—after all, it is exactly the rationale that has been given to economic instruments since WWII (Pestre 2014).

More importantly, compensation remains today quite universal a solution for the health consequences of industrial development—think of compensation for illnesses induced, among hundreds of examples, by asbestos, toxic molecules or pharmaceutical products. Which tells us that industrial societies consider compensation as a banal way to deal with environmental damages; that it belongs to the core of our social, legal and political contract—that it is probably too ingrained in our liberal societies for it not to remain essential. And since industrialists often treat the environmental and health damages they caused as 'externalities' (as economists say), compensating for them is a 'normal' way to act.

An interesting variation of the compensation scheme today is the legal obligation to compensate when one destroys an ecosystem, for example in wetlands: in many countries now, before installing an airport or a large industrial site, the entrepreneur must pay for the restoration, in another place, of an ecosystem said to be 'equivalent' to the one he or she is about to destroy (Méral and Pesche 2016). Of course, the computation of the compensation level is not the one that permitted to compensate for the destruction of olive trees near chemical plants around Marseille in 1810; nor the one that evaluated the cost of a lost arm or leg during a compensation for a work accident near 1900 in Germany (Fressoz and Pestre 2013); but the logics is the same and ecosystemic compensation derives from that very legal tradition.

To organize ecosystems compensation, new rules of equivalence had of course to be invented—from decisions about *what* to measure to the monetary *values* given to each item, from companies making the surveys and assessing ecosystems value *in the fields* to platforms of exchange or *banks*. The rules of equivalence, as the results concretely arrived at by experts, are regularly contested, however—because arbitrariness cannot but be massive in the setting of the rules and their implementation. And often, when demands for compensations are judged, at the end of the process, too high (or too small!) by one or two major stakeholders, the concrete assessments and measures are questioned. As usual, the level of compensation cannot but involve economic-political trade offs; they could be inscribed into the schemes used to make the evaluation, but they could also just happened, notably when what has to be estimated is large and complex. Here as everywhere, the sheer level of what has to finally be paid centrally matters (Méral and Pesche 2016: 183–247; Dauguet 2019).

8.2.2 Norms and Standards: The Public Authority Way

The instruments that make the second group mainly consist in standards of environmental quality, in norms fixing material limits to pollutions. These tools that are mainly in political hands via legislative or administrative bodies are as old as the industrial state. They are the most common over the last 50 years and remain decisive—despite the contrary assertion, often heard today, that 'market instruments' have now become hegemonic, which is false. Norms and standards are still the nerve core of the institutional protection of health and environments at local, national (or EU) levels; conversely, they are less common and ill adapted for situations where no public authority rules—for global affairs for example. And in contexts in which authorities are strong enough (which means rarely in the global South), because they do not offer easy escape routes for people who would like to cheat, they could be quite effective.

Industrialists have been ambivalent vis-à-vis these tools. In general, as for any regulation limiting their autonomy, they tended to lobby and try not to have them. When in place, some could be confrontational (what happened in the United States in 1970), and other more conciliatory (that was more often the case in Europe and Japan) (Cook 1988; Wurzel et al. 2003; Schreurs 2002). The positive aspect of norms is that they clearly define the rules that apply to all—what global business in the 1990s called '*the "level playing field"* for industry'. Norms rely on the definition and enforcement of safety thresholds that are proposed by scientists, notably toxicologists and epidemiologists, working with medical doctors and professional organisations, with industry and state experts, in national contexts and/ or international committees, and sometimes in presence of NGOs.

To norms and standards, one could add *permitting*—an instrument already in use in the early 19th Century (Le Roux 2011; Massard-Guilbaud 2010; Hays 2000) that implied the necessity to get an administrative authorization before opening a polluting plant. Permitting is a way to politically manage space, to geographically condition production (polluting business must be put outside city centres, residential areas or preserved landscape, for example). The idea is to protect portions of a territory from too much damages or pollutions; and to protect the health of large concentrations of population—the question of workers health being taken care independently (Fressoz and Pestre 2013).

Permitting has been revised over the last decades but still occupies a central place—at least in the global North, or for investments in the global South when guaranteed by the World Bank, for example. Designed in the 1970s, in particular at OECD, *Environmental Impact Assessment* procedures were added; they aimed at asserting that environmental considerations were taken into account when developing new industrial projects. Procedures centred on the analysis of risk were also renewed in the recent period. Aiming at evaluating and managing risks (*risk assessment and management*) this technology exploded in the 1980s, when it became more strictly codified (Boudia and Henry 2015; Demortain 2011; Boudia and Jas 2007). In both cases, however, contestation never ceased: the crucial points were the evaluation of potential damages, always more complex and prone to underestimations than the evaluations of costs; to decide who would arbitrate between conflicting evaluations; and to know if an appeal implied the suspension of construction work, a practice not so common (Baya-Laffite 2016).

These instruments centrally rely on scientific data and analyses but of course integrate social values: the level of a norm (the legal threshold for the presence of a carcinogenic in a product for example), or the way to use particularly contested pesticides in agriculture, are political and context dependent; they depend on the strength of the contestation, on the importance, visibility and activism of the victims, on the social and political situation; they are thus often local and idiosyncratic—and the *longue durée* history of protection against lead, for example, sharply differs from one country to the next (Nash 2015). The fixation of a norm or a standard basically depends on arbitrations between the negative effects of the pollution and economic interests, we said it—which also explains why a product or process vital for the good functioning of industry is rarely forbidden before a less damaging technology has been found (Jas 2001).

Up to the 1950s, the fixation of a norm was often done, under state supervision, by direct negotiations between experts and interests, each providing his or her data and claims; in the following decades it tended to rely more on specialists (notably scientists and economists) and on complex forms of calculation and evaluation. Social negotiations about norms were put in place at the turn of the 20th Century but the centrality of computations tools only emerged after WWII—in line with the rise of the welfare state and its own ways of working (Desrosières 2008). In the same way, risk control became far more standardized in the early 1980s, and coordination between national and international norms then became more systematic—international trade *oblige* (Boudia and Jas 2013; for an analysis of the (in)efficiency of this multiplication and scientifization of tools, Jas 2014).

A tool with a large field of application came to play a key role in the last half-Century: cost-benefit analysis. It started to be imposed in the assessment of civil engineering project in the United States in the 1930s but only came to supremacy, for environmental questions, in the early 1970s. Its official rationale was to objectify decision, to withdraw it from the sheer battle of interests—to strictly compare the costs of a measure to its benefits. But that is rhetoric and ideal science, not reality; the exercise faces insurmountable barriers, and trade offs between interests went on behind the scene. The problem is that the number of parameters is infinite; the list of what should count as a cost or a benefit, and to whom, is subject to endless debates; and that made cost-benefit analysis prone to systematic biases and approximations. It is thus a limited form of objectivity—but, on the other hand, an ideal tool of political authority (Porter 1995). Around environmental matters in the United States, for example, it became a tool cherished by powers in place; it was imposed by the executive power (by President Nixon and the Office of Management and Budget) on the Environment Protection Agency and used to limit demands made by environmentalists and populations that would impose too heavy costs on economic activity (Boudia 2014, 2016; Hays 2000; Smith 1984; Kelman 1981; Steven Kelman was

8 Environment and Social Innovation: Why Technology ...

then associate director for management planning at the United States Federal Trade Commission).

8.2.3 Economic and Market Instruments: The Economists' Solution

The third group of tools used to help protect environments is the one that most occupied the media, social sciences and normative discourses in the last decades—the so-called 'economic' or 'market instruments'. This way of talking and posing the problem started to emerge some 50 years ago—a difference with the previous two groups of tools that have far longer a history. What is striking with the notion of economic or market instruments is the central role it played in the 'theological' war that has been waged since the 1970s against Keynesian policies and the welfare state by those who claimed that 'the market' was the only efficient calculator, that market solutions were intrinsically superior to all political regulations, that they were cheaper and more efficient than norms and standards—and that States had to withdraw (Pestre to be published; Short 2012).

The defence of economic or market instruments was at its apex after Thatcher and Reagan elections and they then made the buzz. They were actively promoted by the conservative think tanks like *Entreprise* or *Heritage*; by the direction of OECD, who did it quite systematically; and by most economists (and parts of the social sciences) for whom it became kind of second nature. This new vocabulary and frame, when at the core of political battles, tended to oppose two simple poles: *Control and Command*—a set of ill-defined but rigid, top-down and inefficient ways of regulating, typical of states and norms; and *Market/Economic Instruments*—a group of supple, incentive and clever tools that acted at a far lower cost and led to optimal results. At least that was what proponents of economic instruments and markets claimed (OECD 1985).

Economists were central in the rhetorical victory of economic instruments since they gave them the imprimatur of Science. Most claimed that the efficiency and superiority of economic instruments were proven by theory—even if that has been endlessly discussed, and even if the concrete instruments that were put behind the notion profoundly varied with time.

Initially, the expression of economic instrument was not used systematically: at the turn of the 1970s, what was promoted was essentially the *fee* (OCDE 1972). Borrowed from A. Cecil Pigou, the fee aimed at including the negative environmental externalities of the production process into prices, to have the polluter pays (*or compensates*), via a fee, for the damages he created. In line with theoretical claims, economists said that the fee would lead to *an optimum* for economic growth and environmental protection—a most debatable notion (Barde and Gerelli 1977). There remained a major problem, however. If theory proved the existence of an optimal level of fee, there was no practical way to calculate it—a situation not unknown

184   D. Pestre

in science (Pestre 2006). So it was not easy to justify the level of the fee. Fearing that companies would sue the Environmental Protection Agency for arbitrariness in fixing it, US regulators and politicians kept on with the tools they knew (notably norms and standards) and fees remained anecdotal in practice (Smith 1984).

From the start in the United States, industrialists strongly resisted Environmental Protection Agency (EPA) regulations. They claimed that they were too heavy, and their cost so high that it would lead companies to bankruptcy; and, in certain regions, many did not comply (Cook 1988; Lane 2014). Because national industry and employment could not but be taken seriously, US governments and EPA gave industry more time to comply and negotiations started. The solutions, progressively devised in the second half of the 1970s, were first to let companies compensate, on a site, their varied pollutions; then to let them compensate pollution in one place by reduction made on another of their sites; and finally to let companies trade the 'rights to pollute' they had gained by reducing certain pollutions (below the mandatory threshold) with companies that could not comply (Pestre 2014).

In 1980–81, through conceptual imports from varied fields, notably auctions, the expression of 'markets' of 'pollution rights' became popular in Reaganian politics and conservative Think Tanks (PARA 1981). The practice of pollution rights also reactivated theories previously developed by economists like Dales (1968), and the profession progressively became more positive about those 'markets'.[1] In this frame, a ceiling of pollution is fixed by a political authority and 'the market', as the generic and theoretically perfect solution, is let to optimally distribute the costs among traders. And it is in that context, during the battle needed to impose this tool as the obvious best one that the expression of 'economic' or 'market instruments' became common. The adjective 'economic' was the first to appear; it had the preference of economists and carried with it an idea of scientificity; 'market' appeared later, was more common among Think Tanks—but both opposed the absolute bad way that they started to contemptuously call *Control and Command*.

The development and discursive hegemony of economic instruments meant a major conceptual shift in the way to frame environmental questions—a change from the idea of a given state of the environment that has to be known since it should ground protective action, to that of a given stock of pollution 'rights', in a way inherited and partly possessed by companies, and that they could trade. And, to complement the image, it was in that context of strong business complains that

---

[1] The way these markets of pollution rights were named varied over time and a detailed study of these nominations (depending on people and institutions) would be most instructive. Here are some quick examples. Economist Kolm used the crudest vocabulary and talked about 'un droit à nuire' in 1974. Economists Pearce in 1976, and Barde in 1977 talk about 'the sell of pollution rights'; in 1981, a report on 'experiences' developed in the United States mention 'marketable rights and banking', 'transferable rights' and 'marketable permits'; OECD 1985 talks of 'market creation' ('artificial markets can be created where actors might buy "rights" for actual or potential pollutions or where they can sell their "pollution rights"', p 15); in 1985, Tietenberg talks of 'emissions trading', as did OECD in 1989; in 1991 Barde talks about 'permis négociables' and OECD of 'marketable permits'; in 2001 OECD talks about 'transferable permits'; and in 2007 OECD uses 'price-based instruments (e.g. taxes)' and 'quantity-based instruments (e.g. a 'cap and trade' permit system)' (p 215). Apparently, euphemism has been on the rise.

cost-benefit analysis was imposed on administrations like EPA to limit the rigor of environmental legislations that would have too heavy a cost for the economy.

A last word on the cap-and-trade instruments, as they are now known. Contrary to most speeches, cap and trade were not often in use—even if they are at the core of climate change mitigation, which makes them highly visible. De facto, compensation, permitting, norms and standards remain dominant, and nothing proves that emissions-trading programs were particularly effective—including for CO_2 emissions (Ercmann 1996; Driesen 2003; Comparison of the EU and US 2004; Toke and Lauber 2007). But the reiteration of these endless narratives that promise absolute superiority for one unique instrument is most significant: behind the technical debate between experts, what was crucial was the battle in the public space to win over minds. What was conveyed was the idea that there is one universal way (that's the TINA argument: There Is No Alternative, often attributed to Margaret Thatcher) and that economic/market instruments are ideally efficient—since devised by 'economics' (science) and relying on 'markets' (the only serious option). And that constitutes a central ideological tenet even if economists started to progressively soften their claims—in the late 1990s for some (Fullerton 1998), most of them only in the 2000s (OECD 2007).

8.3 The Business Way

8.3.1 Recycling, Management and Audits

Taking care of environmental damages induced by our modes of development was not the only province of legal and public authorities, or economists—it was also done at the level of production by industrial managers.

In the world of politics, the 1980s were marked by free trade enthusiasm and a fascination for management techniques. In Europe, people mainly turned to Germany, in particular to Georg Winter and BAUM, the business association he founded in 1984 whose goal was to help business taking into account resources, wastes, and environmental impact issues throughout the production value chain. Other models existed in Japan and the United States—the 3M Company, which invented the slogan *Pollution Prevention Pays*, was indeed the preferred standard for American advocates of change (Winter 1988; Royston 1985; Zosel 1990; Zosel was manager of *Pollution Prevention Programs* at the 3M Company).

It was through the creation of GEMI in 1990, the *Global Environmental Management Initiative*, that things picked up pace and pro-environmental management discourses started to significantly spread. GEMI was put in place in 1990 (by Allied Signals, Amoco, Apple, ATT, Boeing, Dow, Du Pont, Merck, Procter and Gamble, etc.) to adapt Total Quality Management to environmental requirements (GEMI 1993; Marshall and Roberts 1992; Kolluru 1994; Borri and Bocchaletti 1995; Miles and Russell 1997. For critiques, see Chatterjee and Finger 1994; van des Pijl 1998; Sklair

2001). Historically, TQM was an answer to globalization—the fact that companies now operated worldwide, that supply chains were long and suppliers geographically spread out (von Molkte et al. 1997). TQM's main principle was the satisfaction of customers and suppliers all along these chains—and TQEM (Total Quality *Environmental* Management) asked managers to now include the demands of 'regulators', 'legislators', 'community' and 'national environmental groups' into their choices and decisions (GEMI 1993).

A consequence is major: with TQEM we go another step further (after markets of pollution rights) in disconnecting the management of environments from an assessment of their state. TQEM does not define any *intrinsic environmental quality*—there are no norms in this world—and 'quality' simply results from the way companies arbitrate between what clients, shareholders and stakeholders expect. Environmental objectives emerge from a judgement made inside the company in face of conflicting demands. A limitation of this management-oriented solution is that the degradation of the environment is not taken into account in itself and for itself, that no one is in charge of it, or has to monitor it.

Lifecycle analysis is another tool considered with attention by managers to avoid unnecessary pollutions and destructions of resources. It could be defined as the analysis of a product or service through all stages of its existence. It mainly developed at the turn of the 1990s—even if it quickly appeared as quite complex a tool. In 1996, for example, the International Organization for Standardization studied the way it was put to use and said it presented strong *practical* limitations: the volume of data to be processed was often too large and its results tended to be *inconclusive* (Global Green Standards Ercmann 1996). One year later, the UNEP's *Environment and Trade* office followed suit and said that lifecycle analyses were 'time-consuming and expensive' and often limited to 'easily measurable and quantifiable impacts on the physical environment' (Lehtonen 1997). In short, lifecycle analyses, whatever their initial promise, remained distant prospects; partly fictional as decision tool, they sometime were, says UNEP's *Environment and Trade* expert, 'mere sales promotion instruments for companies' (Lehtonen 1997).

In the 1980s governments also helped companies develop technical standards for cleaner production—what was known as the Best Available Technologies. This instrument was a way to guarantee 'the best' of what was technically possible; it was sometimes used as a kind of proxy for Environmental Impact Assessments and was accepted by the World Bank for the industrial investments programs it financed in the global South. One must be cautious however: since nobody is ready to save the environment if the price to pay is too high, the complete formulation was that of the Best available technologies *not entailing excessive costs* (BATNEEC)—which let open many ways to escape from too drastic solutions (Baya-Laffite 2016). And in case of disagreement between major industrial interests (between Europe and the United States for example), 'the best' technology was rarely more than a friendly and armed compromise. Which does not mean this tool was hopeless.

Finally codes of good practice and audits were mobilized by managers to help companies become more environmentally friendly. But there were some essential differences between financial and environmental audits that made the latter not so efficient for the environment. Financial audits were statutory, required by authorities, performed according to regulatory texts, by accredited bodies; environmental audits, on the other hand, were designed as voluntary actions, with no mandatory schedule and no agreed requirements in the way they were to be performed (ICC Guide 1991). And that is no accident: according to the International Organization for Standardization (Global Green Standards 1996: 14), for example, 'industry objected strongly' to *EMAS*, the European Community's *Eco Management and Audit Scheme* that 'when first drafted [...] was meant to be mandatory'. After business lobbying, EMAS was introduced as a voluntary scheme. Two quick remarks could finally be added: relations were quite endogamous between business leaders, code designers and auditors around environmental auditing; and audits, when looking at the way industry conceived them, were always closely linked to communication plans.

8.3.2 Private Labelling and Voluntary Commitments

Under pressure from 'civil society' in the late 1980s/early 1990s, some companies also started to promote labels—the *Forest Stewardship Council* label for example—that were to develop sustainable practices and socially responsible production and products (Bartley 2007; Marx 2010). Initial labels were often positive for environment (and social) protection—even if they had only limited impacts in terms of market shares because generally created by companies occupying market niches. But their success among consumers and citizens led to their submersion and the dilution of their impact in the late 1990s: competitors, much bigger on the markets, in turn started to create their own labels with rules as glowing as they were vague and of little importance. This way, they were able to trump the force of initial labels and often dissolved what made them worthwhile in the first place (Abbott and Snidal 2009). But consumers are not necessarily blind or stupid, they often are able to differentiate between what is sold to them—and labels are quite interesting tools.

Initially, labelling programs were mainly designed and managed by states. Committees of experts including consumer organizations and NGOs alongside industry representatives and civil servants assessed the impact of products and issued the label. For the European label, for example, it was necessary to submit an application and to provide evidence of the use of BATNEEC and recyclable, reusable or biodegradable materials (Neitzel 1993).

From 1992/1993 on, however, the *nature of labels changed*. Things were transformed with the creation of the FSC (Forest Stewardship Council) label. A key element was the impossibility to reach an inter-governmental agreement on labels during the Earth Summit in Rio in 1992 (along the lines of what was then building up on climate change). The reason was the pressure from big manufacturers and exporting countries that opposed such an authoritarian idea moving against trade liberalization. That did not prevent Austria to pass a law restricting importation of non-sustainable wood in 1992. But that move was immediately denounced as incompatible with General Agreement on Tariffs and Trade (GATT) rules and, under threats of retaliatory measures, Austria backed down.

From then on, the rules of the new game were established: states were not in a position to provide credible solutions anymore—GATT had the power of depriving states of the possibility to legislate (Anderson and Blackhurst 1992; OECD Trade and Environment 1994; Andersson et al. 1995). In 1995, the creation of the WTO would definitively seal the barriers against the establishment of intergovernmental standards on environmental issues (Sampson and Whalley 2005; Goyal 2006). In other terms, environmental labelling became a private business as a result of the failure of public action—after multinational corporations and the GATT/WTO had rendered states powerless.

Finally, in the 1990s and 2000s, auto-organisation and voluntary commitments on the part of companies—codes of good conduct, guidelines, charters of Environmental and Social Responsibility, sustainable finance—generalized. Around some key tropical agricultural product like palm oil in the mid-2000s, for example, 'multi-actors round tables' were set up to define what would count in international trade as a *sustainable* product. These roundtables gathered, around the major global companies of agro-business like Unilever or Nestlé, representatives of local populations and conservation NGOs like WWF. 'Collectively' they set the norms of sustainable trade—even if the last developments in Indonesia and Malaysia (the key producers of palm oil) show how the palm oil plantations remain destructive of the primary forest and habitats, how the definition of sustainability drastically vary, and why these norms are contested on all fronts (Glasbergen and Schouten 2011; Cheyns 2011; Ruysschaert and Salles 2014).

Let me draw a first round of conclusions about that general move towards 'soft law' making—a move symptomatic of the new attitude of multi-national corporations that emerged between 1988 and 1992, and generalized thereafter. They thought they were now strong enough, at least at global level, to themselves take over environmental protection. In keeping with what they had advocated and done for the previous ten to fifteen years, they proposed to create, on environmental issues, a world of contracts and private law-making, a world in which the role of states was to be limited to the one they had in international trade; that world was to be without mandatory standards, and private tribunals were to be in charge of settling disputes.

In practice, these solutions did not displace the previous ones—*at least at local levels in the global North*; but they quickly became the norm in the global South, where states were too weak to resists global companies but needed investments. On the long run they gained in importance and it was these voluntary commitments (taken by states, industry and financial actors) that finally prevailed in Climate Change conferences after the failure of the Copenhagen meeting in 2009—for example during the Paris COP 21 in 2015. And one reason might be that monitoring their implementation is particularly difficult.

8.3.3 Denial and 'Merchants of Doubts'

Companies are not a homogenous block, and thus call for a more complex analysis. The business world has no head or hierarchy; it is divided by antagonistic interests and guided by competition; in short, it is not as consistent as the world of politics which is based on the legitimacy of election and the verticality of the state apparatus. This leads to a wide range of attitudes and strategies that do not necessarily match with official commitments of bodies like the International Chamber of Commerce. These strategies vary from company to company and depend on their technological advantages, the activity sectors in which they operate, the political options of their leaders—and, for example, on historical differences between Europe and the United States (Schreurs 2002; Wurzel et al. 2003; Vig and Faure 2004; Toke and Lauber 2007; Kelemen and Vogel 2010).

Environmental protests impact all types of companies, but pressure is highest on the energy, automobile, cement, steel, aluminium, chemistry, and paper industries. In these sectors, where vital interests are at stake around environmental and resource protection, there is a permanent temptation to complement public statements with disinformation campaigns and strong political lobbying efforts. At the very time when they supported audits and charters and announced their commitment to sustainability, many companies financed ad hoc 'NGOs' which challenged the reality of environmental damage—endlessly repeating that scientific analyses are marred with 'uncertainties', that other studies are required before taking action, that it is urgent to wait. Exxon, Texaco, General Motors or Ford, for example, played a central role in the creation of the Global Climate Coalition in 1989—whose goal was to create doubt about climate science and the urgency of action (*Company Environmental Reporting* 1994; Oreskes and Conway 2010; Kaiser and Wasserman 2016). Such strategies which consist of denying or minimizing the existence of problems were not exceptional and they were brought into prominence when Republicans 'officially' endorsed climate denial in the mid 1990s; and they have remained central in American politics since then, Donald Trump today being the last proof of it (Dunlap 2008; Hoffman and Forbes 2010).

This refers to differences between American and European political cultures. In the United States, deregulation is motivated by two main considerations: arguments in favour of the universal efficiency of 'the market', but also the belief in the intrinsically corrosive and harmful nature of the state—which has a history largely absent on the European continent, often more 'social democratic' and prone to negotiation. Short (2012) proposes a convincing study on this point. Quantitatively analysing how deregulation was considered in law journals between 1980 and 2005, he demonstrates the growing importance of the argument of the coercive state (towards that of the market) and adds that 'framing regulation as a problem of coercive state power' tends to favor 'a logic of governance uniquely suited to self-regulatory solutions that promised non-coercive ways of governing'. Differences between Europe and the United States also refer to differences in legal cultures. In the United States, for example, what is degraded is mostly the object of assessments by comparison with reference sites with a view to compensation. In the European continent, action often aims at also maintaining functional situations, which makes states key actors in the process (Bouleau 2016).

A quick remark before concluding: the vast arsenal of tools I have described since the beginning of this article is clearly not *systemic*—it rather looks like a baroque tool-box, a cabinet of curiosities. New tools rarely replace old ones and they just tend to pile one onto the other. I think this is no accident: that pilling up allows people with enough power to choose the solution that best fits their intentions and interests; it allows them to choose how and where to act. In other words, it gives them the freedom to display strong commitments without seriously affecting their business.

And this long list of tools should not mask another massive reality—the fact that many practices at world level *ignore any rule* and are just plainly and massively destroying environments. Think of the recycling industry of the world's wastes, which is mainly done in the countries of the global South—where there are few controls; think of production in many regions of Africa or Asia—in the gulf of Guinea, for example, where devastating pollutions due to oil production are at work without serious study, compensation or acknowledgment (Fergusson 2005); think of the non-respect of law, or sheer deception, including in the global North—as showed by the recent VW diesel motors scandal, or Syngenta practices (Syngenta 2015; Green and Berry 1985). Entering that illegal but vast under-world, deploying its complex ramifications and links to criminal activities,[2] compiling the data about unlawful behaviours and trying to uncover that black continent would be most useful—it would be decisive; because that world is quite large indeed, because we know little about it—because it is our role to figure it out, and reduce its opacity.

8.4 Conclusion

No doubt, innovation and technical progress could lead to environmental improvements. On the other hand, when massively used in production contexts, they often are sources of supplementary damages. A fascinating paradox is that, despite massive engagements with green tech and environmental protection over the last 50 years, the rate of environmental destruction continues to grow unabated. The curves defining the Anthropocene remain on their historical negative trajectory, without inflexion (Bonneuil and Fressoz 2013). 'There is no indication of a significant reduction in the rate of biodiversity loss', wrote Dempsey (2016), 'despite conservation-oriented laws and policies at every level of governance'. As for the UN climate change conferences the scale of commitments barely hides the results: 9 Gt of CO_2 were globally emitted in 1960—they were 22 in 1992 and 36 in 2016! (World Scientists' Warning to Humanity 2017).

---

[2]On the place of criminal organizations, http://abonnes.lemonde.fr/europe/article/2010/06/04/l'environnement-a-rapporte-20-5-milliards-d-euros-a-la-mafia-italienne-en-2009_1368086_3214.html.

Probably because this paper looks at day-to-day practices and the mundane ways of dealing with problems, it leads to an image of our relation to environment that is not as optimistic as the one often associated with green technologies. Looking at the tools developed by states, politicians and business, differentiating between regions and according to the North/South divide—and never abstracting from *Realpolitik*—the paper sheds light on the darker side of the story. What it shows is the gap between intentions and actions, between claims and results—the key reason being the unwillingness to change our modes of production and ways of life. We do not want to abandon our carbonated and polluting trajectory, and Growth remains our God. But problems stay, environmental destruction does not seriously recede—and it is at that juncture that *technological promises* are central: they help us remain confident and optimistic.

References

Abbott, K. W., & Snidal, D. (2009). The governance triangle: Regulatory standards institutions and the shadow of the state. In W. Mattli & N. Woods (Eds.), *The politics of global regulation* (pp. 44–88). Princeton: Princeton University Press.

Anderson, K., & Blackhurst, R. (1992). *The greening of world trade issues*. NY: Harvester Wheatsheaf.

Andersson, T., Folke, C., & Nyström, S. (1995). *Trading with the environment. Ecology, economics, institutions and politics*. London: Earthscan.

Barde, J.-P., & Gerelli, E. (1977). *Economie et politique de l'environnement*. Paris: PUF.

Bartley, T. (2007). Institutional emergence in an era of globalization. The rise of transnational private regulation of labor and environmental conditions. *AJS, 113*(2), 297–351.

Baya-Laffite, N. (2016). Black-boxing sustainable development: Environmental impact assessment on the river Uruguay. In J. P. Voß & R. Freeman (Eds.), *Knowing governance. The epistemic construction of political order* (pp. 237–255). London: Palgrave Macmillan.

Blanc, G. (2015). *Une histoire environnementale de la nation, Regards croisés sur les parcs nationaux du Canada, d'Éthiopie et de France*. Paris: Publications de la Sorbonne.

Bonneuil, C., & Fressoz, J.-B. (2013). *L'événement anthropocène. La Terre, l'histoire et nous*. Paris: Seuil.

Borri, F., & Bocchaletti, G. (1995). From total quality management to total quality environmental management. *The TQM Magazine, 7*(5), 38–42.

Boudia, S. (2014). Gouverner par les instruments économiques. La trajectoire de l'analyse coût-bénéfice dans l'action publique. In D. Pestre (Ed.), *Le gouvernement des technosciences. Gouverner le progrès et ses dégâts depuis 1945* (pp. 231–260). Paris: La Découver-te.

Boudia, S. (2016). Des instruments pour mettre en économie l'environnement. L'économici-sation par approximation et occultation. *Ecologie & politique, 52,* 45–61.

Boudia, S., & Henry, E. (2015). *La mondialisation des risques*. Presses Universitaires de Rennes.

Boudia, S., & Jas, N. (2007). Risk and risk society in historical perspective. *History and Technology, 23*(4), 317–331.

Boudia, S., & Jas, N. (Eds.). (2013). *Toxicants, health and regulation since 1945*. London: Pickering and Chatto.

Boulding, K. E. (1966). The economics of the coming spaceship earth. In H. Jarrett (Ed.), *Environmental quality in a growing economy* (pp. 3–14). Baltimore, MD: Resources for the Future/Johns Hopkins University Press.

Bouleau, G. (2016). Ambiguïtés du leadership européen sur l'environnement. Ecological modernisation: Construction and biases of a European environmental ideology. https://hal.archives-ouvertes.fr/hal-00750172.

Chatterjee, P., & Finger, M. (1994). *The earth brokers*. London: Routledge.

Cheyns, E. (2011). Multi-stakeholder initiatives for sustainable agriculture: Limits of the 'inclusiveness' paradigm. In S. Ponte, J. Vestergaard, & P. Gibbon (Eds.), *Governing through standards: Origins, drivers and limitations* (pp. 210–235). London: Palgrave Macmillan.

Company Environmental Reporting (1994). UNEP, I&E, technical report n° 24.

Comparison of the EU and US Approaches Towards Acidification, Eutrophication and Ground Level Ozone (2004). http://ec.europa.eu/environment/archives/cafe/activities/pdf/case_study1.pdf.

Cook, B. J. (1988). *Bureaucratic politics and regulatory reform. The EPA and emission trading*. New York: Greenwood.

Dales, J. H. (1968). Land, water, and ownership. *The Canadian Journal of Economics, 1*(4), 791–804.

Dauguet, B. (2019). La compensation écologique. Etude d'un dispositif environnemental contemporain comme rapport social de production. PhD, Paris: EHESS, to be defended in December 2019.

Demortain, D. (2011). *Scientists and the regulation of risks. Standardizing control*. Cheltenham: Edward Elgar.

Dempsey, J. (2016). *Enterprising nature. Economics, markets, and finance in global biodiversity politics*. Chichester: Wiley.

Desrosières, A. (2008). Pour une sociologie historique de la quantification, L'argument statistique I; Gouverner par les nombres, L'argument statistique II. Paris: Presses des Mines.

Development and Environment. (1972). Report and working paper of a panel of experts (…). Founex, June 4–12, 1971, Paris, Mouton, UN Geneva, and EPHE (VIe section).

Driesen, D. M. (2003). *Does emissions trading encourage innovation?* Washington, DC: Environmental Law Institute. http://www.eli.org.

Dunlap, R. E. (2008). *Climate-change views: Republican-democratic gaps expand*, May 29, 2008. http://www.gallup.com/poll/107569/climatechange-views-republicandemocratic-gaps-expand.aspx.

Ercmann, S. (1996). Enforcement of environmental law in United States and European law: Realities and expectations. *Environmental Law, 26*(4), 1213–1239.

Fergusson, J. (2005). Seeing like an oil company: Space, security, and global capital in Neoliberal Africa. *American Anthropologist, 107*(3), 377–382.

Fressoz, J.-B. (2012). *L'Apocalypse joyeuse. Une histoire du risque technologique*. Paris: Seuil.

Fressoz, J.-B., & Pestre, D. (2013). Critique historique du satisfecit postmoderne. Risque et 'société du risque' depuis deux siècles. In D. Bourg, P.-B. Joly, & A. Kaufman (Eds.), *Du risque à la menace. Penser la catastrophe* (pp. 19–56). Paris: PUF.

Fullerton, D. (1998). How economists see the environment. *Selected Works*, at http://works.bepress.com/don_fullerton/20.

GEMI (The Global Environmental Management Initiative). (1993). *Total quality environmental management*. Washington DC: GEMI.

Glasbergen, P., & Schouten, G. (2011). Creating legitimacy in global private governance. The case of the roundtable on sustainable palm oil. *Ecological Economics, 70*(11), 1891–1899.

Global Green Standards: ISO 14000 and Sustainable Development (1996). Winnipeg: IISD.

Goyal, A. (2006). *The WTO and international environmental law*. Oxford: Oxford UP.

Green, M., & Berry, J.-F. (1985). White-collar crime is big business. *The Nation 240*, June 8, p. 689.

Hays, S. P. (2000). *A history of environmental politics since 1945*. Pittsburgh: University of Pittsburgh Press.

Hoffman, A. J., & Forbes, M. (2010). *The culture and discourse of climate skepticism*. October 6. http://www.eenews.net/assets/2010/11/12/document_cw_01.pdf.

ICC Guide to Effective Environmental Auditing (1991). Paris: ICC Publishing.

8 Environment and Social Innovation: Why Technology … 193

Jarrige, F., & Le Roux, T. (2017). *La Contamination du monde. Une histoire des pollutions à l'âge industriel*. Paris: Seuil.

Jas, N. (2001). *Au carrefour de la chimie et de l'agriculture. Les sciences agronomiques en France et en Allemagne, 1840–1914*. Paris: Editions des Archives Contemporaines.

Jas, N. (2014). Gouverner les substances chimiques dangereuses dans les espaces internationaux. In D. Pestre (Ed.), *Le gouvernement des technosciences. Gouverner le progrès et ses dégâts depuis 1945* (pp. 31–63). Paris: La Découverte.

Joly, P. B. (2019). Reimagining innovation. In S. Lechevalier (Ed.), *Innovation beyond technology* (pp. 25–45). Berlin: Springer.

Kaiser, D., & Wasserman, L. (2016). The Rockefeller family fund vs. Exxon. *The New York Review of Books*, December 8 & December 22.

Kelemen, R. D., & Vogel, D. (2010). Trading places: The role of the United States and the European Union in international environmental politics. *Comparative Political Studies, 43*(4), 427–456.

Kelman, S. (1981). Cost-benefit analysis. An ethical critique. *Regulation, AEI Journal on Government and Society, 33*–40.

Kolluru, R. V. (Ed.). (1994). *Environmental strategies handbook*, foreword by Stephan Schmidheiny, chairman of BCSD entitled *Looking forward. Our common enterprise*. NY: McGraw-Hill.

Lane, R. (2014). Resources for the future, resources for growth. The making of the 1975 growth ban. In B. Stephan & R. Lane (Eds.), *The politics of carbon markets* (pp. 27–50). London: Routledge.

Le Roux, T. (2011). *Le laboratoire des pollutions industrielles, Paris, 1770–1830*. Paris: Albin Michel.

Lehtonen, M. (1997). *Criteria in environmental labelling*, UNEP, Environment and Trade Series, n° 13.

Manulak, M. W. (2017). Developing world environmental cooperation. The Founex seminar and the Stockholm conference. In W. Kaiser & J.-H. Meyer (Eds.), *International organizations and environmental protection. Conservation and globalization in the twentieth century* (pp. 103–127). New York: Berghahn.

Marshall, T., & Roberts, P. (1992). Business and the environment. *Planning, Practice & Research, 7*(2), 25–28.

Marx, A. (2010). *Global governance and the certification revolution: Types, trends and challenges* (November 19). Leuven Centre for Global Governance Studies Working Paper No. 53. https://ssrn.com/abstract=1764563 or http://dx.doi.org/10.2139/ssrn.1764563.

Massard-Guilbaud, G. (2010). *Histoire de la pollution industrielle. France, 1789–1914*. Paris: Éditions de l'EHESS.

Méral, P., & Pesche, D. (Eds.). (2016). *Les services écosystémiques. Repenser les relations nature et société*. Paris: Quae.

Miles, M. P., & Russell, G. R. (1997). ISO 14000 total quality environmental management: The integration of environmental marketing, total quality management, and corporate environmental policy. *Journal of Quality Management, 2*(1), 151–168.

Nash, L. (2015). Un siècle toxique. L'émergence de la santé environnementale. In C. Bonneuil & D. Pestre (Eds.), *Histoire des sciences et des savoirs*, tome 3 *Le siècle des technosciences* (pp. 145–166).

Neitzel, H. (1993). Méthode de travail et problématique de 12 années d'expérience de l'Ange Bleu. In J. Vigneron & C. Burstein (Eds.), *Ecoproduit. Concept et methodologies* (pp. 77–94). Paris: Economica.

OCDE. (1972). *Problèmes d'économie de l'environnement*. Paris: OCDE.

OECD. (1985). *Environments and economics*. Paris: OECD.

OECD. (1994). *Trade and environment. Processes and production methods*. Paris: OECD.

OECD. (2007). *Instrument mixes for environmental policy*. Paris: OECD.

Oki, S. (2019). 'Innovation' as an adaptation of 'Progress': Revisiting the epistemological and historical contexts of these terms. In S. Lechevalier (Ed.), *Innovation beyond technology* (pp. 47–62). Berlin: Springer.

Oreskes, N., & Conway, E. M. (2010). *Merchants of doubt: How a handful of scientists obscured the truth on issues from tobacco smoke to global warming.* USA: Bloomsbury.

PARA, Project on Alternative Regulatory Approaches (1981). *Alternative regulatory approaches: An overview.* http://wetlandia.blogspot.ch/2013/08/jimmy-carter-and-archaeology-of-market. html.

Pestre, D. (to be published). Environment: The business revolution, 1988–1992. Voluntary Commitments, Green Management, Labels, submitted to *Economy and Society.*

Pestre, D. (2006). *Introduction aux Science Studies.* Paris: La Découverte.

Pestre, D. (Ed.). (2014). *Le gouvernement des technosciences.* Paris: La Découverte.

Porter, T. M. (1995). *Trust in numbers. The pursuit of objectivity in science and public life.* Princeton: Princeton University Press.

Royston, M. G. (1985). Local and multinational corporations: Reappraising environmental management. *Environment, 27*(1), 12–43.

Ruysschaert, D., & Salles, D. (2014). Towards global voluntary standards: Questioning the effectiveness in attaining conservation goals. The case of the Roundtable on Sustainable Palm Oil (RSPO). *Ecological Economics, 107,* 438–446.

Sampson, G., & Whalley, J. (Eds.). (2005). *The WTO, trade and the environment.* Cheltenham: Edward Elgar.

Schreurs, M. A. (2002). *Environmental politics in Japan, Germany, and the United States.* Cambridge: Cambridge University Press.

Short, J. (2012). *The paranoid style in regulatory reform.* Washington: Georgetown University, jls272@law.georgetown.edu.

Sklair, L. (2001). *The transnational capitalist class.* Oxford: Blackwell.

Smith, V. K. (Ed.). (1984). *Environmental policy under reagan's executive order. The role of benefit-cost analysis.* Chapel Hill: The University of North Carolina Press.

Syngenta. (2015). Failles dans l'homologation de six OGM en Europe, *Le Monde* 15/10.

Toke, D., & Lauber, V. (2007). Anglo-Saxon and German approaches to neoliberalism and environmental policy: The case of financing renewable energy. *Geoforum, 38,* 677–687.

van des Pijl, K. (1998). *Transnational classes and international relations.* London: Routledge.

Vig, N. J., & Faure, M. G. (Eds.). (2004). *Green giants? Environmental policies of the United States and the European Union.* Cambridge: MIT Press.

von Molkte, K., Kuik, O., Van der Grijp, N. et al. (1997). *Global product chains: Northern consumers, southern producers, and sustainability.* UNEP, Environment and Trade Series, n° 15.

Winter, G. (1988). *Business and the environment.* Hamburg: McGraw-Hill.

World Scientists' Warning to Humanity 2017: A Second Notice. *BioScience.* Published online. November 13.

Wurzel, R. K. W., Jordan, A., Zito, A. R., & Brückner, L. (2003). From high regulatory state to social and ecological market economy? New environmental policy instruments in Germany. *Environmental Politics, 12*(1), 115–136.

Zosel, T. (1990). *How 3M makes pollution prevention pay big dividends* (pp. 67–72). Winter: Pollution Prevention Review.

Chapter 9
Post-disaster Community Recovery and Community-Based Collaborative Action Research—A Case of Process Evaluation Method for Community Life Improvement

Takayoshi Kusago

Abstract Innovation is not an undoubted factor to solve various social and economic hardships and lead us to a more prosperous society. In fact, the Great East Japan Earthquake occurred on 11 March 2011 and shocked both Japan and the world with its scale and seriousness of the adverse impacts on human communities and living environment. The number of natural and man-made disasters continues to rise and create hardships in different parts of the world. It does reflect growing concern over a healthy planet and well-being of people and the members of the United Nations adopted sustainable development goals (SDGs) as the overarching development goal for all in 2015. SDGs state clearly in SDG 11 that we have to find ways to realize sustainable development at cities and communities. Although SDGs become a set of common global development goals, it has never been an easy task to overcome such an adversity and find a way to restore and revitalize communities in any of the post-disaster period. The government assistance is necessary to rebuild basic infrastructure and social services for any community. However, it is not sufficient enough to provide assistance only from outside to recover and rebuild the damaged community. A critical challenge is whether a community building could be sustainable in the long run. The community's recovery and reconstruction require local people's voices, community's future vision by identifying and using local assets and resources. For that end, stakeholders' autonomous endogenous initiatives play a vital role. In this context, collaboration between stakeholders and experts is needed, and community-based collaborative action research has gradually received serious attention as a practical research method. In 2004, *Chuetsu* earthquake occurred and damaged communities in Niigata prefecture in Japan. In the process of a long-run recovery and revitalization of a small community in the area of the epicenter of the earthquake, a team of researchers started collaborative action research with the local residents by applying a process evaluation method for community life improvement. This chapter focuses on the issues of sustainable community development through an experiment of the process evaluation method as a community-based collaborative

---

T. Kusago (✉)
Kansai University, Osaka, Japan
e-mail: tkusago@kansai-u.ac.jp

© Springer Nature Singapore Pte Ltd. 2019
S. Lechevalier (ed.), *Innovation Beyond Technology*, Creative Economy,
https://doi.org/10.1007/978-981-13-9053-1_9

action research. We discuss effectiveness of community-based collaborative action research as co-creative method, which can promote public participation in scientific development and innovation.

9.1 Introduction

Innovation has been recognized as an important factor for any nations to achieve social and economic development. However, we need to be careful to design a development plan and apply innovative technology to improve people's well-being and maintain environment. This has been a challenge and highly industrialized countries, including France and Japan, have not done well on this regard as Pestre (2019) has argued. Then, a big question is that how we transform our stance over innovation from an undoubted determinant for progress to a factor requiring delicate handling, as Oki (2019) has discussed the change in the meaning of innovation in the context of social and economic progress. If we accept a more nuanced treatment on innovation, we have to find a concrete action and practice to transform the conventional development discourse into the one in line with a balanced development outcome consistent with SDGs.

In the field of development, development experts have pointed out that we have to rethink the conventional model of social and economic development. There may be various reasons for this, but one is that economic growth does not necessarily assure the increase in people's well-being, as shown by Richard Easterlin in his seminal study on the economics of happiness (Easterlin 1974). Such a paradoxical situation is particularly noticeable in developed countries including Japan. We need to explore reasons why this paradox occurred, and relationships between the paradox and problems like pollution, depression, and suicide (Kusago 2007).

Another reason why we have to pay more attention to rethinking the conventional development model is related to growing concern over the worldwide environmental destruction, natural disasters related to climate change. In 2011, the Great East Japan Earthquake occurred on 11 March 2011 and shocked both Japan and the world with its scale and seriousness of the adverse impacts of the natural and human-made disaster on human communities and living environment. In 2015, for example, there was heavy flooding in southeastern Africa in January. In Vanuatu, there was a vast cyclone named "Pam." In Nepal, a massive earthquake hard hit its capital city Kathmandu. Then heat waves from India to Pakistan, floods in Pakistan and forest fires occurred in Canada in July. Earthquake in Chile and flooding in Japan in September. In November, forest fires in Australia and landslides in Myanmar occurred. These describe the tendency of recent years with increasing cases of natural calamities, which challenges us, human beings, to mitigate its adverse effects and stay resilient to deal with hardships and reconstruct our society.

Adverse effects of conventional development model and natural catastrophe put us to agree on sustainable development goals (SDGs) under the initiative of the United Nations (UN). SDGs consists of seventeen goals including economic well-being, education, and health, gender, and disability, a wide range of environmental issues. Among the seventeen goals, the goal number 11 targets sustainable cities and communities. If we pursue sustainable development set by SDGs, we need to find a concrete approach and action which leads us to attain societal development envisioned by SDGs at the community level.

In this chapter, we will first introduce sustainable livelihood approach as a reliable community-based development model in line with SDGs. We will explain community-based collaborative action research as an effective method to realize sustainable livelihood at the community level. Then, we will introduce a collaborative action research practice through a case of a process evaluation method for community life improvement experimented in a community devastated by the *Chuetsu* earthquake in *Niigata*, Japan in 2004. As Ruphy (2019) has detailed out the importance of citizen science and people's empowerment for innovation, we will conclude the chapter with the implication of the experiment over a potential of collaborative action research to transform our development path toward a sustainable future through people's autonomous action.

9.2 Importance of People's Well-Being and Sustainable Livelihoods Approach

SDGs have their overarching goal to realize a sustainable society and a healthy planet. SDGs aim at eradication of poverty, hunger zero, health, and welfare for all people, quality education for all, economic growth and job satisfaction, the creation of a sustainable, livable city, reduction of inequality among people and country, clean water, sea environmental protection and combatting climate change. All of the UN member countries have to design a local program to attain the goals by 2030. To achieve SDGs, people's action, as well as a well-designed local program, are needed to pursue high on overall people's well-being and sustainable community livelihood.

First, we need to understand why people's well-being is important. For a long time, economic measures have been used to assess and evaluate people's living conditions following a utilitarian approach advocated by Bentham (1988). In conventional economic thought, to maximize the economic aspect of well-being, a national government gives a high priority on expansion of industrial production and sets a target on GDP. However, after the 1970s, some economists (Easterlin 1974) started questioning if the economic aspect alone could indicate the real level of people's well-being correctly. In 1990, the United Nations Development Programme published its first human development report (United Nations Development Programme 1990) based on capability approach (Sen 1985); with a Human Development Index (HDI), which covers three essential elements of people's well-being: the economic aspect, knowledge and education, and health aspects. Various researches on happiness and well-being (Kahneman et al. 1999; Frey and Stutzer 2001; Graham 2009) began to receive more attention in the search for key elements of people's well-being. In 2007,

OECD launched the Global Project on Measuring the Progress of Societies, which covered multi-dimensional aspects of individual well-being. Also, we have known country-based initiatives like Bhutan's Gross National Happiness (GNH)[1] and the Canadian Index of Wellbeing (CIW)[2] as pioneering efforts in this direction. Besides these national-level measures, community-level measures are needed to search for innovative ideas to improve people's well-being since a local community is a place where people make a living on a daily basis.

Under the age of SDGs, we had to realize a sustainable, healthy community. Chambers and Conway (1991) have proposed an alternative local development approach to make the community sustainable. They call it the sustainable livelihoods approach and characterize it as "The objective of sustainable livelihoods for all provides a focus for anticipating the 21st century and points to priorities for policy and research. For the policy-making purpose, implications include personal environmental balance sheets for the better off, and for the poorer, policies and actions to enhance capabilities, improve equity, and increase social sustainability" (Chambers and Conway 1991: 1). We need to concretize the sustainable livelihoods approach so that it could be applicable in the real world. On this regard, Ashley and Carney (1999) put together six principles of sustainable livelihoods approach as follows:

- People-centred: sustainable poverty elimination will be achieved only if external support focuses on what matters to people, understands the differences between groups of people and works with them in a way that is congruent with their current livelihood strategies, social environment and ability to adapt.
- Responsive and participatory: poor people themselves must be key actors in identifying and addressing livelihood priorities. Outsiders need processes that enable them to listen and respond to the poor.
- Multi-level: poverty elimination is an enormous challenge that will be overcome only by working at several levels, ensuring that micro-level activity informs the development of policy and an effective enabling environment and that macro-level structures and processes support people to build upon their own strengths.
- Conducted in partnership: with both the public and the private sector.
- Sustainable: there are four key dimensions to sustainability—economic, institutional, social and environmental sustainability. All are important—a balance must be found between them.
- Dynamic: external support must recognise the dynamic nature of livelihood strategies, respond flexibly to changes in people's situation, and develop longer-term commitments. (Ashley and Carney 1999: 7)

The six principles tell us that the sustainable livelihoods approach aims at creating a community where sustainable living can be realized through the endogenous action

---

[1]Information on GNH can be found in http://www.grossnationalhappiness.com/ (accessed on 3 April 2019).

[2]Information on CIW can be found in https://uwaterloo.ca/canadian-index-wellbeing/ (accessed on 3 April 2019).

of community members. The six principles can be summarized into four keywords: ownership, autonomy, collaboration, and sustainability.

Then, we could raise some questions. Can we find out a good practice that leads to sustainable community development following the six principles? Would not it be possible to initiate such a practice by a collaboration of community stakeholders and experts? Collaborative action research could be a promising research method, which promotes community development through the collaboration of stakeholders by forming home-grown ideas and endogenous efforts.

9.3 Collaborative Action Research

Social science research has to deal with serious issues like poverty, community revitalization, the school bully, conflict resolution in this age of globalization. We have seen similar problems and challenges across nations and regions. However, solutions to tackle these problems are not always the same; rather, they require an understanding of uniqueness and characteristics of society, mainly because all of these are rooted deep in the complexity of social and economic systems influenced by a different set of local factors. Theoretical work does help to explain main reasons and impacts of these issues; furthermore it cannot provide timely response and action aiming at solving such issues. As Ruphy (2019) has explained, public participation and democratic decision in the adoption of a scientific solution are needed; action research could play an active role in finding a socially valid remedy or solution.

Action research has been developed to improve quality of human-related services such as community activities, social welfare, healthcare, and education (Herr and Anderson 2005). For instance, it aims at improvement of teaching in collaboration with students and effective provision of health services meeting needs of patients. However, action research could vary from problem to problem, and it needs to be modified and invented case by case. We call a type of action research as collaborative action research if researchers and actors (stakeholders) work together to solve a particular social problem. This chapter aims at sharing the importance of collaborative action research to improve people's livelihoods and well-being. Before we introduce the case of collaborative action research in Japan, it is important to review how collaborative action research has been developed, its definition and its key features.

9.3.1 Development of Action Research

The history of action research started with a social psychologist named Kurt Lewin in the USA. He studied social psychology, group activities and the construction of a democratic society at the University of Iowa. After coming to Cornell University from Iowa, he received a reputation as an action-oriented researcher, and he became director of the Center for Group Dynamics at Massachusetts Institute of Technology.

His main contribution was to introduce the concept of action research through his active engagement with minority groups. In 1946, he published a paper referring to action research, and he defined action research as a form of research activity which uses the analysis of the situation and influence of social activities to stimulate the emergence of future practices (Lewin 1946).

After Lewin, application of action research began in various fields, including education, medical, nursing, and social welfare. Indeed, Lewin had a great impact on its subsequent development (Herr and Anderson 2005; Reason and Bradbury-Huang 2013; Rowell et al. 2017). In addition to Lewin, other researchers who have contributed to the development of action research include John Dewey, Steven Corey, Paulo Freire, and Lawrence Stenhouse (Anderson et al. 1994). More people recognize action research through the contribution of researchers in various fields of specialization who pursued social practice or research that could benefit society. Nevertheless, it was through the enthusiasm and the long process of trial and error of those who challenged to improve society by removing its obstacles, which consolidate the basis of action research. In other words, action research did not emerge and develop as a fabrication of researchers, but as an organic outcome of social practice and social demand.

9.3.2 Definition and Key Features of Collaborative Action Research

9.3.2.1 Definition

An all-inclusive definition of action research is difficult to give, considering the wide variety of reasons and trajectories in its development in each particular academic field. This section will present several definitions proposed by researchers in the fields where action research was formulated and advanced, such as psychology, pedagogy, and organizational theory.

McKernan, a psychologist, writes that action research is "a form of self-reflective problem solving, which enables practitioners to understand better and solve pressing problems in social settings" (McKernan 1991). In the field of education, the definition advocated by Kemmis and McTaggart stresses "collaboration" for the improvement of social practices as a necessary identifying feature of action research, in addition to the self-reflective processes undertaken by practitioners (Kemmis and McTaggart 1982). For Elliot and Keynes, action research is a form of inquiry performed by participants in social situations to improve those situations from within (Elliot and Keynes 1991). From the standpoint of organizational theory, Argyris and Schon emphasized action research as a form of action science that makes use of "intervening social experiments" (Argyris and Schon 1978).

Stringer, who engaged in action research for community-building, defined action research as the provision of support for problem-solving within a group, community

9 Post-disaster Community Recovery and Community-Based ...

or organization, by enhancing the members' capacity to grasp their situation and enabling them to reach their solutions (Stringer 1999; McNiff 2013). According to Stringer (1999), community-based action research has strength as follows:

> Community-based action research works on the assumption, therefore, that all stakeholders—those whose lives are affected by the problem under study—should be engaged in the processes of investigation. Stakeholders participate in the process of rigorous inquiry, acquiring information (collecting data) and reflecting on that information (analyzing) to transform their understanding of the nature of the problem under investigation (theorizing). This new set of understandings is applied to plans for resolution of the problem (action), which, in turn, provides the context for a testing hypothesis derived from group theorizing (evaluation). Collaborative exploration helps practitioners, agency workers, client groups, and other stakeholding parties to develop increasingly sophisticated understandings of the problems and issues that confront them. As they rigorously explore and reflect on their situation together, they can repudiate social myths, misconceptions, and misrepresentations and formulate more constructive analyses of their situation. By sharing their diverse knowledge and experience—expert, professional, and lay—stakeholders can create solutions to their problems and, in the process, improve the quality of their community life. (Stringer 1999: 10)

In this way, it can be seen that the differences in the researchers' fields of specialization and focuses correspond to differences in the way they formulate their definitions and in the weight attached to various aspects. Nevertheless, one feature shared by all the above definitions is their emphasis on "action research as a series of research activities aiming to improve social practice by empowering stakeholders." Based on this assumption, following Stringer's definition, the author has defined collaborative action research as follows:

> Collaborative action research deals with issues raised by (practitioners) of an organization or community and researchers collaborate with the stakeholders on the issue and work together to identify its remedy or solution. Collaborative action research continuously conducts a series of activities from finding, implementing and testing solutions, as well as in making adjustments to the content of practice activities, and reflection for improvement.

9.3.2.2 Features of Collaborative Action Research

Distinctive features of collaborative action research can be summarized in four points. First, it is a practical research method to change the quality of society. In other words, collaborative action research aims at inducing endogenous action among stakeholders of an organization or a community to improve the performance of the organization or the level of people's well-being. Given that action research stems from, is conducted within, and is immediately applied to social practice, there is a growing need for it in an increasingly diverse society. The demand for collaborative action research is particularly high in fields such as school education, healthcare, nursing and urban development. In collaborative action research, researchers and practitioners cooperate towards a shared objective, benefiting from the mutual knowledge and putting it into practice. In other words, collaborative action research is a "societal evolutionary approach based on knowledge-sharing and linked with practice." Its uniqueness lies in its emphasis on societal change through the improvement of the real world. This awareness of societal change and societal evolution represents a characteristic missing from the traditional approach of positivist research, which attaches importance to political neutrality.

The second is that collaborative action research needs to be interdisciplinary. It is impossible for everyone to understand social issues from sociological perspectives and knowledge alone. Let's take a case of Japanese schools receiving international (non-Japanese) students. Some of the issues targeted by action research can be handled by an individual stakeholder; other issues require collaborative efforts among stakeholders. The former category includes initiatives such as the improvement of a certain teacher's teaching methods at the classroom level, while the development of educational strategies for international students at the level of the entire school would fall under the latter. When considering the education of international students who cannot communicate in Japanese, what sort of activities would emerge if all the team members were Japanese language education experts? Research meetings would probably become a forum for discussing the teaching method relevant for Japanese language classes, and theories and practices of Japanese language education would be studied. Then, the meeting would probably end with the selection of activities to be used in Japanese language classes for international students. Educational activities centered on Japanese language acquisition are crucial to equip the children with the necessary skills to receive education in a Japanese school. However, there are cases in which school attendance becomes a problem for international students because of factors unique to each student including living conditions and ethnic or cultural. In such situations, discussion and formulation of measures to improve teaching methodology at the class cannot solve all the problems inherent in the education of international students. Satisfactory outcomes cannot be produced only by focusing on theories and practices of Japanese language education. While a research team consisting only of researchers and practitioners (teachers, etc.) belonging to the same field may have the advantage of a deep insight into the nature of the problem, supported by a high level of specialization, there must be some risk in that such team composition might actually limit effectiveness of teaching methods and activities proposed for addressing the respective issue. In contrast, collaborative action research provides a framework for researchers and practitioners to act as partners who consider and evaluate teaching actions in close collaboration. While its grasp may be broad rather than deep, action research is expected to analyze and examine practice from a diverse and multifaceted perspective, to propose improvement taking into consideration the practitioners' perspectives, to provide advice on introduction of experiments, and to indicate evaluation and feedback methods for practice. To effectively address issues related to teaching method used in the class for international students, the research team should consist of experts in various fields ranging from Japanese language education, educational curriculum, foreign languages and cultures, counseling, and others. Collaborative action research does not necessarily seek to prove whether advanced theory developed within a narrow field of specialization, but to realize the improvement of student's performance. Therefore, it is characterized by an "interdisciplinary style," deriving from the broad use of knowledge across a variety of

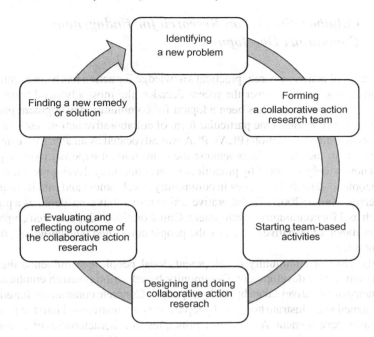

Fig. 9.1 Cycle of collaborative action research

fields, rather than by the fusion of narrowly-focused but deeply rooted specializations (Herr and Anderson 2005; Reason and Bradbury-Huang 2013). In the case of community development, the ultimate goal is to increase the level of overall well-being of the community members. It does require different realms of one's livelihood from economic, social, political, environmental, psychological, medical, and so on.

Third, collaborative action research applies participatory research method and existing social research methods like quantitative and qualitative methods of data analysis such as questionnaire survey or interview. Collaborative action research should utilize scientific evidence to assist the stakeholders in any stage of research investigation and reflection.

Fourth, dynamism among the collaborative action research team is extremely important from planning, action, and fact-finding of the action research. Looking at the illustration of Fig. 9.1, similar to what Lewin calls cyclical process (Lewin 1946), we begin with identifying a new issue and form a collaborative action research team. After designing action research, the team collaborates on designed research. Sharing outcomes after evaluating and to reflect on action research activities and once new recommendations or ideas were made to improve the activities, it will lead to a new phase of taking action dealing with another issue. In other words, it assumes that things always do evolve and the process of the collaboration becomes a critical factor for collaborative action research. Thus, such a cyclical aspect constitutes the core of the collaborative action research method.

9.3.3 Collaborative Action Research for Endogenous Community Development

For decades of action research, practical knowledge for action has been accumulated to improve one's action. Over the recent decades, the most advanced form of collaborative action research has been adopted for community development programs in developing countries. One particular form of collaborative action research is participatory learning and action (PLA). PLA was advocated as an alternative approach involving with the stakeholders against the conventional experts-driven approach. PLA is now widely accepted by practitioners on community development and assists local people to identify key issues in community development and find its remedy by themselves (Kumar 2002). Collaborative action research is considered as a powerful research tool for community development. Collaborative action research emphasized the importance of initiatives taken by the people concerned (stakeholders), over the relevant issue.

In the case of community development, local people can influence the direction of community development. Community-based action research emphasizes the importance of initiatives taken by the local people. Concrete community-based action research methods illustrate how local people can be mainstreamed into the process of community development. A set of core principles and characteristics of community-based action research are summarized by Minkler and Wallerstein, who are pioneers in community-based participatory research, as follows:

- It is participatory
- It is cooperative, engaging community members and researchers in a joint process in which both contribute equally
- It is a co-learning process
- It involves systems development and local community capacity building
- It is an empowering process through which participants can increase control over their lives
- It achieves a balance between research and action (Minkler and Wallerstein 2008: 9)

In the case of community development, local people should become a change agent of their community, which is in line with endogenous development theory proposed by Kazuko Tsurumi, a Japanese sociologist (Tsurumi 1996). To understand the importance of endogenous development for community development, we can learn from the recovery process of the city of Minamata from an industrial pollution city to a leading environmental model city through the invention of neighborhood study method (Yoshimoto 2008).

In the city of Minamata severely damaged by the Minamata Disease (organic mercury poisoning caused by the discharge of contaminated water from a chemical company), community restoration was the daunting task for decades. Besides the Minamata disease problem, communities in the mountainous area faced aging and depopulation problems. Many residents, especially young ones, left and the average

age of the local people went up. Because this trend continued for a long time, those who remain in the communities have accepted the notion of the demise of their rural community as a fate. However, in the 1990s, the local city office and a group of community members of a small community in Minamata started "neighborhood study method" to revitalize it. The neighborhood study method is to operate a community as a living museum once the community declares its environmental policy specific to the community. For example, keeping clean river and water in the community and respecting nature are included in the community-made policy. After the opening of the whole village as a living museum, visitors, who mostly come from big cities to the community can explore freely any part of the community with a local curator. The local curator has to walk together with them and respond any inquiries they ask. Interestingly, the local curator receives many questions over local things (houses, food, woods, plants, a way of life) taken for granted by him which influence the curator's mindset on the local community. This neighborhood walk allows local curators to rediscover local resources through the interaction with the outsider. For the visitor, this community walk gives a chance to accept a value of rural community life and rethink of their way of life in the urban center.

This method is to create an opportunity for local people to interact with people from outside of the community. It comes with the initiation of a collaborative action among the stakeholders of the community by exposing perspectives different from theirs. With the adoption of this method, the number of visitors attracted by the uniqueness of local resources and way of life to the community increased. Through the interactions, local people's views on their community drastically changed from negative to positive. Over the decade of continuous effort with the neighborhood study method, a group of women recognized the value of local agricultural products and they successfully developed a locally produced food business process. It has made the local people reflect their community from the eyes of the outsiders and encouraged them to take actions to change their community. In a nutshell, the neighborhood study method is to learn something from a local way of life. Outsiders are the key for local people to be aware of elements of people's well-being in local life and act for the progress of their own community from planning, implementation, reflection, and improvement.

9.4 Process Evaluation Method for Community Life Improvement

Process evaluation method was invented by a joint team of researchers and residents of a small village in the *Niigata* prefecture in Japan. In this section, we look at the purpose and outline of the process evaluation method before we introduce its application into the community.

The process evaluation method for community life improvement induces local people's own ideas and actions over measures to improve their community life and their living conditions. With the adoption of this method, local people can evaluate the present situation of their local community, and identify what needs to be maintained/changed in the community. In this manner, local people can modify community development activities to improve the conditions of their own lives in their communities.

Before exploring the mechanism of this method, it is important to explain how unique the process evaluation method for community development is by comparing it to conventional research method.

As shown in Fig. 9.2, in conventional research method, researchers conduct community assessment with scientific tools such as questionnaire surveys and analysis of objective data collected by the government. On the other hand, in the case of the process evaluation method for the improvement of community life, researchers collaborate with local people in a horizontal relationship. The process evaluation method finds facts using surveys, interviews and community meetings. Various aspects of gathered community data are given back to local people for community-based discussion and to make concrete actions for community development. For this reason, an interdisciplinary approach needs to be incorporated into the process evaluation method. Local people play an active and positive role in the process evaluation method although they are seen as inactive and passive in the conventional research method. In this sense, there is a clear difference in research methodology between the two. The conventional method relies heavily on assessment of a community's living conditions measured by data with economic and social indicators. On the other hand, the process evaluation method strives to trace an economic and social change of the community by utilizing not only extensive data on basic local living conditions but also on the people's subjective satisfaction and evaluation from the vantage point of local people trying to realize sustainable community development. Differences can also be found in the style of outputs. The process evaluation method for the improvement of community life does not end by publishing and reviewing academic papers. Rather, the process evaluation method focuses on giving feedback to local people in community meetings and workshops, using community improvement proposals, and in providing action reports. In creating an implementation plan, the difference between the process evaluation method for the improvement of community life and the conventional research method is clear. The process evaluation method requires flexibility in implementation which allows different stakeholders of the community to adjust original plan and policy ideas to the process of community development.

Figure 9.3 illustrates the outline of this process evaluation method for improvement of community life. In the first stage of the evaluation process, an initial local life assessment survey is conducted. This baseline survey has been designed and implemented jointly by a team of researchers and local people, and the full results of the baseline assessment will be given back to the local people. After this survey is conducted, the locals discuss their present and future roles in their community, based on what they have learned from the survey. They can decide what kind of local activities are needed and what can be done to improve the condition of their community's life. To prepare the second survey, the researchers reexamine the survey questionnaire by consulting local people to check whether any revisions are needed.

	Conventional research method	Process evaluation method
Core members	Researchers/experts	Local people and researchers/experts
Role of researchers/experts	Plan and do research and one-way report from researchers/experts to local people	Plan and research in a team with local people, and mutual dialogue over research findings with local people
Role of stakeholders	Knowledge recipient Passive and inactive	Knowledge creator Positive and active
Methodology	Analysis and evaluation of objective data collected by the government	Fact-finding and analysis of community life conditions by tailor -made surveys and interviews, and conduct reflection and evaluation by workshops
Area of expertise	Particular field of discipline	Interdisciplinary
Research planning	Set a detailed research plan in advance	Design a general plan and flexibility in the research process
Output	Research articles, research reports and policy recommendations	Workshops and practical reports
Outcome	Accumulation of scientific knowledge and evidence	Local empowerment and autonomy

Fig. 9.2 Comparison of research methods. Figure 9.2 is a revised version of Fig. 9.1 in Kusago and Miyamoto (2014)

Once the survey tool is prepared, a second survey is conducted, and its results can be shared with local people again for further assessment of their own local community lives and activities, and once again, they can modify their activities to improve the local conditions of their lives further. This method repeats the cycle of conducting the community assessment survey and sharing its results with community members, who assist the locals in initiating proactive local action to improve their lives. This method, although it has commonality with the neighborhood study method discussed in the previous section in collaboration with local people, differs in that it puts a systematic bottom-up scheme in place for endogenous community development.

The key to this process evaluation method is to encourage local people to use the survey results to review both positive and negative outcomes of local community activities from various viewpoints of certain community members. If locals assess some community activities as positive, locals can think of a way(s) to maintain the positive activities; on the other hand, if they identify negative or weak activities, they

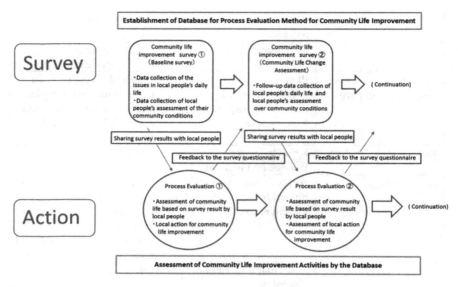

Fig. 9.3 System of process evaluation method for the improvement of community life

will have the opportunity to think of new ideas to correct negative situations. In the next section, we discuss the case of the Kizawa community in Niigata prefecture that has introduced this process evaluation method since 2010 to understand how it works in practice.

9.5 Practice of the Process Evaluation Method: The Case of the Kizawa Community

9.5.1 Needs for Rebuilding the Kizawa Community After the Earthquake

Kizawa is a mountainous community over 300 m high located in Kawaguchi district, Nagaoka city, Niigata prefecture. Kizawa receives some of the highest snowfall in Japan with approximately 3 m or more of snow each winter. On the 23rd of October, 2004, a huge earthquake called the Niigata Chuetsu earthquake struck the Chuetsu area in Niigata. Kizawa was the epicenter of the earthquake and suffered severe damage. Most houses were destroyed, and one senior woman was killed. Although the Kizawa community had had aging and depopulation issues like other Japanese rural areas even before the disaster occurred, the earthquake aggravated their problems. Just before the earthquake, 138 people and 52 households resided in Kizawa, but by

March 2014, after the earthquake, there were only 71 people and 33 households, and the percentage of people over 65 years old increased from 35 to over 50%.

In April 2006, local people in Kizawa formed a community-based organization called "Friendship Kizawa" to address the aging and depopulation issues. After the earthquake, Friendship Kizawa became active in restoring the community and many young volunteers, who were mainly university students from big cities outside Niigata prefecture, participated in these activities. The volunteers admired Kizawa's abundant local resources such as delicious rice and vegetables grown in the village, as well as the various types of edible wild plants and the beautiful landscape with a sea of clouds. The local people in Kizawa did not value their natural resources as highly as the outsiders because after living in the area for many years, they became indifferent to the beauty and abundance of the local resources. However, they gradually realized the richness of their local community through frequent interactions with the young volunteers.

Friendship Kizawa initiated to organize local events. For example, they started several tours such as "an edible wild plants tour" for visitors. They also developed a unique map of Kizawa which showed many of the local resources. In parallel with these events and activities, the locals convened workshops to discuss their future. Especially during winters of 2007 and 2008, they set goals and strategies to receive newcomers from the urban areas to revitalize their community. In April 2010, they finally decided to reuse the closed local elementary school as a municipal guest house, called *Yamaboushi*,[3] so that visitors could easily stay and enjoy the Kizawa community, and the local economy could get on its feet. When the research team[4] and the locals agreed to collaborate on the process evaluation method for the improvement of community life within the Kizawa community, Kizawa was faced with a new challenge; namely, how could they achieve sustainable community development with local resources?

9.5.2 Progress of the Process Evaluation Method in the Kizawa Community

The research team conducted fieldwork there since 2009 on the community's revitalization process.

In the Spring of 2010, the Kizawa community made an important transition by creating *Yamaboushi*. The operation of *Yamaboushi* was a challenge to the community organization already in place, Friendship Kizawa, because *Yamaboushi* is a trial to bring not only vitality but also sustainability to the community. *Yamaboushi* created jobs right in the Kizawa community so that local people could earn incomes in their community. *Yamaboushi* might be effective in bringing back to Kizawa out-migrated children who live nearby. It is hoped that Kizawa can utilize *Yamaboushi* to resolve

---

[3] *Yamaboushi* is the name of a locally grown tree.

[4] The team consists of two researchers (Miyamoto and Kusago 2014).

aging and depopulation issues which are not solved through frequent interactions with young volunteers.

The president and the vice president of Friendship Kizawa and a team of researchers including the author, informally met several times to exchange views on the future of the Kizawa community and shared the local people's concerns. The president and the vice president of Friendship Kizawa said that they wanted to check whether current activities including *Yamaboushi* can contribute to improving community life or not. The research team recognized the strong needs of this community to have a comprehensive assessment of the present situation of their community. The team and the local members agreed to collaborate by using the process evaluation method for the improvement of community life. The research team prepared the survey questionnaire in consultation with the key members of Friendship Kizawa (chairperson, vice-chairperson, and treasurer). The questionnaire consisted of individual attributes (age, gender, educational background, and experience of migrant work) and household characteristics (household structure, level of the household economy, and degree of housing damaged by the earthquake). It included subjective questions about well-being such as happiness and life satisfaction, anxiety and concern, assessment of institutions and organizations dealing with the Kizawa community, participation of the people of Kizawa in local events, and a general, freely descriptive part asking the locals about their favorite parts of Kizawa and where they would like to bring guests. The complete responses of the local people were considered, and the baseline survey was conducted in May 2010, and follow-up surveys were conducted in December 2010 and March 2013. In the Spring of 2012, the purpose of the process evaluation method and the result of the baseline survey were shared with the residents of Kizawa by distributing an article produced by Kusago and Miyamoto (2012) with detailed survey results. Furthermore, in August 2012, the research team conducted focus group interviews with local men and women and received the local people's views on the survey results and the process evaluation method itself. The views expressed in the interview meetings greatly helped the authors to modify the survey questionnaire for the second and the third follow-up surveys.

In November 2013, the research team and Friendship Kizawa co-hosted workshops based on the result of the third follow-up process evaluation survey. We conducted two workshops, one in the afternoon and the other in the evening. The number of participants in the afternoon workshop was seven (five men and two women) and in the evening workshop twenty (fifteen men and five women). Participants of this workshop included local people, the city office staff, and Kizawa community supporters. In the workshop, these groups shared their views on local living conditions in Kizawa by evaluating the pros and cons of Kizawa. In this way, the process evaluation method for the improvement of community life progressed as shown in Fig. 9.3. In the first step, the baseline survey was designed and conducted; in the second step, assessment of the baseline data by members of community was completed; in the third step, discussion and dialogue among local people about the conditions of their community based on the assessment was discussed; in the fourth step, reflections on local activities and continuation of local actions were done by the local people involved in the activities; and in the fifth step, the second survey was designed, and finally, in the sixth step, the whole cycle was repeated again.

9.5.3 Effectiveness of the Process Evaluation Method in the Kizawa Community

In this section, we review how effective the process evaluation method applied in the Kizawa community has been in improving local living conditions from the 1st survey in 2010 to the 3rd survey in 2013.

(1) Survey design and data gathering of the 1st and 3rd surveys

The research team formed a survey team with graduate students and local people and developed the initial survey questionnaire. In particular, we obtained advice from local people, such as what kind of questions were relevant to evaluate the living conditions of their community and the best format to use for the questionnaire. The team conducted all of the surveys door-to-door. The total number of local people who participated in the 1st and 3rd surveys was 36 men and 19 women, and the average age of the respondents was around seventy years old.

(2) Example of survey report and assessment of the local conditions of life through the process evaluation method in Kizawa

To illustrate what kind of reports were prepared by the research team, a part of the survey report made after the 3rd survey done in 2013 will be introduced below with key findings regarding local people's assessment of their quality of life and community conditions.

(a) Happiness and its determinants

Two questions were asked to capture the level of happiness and the elements of happiness of the Kizawa people.

1. What is your level of happiness between 0 (very unhappy) and 10 (very happy)?
2. Which things do you consider important when you think of your level of happiness? (choose all relevant)
    Household economy, Job, Health, Free time and leisure, Work/Hobby/Social Contribution,
    Family relations, Friendships, Working relations, Local community relations

These two questions were adopted from the National Survey on Lifestyle carried out by the Japanese Cabinet Office in 2009–2010. Figure 9.4 shows the results of the first questionnaire given on the level of happiness. The average level of happiness was 7.3 for the 1st survey and 6.9 for the 3rd survey. In the 3rd survey, people with a low level of happiness, 2 and 3, were identified, while there were none with these scores in the 1st survey.

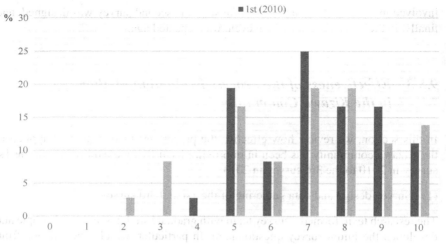

Fig. 9.4 Level of happiness among the Kizawa community people (N = 36, %)

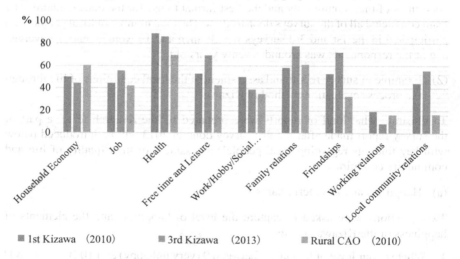

Fig. 9.5 Important items for community members' level of happiness. Data are from Kizawa surveys (2010, 2013) and National Survey on Lifestyle, Cabinet Office (CAO), Japan (2010) (N = 36, %)

Figure 9.5 shows the results of the question: *Which things do you consider important when you think of your level of happiness?*

The overall trend did not change much between the 1st and 3rd survey results. Health, family relations, friendship and household income, were considered important by many of the community people. Hobbies, social contributions, and human relationships at work were chosen as less important while jobs, free time and leisure, family relations, friendship, and local community relationships were chosen as more important. In the Kizawa community, between the 1st and the 3rd surveys, some respondents had retired from work and their community relations became more significant.

The comparison between the Kizawa survey data and the National Survey on Lifestyle data (Rural CAO data[5]) reveals the uniqueness of the Kizawa people in their perception of a happy life and a happy community. The CAO data shows that 16.7% of the respondents in rural communities in Japan considered local community relations as important, while more than 40% of the Kizawa people considered it as important. For the people in Kizawa, the local community itself was described as critical to maintaining their level of happiness. Over the two years from the 1st to the 3rd surveys, the number of local people who considered local community relations, friendships and family relations as an important factor went up. It suggests that after the earthquake the Kizawa community began to take on a more significant meaning, and the level of social capital grew year by year.

Next, the survey asked about a means to increase one's level of happiness as follows:

Please tell us effective measures to keep and increase the level of happiness by selecting one or two close to your thought.

Figure 9.6 shows the result of this question. The 1st and the 3rd survey results were not much different. The Kizawa people considered good relations with their own family the most important factor in keeping a high level of happiness, and a good relationship with their friends was considered equally important. If we compare the responses of Kizawa's local people to the national government survey responses (Rural CAO), it appears that the Kizawa people rely more on others than in the national average. The authors assumed that the Kizawa local people considered government support important because Kizawa was hit hard by the earthquake in 2004. However, the local people viewed local relations—family, neighbors, and friends—as being much more important than government support.

An open-ended question was also asked about the local people's perceptions of happiness: *what do you need for your happiness?* Changes in the local people's views about their happiness were illustrated by this question. We reported our analysis of the data obtained by the open-ended questions after we extracted keywords referred to by the Kizawa people. The most used keywords were "family" and "health." These most often used keywords were consistent with the results on the question for factors of happiness. In their free descriptions, the local people described how special the Kizawa community is for them. For instance, in the 3rd survey, local people expressed how special their relationships were with their friends in Kizawa. "Born in Kizawa. Always with my friends who went to school together. There are no strangers in this community, and I appreciate the strong bonds among us in Kizawa" (female, 80s).

Also, we asked the following open-ended question: *When was the happiest moment in your life?* For this question, we extracted keywords and learned that

---

[5]The Cabinet office data consists of urban and rural data. Since Kizawa is a small rural community, rural CAO data is relevant for comparison.

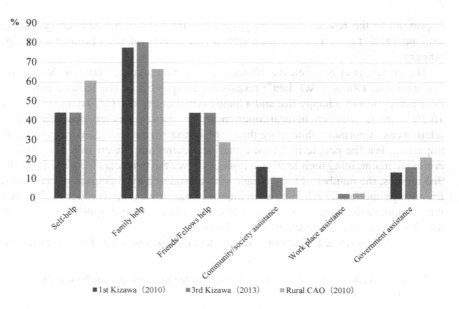

Fig. 9.6 Effective measures to increase the level of happiness Data are from Kizawa surveys (2010, 2013) and National Survey on Lifestyle, Cabinet Office (CAO), Japan (2010) (N = 36, %)

the most used keywords were health, self, and family. One respondent wrote "As long as I feel healthy, I can do anything I like to do. But, without health, money means nothing" (male, 60s). Another wrote, "Two of us as husband and wife can do farming together and help each other" (male, 60s), and "two of us can go anywhere and have money to eat out with our grandchildren" (female, 70s).

(b) Changes in happiness and life satisfaction according to age

Reporting changes in community life is a critical step in the process evaluation method because it helps local people assess the conditions of community life based on the data. The research team presented one survey outcome by showing the frequency distribution chart of the level of happiness with the ratio of the 3rd survey score divided by the 1st survey score according to age. Figure 9.7 shows the distribution of the level of happiness by age. It appears that the level of happiness of ages in the 60s, 70s, 80s and above changed little.

However, the age group of the 50s showed a drastic change from the 1st to the 3rd survey. The level of happiness went down to almost 0.6 (=60%) after the 1st survey was conducted. In the feedback session, this finding caught the local people's eyes, and they discussed why the level of happiness dropped so much in their 50s. They discussed issues related to the situations and issues surrounding local people in their 50s in Kizawa. Aging and depopulation problems have caused people in their 50s to still have to take on the responsibilities of young adults. They often had to take care

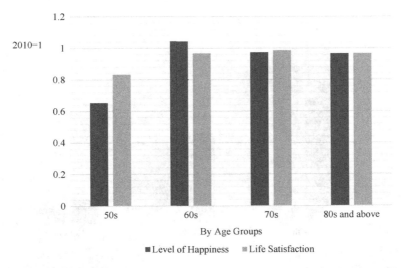

Fig. 9.7 Changes in the level of happiness and life satisfaction from 2010 to 2013 (By age group; 2010 = 1)

of older family members and attend various local activities besides working daily in their regular jobs.

(c) Anxiety and concern

The community life survey also asked a question about anxiety and concern. The question was phrased as follows: *Do you feel anxiety or concern in your daily life? If you do, please describe such anxiety or concerns?*

Figure 9.8 shows the anxiety and concern shared by some locals from Kizawa. Those who responded that they have anxiety or concerns was just above 60%. This percentage went up from the 1st to the 3rd survey. The local people were mostly concerned or anxious about their health or the health of their family. The research team applied coding analysis to the freely descriptive answers and found that many people worried about the possibility of living and being alone if her/his partner passes away. This concern does reflect a harsh reality of the Kizawa community. One local wrote, "In the future, one of us will die. When I think of that day, I am very much worried about my life" (female, 60s). In the 3rd survey, similar concerns were voiced.

(d) Evaluation of people's participation in community events

This process evaluation method aims at improving community life; thus, the method should evaluate the local people's interests and involvements in community activities. The team asked local people about the frequency of their participation in local events.

Figure 9.9 shows the percentage of local people who participated in major community events in 2013. The Kizawa community has three major events: a local field day, an informal get-together (assembly) with neighbors (*Yoriaikko*), and the Kizawa *Bon Odori* festival (dance honoring the spirits of one's ancestors). Local people are

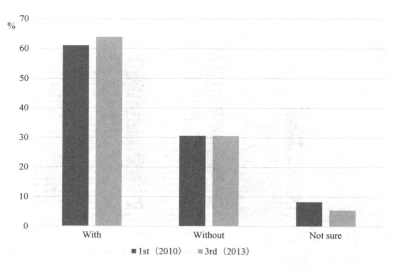

Fig. 9.8 Anxiety and concern (with and without) (N = 36, %)

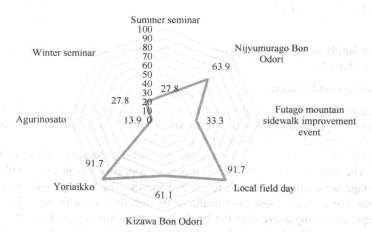

Fig. 9.9 Local participation in major community events (N = 36, %)

expected to participate in these events. The local field day started in 2004 as a continuation of the school's sports day event when the local elementary school was closed down. The *Yoriaikko* event started, before the 2004 earthquake, to create an opportunity to promote friendship among local people and also to celebrate the Autumn harvest. This festival requires local people to prepare local foods and run activities for the festival. The Kizawa *Bon Odori* festival has been run annually by the local community for generations.

Another *Bon Odori* festival in the area that includes the Kizawa community is the *Nijyumurago Bon Odori*. Four communities in *Nijyumurago* decided to form a joint *odori* committee after these communities also suffered devastation after the 2004 earthquake. Every four years, four different communities rotate hosting the festival.

The Kizawa community has organized the *Futago* mountain sidewalk improvement event. *Agurinosato* is a road-side station run by a local organization in the town of Kawaguchi, the nearest town to the Kizawa community, where local people can sell their agricultural products. Summer and winter festivals are retreats for visitors started by a group of university students who formed a supporting group to assist the recovery of the Kizawa community.

Figure 9.9 shows that more than 90% of the local people participated in both the local field day and *Yoriaikko*. Interestingly, the participation rate for the area-based *Nijyumurago Bon Odori* festival was higher than that for the Kizawa community's *Bon Odori* festival. The *Nijyumurago Bon Odori* festival is a new event that started as a symbol for recovery from the earthquake by promoting mutual assistance among the four communities. One community could not maintain its community-based *Bon Odori* because of the decrease in the local population. However, the start of the *Nijyumurago Bon Odori* offered hope for the residents in this community. The *Nijyumurago Bon Odori* has become a popular local event, and people in all of the four communities get along well with each other. This survey result reveals cultivation of a new local way of life which could go beyond the boundary of a single local community.

(3) Feedback sessions with local people

The research team prepared a report based on the survey results to share with local people. In November 2013, a feedback session at the Kizawa community was organized so that local people could learn the key findings of the process evaluation surveys. In this feedback session, local people, leaders of key local organizations, city office staff, and local NPOs supporting Kizawa participated and discussed Kizawa community life. The process evaluation method helped provide feedback to the community and encouraged the community to share ideas on their improvement. In the feedback session in the Kizawa community, opinions and ideas expressed by the participants were:

- Some local people did not know about new local businesses, such as running *Yamaboushi*, which exemplifies the importance of getting information out to the community.
- The survey data should be analyzed by individual attributes such as gender and age group, which would provide concrete measures for improving the Kizawa community and other communities.
- On a personal level as a member of the supporting agency for Kizawa, I found the information in this survey helpful in realizing how active the Kizawa people are in revitalizing their community after the earthquake.
- From the data, I was surprised to learn of the low level of happiness among local people in their 50s. I think we should act immediately to remedy this situation because it is a problem related to the future and well-being of the whole community.

Although the local people in Kizawa felt somewhat different extents of happiness amongst themselves, they didn't know that there was such a huge gap between people in their 50s and the other locals. These comments suggest that the local people in Kizawa have realized current pressing issues in their community and have felt a sense of urgency about them.

(4) Local action after the feedback session

One more important step of this process evaluation method is whether local people reflect what they have been working on to improve community life and initiate "concrete action" after the survey results are shared through a feedback meeting.

Surveys were conducted, and their results were shared among local people. In particular, key members of Friendship Kizawa and community association were informed of the situation of their community. After the feedback session, they started thinking of learning from other communities that have been successful in attracting people from outside their immediate community, and they discussed visits to such communities.

Also, in the Kizawa community, there was a young male intern who assisted the Friendship Kizawa in its operation of *Yamaboushi*, a municipal guest house, for one year from April 2013. Immediately after the meeting in November 2013, the intern proposed starting an informal gathering over informal food and drink to talk more about the community issues openly and candidly. This gathering started in late December 2013 and continued six times until March 2014. In one meeting, those who joined this gathering exchanged views about snow-removal, hardship in Kizawa, and set forth a concrete plan to revise the present snow-removal scheme to ease the burden on people in the 50s and under, which was revealed through the surveys. To this purpose, the meeting also invited a resource person from a neighboring community who had successfully utilized a public financial support scheme for snow-removal to study if the Kizawa community could apply for similar support. In this way, both reflections on the activities initiated by local people and discussions for future community-based actions have been spurred on by survey results and feedback sessions.

9.6 Collaborative Action Research as Co-Creating Social Innovation Method

This chapter has paid serious attention to development issues and sustainability in the context of SDGs. We have reviewed fundamental changes occurring at the international, national, and community levels, elaborating theoretical discussions on economic growth model and comprehensive well-being model.

We have highlighted sustainable livelihood approach as an effective tool to transform the core of development from economic growth to people's well-being. We have emphasized endogenous development approach as a key to implementing the sustainable livelihood approach. One challenge we have faced is how to find a way to work with autonomous initiatives of local people toward sustainable community development. Then, we have introduced collaborative action research as an effective tool to co-create sustainable community.

Collaborative action research is not top-down but bottom-up, which makes stakeholders as the core members of action research activities. It means that those who do design and implement action research are not limited to professional researchers. Rather, they include local people (community development case), teachers and students (school case), and clients and medical staff (hospital case). Then, the role of professional researchers is to participate actively in co-designing and co-learning activities through dialogue and collaboration with these stakeholder members.

We have reviewed the history and main features of collaborative action research and have discussed a collaborative action research method: Process Evaluation Method for Community Life Improvement. The process evaluation method has potential as a new tool for community development as seen in the case of the Kizawa community damaged by Chuetsu earthquake in 2004. This method assisted people of the Kizawa community in reflecting on both their accomplishments and needs in community recovery and reconstruction with the use of data, both objective and subjective, gathered and analyzed by qualitative and quantitative research tools. The process evaluation method has made local people in the Kizawa community assess the level of well-being and the living condition of the community.

The method is unique because it depends highly on local people's voluntary actions. The conventional approach to community revitalization is often a top-down solution which assumes that local people will follow the government's plans and instructions. In the case of the process evaluation method, if people do not take autonomous action to improve their community, change will not be sustainable. The process evaluation method cannot be effective without people's motivated actions, which push them to reflect, to discuss, and to find solutions to improve living conditions in their community. This method, although it includes the word "evaluation" in its name, is not used to determine if the local effort is a success or a failure in the way that external evaluation agencies usually do. Rather, it supports the local people to initiate actions addressing their problems and concerns to achieve a high level of community life. Moreover, the process evaluation method can be a co-creation tool which allows the bottom-up scheme to nurture knowledge and idea through mutual interactions among the stakeholders and researchers/experts.

The process evaluation method, an action research tool, has the potential to create a practical bridge between action researchers and experts, since the process evaluation if it is applied to a community setting, requires an extraordinary understanding of local resources regarding its social, economic, cultural, political and environmental aspects. The method can be viewed as a practical research tool which not only expands knowledge, but also encourages local people to learn actively, cultivate, and use the tool for sustainable development of their communities.

We also need to look at the potential and challenge of collaborative action research in future. As for the potential, it could change conventional way of research collaboration from experts-driven to flat-based. As a result, we could empower both collaborating researchers and practitioners/stakeholders. Researchers could widen and deepen understanding of a social issue from multiple angles, which enhance linkage between theory and practice. Stakeholders become equipped with alternative ways to examine issues they face, recognize strength and weakness, identify local resources, and so on. In other words, the collaborative action research can assist continuously evolving communities and institutions to make our society better.

To expand the number of communities and organizations that adopt collaborative action research, we need to secure funds for implementing the collaborative method and to receive supports from leaders of communities/organizations. If we want to convert a company or a community in its management style from top-down to bottom-up, a collaborative action research method could be effective. However, if the leaders of the company or the community do not buy into the idea, such change would not happen easily.

If we challenge and overcome such obstacles, collaborative action research could help us to lead people-initiated social innovation through co-learning and co-creation.

References

Anderson, G., Herr, K., & Nihlen, A. S. (1994). *Studying your own school: An educator's guide to qualitative practitioner research*. Corwin Press.

Argyris, C., & Schon, D. A. (1978). *Organizational learning: A theory action perspective*. Addison-Wesley.

Ashley, C., & Carney, D. (1999). *Sustainable livelihoods: Lessons from early experience*. London: Department for International Development.

Bentham, J. (1988). *A fragment on government, Cambridge texts in the history of political thought*. Cambridge University Press.

Chambers, R., & Conway, G. R. (1991). Sustainable rural livelihoods: Practical concepts for the 21st century. IDS Discussion Paper 296.

Easterlin, R. (1974). Does economic growth improve the human lot? In P. A. David & M. W. Reder (Eds.), *Nations and households in economic growth: Essays in Honor of Moses Abramovitz* (pp. 89–125). New York: Academic Press Inc.

Elliot, J., & Keynes, M. (1991). *Action research for educational change*. Open University Press.

Frey, B. S., & Stutzer, A. (2001). *Happiness and economics: How the economy and institutions affect human well-being*. Princeton University Press.

Graham, C. (2009). *Happiness around the world*. Oxford University Press.

Herr, K., & Anderson, G. L. (2005). *The action research dissertation*. SAGE.

Kahneman, D., Diener, E., & Schwarz, N. (1999). *Well-being*. The Russell Sage Foundation.

Kemmis, S., & McTaggart, R. (Eds.). (1982). *The action research planner*. Deakin University Press.

Kumar, S. (2002). *Methods for community participation*. Vistaar Publications.

Kusago, T. (2007). Rethinking of economic growth and life satisfaction in post-WWII Japan? A fresh approach. *Social Indicators Research, 81*(1), 79–102.

Kusago, T., & Miyamoto, T. (2012). Jyuminniyoru chiikiseikatsu purosesu hyokashuhou no kokorom: niigataken nagaokashi kawaguchi kizawa chiki no donyujirei (Community life process evaluation method: A pilot case study in Kawaguchi-Kizawa, Nagaoka, Niigata, Japan). *Journal of Kansai University Faculty of Sociology, 43*(2), 33–60.

Kusago, T., & Miyamoto, T. (2014). The potential for community-based action research for area studies: A process evaluation method for the improvement of community life. *Psychologia, 57*(4), 275–294.

Lewin, K. (1946). Action research and minority problems. *Journal of Social Issues, 2*(4), 34–46.

McKernan, J. (1991). *Curriculum action research: A handbook of methods and resources for the reflective practitioner*. Kogan Page.

McNiff, J. (2013). *Action research* (3rd edn.). Routledge.

Minkler, M., & Wallerstein, N. (2008). *Community-based participatory research for health: From process to outcomes* (2nd edn.). Jossey-Bass.

Miyamoto, T., & Kusago, T. (2014). Jyuminshutai no saigaifukkou ni shisuru tiikiseikatsukaizen purosesu hyoukashuhou no yukousei: Niigataken nagaokashi kawaguchikizawa no jirei (Effectiveness of the process evaluation method for community life improvement to post-disaster reconstruction: A case study of Kawaguchi-Kizawa, Nagaoka, Niigata, Japan). *Journal of Disaster Recovery and Revitalization*.

Oki, S. (2019). 'Innovation' as an adaptation of 'Progress': Revisiting the epistemological and historical contexts of these terms. In S. Lechevalier (Ed.), *Innovation beyond technology* (pp. 47–62). Berlin: Springer.

Pestre, D. (2019). Environment and social innovation: Why technology never was the solution. In S. Lechevalier (Ed.), *Innovation beyond technology* (pp. 175–194). Berlin: Springer.

Reason, P., & Bradbury-Huang, H. (2013). *The SAGE handbook of action research: Participative inquiry and practice* (2nd edn.). SAGE.

Rowell, L., Bruce, C., Shosh, J. M., & Riel, M. (Eds.). (2017). *The Palgrave international handbook of action research*. Palgrave.

Ruphy, S. (2019). Public participation in the setting of research and innovation agenda: Virtues and challenges from a philosophical perspective. In S. Lechevalier (Ed.), *Innovation beyond technology* (pp. 243–261). Berlin: Springer.

Sen, A. K. (1985). *Commodities and capabilities*. Oxford University Press.

Stringer, E. T. (1999). *Action research* (2nd edn.). SAGE.

Tsurumi, K. (1996) *Naihatsuteki hatten ron no tenkai (Study on endogenous development)*. Chikumashobo.

United Nations Development Programme (1990). *Human development report*. Oxford University Press.

Yoshimoto, T. (2008). *Jimotogaku wo hajimeyo (Let us start neighborhood study method)*. Iwanami Junior Shinsho.

Chapter 10
Lessons from Fukushima for Responsible Innovation: How to Construct a New Relationship Between Science and Society?

Yuko Fujigaki

Abstract The present study focuses on a relationship between NPPs (Nuclear Power Plants) and society in Japan relating to the Fukushima Daiichi Nuclear Accidents in March 2011. Analyzing the process through which NPPs are embedded in political, economic and social contexts in Japan, it is revealed that community-divide was established between sites that accepted NPPs before the 1970s and sites without NPPs. After the accidents, this community-divide expanded between these sites as well as within each site. How can the Japanese society bridge this community-divide for responsible innovation regarding to the future energy? Focusing on the National Diet Report, I will show the recommendation the report made in 2012 and will introduce the Cabinet Office's reaction reports of 2017. After these analyses, I look into these recommendations and reactions in the context of Responsible Research and Innovation (RRI). RRI implies that societal actors work together during the whole research and innovation process (Horizon 2020). Based on the essence of the RRI, such as (1) Open up questions, (2) Mutual discussions, and (3) New-institutionalization, the present situation of Japanese NPPs are examined. Through this analysis, this paper shows one example of governance, public engagement and inclusion in the responsible R&D and Innovation process, dealing with Fukushima NPP accidents. These are "societal and institutional innovations" for the future.

10.1 Introduction

The definition of innovation is "a new idea, method, or invention" or "introduction of new things[1]". Therefore, innovation beyond technology includes institutional innovation. At the same time, social protests are considered as a driving force of innovation. The present study focuses on a relationship between NPPs and society in Japan relating to the Fukushima Daiichi Nuclear Accidents in March 2011. An

---

[1] Longman dictionary of contemporary English, 1987.

Y. Fujigaki (✉)
The University of Tokyo, Tokyo, Japan
e-mail: fujigaki@idea.c.u-tokyo.ac.jp

© Springer Nature Singapore Pte Ltd. 2019
S. Lechevalier (ed.), *Innovation Beyond Technology*, Creative Economy,
https://doi.org/10.1007/978-981-13-9053-1_10

earthquake on March 11, 2011, triggered a large tsunami along the east coast of Japan, which damaged the cooling system of the Fukushima-Daiichi nuclear power plant and led to a hydro-explosion of the plant's core. This accident became a key event that made the Japanese society consider responsible innovation, that is, the rebuilding of the relationship between NPP, society and new institutional innovation for regulation.

First, the present study analyzes the process through which NPPs are embedded in political, economic and social contexts in Japan, focusing on the attempted siting of NPP by several municipalities as well as protests and refusals of NPP. Why do these two different directions co-exist in society? How did these two communities co-develop after Fukushima accidents? Using historical analysis before Fukushima accidents and communication analysis after the accidents, I will describe the relationship between NPPs (Nuclear Power Plants) and society.

Second, the present study surveys institutional facet for NPP regulation. After the accident, three reports had been published in 2012. The first one is by National Diet (National Diet official report of Fukushima nuclear accident independent investigation commission 2012), second one is by Cabinet Office (Cabinet Office Investigation Committee on the Accident at the Fukushima Nuclear Power Stations 2012), and the third one is by an independent organization (Independent Investigation Commission on the Fukushima Daiichi Nuclear Accident 2012). The present study focuses on the National Diet Report on this triple disaster (earthquake, tsunami, NPP accident), and will show the recommendations issued by the 2012 report, comparing them to the reaction reports issued by Cabinet Office in 2017.

After these analyses, I look into the relationships between NPP and society, and institutional innovation on NPP governance, integrating historical analysis, communication analysis and institutional reports analysis. Based on the essence of the RRI, such as (1) Open up questions, (2) Mutual discussions, and (3) New-institutionalization, the present situation of Japanese NPP is examined. Through these analyses, this paper shows one example of governance, public engagement and inclusion in the responsible R&D and Innovation process, dealing with Fukushima NPP accidents. As Pierre-Benoit Joly (2019) indicated, there are three literature streams in innovation study. The present study focuses on responsible innovation among these three streams.

10.2 Historical Analysis of the Relationship Between NPP and Society

10.2.1 Community-Divides Between Sites After WWII

How are NPPs embedded in political, economic and social contexts in Japan? After the atomic bombs detonated in Hiroshima and Nagasaki in August 1945 and U.S. President Eisenhower's address on "Atoms for Peace" in December 1953, the

Japanese Diet enacted the basic law for nuclear power in 1955. In the 1950s, nuclear power was a kind of dreamy media for Japan's come-back story after World War II and the government succeeded in siting nuclear power plants. In the construction process of nuclear power plants, the residents' "dream for regional developments" and the central government system's "dream for independence of the resource supply of Japan" led the two parties to cooperate[2] (Kainuma 2011). By 1970, the government's attempted siting of nuclear power plants succeeded in 17 regions (e.g., Fukushima, Fukui, Kashiwazaki-kariwa); however, at the beginning of the 1970s, under the influence of global environmental movements, anti-nuclear activities gained momentum in Japan, and many residents began to resist plant construction. As a result, Japan experienced a community-divide of promoters and opponents of nuclear power plants after 1970.

The pronuclear government, facing many anti-nuclear activities after 1970, promoted strategically concentrating nuclear power reactors in the sites where residents had already accepted nuclear power before 1970. At such sites, "fundamental problems and issues, which would have hampered progress, were ignored, downplayed, neglected or shunted aside" (Juraku 2013: 52). Instead, pronuclear supporters focused on the local economic benefit and development through subsidies (e.g., Dengen Sanpou Ko-fu-Kin Seido, which means a law on electricity to provide subsidies to local governments that support the generation of electricity). At these sites, any problems posed were seen as being manageable; therefore, residents came to believe that problematic safety factors would never become critical issues. On the contrary, citizens who lived in different areas did not see those problems as manageable and did not believe that safety factors would never become a critical issue. In this way, social community-divide on the basis of safety issues arose between residents in sites with nuclear power plants and those without them.

Thus, pronuclear individuals who benefitted from institutional politics to enhance economic development using subsidies at sites with nuclear power plants used strategic agenda-setting to successfully promote the safety statements at these sites, segregating between pronuclear and anti-nuclear citizens. With this social community-divide, nuclear power plants are embedded in political, economic, and social contexts in Japan. In Japanese society, anti-nuclear activities existed, but their power did not reach to the sites with nuclear power plants. The strong community-divide between pro- and anti-nuclear power activities developed in parallel with community-divide in statements on the safety of nuclear power. The Fukushima accident in 2011 occurred within this situation.

The above explanation on community-divide gave us some insights into several points. First, whereas the "precautionary principle" had an effect on environmental problems of chemical contamination like the Itai-itai disease case (Cadmium pollution) (Kaji 2015), this principle coming from the environmental field could not reach the sites with nuclear power plants. The reasons were: atomic power was promoted in the "atoms for peace" context and any problems posed were seen as being

---

[2]Hecht (2009) indicated that in French case, nuclear program epitomized the link between French radiance and technological prowess, which was also linked to national identity.

manageable at these sites, as I described above. Second, public engagement and the construction of the public sphere were not enough in the field of nuclear power plants because of the community-divide mentioned above. Why were the points that came to light after the controversy in the administrative lawsuit, for example, the lawsuit on the Monjyu prototype fast-breeder reactor (Fujigaki 2009; Kobayashi and Kusafuka 2015)—that is, the lack of public engagement—not applied to nuclear power safety discussions or risk communication after the lawsuit? The reason is the existence of community-divide. For example, the Japanese government (specifically) approved the establishment of the Monjyu nuclear power plant in the Tsuruga District, Fukui Prefecture, in May 1983. In response, residents began legal action against the government in September 1985. Although any problems posed were seen as being manageable at sites with nuclear power plants in areas that had accepted nuclear before the 1970s, the local residents who brought the Monjyu lawsuit did not believe the "manageable" or safety myth. Therefore, residents who pursued legal action against the government in the 1980s did not have the same safety beliefs as residents who accepted the nuclear power plants before the 1970s. The former's skepticism did not reach to the latter's belief and could not deconstruct the belief. Third, the new relationship between science, technology, and society resulted in new technology fields like food science or information technology; however, the new relationship has had little effect on the historically-rigidly constructed relationship in the field of nuclear energy (Fujigaki and Tsukahara 2011; Fujigaki 2015). The reason and basis for this "rigidness" is the community-divide mentioned above. That kind of community-divide makes mutual discussions impossible, and the "public sphere" for constructing new relationships can hardly become a reality.

10.2.2 Community-Divide After the Accident

How did the community-divide between sites develop or change after the accidents? First, new community-divide developed within the sites with nuclear power plants. It is not hard to imagine how these residents felt when their belief in safety was shattered after the nuclear power plant accidents. Some people lost trust in authorities (engineers and policy-makers), while other people tried to keep their trust in authorities. To explain these situations better, I will introduce a salient value similarity (SVS) model as follows.

The SVS model postulates that shared values determine social trust in institutions and persons related to a technology (Siegrist et al. 2000). In this model, if an individual thinks that the person in front of him/her shares similar salient values with him/her, then he/she will trust that person. Therefore, one who holds the salient value to ease the public's worry trusts other people who hold the salient value to ease the public's worry. Likewise, one who holds the salient value to open neutral data trusts other people who hold the salient value to open neutral data. The same holds true for those who wish to abolish nuclear power. In the Fukushima case, some local governments and citizens still support nuclear and other citizens do not. In this way, one trusts people who hold similar salient values, and this tendency accelerates the community-divide of groups that have different salient values.

Within the sites with nuclear power plants, as I described, some people lost trust in authorities (engineers and policy-makers), while other people tried to keep their trust in authorities. Applying the SVS model, one who holds the salient value to want to know impartial, non-partisan information trusts other people who hold the salient value to want to know impartial, non-partisan information. On the contrary, one who holds the salient value to ease the public's worry trusts other people who hold the same salient value. This kind of community-divide was pushed forward by their decision-making on whether to stay in the land of their birth or to evacuate to other prefectures. Thus, new community-divides developed within the sites.

At the same time, residents who lived in sites without nuclear power plants also lost trust in specialists and the government since these authorities released only one-sided safety information after the accidents. One who holds the salient value to abolish nuclear power trusts other people who hold the salient value to abolish nuclear power. This distinction accelerated the community-divide between sites with nuclear power plants and sites without them. Social trust toward international agencies (e.g., International Atomic Energy Agency (IAEA)) was also divided: some people clung to the hope that the IAEA would bring the Japanese government toward the right direction. On the contrary, others criticized the IAEA as the organization that enhanced the nuclear energy generation (Shimazono 2013; Watanuki 2012). In this way, the communication disaster after the accidents accelerated the segmentation of the Japanese society.

This fragmentation of the society makes attempts to survey Fukushima residents' health difficult. In doctor–patient communication, both parties can easily share the salient value of fighting the disease or of improving the quality of life. However, in doctor–public communication, there are so many different salient values, and doctors seldom share their salient values with the public. For example, in a crisis, the doctors tend to try to avert panic or to ease the public's worry, while the public—presumably suffering from radiation—wants to abolish nuclear power. Thus, in doctor–public communication, the doctor and the public rarely share salient values; therefore, it is very difficult to build trust among them. Several doctors in the Fukushima Medical University (FMU) noted this situation (FMU-IAEA 2013, 2014).

In this way, we can see that community-divide has expanded after the Fukushima accident. How can we bridge these community-divides to prevent the next disaster? Before pursuing an answer to this question, I will focus on institutional facet.

10.3 Institutional Analysis

In this section, I will focus on the institutional facet of NPP regulation through reports analysis. Many reports and statements have been produced over the last 6 years on triple disasters. Did these reports trigger some change in Japanese society? This paper verifies the countermeasures to these disasters by Japanese government focusing on the National Diet Report. I will show the report's recommendations in Sect. 10.3.1 first, and then will introduce in Sect. 10.3.2 the Cabinet Office's 2017 reaction reports to National Diet Reports. Note that these recommendations and reaction reports are issued in a political context that promotes the restart of nuclear plants after they were stopped for several years.

10.3.1 Recommendations by the National Diet Report

The National Diet Report (2012) proposed 7 recommendations based on the analysis of the NPP accidents as follows.

Recommendation 1: Monitoring of the Nuclear Regulatory Body by the National Diet
A permanent committee to deal with issues regarding nuclear power must be established in the National Diet in order to supervise the regulators to secure the safety of the public.[3]

Recommendation 2: Reforming the Crisis Management System
A fundamental reexamination of the crisis management system must be made. The boundaries dividing the responsibilities of the national and local governments and the operators must be made clear.[4]

Recommendation 3: Government Responsibility for Public Health and Welfare
Regarding the responsibility to protect public health, three points must be implemented as soon as possible.[5]

---

[3]Its responsibilities should be: (1) To conduct regular investigations and explanatory hearings of regulatory agencies, academics and stakeholders. (2) To establish an advisory body, including independent experts with a global perspective, to keep the committee's knowledge updated in its dealings with regulators. (3) To continue investigations on other relevant issues. (4) To make regular reports on their activities and the implementation of their recommendations.

[4]This includes: (1) A reexamination of the crisis management structure of the government. A structure must be established with a consolidated chain of command and the power to deal with emergency situations. (2) National and local governments must bear responsibility for the response to off-site radiation release. They must act with public health and safety as the priority. (3) The operator must assume responsibility for on-site accident response, including the halting of operations, and reactor cooling and containment.

[5](1) A system must be established to deal with long-term public health effects, including stress-related illness. Medical diagnosis and treatment should be covered by state funding. Information should be disclosed with public health and safety as the priority, instead of government convenience. This information must be comprehensive, for use by individual residents to make informed decisions. (2) Continued monitoring of hotspots and the spread of radioactive contamination must be undertaken to protect communities and the public. Measures to prevent any potential spread should also be implemented. (3) The government must establish a detailed and transparent program of decontamination and relocation, as well as provide information so that all residents will be knowledgable about their compensation options.

Recommendation 4: Monitoring the Operators

TEPCO must undergo fundamental corporate changes, including strengthening its governance, working towards building an organizational culture which prioritizes safety, changing its stance on information disclosure, and establishing a system which prioritizes the site. In order to prevent the Federation of Electric Power Companies (FEPC) from being used as a route for negotiating with regulatory agencies, new relationships among the electric power companies must also be established—built on safety issues, mutual supervision and transparency.[6]

Recommendation 5: Criteria for the New Regulatory Body

The new regulatory organization must adhere to the following conditions. It must be[7]: Independent, Transparent, Professional, Consolidated, and Proactive.

Recommendation 6: Reforming Laws Related to Nuclear Energy

Laws concerning nuclear issues must be thoroughly reformed.[8]

Recommendation 7: Develop a System of Independent Investigation Commissions

A system for appointing independent investigation committees, including experts largely from the private sector, must be developed to deal with unresolved issues, including, but not limited to, the decommissioning process of reactors, dealing with spent fuel issues, limiting accident effects and decontamination.

---

[6](1) The government must set rules and disclose information regarding its relationship with the operators. NAIIC 23. (2) Operators must construct a cross-monitoring system to maintain safety standards at the highest global levels. (3) TEPCO must undergo dramatic corporate reform, including governance and risk management and information disclosure—with safety as the sole priority. (4) All operators must accept an agency appointed by the National Diet as a monitoring authority of all aspects of their operations, including risk management, governance and safety standards, with rights to on-site investigations.

[7](1) Independent: The chain of command, responsible authority and work processes must be: (i) Independent from organizations promoted by the government (ii) Independent from the operators (iii) Independent from politics. (2) Transparent: (i) The decision-making process should exclude the involvement of electric power operator stakeholders. (ii) Disclosure of the decision-making process to the National Diet is a must. (iii) The committee must keep minutes of all other negotiations and meetings with promotional organizations, operators and other political organizations and disclose them to the public. (iv) The National Diet shall make the final selection of the commissioners after receiving third-party advice. (3) Professional: (i) The personnel must meet global standards. Exchange programs with overseas regulatory bodies must be promoted, and interaction and exchange of human resources must be increased. (ii) An advisory organization including knowledgable personnel must be established. (iii) The no-return rule should be applied without exception. (4) Consolidated: The functions of the organizations, especially emergency communications, decision-making and control, should be consolidated. (5) Proactive: The organizations should keep up with the latest knowledge and technology, and undergo continuous reform activities under the supervision of the Diet.

[8](1) Existing laws should be consolidated and rewritten in order to meet global standards of safety, public health and welfare. (2) The roles for operators and all government agencies involved in emergency response activities must be clearly defined. (3) Regular monitoring and updates must be implemented, in order to maintain the highest standards and the highest technological levels of the international nuclear community. (4) New rules must be created that oversee the backfit operations of old reactors, and set criteria to determine whether reactors should be decommissioned.

10.3.2 Cabinet Office's 2017 Reaction Report

How has the government reacted to the National Diet's recommendations? It has past 6 years from the accidents and the Cabinet office summarized the 2017 report and submitted to the No. 193 regular session of the Diet on June 16th, 2017. The reactions to the recommendations are as follows.

To Recommendation 2: Reforming the Crisis Management System
The National Diet revised the Act on Special Measures concerning Nuclear Emergency Preparedness on September 2012, and on that basis the government expanded the Task force on Nuclear Emergency Preparedness. In addition, the National Diet revised the Atomic Energy Fundamental Act on September 2012, and based on it the government established the Nuclear Emergency Preparedness committee to coordinate measures to prepare for emergency in ordinary times.

To Recommendation 3: Government Responsibility for Public Health and Welfare
The government provides subsidies to the "Public health funds for Fukushima residents." Using these funds, the Fukushima prefecture conducted a Health Survey of the residents. The government also utilize the UNSCEAR (United Nations Scientific Committee on the Effects of Atomic Radiation) publication titled 'Levels and effects of radiation exposure due to the nuclear accident after the 2011 great east-Japan earthquake and tsunami' which was published on April 2014.

In addition, the government conducted countermeasures on decontamination, temporary storage, reexamining an evacuated area, recompense, reconstruction support.

To Recommendation 4: Monitoring the Operators
The Nuclear Regulation Committee sets up the transparency plan to monitor NPP operators (e.g. TEPCO). The JANSI (Japan Nuclear Safety Institute) evaluates operators like TEPCO, and enhances operator's self-reform.

The JANSI evaluates, makes proposals, and supports operators to pursue the highest safety level in the world.

To Recommendation 5: Criteria for the New Regulatory Body
The government established the Nuclear Regulation Committee in September 2012 and this committee was set down by article 3 of the National Government Organization Act. The establishment law of this regulation committee specifies the duty, how to exercise the committee's authority, organization, decision, etc. There are 5 principles: Independent decision making, effective exercise, open and transparent organization, aspiring and responsibility, and rapid-response in an emergency.

The IAEA (International Atomic Energy Agency) has an evaluation service on law and organization concerning Nuclear Power, like IRRS (Integrated Regulatory Review Service). An IRRS mission team visited Japan from January 11th to 22nd, 2016, and reported 13 recommendations and 13 proposals. In this report, the independency and transparency of the NRA (Nuclear Regulation Agency) are evaluated as good practice.

To Recommendation 6: Reforming Laws Related to Nuclear Energy

The Atomic Energy Fundamental Act sets the main objective of Nuclear energy to contribute to citizen's health and safety. Regulations on the atomic reactor are relegated from the Electricity Business Act to the Nuclear Reactor Regulation Law.

As for Recommendations 1 and 7, the Cabinet office made no comments. However, the National Diet established the Select Investigation Commission on Nuclear Power to deal with Recommendation 7. In addition, in this commission, an Advisory Board was established on May 25th, 2017, to address Recommendation 1.

10.4 Reconsideration of the Relationship Between NPP, Society, and New Institutional Innovation

In this section, I will integrate the contents of Sect. 10.2 and 10.3. As we have seen in Recommendation 2 in Sect. 10.3.1, reexamination of the crisis management structure of the government is recommended. It says: "A structure must be established with a consolidated chain of command and the power to deal with emergency situations". This recommendation symbolically reveals that the beliefs people in the sites with NPP before the accidents had—that is, "any problems posed were seen as being manageable; therefore, residents came to believe that problematic safety factors would never become critical issues"—were just a myth. Instead, the Cabinet Office's reaction report focused on "the independency, effective exercise, open and transparent organization, aspiring and responsibility, and rapid-response in emergency" as we see in the countermeasures for Recommendation 5. It means that the myth is now dispelled and it is time to construct crisis management for critical issues by using open and transparent processes. *It also implies that the driving force of the institutional innovation of the Japanese NPP regulation body was not a social protest and refusal, but the disaster and accidents.*

In addition, the government declares that they seek "the highest safety level in the world" (e.g. Recommendation 4), but criteria for this highest safety level were decided in closed space by experts: there is no space to reflect residents' voice. On this point, the American historian T. M. Porter, who studied severe public scrutiny of flood control in the U.S. (Porter 1995), indicated that the "Japanese nuclear engineers were insulated to a striking degree from public scrutiny of the sort faced by American ones" (Porter 2013). Lack of democratic control and public scrutiny in Japan was exposed to the light of day by the accident. To construct democratic control, mutual discussion between residents and the government is inevitable.

At the same time, the community-divide which I described in Sect. 10.2 makes mutual discussions difficult. The same holds true for Recommendation 3, which, for the record, was about government responsibility to public health and welfare. To build the mutual trust necessary for conducting a health survey of residents, doctors in Fukushima Medical University had held IAEA-FMU international conference for several times.[9] However, there still exists a community-divide among residents and distrust of doctors and governments, as I mentioned in Sect. 10.2. There are several attempts to include citizens in discussions about health, but they were not successful (Iwata 2013). To set a successful citizen conference on health survey, we have to deal with community-divide among residents.

Given how the "public sphere is configurated," not only central management, but also local governments should be considered. In Japan, local governments do not have legal authority in NPP running processes (Sugawara 2011). There is no statement on responsibility or commission of local governments in Japanese law. Instead, "Safety agreements" between local government and operators are concluded.[10] The reason why the National Diet's report includes little recommendation on local government comes from this legal structure. However, information disclosure on the safety of NPP to local governments and the safety agreements play an important role.

Thus, if we try to reconstruct the relationship between NPPs and society, and if we anticipate the new institutional innovation on regulation of NPPs, we can understand that dealing with the community-divide and making "public sphere" including local governments is the most important thing. How can we construct the public sphere on several levels bridging community-divide? These points are investigated through the use of the concept of RRI (Responsible Research and Innovation) in the next section. What is required to make nuclear power technology responsible?

10.5 Discussion from the Point of View of RRI

10.5.1 The Concept of RRI

RRI is now making a main stream for research funding program in the European Union (Horizon 2020). It is described as "RRI implies that societal actors work together during the whole research and innovation process in order to better align both the process and its outcomes with the values, needs and expectations of society."[11] Von Schomberg, who is considered as one of the concept makers explains: "Responsible Research and Innovation is a transparent, interactive process by which societal actors and innovators become mutually responsive to each other with a view to the (ethical) acceptability, sustainability and societal desirability of the innovation process and its marketable products (in order to allow a proper embedding of scientific and technological advances in our society)" (von Schomberg 2010, 2011).

This concept has evolved based on two streams: one is programs supporting the study of ethical, legal and social implications/aspects (ELSI for the US and ELSA for

---

[9]IAEA-FMU International Conference, Fukushima, 22–24, November, 2013 and IAEA-FMU International Conference, Fukushima, 24–27, July, 2014.

[10]In addition, in siting NPP, agreement by governor of local government is required.

[11]https://ec.europa.eu/programmes/horizon2020/en/h2020-section/responsible-research-innovation.

Europe) of scientific and technological developments[12] and the other is upstream public engagement and constructive technology assessment in Europe from the 2000s. In Europe, BSE (bovine spongiform encephalopathy) scandal in the U.K. in the middle of the 1990s, GMO (genetically modified organization) controversy from the end of the 1990s and discussions on Nanotechnology at the beginning of the 2000s enhanced the developments of public engagement. For example, citizen foresight on "future of food" was conducted in 1999 and Nano-jury (Jury for nanotechnology) was conducted in 2005 in the U.K. The experience of controversy on GMO leads to the discussion of "upstream" engagement. Once the commodity (e.g. GMO) is on sale, it is too late to discuss the ethical aspect of the commodity; therefore, citizens demanded to participate in the early stage of research and innovation. This kind of "upstream" engagement is consolidated into the concept of RRI.

Now RRI is used as an umbrella term[13] covering several areas such as; technology assessment, ELSI, applied ethics, CSR (Corporate Social Responsibility), value sensitive design, midstream modulation, social-technical system, and anticipatory governance (Timmermans and Blok 2018). RRI includes open innovation, open access, open space, engagement, mutual learning. For example, this concept is effective in a domain like ICT (Information and communication technology), since societal actors can work together during the whole research and innovation process and can participate equally in open space. From the private company side, RRI is said to be a means to remedy excesses of free market capitalism. At the same time, RRI is criticized for being the "new ideal management instrument[14]" in research and innovation.

10.5.2 Applying RRI to the Japanese NPP Case

The essence of the RRI is considered as (1) Open up questions, (2) Mutual discussions, and (3) New institutionalization.[15] From these points of view, for the establishment of a new regulatory body (Recommendation 5), it is inevitable to set up a space for open questions and mutual discussions.

---

[12]In U.S., NIH introduced ELSI study using from 3 to 5% of total funds relating to Human Genome Project. ELSI study introduced not only bio-technology domain, but also new material domain, e.g. nanotechnology. In EU, ELSA is included the 6th and 7th Framework program (2002–2006, 2007–2013, respectively).

[13]"Umbrella terms like 'nanotechnology' and 'sustainability research' have emerged as part of the new regime of Strategic Science. As mediators between science and society they have a dual role. Their overall promise allows resources to be mobilized for new fields which can then be productive in their own right. At the same time, however, they also put pressure on these fields to take relevance considerations into account" (Rip and Voß 2013).

[14]A word used in the discussion in the 4S (Society for Social Studies of Science), at the session on "Responsible Research and Innovation in Academic Practice: Institutions, Careers, Evaluation and Academic Integrity", on Sept. 2nd, 2017, Boston.

[15]Statement by Ulrike Felt in the 4S/EASST conference at the session on "Case studies for responsible innovation: Lessons from Fukushima" as a discussant, on Sept. 3rd, 2016, Barcelona.

In the Japanese case, as we have seen in Sect. 10.2, there had been little attempts for "open-up questions" or "mutual discussions" in crisis management and safety issues, since "any problems posed were seen as being manageable" before the Fukushima accident. After the accident, society requested operators several attempts to "open-up questions" or "mutual discussions". However, TEPCO says that the NPP operators believe that "If we open up new risks, then we will receive too much demand to countermeasure such risks from the residents in sites as well as from the regulatory body, and NPPs will stop operations for a long time.[16]" This kind of belief is a myth, coupling with the myths by residents as "any problems posed were seen as being manageable." Thus, "open-up questions" or "mutual discussions" in Japanese NPPs are just in a beginning phase and so is mutual trust.

10.5.2.1 Mutual Discussion: Building Trust

It is said that local governments' ability to control enhances the trust by residents on safety (Slovic 2000). In one French case, a transparency law enacted in 2006 gave the Commission Locale d'Information (CLI) legal authority.[17] The CLI plays a role in enhancing communication between operators and residents. Mutual discussion is clearly excluded from the government's decision-making process; however, this kind of discussion can help building trust between operators and residents. Indeed, not only does the CLI play a role in sharing information on sites, but also in building an accident-prevention-system such as; voluntary engagement for emergency drill, independent investigation into post-disaster management, and engagement in development and utilization of simulation system (Sugawara 2013).

In Japan, there is no such thing as a CLI empowered by law and only a few sites host citizen meetings on safety agreements. This is why the community-divide I mentioned in Sect. 10.2 expanded after the accidents. Since there are no laws giving legal authority to citizen meetings, communications on safety were conducted only voluntarily based on the safety agreement in each site. The conduct of meetings is left to the local governments. Sometimes, the central regulation body facilitates communication between residents and operators, but such a government-initiated communication can only fail to account for the characteristics that are key to a mutual discussion. Thus, lack of mutual discussion invites lack of information, which leads to an increased community-divide (refer to the SVS model mentioned in Sect. 10.2).

Of course, establishing CLI in Japan is not the only solution for mutual discussion to resolve community-divide. There are several levels of public engagement; for example, (1) public engagement for understanding, (2) that for mutual discussion, (3) that for empowerment, and (4) that for decision-making. At the same time, decision-making goes through different stages; (1) deciding on the NPP's site, (2) setting a

---

[16]Plan for safety NPP by TEPCO, 2013.

[17]La loi sur la transparence nucléaire et la sécurité en matière nucléaire, 2006.

NPP regulatory body, (3) managing independent investigation, (4) re-operating NPP after accidents, and (5) constructing accident-prevention-system including emergency drill. In the French case, mutual discussion is clearly independent from central government's decisions.

When Japanese society conducted a consensus conference on GMOs in 2000, there were also discussions on how we can distinguish the function of mutual discussions from that of decision-making.[18] A citizen meeting like the consensus conference reveals a variety of citizen opinions and differences in values, and it is very difficult to build a consensus. However, this kind of experience will enhance citizens' motivation for engagement, which leads to building trust. Therefore, even if there is little link with decision-making, mutual discussions are important to build trust. Building trust is the first step to settle community-divide.[19]

The government established the Nuclear Regulation Committee in September 2012 (article 3 of the National Government Organization Act). The law that gave rise to the regulation committee also specifies its duties. However, this committee operates only at the nation-level. Citizen meetings by local governments are now not based on law but based on agreements. The National Diet established the Select Investigation Commission on Nuclear Power and in this commission, an Advisory Board was established in 2017. This commission, however, is national in scope and only includes Diet members. In the future, relationship between local assembly members and this commission should be constructed. Institutional innovation of regulation body is needed both in national level and in local government level. For the settlement of the community-divide, making the link between these two levels is required.

10.5.2.2 Re-institutionalization: Breaking Walls

The essence of RRI includes open up questions, mutual discussions, and new-institutionalization. The last one, new-institutionalization means "Innovation beyond technology", namely. It implies to break walls of established institutions, that is, to scrap and build historically established structure.

Let us show an example. In Japan, the levels of research in nuclear technology and simulation technology, as well as the levels of research regarding tsunamis and earthquakes, were not low. However, this research and these technologies were not integrated for risk-prevention. In reality, there was no "sphere" to discuss this integration (Imada 2014). We have to admit that there is segregation not only between the sites but also in fields of research. For example, Makino (2011) showed that the Japan Nuclear Energy Safety Organization had already released a simulation report

---

[18]Komayashi (2007).

[19]Community-divide in Japanese society should be re-considered in the characteristics of the Japanese society like: Japanese society rely on "Not rule, but hierarchical relationship," Nakane (1967).

predicting the "loss of electric power supply of cooling system" five months before the earthquake (Japan Nuclear energy Safety Organization 2010). But because of the segregation between the research fields as well as between institutions, this simulation were not utilized. In addition, Soeda (2014) indicated that the risk of melt down of fuel by damaged cooling system triggered by large tsunami was predicted and was shared by TEPCO and Regulation body (National Diet Report 2012: 27). Whistle brewing by researchers of tsunami and of earthquake were summarized to guideline by 7 Ministers (1997) and by Long term estimation report by Earthquake Headquarter (2002). However, this kind of whistle brewing and recommendation were not to utilized in the NPP institutions, especially operators like TEPCO.

Therefore, re-institutionalization of operators and regulatory bodies is inevitable to strengthen the integration of nuclear power engineering, tsunami research, and earthquake research. Hitherto decision making in Japan was done in a closed space and responsibility of accident was undertaken by established institutions whose walls are firmly fixed. The Public accused operators and regulation bodies when the accident happened. Social community-divide mentioned in previous sections has a close relationship with this responsibility allocation to each institution. However, if we apply RRI, decision making should be done in an open space, and we should engage in a re-institutionalization that is effective for building responsible system. The former point, open discussion, is also indicated in the Nation-Diet recommendation (Recommendation 5). The latter point, re-institutionalization that is effective for building responsible system, relates to "intuitional innovation." This kind of innovation beyond technology cannot be conducted with an ongoing community-divide and unchallenged institutions. Collective responsibility will be considered in the re-configuration of responsible system.

Japanese nuclear engineers have a sense of crises[20] and do not share the rosy, optimistic picture of nuclear power the Ministry of Economic, Trade, and Industry has. In addition, the Fukushima nuclear power plant accidents and the Japanese Deliberative Poll attempt have invoked many international reactions.[21] Japanese policy and citizen movements seem to be attracting worldwide attention. Therefore, for the responsible R&D, the Japanese Nuclear engineering should consider how to include the essence of RRI in NPPs.

---

[20]For example "If the situation do not change, there will be no nuclear power plants within 50 years", "If we cannot describe a future perspectives of nuclear energy, then good, young students will not come in this domain", "Engineers should be mentally prepared that if we have once more accident, then, nuclear power cannot survive in the Japanese society" (Mr. Yagawa, Emeritus Professor of University of Tokyo, Fellow of Atomic Energy Society in Japan, in his statement in Symposium on Atomic Energy at Science Council in Japan, July 8th, 2017).

[21]For example, a Dutch sociologist at the International Joint Conference of EASST (European Association of Studies of Science and technology) and 4S (Society for Social Studies of Science) (2012) expressed that "people in European countries are curious about the future of Japanese nuclear power as well as about the effect of citizen movements on future policy." A French social economist at the same conference showed strong interest in the effect of Japanese nuclear power policy on similar policies in Europe. In addition, a German researcher at the same conference told me that it was an epoch-making event that the agency of Energy Resource, Ministry of Economy, Trade and Industry concluded that "Japan should set a goal for 0% NP by the 2030s (Kumagai 2012)."

10.6 Conclusion

From the analysis of the processes through which nuclear power plants are embedded in political, economic, and social contexts in Japan, we can determine that community-divide was established between sites that accepted nuclear power plants before the 1970s and sites without nuclear power plants. After the accidents of March 11, 2011, this community-divide expanded between these sites as well as within each site. For example, those who hold the salient value to trust officials continued to support nuclear power while those who developed the salient value to distrust sought to abolish nuclear power. Given this community-divide among the public with several different salient values and the historical community-divide between the sites, social protests could not be a driving force of institutional innovation of NPP regulatory bodies.

The National-Diet-recommendation-report analysis and the Cabinet-office-reaction-report analysis showed that the National Diet recommended an "Independent, Transparent, Professional, Consolidated, and Proactive" regulatory body. The Nuclear Regulation Committee has five statutory obligations: Independent decision making, effective exercise, open and transparent organization, aspiring and responsibility, and rapid response in case of emergency. It implies that the driving force of the innovation of the Japanese NPP regulation body was not a social protest, but the Fukushima accident.

Applying RRI to these historical and institutional analyses of NPP cases, we can conclude that (1) Decision making in NPPs should be done in an open space, as indicated in the Nation-Diet recommendation, with 5 principles mentioned above. (2) We should engage in re-institutionalization that is effective for building responsible system. This kind of innovation beyond technology can only occur if community-divide is addressed. The concept of collective responsibility in RRI leads to the re-configuration of responsible system with re-institutionalization. The advisory board to the committee on Nuclear Plants problem in National Diet has just started to consider these re-configurations.

References

Cabinet Office Investigation Committee on the Accident at the Fukushima Nuclear Power Stations (2012). Final report. Retrieved August 5, 2014, http://www.cas.go.jp/jp/seisaku/icanps/eng/final-report.html.

FMU-IAEA. (2013). International Academic Conference: Radiation, Health, and Society: Post-Fukushima Implications for Health Professional Education, November 21–14, Fukushima.

FMU-IAEA. (2014). International Academic Conference: Radiation, Health, and Population: The Multiple Dimensions of Post-Fukushima Disaster Recovery July 25–27, Fukushima.

Fujigaki, Y. (2009). STS in Japan and East Asia: Governance of science and technology and public engagement. *East Asian Science, Technology and Society: An International Journal, 3,* 511–518.

Fujigaki, Y., & Tsukahara, T. (2011). STS implication of Japan's 3/11 crisis. *East Asian Science, Technology and Society, 5*(3), 381–394.

Fujigaki, Y. (Ed.). (2015). *Lessons from Fukushima: Japanese Case Studies on Science, Technology and Society*. Springer.

Guideline by 7 Ministers (1997).

Hecht, G. (2009). *The radiance of France: Nuclear power and national identity after WWII*. MIT Press.

Independent Investigation Commission on the Fukushima Daiichi Nuclear Accident. (2012). *Fukushima genpatsu jiko dokuritsu kenshyou iinkai chyousa kensyou houkokusyo* (Independent investigation commission on the Fukushima Daiichi nuclear accident, final report). Tokyo: Discover 21.

Imada, T. (2014, June 4). Presentation at the Science Council of Japan.

Iwata, W. (2013). After two years: Through the activities in CRMS Institutes of citizen radio-activity measurement (in Japanese). Gendai-Shiso (revue de la pensee d'aujourd'hui), 123–133.

Japan Nuclear Energy Safety Organization. (2010, October). Jishin ji reberu 2PSA no kaiseki: BWR (Level 2 PSA analysis for seismic events: BWR). Retrieved August 5, 2014 from http://www.nsr.go.jp/archive/jnes/content/000017303.pdf.

Joly, P. B. (2019). Reimagining innovation. In S. Lechevalier (Ed.), *Innovation beyond technology* (pp. 25–45). Berlin: Springer.

Juraku, K. (2013). Social structure and nuclear power siting problems revealed. In R. Hindmarsh (Ed.), *Nuclear disaster at Fukushima Daiichi: Social, political and environmental issues* (pp. 41–56). New York: Routledge.

Kainuma, K. (2011). *'Fukushima'ron: Genshiryoku-mura wa naze umaretanoka* (Why was the "genshiryoku-mura" (nuclear power village) born?). Tokyo: Seidoshya.

Kaji, M. (2015). Itai-iati Disease: Lessons for the ways to environmental regeneration. In Y. Fujigaki (Ed.), *Lessons from Fukushima: Japanese case studies on science*. Springer: Technology and Society.

Kobayashi, T. (2007). *Teans-Sceince no jidai* (The age of trans-science: Linking science and society). Tokyo: NTT publishers.

Kobayashi, T., & Kusafuka, M. (2015). In Y. Fujigaki (Ed.), *Lessons from Fukushima: Japanese case studies on science*. Technology and Society: Springer.

Kumagai, T. (2012). *Naze Merkel wa tennkou shitanoka* (Why Merkel changed her decisions?). Tokyo: Nikkei BP.

Long term estimation report by earthquake headquarter (2002).

Makino, J. (2011). 97. Fukushima genpatsu no jiko (2011/3/19–21) (Accident at the Fukushima nuclear power plant on March 19–21, 2011). Retrieved August 5, 2014, from http://jun-makino.sakura.ne.jp/articles/future_sc/note098.html.

Nakane, C. (1967) *Tate-sakai no ningen-kankei* (Human relationships in hierarchical society). Kodansya.

National Diet. (2012). *Kokkai jiko cyou houkokushyo: Tokyo denryoku Fukushima genshiryoku hatsudenshyo jiko chyousa iinnkai* (National Diet official report of Fukushima nuclear accident independent investigation commission). Tokyo: Tokuma shyoten.

Porter, T. M. (1995). *Trust in numbers: The pursuit of objectivity in science and public life*. Princeton: Princeton University Press.

Porter, T. M. (2013). Nihongo ban (2013 nen) eno jyo (Preface for the Japanese edition of *Trust in numbers: The pursuit of objectivity in science and public life*). T. M. Porter, *Su-chi no Shinraisei* (Y. Fujigaki, Trans.). Tokyo: Misuzu syobo.

Rip, A., & Voß, J. P. (2013). Umbrella terms as mediators in the governance of emerging science and technology. *Science, Technology & Innovation Studies, 9*(2), 39–59.

Shimazono, S. (2013). *Tsukurareta housyasen 'anzenron'* (Man-made radiation safety). Tokyo: Kawaide shobo shinshya.

Siegrist, M., Cvetkovich, G., & Roth, C. (2000). Salient value similarity, social trust, and risk/benefit perception. *Risk Analysis, 20*(3), 353–362.

Slovic, P. (2000). Perceived risk, trust and democracy. The Perception of Risk. Earthscan Publication Ltd.

Soeda. (2014). Genpatsu to Ootsunami: Keikoku wo houmutta hitobito (Nuclear Power Plants and Large Tsunami: People who neglect whistle brewing). Tokyo: Iwanami-shinsyo.

Sugawara, S., & Shiroyama, H. (2011). A comparative analysis between France and Japan on local government' involvement in nuclear safety governance (in Japanese). *Japanese Journal of Civil Engineering, 67*(4), 441–454.

Sugawara, S. (2013). Institutional reforms of nuclear emergency preparedness in Japan and its challenges—Case studies on stakeholder involvement in establishing nuclear emergency: Preparedness in France and its implication for Japan (in Japanese). Socio-economic Research Center Report. No. Y12013, Centre Research Institute of Electric Power Industry.

Timmermans, J., & Blok, V. (2018). Hermeneutic reflection on the paradigm-level assumptions underlying RRI. In F. Ferri et al. (Eds.), *Governance and sustainability of responsible research and innovation processes: Cases and experiences* (pp. 83–90). Springer.

von Schomberg, R. (2010). Organizing collective responsibility: On precaution, code of conduct and understanding public debate. In Fiedeler et al. (Eds.), *Understanding nanotechnology* (pp. 61–70).

von Schomberg, R. (2011). Prospects for Technology Assessment in a framework of responsible research and innovation. In M. Dusseldorp & R. Beecroft (Eds.), *Technikfolgenabschätzen lehren: Bildungspotenziale transdisziplinärer Methoden*. Wiesbaden.

Watanuki, R. (2012). *Housyanou osen ga mirai sedai ni oyobosumono* (Chernobyl research: Effect of radiation contamination on next generation). Tokyo: Shinhyouronsya.

Part IV
Innovation for Whom and for What?

Chapter 11
Public Participation in the Setting of Research and Innovation Agenda: Virtues and Challenges from a Philosophical Perspective

Stéphanie Ruphy

Abstract Inclusiveness in scientific research and innovation is more and more valued by many scientific institutions, as attested by the increasing visibility and displayed institutional support in favour of "citizen science", "participatory science" and other forms of science involving in one way or another lay people. Could science benefit from being more inclusive and, in turn, could society benefit from a more inclusive science? The general aim of this chapter is to investigate how public participation may challenge and renew traditional epistemological and organisational features of scientific research, thereby providing a basis to assess the merits of public participation in this sphere. It will in particular offer epistemological arguments disqualifying common sources of resistance to public participation and discuss pending issues that need to be addressed if one wants to make a strong case in favour of public participation in science. In doing so, the chapter will (hopefully) contribute to going beyond an isolationist, decontextualised view of scientific developments and redefine the role that society is expected to play in new models of scientific research and innovation aiming at a better alignment of its outputs with society needs and interests.

11.1 Introduction

In a recent editorial entitled "Beyond the science bubble", the influential scientific journal *Nature* (2017) calls for a better alignment between the outputs of scientific research and innovation and the needs and expectations of society. The charge is rather virulent: "the needs of millions of people in the United States are not well enough served by the agendas and interests that drive much of modern science. (…) Research leaders in the United States and elsewhere should address the needs and employment prospects of taxpayers who have seen little benefit from scientific advances". This editorial echoes a seemingly growing dissatisfaction with scientific research and innovation: global contribution to economic growth is still of course

S. Ruphy (✉)
Université de Lyon—Jean Moulin, Lyon, France
e-mail: stephanie.ruphy@univ-lyon3.fr

© Springer Nature Singapore Pte Ltd. 2019
S. Lechevalier (ed.), *Innovation Beyond Technology*, Creative Economy,
https://doi.org/10.1007/978-981-13-9053-1_11

centrally on the agenda but it does not exhaust today society expectations: a *socially relevant* and *desirable* research and innovation is also expected. On the institutional side, these additional expectations are displayed for instance as lying at the core of the concept of "Responsible Research and Innovation" (RRI) put forward by the European Commission in its Horizon 2020 programme. Aiming at fostering "the design of inclusive and sustainable research and innovation", RRI implies that "societal actors (researchers, citizens, policy makers, business, third sector organisations, etc.) work together during the whole research and innovation process in order to better align both the process and its outcomes with the values, needs and expectations of society."[1] Public participation in research and innovation is thus seen and advertised as a mean to foster and achieve responsible research and innovation. More generally, inclusiveness in scientific research and innovation is more and more valued by many scientific institutions, as attested by the increasing visibility and displayed institutional support in favour of "citizen science", "participatory science" and other forms of science involving in one way or another lay people.[2] In that perspective, scientific research is no exception to a broader societal demand for more direct participation of the citizens in various areas of public and political life. Political valorisation of direct participation of citizens has become ubiquitous and leads to a variety of concrete participative forms of democracy at various levels (participatory budgets at municipal levels, crowd-sourcing in electoral campaigns, citizen consultations, etc.). From the perspective of democracy theorists, participative forms of democracy are often seen as a way to renew and enrich representative democracy, in response to its diminishing legitimacy and appreciation in the eyes of the citizens of our contemporary democratic societies.

Similarly, could science benefit from being more inclusive and, in turn, could society benefit from a more inclusive science? On the face of it, opening the scientific sphere to non scientists appears quite challenging in many respects, and especially from an epistemological point of view. After all, as much of historical, philosophical and sociological thinking about science has taught us, science is characterized, as a social field, by a very high level of closure ("among peers" is the rule in science). The general aim of this chapter is to investigate how public participation may challenge and renew traditional epistemological and organisational features of scientific research, thereby providing a basis to assess the merits of public participation in this sphere. It will in particular offer epistemological arguments disqualifying common sources of resistance to public participation and discuss pending issues that need to be addressed if one wants to make a strong case in favour of public participation in science. In doing so, the chapter will (hopefully) contribute to going beyond an isolationist, decontextualised view of scientific developments and redefine the role that society is expected to play in new models of scientific research and innovation aiming at a better alignment of its outputs with society needs and interests.

---

[1] https://ec.europa.eu/programmes/horizon2020/en/h2020-section/responsible-research-innovation. Accessed December 2017.

[2] For a typology see for instance Bucchini and Neresini (2008).

More precisely, I will proceed as follows. Starting with some preliminary remarks, I will first recall recent contributions from science and technology studies (STS), as well as from philosophy of science, emphasizing an evolution of the very aims assigned to scientific research in our societies, which can be broadly captured by the notion of contextualisation of these aims. As I shall explain, this background evolution is what makes room for the very idea of public participation in scientific research, leading also to a principled limitation of the autonomy of scientific communities. Distinguishing (classically) between two phases of the scientific enterprise (the choice of the problems to be addressed and their resolution), I will then discuss a first form of limitation of scientific autonomy, namely, a limitation of freedom of scientific communities when it comes to the setting of their research priorities. My main contention will be that resistance to any form of "external" piloting of research priorities on the grounds that it would hamper the fecundity of science (a widespread stand in public debates about scientific freedom) turns out to rest on misplaced epistemological views on the very nature of the dynamics of science and to remain in the grip of a linear model of innovation. Having established the epistemological acceptability of an externalisation of the setting of research agenda, I will then address the issue of which form of such "external" piloting (more on this notion later) is preferable when a better alignment between the outputs of scientific research and the needs and expectations of society is sought for. This part of the chapter will be primarily exploratory (rather than conclusive), discussing pro's and con's of various options, especially in comparison with the option of direct involvement of lay citizens.

11.2 Preliminary Remarks on the Evolution of the Aims of Science

It is now commonly acknowledged that science has gone through significant changes in the past few decades and especially in its relationship with other components of the society. Influential works in science and technology studies have proposed various conceptual tools to grasp these changes that affect in particular modes of research funding and the setting of research agendas.[3] For instance, the concept of triple helix of entrepreneurial science, developed by Etzkowitz (2003), puts forward the high level of intertwining between government, industry, and academia. The widely discussed 'mode-2' of knowledge production proposed by Gibbons et al. (1994) emphasizes a new social contract between science and society characterized, amongst others, by a research agenda much more open to "external" problems, that is, to problems defined in response to some identified needs of the society, by contrast with 'mode-1' of knowledge production, in which problems addressed by science are mainly defined according to interests and needs internal to a scientific discipline.

---

[3]For a useful historical perspective on these STS contributions, see Pestre (2003).

11.2.1 Decontextualized Versus Contextualized Views on the Aims of Science

As regards more specifically the aims of science, these contributions from science and technology studies coincide, on the philosophical side, with "contextualized" views on what makes science valuable, by contrast with "decontextualized" ones. Broadly speaking, decontextualized views conceive the ends of science in terms of gaining knowledge about how the world is, its structures, its constituent parts, independently of what could be the specific needs of a society at a given time of its history, be they epistemic (e.g. expertise) or practical. Within this decontextualized perspective, philosophers may differ about what exactly scientific inquiry is after, but they at least agree on the fact that these goals do not depend on contingent, socio-economical or cultural expectations. Various lists of goals have been proposed, including general items such as identifying the laws of nature, providing objective explanations, providing reliable predictions, formulating unitary principles, or more specific ones such as depicting and making use of causal patterns by using idealizations (Potochnik 2017).

Contextualized views on the ends of science, on the other hand, do not reject these purely epistemic goals, but acknowledge that other, non-epistemic considerations must be taken into account as well. After all, there are many, if not an infinity of questions that can be asked about the world, and many, if not an infinity of phenomena that could be the object of predictions and explanations. But the fact is that we do not deem them all equally worth being the objects of scientific inquiry. Depending on our needs and interests, we make choices: for instance modelling climate evolution is today given high priority. Kitcher (2001, Chap. 6) proposes a notion of "scientific significance" accounting for this dependency, by combining curiosity-driven, context-independent considerations with context-dependant ones. He gives the example of a research program aiming at cloning mammals and asks what makes such programs valuable and worth being pursued. The answer combines purely epistemic reasons (gaining, for instance, a better understanding in developmental biology of the first stages of development and the migration of DNA) and interest-driven (hence context-dependant) ones such as improvement of livestock or improvement of drug production processes using animals. Kitcher's mixed conception of scientific significance thus offers an integrative articulation of curiosity-driven, context-independent ends and interest-driven, context-dependant ones. From Kitcher's perspective, views of the aims of science must thus overcome the traditional contrast, if not opposition, between what is also often described as "disinterested" aims and "utilitarian" aims, corresponding to two broad types of expectations toward science. On the one hand, one can expect from science that it provides us with reliable knowledge about the world, and this knowledge is valuable in itself, independently of any practical use that can be made of it. On the other hand, one can adopt a more utilitarian stance toward science and expect primarily some practical usefulness of the outputs of scientific inquiries.

11.2.2 Scientific Autonomy and Utilitarian Expectations

Disinterested and utilitarian expectations towards science coexist today, but not always as harmoniously as suggested by normative philosophical views such as Kitcher's. They can be on the contrary experienced as being in tension, or even incompatible, especially by some practicing scientists. Just as an example among many, here is a recent public statement made by an eminent British chemist, Sir J. Cadogan, also endorsed by forty-one of his fellows from the Royal Society:

> The nature of all politics and politicians means it is easier for our pay-masters to feel comfortable about the proclaiming of programmes relating to Energy, Health, Materials, Climate Change, the Hydrogen Economy and so on, rather than to announce, let alone trumpet, that money is available for scientists to follow their curiosity in their own disciplines. (Cadogan 2014)

Grounds for resistance to a driving of scientific inquiry by utilitarian considerations are easy to identify. Such driving may first be perceived as running counter to values that are taken as central to the scientific enterprise such as disinterestedness and autonomy from other components of the society, especially the political sphere. Note, though, that utilitarian views of science are not necessarily incompatible with a defense of its autonomy, on the contrary. A historically central and well-known example of this compatibility is Vannevar Bush's claim that autonomy is not only compatible with utilitarian expectations, but even a necessary condition for science to be able to deliver benefits to society. In his influential science policy report, *Science, The Endless Frontier* (1945), Bush, who was at the time Roosevelt's scientific counselor, formulates these utilitarian expectations in the following broad terms: "scientific progress is one essential key to our security as a nation, to our better health, to more jobs, to a higher standard of living, and to our cultural progress" (1945: 2), adding immediately that "scientific progress on a broad front results from the free interplay of free intellects, working on subjects of their own choice, in the manner dictated by their curiosity for exploration of the unknown. Freedom of inquiry must be preserved under any plan for government support of science" (1945: 12). This kind of utilitarian justification of scientific autonomy goes hand in hand with what can be described as a "cascade model" of the social contract between science and society (e.g. Guston 2000), according to which policies of research oversight and funding should limit themselves to inject money in scientific communities, and let them self-organize and self-regulate.[4] Society will then receive in return all kinds of benefits (technological innovation fueling economic growth, expertise and knowledge improving living conditions, etc.). But the fact is that this classical cascade model has proved unsatisfactory on several grounds,[5] as acknowledged quite vividly in the *Nature* editorial evoked at the beginning of this chapter. When complaining

---

[4]See also Wilholt and Glimell (2011) for an analysis of this kind of mode of research oversight that they call "blind delegation".

[5]It has been for instance challenged on the grounds that its underlying linear model of innovation linking fundamental science to technological innovations neglects some degree of independence of the latter from the former (e.g. Rosenberg 1992; Edgerton 2004).

that science response to the needs of society is insufficient, the authors immediately warn that "just telling the same old stories won't cut it. The most seductive of these stories—and certainly the one that scientists like to tell themselves and each other—is the simple narrative that investment in research feeds innovation and promotes economic growth" (Nature 2017). I want to draw attention here to a lecture of the decline of this model in terms of evolutions of the expectations toward science.

11.2.3 Shift Towards More Targeted Expectations

It is commonplace to emphasize that science and innovation are considered as playing a central role in development projects of our societies. But what distinguishes our 'knowledge societies' from Bush's time (after World War II), is that our expectations towards science have become, I suggest, both more pressing and more targeted. This can be seen as the other side of the coin of the very success of science and innovation as a key element of so many aspects of the development of our societies. Given this central and ubiquitous role, it shouldn't come as a surprise that public science funders do not expect from science more knowledge and more technological innovation *tout court* (as Bush did), but more knowledge and more innovation in specific domains, considered as having priority because they correspond to currently pressing needs and expectations of society. This evolution can be formulated in terms of a shift away from what I would describe here as an "offer mode" and towards a "demand mode". In the first mode, scientific communities are expected to produce, following their curiosity, new reliable knowledge, which is then made available to society and, in turn, may lead to very useful developments (the laser is a case at hand, being a remote bonus from very theoretical, curiosity-driven developments of quantum mechanics at the beginning of the XXe century). In the second mode, some particular problems and needs of society are identified and deemed as having priority, and addressing them will then constraint and direct research programs towards specific topics, given, again, the central role ascribed to science in our societies.

11.2.4 Is the Shift Legitimate?

A crucial normative issue is then whether this shift towards more targeted, hence contextualized, expectations is legitimate and desirable. Two types of considerations, epistemological and political, need to be distinguished to address this normative issue. From an epistemological point of view, what are the consequences, in terms of the epistemic productivity of scientific research, of a shift towards a more interest-driven science?[6] In other words, how does a limitation of the autonomy of science with regards to the setting of research agenda impact the fecundity of sci-

---

[6]Note that utilitarian expectations towards science are by no means new.

ence? Independently of this epistemological dimension (which will be addressed in the next section of the chapter), the normative issue of the legitimacy and desirability of this shift has also a political dimension, which is two-fold. First, whether or not a contextualized view on the ends of science is preferable to a decontextualized one is a political issue, and should be considered and treated as such, which means (minimally) that it is not up to scientists, of for that matter to philosophers to decide, what the ends of science and innovation are. Much more could be said here to make a case in favor of a contextualized view on the ends of science. I will take for granted in the rest of the chapter that such a view is both descriptively and normatively more adequate, if only because it is a preliminary necessary condition for raising the very issue of the virtue and challenge of public participation in scientific research. Let me briefly spell out why. If one sticks to a decontextualized view on the ends of science, choices of research priorities remain internal to scientific communities, and rightly so: which problems should be addressed, when aiming at discovering the laws of nature or explaining natural phenomena, regardless of society specific needs and interests, is certainly a matter upon which scientists are in the best position to decide. But once acknowledged that science should also respond to society specific needs and interests, then it is not obvious at all that scientists are still in the best position to do so. Indeed, the priorities that would be defined by scientific communities "following their curiosity in their own discipline" as the British scientist J. Cadogan puts it in the above mentioned quotation, are unlikely to coincide with the ones defined in light of society needs.

Who, then, should be in charge? This issue will be addressed in the last part of my chapter, and the option of direct public participation in these matters is certainly an increasingly considered option worth being assessed. But let us turn before to the epistemological dimension of the normative issue of the acceptability of a limitation of scientific autonomy.

11.3 Epistemological Soundness of the Unpredictability Argument in Favour of Scientific Autonomy[7]

"I didn't start my research thinking that I will increase the storage capacity of hard drives. The final landscape is never visible from the starting point." This statement made by the physicist Albert Fert (2007), winner of the 2007 Noble Prize for his work on the giant magnetoresistance effect, expresses a very common belief, especially among scientists, about the unpredictable nature of the development and results of a research program. Such retrospective observations feed a type of 'unpredictability argument' often invoked in favor of curiosity-driven science, in contrast with interest-driven science. Polanyi gave a somewhat lyrical form of this kind of unpredictability argument in his classical essay "The Republic of Science" (1962). Science, says

---

[7]The following section draws directly on Bedessem and Ruphy (2019) which offers a more elaborated version of the arguments.

Polanyi (1962: 62), "can advance only by unpredictable steps, pursuing problems of its own, and the practical benefits of these advances will be incidental and hence doubly unpredictable. ... Any attempt at guiding research towards a purpose other than its own is an attempt to deflect it from the advancement of science... You can kill or mutilate the advance of science, but you cannot shape it." In Polanyi's view, claims about the unpredictable nature of scientific development go hand in hand with a plea for an *internal* definition of research priorities: a problem should be considered important in light of considerations internal to a field of scientific inquiry and not (at least not primarily) in light of external considerations, such as practical utility or relevance for political decisions (expertise). The orientation of the inquiry by such external objectives is then deemed epistemically counter-productive and vain: one should not attempt to predict the unpredictable. In this section, I will challenge a crucial but often implicit assumption in the traditional defense of scientific freedom based on scientific unpredictability (such as Polanyi's or Fert's), namely the assumption that a free, curiosity-driven science is more likely to generate unexpected facts and hence to be pioneering, creative and fecund. But what are actually the conditions favoring the emergence of novelty in the course of a scientific investigation? This important issue has not received much epistemological attention.[8] I will fill this gap by first distinguishing two kinds of unpredictability arguments often mixed when debating on scientific freedom, to wit, unpredictability as unforeseen practical applications and unpredictability as unforeseen new lines of research and discoveries. Focusing on the latter, I will identify epistemological conditions that favor the occurrence of unexpected facts in the course of a scientific investigation and discuss, in light of these conditions, whether curiosity-driven research is more, or less, hospitable to the unpredictable than interest-driven research.

11.3.1 Two Kinds of Scientific Unpredictability

When unpredictability refers to unexpected applications, the argument is the following: freedom of research should be preserved since a free, curiosity-driven science is needed to generate a reservoir of fundamental knowledge, which then can be used to develop applications. This argument was typically developed by Vannevar Bush who appealed to the now classically called linear model of innovation linking pure science and practical applications:

> Basic research leads to new knowledge. It provides scientific capital. It creates the fund from which the practical applications of knowledge must be drawn. New products and new processes do not appear full-grown (1945: 20).

---

[8]Wilholt and Glimell (2011: 353) do touch upon this issue when discussing the link made by proponents of the autonomy of science between freedom of research and diversity of approaches favoring the epistemic productivity of science. But they just note that it is a strong assumption and do no further discuss its validity.

The development of the A-bomb in the frame of the Manhattan project is a paradigmatic case. As Bush emphasizes (1945: 20), accumulating fundamental knowledge about the structure of the matter is what allowed the development of the A-bomb. Another frequently cited example of unpredictable application is the invention of the laser, a widely-used technological device nowadays, made possible by pure theoretical developments in quantum physics during the first half of the XXe century. I will not discuss further this first version of the unpredictability argument, if only because its underlying linear model of innovation linking pure science and practical applications has already been challenged on several grounds, as mentioned earlier (see footnote 5). Rather, I want to focus on the second (and also widespread) type of unpredictability arguments, whose validity has been much less scrutinized.

In this second type of argument, unpredictability refers to cases when unexpected observation or result opens up a new line of research leading to a fundamental discovery. A very well-known historical episode illustrating this kind of unpredictability is the invention of the first antibiotic by Fleming, after he had accidentally observed the effect of a fungus (Penicilium) on bacteria colonies (Fleming 1929). Also often cited is the discovery of radioactivity by Becquerel (1896): when working with a crystal containing uranium, Becquerel noted that the crystal had fogged a photographic plate that he had inadvertently left next to the mineral. This observation led to posit that uranium emitted its own radiations.

When unpredictability refers to such unexpected developments, freedom of research is defended on the grounds that scientists should be able to freely change the direction of their research or open up new lines of inquiry in order to be able to follow up on unexpected results, thereby generating new knowledge and innovation. But to properly work in favor of scientific autonomy, the argument actually presupposes that the occurrence of surprising facts is more likely to happen in a curiosity-driven system of science than in an interest-driven one. For increasing the production of new knowledge and innovation does not only depend on being able to freely follow up on unexpected facts, it also (obviously) depends on whether occurrences of unexpected facts are favored, to start with. It is thus necessary to clearly distinguish between two types of considerations, too often mixed in defense of scientific freedom: considerations on the occurrence of unexpected facts and considerations on the (institutional, material) possibility to follow up on them.

I will not discuss for the moment the second type of considerations (management of the unexpected) and focus on the first (genesis of the unexpected), which has been largely neglected in the literature on scientific freedom, namely the epistemological conditions that actually favor the occurrence of surprising facts. The central epistemological issue can then be reformulated as follows: is it the case that when the inquiry is interest-driven, unexpected facts are less likely to occur than when the orientation of the inquiry is set internally by scientific communities following their curiosity?

11.3.2 Epistemological Conditions Favoring the Occurrence of Unexpected Facts

By 'unexpected facts' occurring in the course of an inquiry, I simply mean here results (observations, outcomes of an experiment, etc.) that cannot be accounted for within the theoretical framework in which the empirical inquiry has been conceived and conducted. This kind of "exteriority" is what leads scientists to move away from the initial explanatory framework and open up new lines of inquiry in search of an alternative one that could accommodate the unexpected results. My central claim is that occurrence of unexpected facts follows from our partially uncontrolled intervention on the (complex) real world. Consequently, as I argue in more details below, there are no good epistemological reasons to claim that curiosity-driven research is more hospitable to the unexpected than interest-driven research. Let us turn now to a first epistemological condition favoring the unexpected.

Isolation and purification of phenomena It is now a well-known feature of contemporary experimental sciences that many of their objects under study are "created" in the laboratory rather than existing "as such" in the real world. When drawing our attention to this epistemologically important feature, Hacking (e.g. 1983, Chap. 13) specified that we should not read this notion of "creation" of phenomena as if *we* were *making* the phenomenon, suggesting instead that a phenomenon is "created" in the laboratory to the extent that it does not exist outside of certain kinds of apparatus. This is typically the case for a phenomenon like the Hall effect: it did not exist "until, with great ingenuity, [Hall] had discovered how to *isolate, purify* it, create it in the laboratory" (Hacking 1983: 226, *our italics*). In other words, Hall created in 1879 the material arrangement—a current passing through a conductor, at right angles to a magnetic field, for the effect to occur and "if anywhere in nature there [was such an arrangement, *with no intervening causes*, then the Hall effect [would] occur" (1983: 226, *our italics*). Isolation, purification, control of intervening causes (i.e. control of physical parameters) are noticeable features of an experimental protocol that have a straightforward consequence directly relevant: they tend to limit the number of causal pathways which can influence the response of the object or phenomenon under study experimentally. Unknown causal pathways existing in the real world are thus inoperant (or less operant), thereby limiting the occurrence of unexpected results. Hence our first criterion to evaluate whether a certain system of science favors the occurrence of surprising results: the more the phenomena under study in that system are isolated, purified in highly regimented experimental conditions, the less likely the occurrence of unexpected results is.

Theoretical unifying ambition Another relevant factor is the degree of generality of the theoretical framework within which the inquiry takes place. Scientists working within a theoretical framework with a large unifying scope will be reluctant to "leave" it and search for an alternative one when facing an unexpected result, and for good epistemological reasons: there is (obviously) a high epistemic cost of abandoning a theoretical framework that provides explanations for a large set of phenomena.

The right move is rather to try to accommodate the surprising result by adopting, if necessary, ad hoc hypothesis or tinkering with some ingredients of the existing theoretical framework, so that the result loses its "exteriority" and ends up being integrated. And because of this well-known "plasticity" and integrative power of well-established theoretical frameworks with a large unifying scope,[9] when a (at first sight) surprising result occurs, it rarely leads to the opening up of a new line of inquiry in search of an alternative explanatory framework, but rather gets integrated within the existing one, thereby losing its unexpectedness.

There is another reason why a high degree of theoretical generality does not favor the occurrence of unexpected results. By constraining the type of experimental procedures developed and the type of data generated, a theoretical framework with a large unifying scope tends to *homogenize* the experimental works conducted to probe the various phenomena that it accounts for. And since a diversity of experimental approaches increases the possible sources of emergence of surprising facts, we can conclude that by reducing this diversity, theoretical generality makes the occurrence of unexpected facts less likely to happen.

11.3.3 Comparative Analysis

In light of the criteria proposed above, how does curiosity-driven science score compared to interest-driven science when it comes to favoring the occurrence of unexpected facts? Let us first compare the two in light of our first criterion based on the degree of isolation and purification of the phenomena under study. A directly relevant feature of interest-driven science is the use of what Carrier (2004) calls "contextualized causal relations" rather than full causal chains. Interest-driven science, or use-inspired science as it is also called, typically aims at directly intervening on a process or phenomenon often disposing only of a partial knowledge of the causal chains involved and without being able to isolate it from various causal influences exerted by the rest of the physical world. A direct consequence of this feature of use-inspired science is the low degree of control of its experimental protocols. By contrast, to the extent that pure, curiosity-driven science aims primarily at answering fundamental theoretical questions about the world, it designs highly regimented experimental procedures that isolate and purify phenomena in order to be able to get empirical answers about the specific fundamental processes questioned in the theoretical investigation.[10] Moreover, building highly regimented experimental procedures requires knowledge of full causal chains in order to be able to better control

---

[9]Classical references on these ideas of plasticity or integrative power are of course Kuhn's description (1962) of scientists being busy working on resolving anomalies in normal science and Lakatos' concept of "protective belt" of a research program (1978).

[10]Carrier sums up this contrast as follows: "Empirical tests often proceed better by focusing on the pure cases, the idealized ones, because such cases typically yield a more direct access to the processes considered fundamental by the theory at hand. But applied science is denied the privilege of epistemic research to select its problems according to their tractability (…). Practical challenges

the response of the system under study. The outcome of the application of our criterion is straightforward: compared with pure, curiosity-driven science, use-inspired, or interest-driven science favors the occurrence of unexpected facts to the extent that its experimental procedures tend to be less controlled and based only on partial knowledge of the causal influences exerted on the phenomenon under study.

The etiology of cancer provides an interesting illustration of this claim. Indeed, many current cancer therapies built in the frame of use-inspired research are based on contextualized causal relations. Typically, if a cellular agent is found to be massively expressed in cancer cells, drugs are designed to inhibit it, even if the whole causal chain determining its action is not known. For instance, a large amount of proteins promoting angiogenesis (the growth of blood vessels), notably VEGF (Vascular Endothelial Growth Factor), was found in tumoral cells, leading to the design of anti-VEGF molecules (Sitohy 2012). These molecules are used without considering the complete causal chain in which the VEGF is embedded. Only their known action on angiogenesis is considered. The clinical tests have led to unexpected observations: the use of an anti-VEGF molecule (Avastin) can stimulate tumor growth (Lieu et al. 2013). This example shows that the use of contextualized causal relations promotes the occurrence of surprising facts by allowing unknown mechanisms to intervene in the experimental procedure.

Let us now compare curiosity-driven science and interest-driven science in light of our second criterion. Whereas pure, curiosity-driven science often aims at providing comprehensive and unifying theoretical frameworks (think of the Standard Model in particle physics or the Big Bang model in cosmology), interest-driven research is often characterized by the coexistence of numerous local models, each determining the development of specific experimental procedures. An extreme case of this locality are for instance the design-rules used in the industry, which are built as laws guiding action (Wilholt 2006). They are experimentally confirmed rules providing relations among different relevant parameters to manufacture industrial products. These rules are extremely specific: they apply to a very few numbers of situations and each of them determines a singular experimental practice. The use of local models is also widespread in the biomedical sciences, a typically interest-driven field of research. I will draw again on oncology to illustrate my point. Consider for instance the case of the development of radiotherapy protocols in the first half of the XXe century. The aim was to intervene on cancer to cure it, without any general model describing the mechanism of carcinogenesis. This program promoted the development of a variety of exploratory approaches using X-rays against cancer (Pinell 1992). As there were no standardized protocols, many experimental procedures were tested, changing the density of X-rays received, the distance of emission, the frequency of the radiotherapy sessions. In order to improve the efficiency of the therapeutic methods, scientists tried to build various local models describing the action of X-rays on cancer, corresponding to the variety of experimental procedures implemented. Grubbe (1949) formulated a model based on the inflammatory reaction to explain the effects of radiotherapy on

---

typically involve a more intricate intertwinement of factors and are thus harder to put under control" (2004: 4).

cancer: the inflammation of the surrounding tissue beyond the effects of X-rays is responsible for the decrease of tumoral mass. This model reflects his specific use of X-rays: he applied very high doses, necessary to generate an inflammatory response. In parallel, Tribondeau and Bergonié, using more moderate doses, developed a model based on the proliferation of the cells in tumoral context, which led to the "Bergonié law": X-rays have a higher impact on proliferating cells (Bergonié and Tribondeau 1959). The outcome of the application of our criterion is then again straightforward. By promoting the use of a diversity of local models and heterogeneous experimental protocols, interest-driven science favors the occurrence of unexpected facts, whereas the penchant of pure, curiosity-driven science for comprehensive unifying theoretical and explanatory frameworks, hence homogenized experimental protocols, does not.

11.3.4 Intermediate Conclusion

Our previous analysis has established that several features of pure, curiosity-driven science make it no more hospitable than use-inspired, interest-driven science to the occurrence of unexpected facts. For all that, it does not follow that proponents of freedom of science cannot appeal anymore to the unpredictability argument to make their case. For the issue of which conditions favor the occurrence of unexpected facts is only half of the story. The other half is the possibility to actually follow up on these occurrences and open new lines of inquiry. And this other half raises different issues. What are the institutional, organizational structures of science that make it easier for scientists to re-orient their research when needed? To what extent an initial orientation of a scientific investigation by external practical needs is less compatible with the opening of new lines of inquiry than an initial orientation by epistemic considerations internal to the dynamics of a scientific field? When appealing to the unpredictability argument, proponents of free, disinterested science not only presuppose that it is the best system of science to generate unexpected facts to start with—a contention that I have challenged in this section—but also that it actually gives more freedom to scientists to follow up on unexpected results. In other words, the issue of the possibility for researchers to change the direction of their line of inquiry when needed is somewhat mixed, confused with the normative issue of what the aims of science should be (in short, increase knowledge following considerations internal to science *vs.* answer external needs). But the two issues, I contend, should be kept separate. After all, one can very well conceive a system of science whose aims are primarily to answer society needs but which nevertheless leaves scientists free to choose the lines of inquiry that seem *to them* the most promising ways of fulfilling these needs (which includes changing research directions if needed). Otherwise put, one can very well conceive a use-inspired, interest-driven science which is not a *programmed* science in which scientists are asked to plan every step of their inquiry in order to achieve a given aim. And note that a pure, curiosity-driven science may be as much programmed as an interest-driven one: the fact that scientists are left free to choose the aims of their research does not protect them from having to plan every step to reach these aims. In any case, my purport in this section is not to attack pure, curiosity-driven science. There may be, no doubt, many good reasons to defend it, but the widespread, traditional one appealing to the unpredictability of scientific inquiry is certainly not the most cogent and solid one. Consequently, from an epistemological point of view, resistance to a limitation of the autonomy of science (hence in particular to public participation in the setting of research agenda) grounded in views on the very nature of the dynamics of scientific development and innovation is not well-founded.

11.4 Pro's and Con's of Public Participation

Now that epistemological room has been made for external, interest-based guiding of scientific research, let us turn to a comparative discussion of the shortcoming and virtues of various possible options to define priorities in the setting of research agenda, focusing in particular on the public participation option. When discussing such options, a first step, I suggest, is to distinguish between two main ways of identifying the interests that should shape research and innovation agenda, which are 'objectivist, substantialist' and 'non-objectivist' ones. According to an objectivist, substantialist conception, the needs and interests of society that scientific research and innovation should respond to can be defined independently of what members of the society, the citizens, would identify and express as being these needs. By contrast, according to a non-objectivist conception, these needs and interests are just those identified and expressed by the citizens (by some appropriate process—more on this crucial issue later).

11.4.1 Objectivist, Substantialist Conceptions of the Goals of Scientific Research and Innovation

In an objectivist, substantialist approach, some subset of citizens are in charge of defining the needs of society, that is, "the collective good that scientific inquiry is supposed to fulfill", as Kitcher puts it (2001: 137). Who are the candidates and by virtue of what quality can they be considered as being legitimately in charge of defining this collective good? Given the antecedents of philosophers in matters pertaining to the definition of the common good, it should come as no surprise that philosophers of science are inclined to take up the task. And indeed, some philosophers of science with a taste for a socially relevant philosophy of science (admittedly a rather rare species in the contemporary philosophical landscape) have come up with propositions. Kourany (2012) for instance developed an ideal of "socially responsible science", whose agenda should be shaped by "sound social values", so that its outputs meet the needs and expectations of society (2012: 348). This kind of propositions clearly partakes of an objectivist, substantialist approach: the guiding "sound social values", whatever they are exactly, are taken as being universally shared and Kourany insists that neither "the market" nor "the politicians" should be in charge of defining them (2012: 346). Note that when defined in an objectivist, substantialist way, the goals of science and innovation may admittedly coincide with the goals that would be defined in a non-objectivist way by the whole set of members of society, but it *needs not* be so.

11.4.2 Epistemic Elitism

An objectivist, substantialist approach of the definition of the main goals of science and innovation such as Kourany's goes hand in hand with what can be described as 'epistemic elitism': a subset of members of a society is considered as being legitimately in charge in virtue of having some privileged epistemic position in that society. This is by no means a recent feature of the organization of science. As Kitcher (2001: 137–138) for instance reminds us, epistemic elitism was at the core of what can be considered the first document of science policy, namely, Francis Bacon's description of Salomon's House in his fable the *New Atlantis* (Bacon (1627) 1966). The wise inquirers of Salomon's House were in charge of defining the human needs, taken as being universal, that scientific inquiry should fulfill, independently of the actual needs that the rest of the citizens might have expressed, had they been consulted.

In our contemporary societies, given the central role assigned to the natural sciences and technology, researchers in these fields (rather than from the social and human sciences) account, not surprisingly, for most of the members of our modern versions of Salomon's House. Consider for example in France the *Conseil stratégique de la recherche* (Research Strategic Council) reporting to the French Prime Minister, whose mission is to "identify and propose a limited number of big research and technological priorities to prepare and construct the future of France".[11] Looking at who is involved in the choices made about research priorities at the national level in France today is telling. Eminent researchers from the natural sciences make the bulk of it and France is, in this regard, no exception. I will comment later on the other members of the Council (a minority, at least numerically). For the moment, I just want to emphasize that the option of epistemic elitism is (still) alive, both descriptively and normatively, in our democracies. But is it satisfactory?

There are, at least, two reasons to be unhappy with epistemic elitism (restricted to the natural sciences). First, one can challenge that the privileged epistemic position of scientists is *relevant* in those matters. Second, one can challenge the very idea of an objectivist, substantialist conception of the goals of science underlying epistemic elitism.

---

[11] http://www.enseignementsup-recherche.gouv.fr/cid75958/www.enseignementsup-recherche. gouv.fr/cid75958/conseil-strategique-de-la-recherche.html. Accessed August 2016.

With regards to the first source of concern, remember first that, in this chapter, a *contextualized* view of the aims of science and innovation is taken as being the appropriate framework of discussion, both for normative and descriptive reasons (see end of Sect. 11.2). That means, I would remind, that scientific research is supposed to trigger new knowledge and innovation *responding to the needs of society*, not only to produce new knowledge for its own sake. Eminent scientists are members of research guiding bodies as epistemic experts in their field of speciality. That would suffice to qualify them for the task if the aims of science were decontextualized. In that case, yes, practicing scientists are in the best (epistemic) position to determine what are the most promising lines of research to increase knowledge in their fields. But why would this kind of expertise put them in an epistemically privileged position when it comes to defining what the needs and interests of society are? To put it otherwise, their epistemic expertise is not the kind of epistemic expertise needed to grasp what the needs of society are at a certain time of its history. Who, then, could have this relevant kind of expertise?

It would certainly be interesting to contemplate an articulation of epistemic expertise coming from both the natural sciences *and* the human and social sciences (after all, the epistemic aims of the latter include precisely providing knowledge about the needs and interests of society). This kind of interdisciplinary endeavour is for instance what Kourany has in mind to define the proper goals for science (2012: 346). I will not, however, pursue here this line of thought, because I want to question the very idea of defining the goals of science and innovation in an objectivist, substantialist way. In other words, rather than trying to improve the functioning of Salomon's house, one should, I contend, rebuild it on new foundations altogether.

11.4.3 Non-objectivist Views on Defining the Goals of Science and Innovation

The main reason for giving up an objectivist, substantialist approach is straightforward: democracy. Indeed, pleas for a democratisation of the setting of research and innovation agenda are easily made on political grounds[12]: citizens are affected in their daily life by scientific developments and innovations (just think of genetic tests, nanotechnologies, genetically modified food (GMO), etc.), research is (at least partly) funded by their taxes, so why shouldn't citizens have their say? But if so, in what matters exactly should citizens have their say and how? It could first be noted that various kinds of participatory devices, as for instance deliberative forums open to lay citizens, have already been implemented in relation to science and innovation. However, they usually focus on a particular issue (e.g. innovations in nanotechnology), not on the broader issue of what are the needs and interests that science and

---

[12]A more sophisticated philosophical case in favor of a non-objectivist approach to the definition of the goals of science taking the form of a democratisation of the setting of research is offered by Kitcher (2001, Chap. 11).

innovation should respond to in priority. Moreover, many of these democratic experiments have been a recurrent source of dissatisfaction, and rightly so, for the people involved, and criticised on the ground that, to put it briefly citizen participation was only an alibi for diminishing resistance to new technologies. It is not my purpose here to further discuss the actual role played by these democratic experiments, nor the actual influence of their outputs, nor either the actual intentions and aims of the institutions implementing them.[13] The rest of the chapter will rather map out, from a philosophical point of view, pro's and con's of various possible ways of democratizing the setting of research agenda.

11.4.4 Comparative Discussion

Let us start by going back to the composition of the French research guiding body evoked earlier, the *Conseil stratégique de la recherche*. Along with eminent scientists, three other types of people are involved (again, seemingly marginally, at least by their number): a few representatives of big French companies (e.g. Total, Orange, EADS), three elected representatives and… a rather well-known novelist, Marie Darrieussecq. It is not clear by virtue of what quality this novelist is included in the council, but let us suppose here that it is as a lay citizen. This composition is telling in that it reflects the main options currently on the table, implicitly mixing objectivist approaches and non-objectivist ones. The epistemic elitism option, lying within the objectivist framework, is (still) dominant (at least, again, by the number of eminent scientists involved), but our modern version of Salomon's house has become a bit more inclusive: citizens are invited in, via their elected representatives or directly (the novelist) and "the market" is also on the guest list. What these new guests have in common is that their expectations towards science go beyond "seeking the knowledge of causes and secret motions of things", which was the core expertise of the members of Salomon's House (Bacon (1627) 1966: 288). Let us discuss each of these options in turn, while keeping in mind that what is sought for is a better alignment between the outputs of scientific research and innovation and the needs and expectations of society.

Assessing the "market option" as a mean to respond to the needs and interest of society takes us back of course to a much broader and long-standing political debate. It suffices here for our purpose to emphasize that when guided by economic interests (be it directly when conducted by private companies or indirectly by cooperation agreement between private and public laboratories), research and innovation can only respond to a limited (albeit still central) subset of the needs of society (to wit, the economic ones). Moreover, as Hiroi (2019) suggests, this limited subset may even become less central in our societies, as alternative measurements of wealth, such as "happiness studies", are on the rise.

---

[13]This issue is especially worth being addressed in the case of RRI (Responsible Research and Innovation) actions implemented in H2020.

On the face of it, the two other options (our elected representatives and direct participation of lay citizens) allow avoiding the pitfall of a scientific and innovation agenda overly restricted to economic interests. After all, our elected representatives are supposed to convey the whole range of needs and interests of the people they represent. But the fact is that the rhythm and demands of political life are hardly compatible with the kind of long term engagement needed for the development of a scientific program. Consequently, our elected representatives may be biased toward short-term, practical expectations, neglecting long-term needs and interests in matters of science and innovation of the citizens they represent.

In principle, contrary to the two preceding options ("the market" and our elected representatives), the option of direct participation of lay citizens in the setting of research agenda avoids, by design so to speak, the pitfall of a possible gap between the actual needs and interests of the citizens and the needs and interests actually taken into account in the setting of research and innovation priorities. This presupposes, admittedly, that the participatory processes are well designed so that their outcomes do correspond to the collective needs and interests of the concerned citizens. The implementation in the real world of such participatory devices is notoriously difficult, with all kinds of unwanted biases, and I can only refer here to the numerous studies in sociology and political sciences dealing with these issues, as well as to the lessons drawn from past experiences (e.g. Fishkin 2009). I will take for granted that appropriate participatory devices can be implemented and discuss another problem facing, this time in principle, the public participation option. To what extent is the small subset of citizens involved in a participatory device representative of the rest of the citizens? The participating citizens are not elected, so they cannot "act for" the rest of the citizens and be accountable to them in the way that elected representatives "act for" and are accountable to their constituents. As Brown (2004: 86) explains, participating citizens, at best, just "stand for" the rest of the citizens. But then how do they grasp and make representations of the views of the rest of the citizens on what the agenda of research should be? "Without input from their constituents, the deliberators must rely upon introspection, intuition, or speculation to assess popular preferences", says Brown (2004: 86). This might be all very nice, but incompatible, as Brown warns us, with the expectation that the recommendations so obtained "have binding force on elected officials" (2004: 86). I thus see this lack of political representativeness of the participating citizens as a serious, in principle, shortcoming of the public participation option, especially when one requires more than the granting of a mere consultative role to these participatory devices.

11.5 Concluding Remarks on Pending Issues

As could be expected, no clear winner has emerged from the previous comparative analysis, so that a crucial pending issue is the following: how should these various options (including the 'epistemic elitism' option) be articulated? In the present state of affairs, the articulation mainly boils down to a mere *juxtaposition* of them: eminent scientists, elected representatives, representatives of the private sectors, sometimes other stakeholders from the lay society (but the participation of lay citizens remains anecdotal) sit around a table and deliberate (see for instance, again, the French Research Strategic Council). This is unsatisfactory because it tends (not surprisingly) to lead to a play of power between various groups defending their own agenda (not to mention the accompanying lack of transparency unfortunate in a democracy). In particular, fundamental research is then held, regrettably, in tension with interest-driven research. What is needed is a *non-competitive, integrative* articulation. Such an integrative framework should be based on a contextualized view of the ends of science. Note that there can be plenty of room for fundamental, curiosity-driven research within this framework [see for instance the notion of "use-inspired basic research" analyzed by Stokes (1997)]. Another specification for the integrative framework is that our elected representatives cannot be left out of the picture, as it is the case in Kitcher's widely-discussed (at least in philosophy of science) ideal of "well-ordered science" (2001), nor can they just occupy a back seat, given their accountability and central roles in our *representative* democracies. How then direct participation of the citizens can be articulated with indirect participation (via their elected representatives) is, no doubt, a central challenge to be met, but not one specific to the science and technology sphere. Also, epistemic experts (practicing scientists both in the natural and human and social sciences) must keep a central role in the integrative framework but this role should be redefined as being informative and not decisional. Moreover, interdisciplinary work between the natural and social and human sciences is needed to clearly identify the needs and interests of society that cannot be addressed by the market. Interdisciplinary work is also needed to anticipate on the evolution of the needs of society, so that scientific research can adjust its agenda in time.

I have only offered in this chapter some general specifications for the building of an integrative framework. Much more work remains to be done to elaborate detailed blueprints for the democratic rebuilding of Salomon's house. Successful experiments at local levels of inclusive research practices such as "community-based collaborative action research" (Kusago 2019) may provide insights for more general plans, the aim being to come up with a renewed, more democratic and workable conception of the role that society should play in the course taken by scientific developments and innovation.

Acknowledgments This work was supported financially by The French National Agency ANR under grant n° ANR-14-CE31-0003-01 (DEMOCRASCI project).

Many thanks to the PhD students and the post-doc of the project DEMOCRASCI (www.democrasci. com), Ismaël Benslimane, Renaud Fine, Haris Shekeris, and especially Baptiste Bedessem for Sect. 11.3 of the chapter.

References

Bacon, F. (1627) (1966). *New Atlantis*. Oxford University Press.
Bedessem, B., & Ruphy, S. (2019). Scientific autonomy and the unpredictability of scientific inquiry: The unexpected might not be where you would expect. *Studies in the History and Philosophy of Science., 73*, 1–7.
Becquerel, H. (1896). Sur les radiations émises par phosphorescence. Comptes-rendus de, l'Académie des sciences. C.R. T: Vol. 122, pp. 420–421.
Bergonié, J., & Tribondeau, L. (1959). Interpretation of some results from radiotherapy and an attempt to determine a rational treatment technique. *Yale Journal of Biology & Medicine., 76*, 181–182.
Brown, M. B. (2004). The political philosophy of science policies. *Minerva, 42*, 77–95.
Bush, V. (1945). *Science, the endless frontier*. A Report to the President by Vannevar Bush, Director of the Office of Scientific Research and Development. Washington D. C.: National Science Foundation.
Bucchini, M., & Neresini, F. (2008). Science and public participation. In E. J. Hackett, O. Amsterdamska, & M. Lynch (Eds.), *Handbook of science and technology studies* (3rd edn., pp. 449–473). Cambridge, Mass: MIT press.
Cadogan, J. (2014). Curiosity-driven blue sky research: A threatened vital activity? The learned society of wales.
Carrier, M. (2004). Knowledge gain and practical use: Models in pure and applied research. In D. Gillies (Ed.), *Laws and models in science* (Vol. 1, pp. 17). London: King's College Publications.
Edgerton, D. (2004). The linear model did not exist. Reflections on the history and historiography of science and research in industry in twentieth century. In K. Grandin & N. Wormbs (Ed.), *Science-industry nexus: History, policy implications* (pp. 31–57). New-York: Watson.
Etzkowitz, H. (2003). Innovation in Innovation: The triple helix of university-Industry-Government relations. *Social Science Information, 42*, 293–337.
Fert, A. (2007). Interview published in *Le Monde*, October, 25, 2007.
Fishkin J. S. (2009). *When the people speak*. Oxford: Oxford University Press.
Fleming, A. (1929). On the antibacterial action of cultures of a penicillium with special reference to their use in the isolation of *B. influenza*. *Journal of Experimental Pathology, 10*, 226–236.
Gibbons, M., Limoges, C., Nowotny, H., Schwartzman, S., Scott, P., & Trow, M. (1994). *The new production of knowledge: The dynamics of science and research in contemporary societies*. Sage.
Grubbe, E. (1949). *X-ray treatment: Its origins, birth, and early history*. St. Paul, Minneapolis, MN: Bruce Publishing Company.
Guston, D. H. (2000). *Between politics and science*. Cambridge: Cambridge University Press.
Hacking, I. (1983). *Representing and intervening*. Cambridge: Cambridge University Press.
Hiroi, Y. (2019). Science as care: Science and innovation in post-growth society. In S. Lechevalier (Ed.), *Innovation beyond technology* (pp. 301–324). Berlin: Springer.
Kitcher, P. (2001). *Science, truth, and democracy*. Oxford: Oxford University Press.
Kourany, J. (2012). The ideal of socially responsible science: Reply to Dupré, Rolin, Solomon, and Giere. *Perspectives on Science, 20*, 344–352.
Kuhn, T. S. (1962). *The structure of scientific revolutions*. The University of Chicago Press.
Kusago, T. (2019). Post-disaster community recovery and community-based collaborative action research—A case of process evaluation method for community life improvement. In S. Lechevalier (Ed.), *Innovation beyond technology* (pp. 195–221). Berlin: Springer.
Lakatos, I. (1978). *The methodology of scientific research programs*. Cambridge: Cambridge University Press.
Lieu, C. H., et al. (2013). The association of alternate vegf ligands with resistance to anti-vegf therapy in metastatic colorectal cancer. *PLoS ONE, 8*(10), e77117.
Nature, (2017). *542*, 391.
Pestre, D. (2003). Regimes of knowledge production in society: Towards a more political and social reading. *Minerva, 41*, 245–261.

Pinell, P. (1992). *Naissance d'un fléau. Histoire de la lutte contre le cancer en France (1890–1940)*. Métailié.

Polanyi, M. (1962). The republic of science: Its political and economic theory. *Minerva, 1,* 54–73.

Potochnik, A. (2017). *Idealization and the aims of science*. The University of Chicago Press.

Rosenberg, N. (1992). "Science and technology in the twentieth century". In *Technology and enterprise in historical perspective*. Oxford: Clarendon Press.

Sitohy, B. (2012). Anti-vegf/vegfr therapy for cancer: reassessing the strategies. *Cancer Research, 8,* 1909–1914.

Stokes, D. E. (1997). *Pasteur's quadrant*. The Brookings Institution.

Wilholt, T., & Glimell H. (2011). Conditions of science: The three-way tension of freedom, accountability and utility. In M. Carrier & A. Nordmann (Eds.), *Science in the context of application* (pp. 351–370). Boston Studies in the Philosophy of Science.

Wilholt, T. (2006). Design rules: Industrial research and epistemic merit. *Philosophy of Science, 73*(1), 66–89.

Chapter 12
Innovation for Whom? City Experiments and the Redefinition of Urban Democracy

Brice Laurent

Abstract As "smart cities" or "eco cities" proliferate, innovation has become a central component of urban policy. This chapter discusses the politics of innovation in urban contexts by focusing on city experiment, that is, experiments conducted *in* the city and *with* the city. The analysis of city experiments is a path for displacing oppositions between (1) the stability of urban space and the "disruption" introduced by innovation, (2) "technical" innovation and "social" innovation, (3) the local life of cities and the global flows of technologies and capital. Instead, one can contrast various propositions for organizing innovation in the city. The example of innovation policy in San Francisco and its associated controversies shows that these propositions offer various imaginations of the beneficiaries of innovation, and eventually different understandings of urban democracy. In particular, the imagination of the city as a place for real-time experiments and the increasing role of global investment can be contrasted with other propositions, which make collective life the means and ends of urban innovation.

12.1 Introduction

In December 2017, news was reported that San Francisco was restricting the use of the delivery robots that had been introduced on the city's sidewalks by companies eager to automatize at home delivery.[1] The San Francisco Board of Supervisors decided on December 5 that companies would need to apply for permits to operate their robots, and that they could do so only in particular zones with low foot traffic, and only for research purposes.

---

[1]"San Francisco just put the break on delivery robots", *Wired,* December 6, 2017; https://www.wired.com/story/san-francisco-just-put-the-brakes-on-delivery-robots, accessed December 29, 2017.

B. Laurent (✉)
CSI—Centre de Sociologie de l'Innovation, i3 UMS CNRS, PSL Research University, MINES ParisTech, Paris, France
e-mail: brice.laurent@mines-paristech.fr

© Springer Nature Singapore Pte Ltd. 2019
S. Lechevalier (ed.), *Innovation Beyond Technology*, Creative Economy,
https://doi.org/10.1007/978-981-13-9053-1_12

This episode is a perfect illustration of the ambivalence regarding technological innovation that San Francisco might be a scene of. After decades of being little more than a place to sleep and party for Silicon Valley tech workers, San Francisco has been active in attracting tech companies. That Twitter decided to locate its headquarters in downtown San Francisco, in an impoverished part of the city, was a sign of urban renewal and, more generally, of the new character of the city as the "innovation capital of the world". Yet the restrictions put on delivery robots also point to a pervasive ambivalence in San Francisco, regarding who should benefit from innovation. This question directly relates to the material ordering of the city as a place where space is allocated across users, some of them aiming to make private profits out of spatial use (Graham and Marvin 2001). Seemingly benign issues such as who (or what) can use sidewalks acquire pressing political dimensions, as they pertain to the allocation of space for public use or private profits, and force to reflect on the ways in which cities can (and should) be redesigned according to technological advances. For all its anecdotal appearance, the delivery robot episode suggests reflecting on the contested ways in which technological innovation changes (or is expected to change) city life, at economic, social and material levels.

A familiar reading of the delivery robot episode would oppose the stability of urban settings and the disruption caused by innovation, the social life of the city and the change caused by technological development, the local characteristics of the city and the global flows of technologies and capital that private companies make circulate, and for which San Francisco is one site among many, soon to be replaced if too reluctant to accept innovation. These oppositions echo some pervasive modes of reasoning about innovation, such as the "deficit model" (which explains critical positions toward innovation by a lack of understanding), which tend to introduce an asymmetrical understanding of who has the ability to innovate, who can problematize innovation, and who should benefit from innovation (Jasanoff 1998). By contrast, works in Science and Technology Studies (STS) have proposed to refine these oppositions by discussing the distribution of the ability to innovate across society (Callon et al. 2009).

This chapter discusses some examples of urban innovation and the opposition it faces in San Francisco[2] in order to develop a critical reflection on the transformation of innovation in the city. It argues that understanding the politics of innovation in the city requires displacing oppositions (such as stable/instable, social/technological, local/global) that might come to mind when accounting for episodes such as the San Francisco delivery robot story. The chapter argues that the politics of innovation in the city can be examined in the context of a way of governing innovation based on experiments, which one can identify in San Francisco but is much wider—as a

---

[2]I use empirical material collected in 2016 in the framework of a collective study, undertaken with Madeleine Akrich, Stève Bernardin, David Pontille and Félix Talvard, as well as graduate students from Mines ParisTech. I draw on a more detailed case study written by Félix Talvard and I, and forthcoming in an edited volume directed by Sheila Jasanoff on sociotechnical imaginaries of innovation in urban contexts (Laurent and Talvard 2017). I also refer to other fieldworks in Medellin and Singapore conducted within the City Experiments research project, coordinated by David Pontille and myself (see: Talvard 2018 about Medellin).

growing literature focusing on "urban laboratories" (Karvonen and van Heur 2014), "experimental cities" (Evans et al. 2016) or "test-bed urbanism" (Halpern et al. 2013) shows. Accordingly, I propose to use San Francisco as a lens to examine current transformations of urban innovation, and cities themselves, through experiments, and eventually discuss the possibility of counter-experiments.

Urban innovation, then, allows us to better understand innovation in general as an outcome of sociotechnical processes, not only because it stems from policy choices and the economic interests of private actors but also because it shapes individual agencies and collective organizations. The examples discussed in this chapter, as others in this volume, show the importance of a concern for "public participation" or "community-based intervention" and the ways in which it impacts innovation (Kusago 2019; Ruphy 2019; Hiroi 2019). They also demonstrate that this very concern is a sign that innovation is a site of democratic struggle, where pervasive political questions need to be asked, including: who are the "participants" to innovation processes? In the name of whom is innovation conducted? For the sake of what objectives? In this chapter, I show that the analytical focus on city experiments offers a path for exploring these questions, as proponents and critics of urban innovation propose different (and sometimes conflicting) statements about who can experiment, who can attest that experiments are successful, and how the value of experiment is defined.

In the following sections, I start by discussing the oppositions in San Francisco as an echo to current fractures around city space. I then argue that a way to analyze them in ways that do not simplify the oppositions at stake is to explore the politics of innovation in greater details, and in particular a mode of governing the city based on experiments. This will lead me to discuss counter-experiments as a basis for alternative imaginations of the city, again using examples in San Francisco as empirical entry points.

12.2 Frictions in the Innovation Capital of the World

12.2.1 A Global City and the Innovation Capital of the World

The 2012 election of Edwin Lee as mayor of San Francisco owed a lot to the "tech community" or "tech sector", that is, the network of companies active in technological development, venture capital firms, and investors in search of potential highly valuable start-ups—the so-called "unicorns". This community had taken an institutional shape when powerful investor Ron Conway created the San Francisco Initiative for Technology and Innovation. Known as sf.citi, this organization has been serving as a platform for advocacy for the tech sector in local politics. Geographer Donald McNeill has described the tight connections between the "tech sector" (as constituted through initiatives such as Conway's) and Mayor Lee's elections and subsequent policy initiatives (McNeill 2016). These connections were made explicit as pro-business initiatives passed, such as Proposition E, which replaced a payroll tax with a gross receipts tax varying across industrial sectors—a measure that was supported by Ron Conway, and interpreted as beneficial to technology firms (which tend to hire before earning revenue).[3] The connections between the city of San Francisco and the "tech sector" were publicly displayed on downtown Market Street, when Twitter moved its headquarters there. Mayor Lee participated in the opening ceremony in 2012. As numerous press accounts stated, he was then celebrating the success of a tax policy allowing the company to avoid payroll taxes as an incentive to move to a previously under-developed part of the city, the promised renewal of downtown San Francisco thanks to the involvement of a major tech company, and the affirmation of the city as a significant player in the global and local competitions for technological activities.[4] Turning parts of the city into special zones dedicated to private investments is of course not limited to San Francisco. In fact, the making of the "global city" can be read as a re-direction of urban policy to a global public of would-be investors that public bodies try to lure by designating targeted tax policies. As Michael Goldman's study of Bangalore shows, making the "global city" often articulates the development of technological sectors with various forms of land speculation, thereby redirecting the beneficiaries of urban policies from local inhabitants to a global public of investors and entrepreneurs (Goldman 2011). In San Francisco as in other global cities, this dynamics is tied to a recurrent housing problem, driven by rising prices and the ever-increasing flows to and from the entire Bay area that crisscross the city—as the architects of the "innovation capital of the world" hope not only to attract tech workers working in Silicon Valley but become a place of innovation in its own right.

12.2.2 Protests and a New Class Warfare

The recent transformations of San Francisco have given rise to various forms of protests, perhaps best epitomized by the Google bus controversy. In 2014, the *Guardian* spoke of "guerrilla protest" to describe how activists repeatedly stopped the luxury shuttle buses transporting employees of Silicon Valley based companies such as Facebook and Google from San Francisco (where they lived) to their work place.[5] There are several ways of accounting for these protests. Officials in San Francisco tended to see them as misguided, drawing undue connections between

---

[3] See: https://ballotpedia.org/San_Francisco_Gross_Receipts_Tax_on_Businesses,_Proposition_E_(November_2012; "San Francisco tech companies win a proposition to save on taxes", *The New York Times*, July 7, 2011.

[4] See for instance "Twitter will get payroll tax break to stay in San Francisco", SFGates April 6, 2011; "Twitter headquarters opens: San Francisco mid-market offices revealed", The Huffington Post June 13, 2012.

[5] "San Francisco's guerrilla protest at Google buses swells into revolt", *The Guardian*, January 25, 2014.

rising housing costs and bus riding tech employees (Maharawal 2014).[6] The critical voices, on the contrary, framed the oppositions not just as a local protest, more or less adjusted to the pricing dynamics of housing, but also as a new "class warfare". The expression was then regularly used in the media and in scholarly accounts of the bus protest.[7] It reads the oppositions in San Francisco as a fight between affluent new residents working in the tech sector, and the victims of high rents and potential evictions. This language requires drawing lines between relatively stable social groups, a "tech class" that would be responsible for the transformation of the city, and another one that would suffer from it. This is what protesters have been attempting to do, targeting buses that would benefit an affluent minority of people also constitutes the riders of these buses as the enemy group, however ambivalent the relationships of its members with the city might be.

Some of the activists also engage in operations that constitute collectives able to fight against increases in rents or evictions. During a collective fieldwork, colleagues and I met Joseph Smooke and Dyan Ruiz, who run the independent online media platform *People. Power. Media*. We spoke about the numerous housing right initiatives they engaged in—such as organizing local communities so that they can voice their concerns about future developments, and ensuring that enough participants intervene in public meetings for these concerns to be heard.[8] Smooke and Ruiz were harsh critics of the fact that San Francisco's public bodies tend to come up with "simple technological solutions" to "simple problems" instead of tackling what they define as "complex issues" pertaining to the allocation of resources in the city. Instead, they construed their interventions as a matter of mobilizing local communities and opposing their replacements by flows of affluent newcomers. Community organizing was an answer to the current transformations of San Francisco and a necessary complement to demonstrative protests such as those stopping private buses.

12.2.3 Oppositions to Refine

These debates, and the very language of class warfare, map onto a series of oppositions. They oppose the stability of urban life and the instability introduced by permanent flows of technologies, people and capital, the social identities of local communities and technology-based transformations, the locality of urban life and the global characteristics of a "world city" attracting capital investment. These three couples of oppositions are only rough descriptions though, and need to be refined.

---

[6]One official in San Francisco criticized during an interview the connections drawn by activists between the trajectory of the private buses and rising rent prices.

[7]See de Kosnik (2014); Maharawal (2014), and among numerous examples in the press: "The class war is back on in San Francisco", Time Magazine, April 2, 2014; "In this Silicon Valley tech culture and class war, we're fighting about the wrong things", Wired, December 16, 2013.

[8]Interview with Joseph Smooke and Dyan Ruiz, February 15, 2016.

First, oppositions in San Francisco do not simply originate from the clash between the disruptions introduced by innovation on the one hand, and the stability of social groups on the other. The language of disruption should not hide the fact that the instability resulting from the flows of technologies, people and capital is the product of stable arrangements, including those resulting from advocacy politics in San Francisco that has turned the tech sector into a powerful political actor of its own. By contrast, oppositions in San Francisco are as much about the stability of social groups as related to the emergence of new coalitions of protests, associating for instance anti-eviction movements with wealthy owners eager to limit high-rise buildings in the city. The initiatives undertaken by people such as Smooke and Ruiz are only efficient if they manage to extend the collectives voicing their concerns, and indeed destabilize the existing passive social groups.

Second, reading the opposition as that of "social identities" reacting against technological development would ignore the dual fact that protesters and activists are very much prone to use technology, and that technological developments are also social projects. Activists in San Francisco have been engaged in the "Anti-Eviction Mapping Project". This project aims to collect various data (about housing prices, evictions, types of retailing activities…) and draw correlations among them. In turn, technology development projects in San Francisco are also political programs aiming to turn the city into the "innovation capital of the world". The trajectory of Edwin Lee is revelatory of the dual role of technology development programs, as technological innovation was for him an engine in the redevelopment of downtown San Francisco.

Third, the oppositions in San Francisco can only partly be described as local resistance to global transformations. The locality of the protest is also associated to global movements of resistance, and draws on repertoires of activism that cut across geographical and moral boundaries, such as those separating "developed" from "developing", "legal" from "illegal" (Roy 2003). By contrast, the alleged "globalism" of urban transformations is also fractured by tensions that are inherent to the ways in which the contemporary forms of liberalism are shaped. In a study that resonates with the case of San Francisco, Katharyne Mitchell has analyzed how the growing flows of foreigners investing in real estate in Vancouver disrupt national liberal discourses about the role of communities in political and economic life (Mitchell 2004).

These considerations invite us to adopt theoretical and empirical approaches that displace the oppositions between stable/unstable, social/technology, and local/global. Below, I argue that Science and Technology Studies (STS) have much to offer in that regard, particularly as they propose to explore the politics of innovation in ways that do not take for granted the distribution of the ability to innovate, and explore processes of joint social and technological ordering. Building on this body of work, one can envision an analysis of the politics of innovation, particularly as it is conducted in formats, such as *city experiments*, that cut across the too simple oppositions we need to refine.

The study of city experiments, as the remainder of this chapter will argue, makes it possible to unpack the notion of innovation, seeing it as a mode of producing political legitimacy and political subjectivities. But before we discuss these points, we need to discuss the notion of experiment and how it is manifested in contemporary urban innovation.

12.3 From Experiments in San Francisco to City Experiments

12.3.1 Experimental Situations

The vocabulary of experiments has become a pervasive trope in contemporary discourses about the city. Multiple examples in San Francisco can be seen as illustrations of this trend. The language of experiments is a recurrent part of the official discourse of public bodies like the San Francisco Municipal Transportation Agency (SFMTA). Consider for instance the Muni Mobile application, which presents transportation data for users of public transportations to plan their journeys. The experimental dimension of the Muni Mobile App was explicit in the initial testing phase, which was managed by a dedicated private company, and during which self-registered users tested a beta version and offered feedback to the SFMTA. But the experiment extends far beyond the initial testing phase of the app. Once in place, the app offers a platform gathering data, which can be used to test various mechanisms related to pricing and incentives. As the person in charge of innovation at the SFMTA said during an interview:

> We're experimenting with what the customers actually care about—what they care about is getting free things. We call that gamification. We don't have the money to pay for these things so we think the right approach is to partner with the private sector and have them do it. (SFMTA Office of Innovation, 10/02/2016)

Another example is SFParks, the parking management program based on the real-time definition of parking prices according to availability, or, in other words, "smart parking". Launched in 2011, the project was expected to test new management and pricing technologies, and meant to be alternatives to road pricing in downtown San Francisco—an option that the chamber of commerce and then mayor Gavin Newsom refused.[9] In this case as in the previous one, and in San Francisco as in many cities across the globe (Kitchin 2014), experiments are based on the ability to collect large amount of data, assemble them to gain knowledge about transportation or parking behaviors, and use them to introduce incentives in the form of differentiated prices.

Experiments are not limited to this format though. Consider for instance small-scale, citizen-induced tests of potential transformations of the public space, such as those occurring in the so-called "Living innovation zones", or within the "Pavement to Park" program, which aims to offer inhabitants the possibility to redesign portions

---

[9]"San Francisco is not London", *SFGate*, December 22, 2008; "San Francisco studies fees to ease traffic", *The New York Times*, January 3, 2009.

of public space. These tests are intended as material interventions on city space, and are directed towards inhabitants expected to be turned into day-to-day innovators.

Apps developed by private companies or individuals thanks to the Open Data policy of San Francisco, or material interventions in city space as framed by initiatives such as the "Living Innovation zones" or the Pavement to Park program are seen by officials such as the city's chief data officer as powerful ways of turning "problems" into "opportunities" for the development of future solutions.[10] In each of these cases, public bodies draw the legitimacy of their intervention in their ability to act in experimental ways, adaptable to both potential issues as they emerge, and the available competencies of private companies or individuals seen as partners. Experimenting thereby appears as a way of negotiating with a series of time or money related constraints, demonstrating an ability to act in multiple small-scale sites, while permanently re-interrogating the demand for and the supply of solutions meant to answer urban problems.

When the SFMTA answered the U.S. Department of Transportation's "Smart City Challenge" in 2015, it proposed a synthetic vision of the city as a place dedicated to experimentation. In proposing to turn San Francisco into a city that would "expand and integrate shared mobility services" (SFMTA 2015: 1), the SFMTA saw experiments as appropriate operations meant to introduce innovations in local transportation practices, the most visible of them being autonomous vehicles, possibly "integrated" into the other components of the local transportation system and "shared" by users according to the similarities of their trips with the help of digital devices. The proposal expected that the concept of "integrate shared mobility services" would be reached in the following way:

> To test and scale this concept, the City will challenge neighborhoods to participate and apply with participating residents, businesses and stakeholders (...) Pilots could include but are not limited to: Wi-Fi, charging, smart signals, lanes, sensors and beacons, fleet operations, first-last mile transit shuttles, flexible loading zones and open space, delivery services, parking management, geo-fencing, demand management pricing and incentives, and bike/car/scooter/cargo share pods. This iterative, community supported process will include dashboards to track and monitor progress and outcomes (...). (SFMTA 2015: 2)

In this excerpt, experiments appear as small-scale, controlled operations allowing the public bodies to harness the participation of "residents, businesses and stakeholders" in order to test what can be extended at a later time. Taken together, they suggest that:

> The city is an urban laboratory that has several locations ideally suited to create demonstration sites. (SFMTA 2015: 8)

This latter quote suggests considering that any experiment comes with a demonstration, addressed to particular audiences, be they inhabitants attesting the value of public policy intervention, investors ready to contribute to future scaling-up operations, or potential partners interested in future replications of the tests. It connects

---

[10]She used those terms during a public presentation (cf. a discussion in Laurent and Talvard, 2017).

these demonstrations within a city understood as an "urban laboratory"—an expression that echoes both the long-time sociological tradition of the Chicago school and a renewed scholarly interest (Gieryn 2006; Karvonen and van Heur 2014). San Francisco can indeed be described as an "experimental city" (Evans et al. 2016), as experiments are used as a mode of governing and organizing urban life, and the city itself made an "urban laboratory". The evolution making experiments a basis for governing cities parallels the transformation of private interventions, as companies undertake tests "in the wild" to experiment with innovative technologies and services (Laurent and Tironi 2015).

This invites us to theorize further the notion of experiment and discuss the ways in which it offers a renewed understanding of innovation in the city.

12.3.2 Experiment as an Analytical Category

The recent literature on cities and urban innovation invites us to study experiments in cities, and to consider cities themselves as experimental sites (Halpern et al. 2013; Evans et al. 2016; Laurent and Tironi 2015; Tironi and Sánchez Criado 2015). One can then speak of "city experiments" to point to a dual process, whereby: (1) initiatives such as those I mentioned in San Francisco are urban related projects intended to serve as tests, assembling a sociotechnical apparatus for the sake of a learning objective, at least partly uncertain, and tied to public demonstrations, and (2) the city itself (or part thereof) is experimented with: as transportation tests re-route flows of passengers, or parking behaviors are transformed, various configurations of the material and human organization of the city are tested.

The analysis of city experiments can build on a body of scholarly works in STS that have discussed the politics of experiments. Early works in the field discussed experiments as operations that simultaneously act on the production of knowledge and social ordering. Shapin' and Schaffer's seminal study of the nascent experimental physics in 17th century England (Shapin and Schaffer 1985) and detailed studies of testing practices (Pinch 1993) have been followed by analysis that have extended the discussion of experiments to situations where economists test, in vitro or in vivo, their theories or models and thereby re-arrange the economy itself (Muniesa and Callon 2007; Mitchell 2005), protesters reinvent the forms of political activism (Barry 1999; Doubleday and Wynne 2011), experts test "technologies of democracy" (Lezaun and Soneryd 2007; Laurent 2011), users of mundane technologies make sustainable development a matter of personal engagement (Marres 2012), and actors engage in various types of political experiments (Laurent 2016; Millo and Lezaun 2006). These works have used experiments as an analytical category that allows the analyst to account for situations where a sociotechnical apparatus is aimed at demonstration practices, for the sake of a learning objective that is at least partly uncertain upfront.

Seen through the analytical lens of STS, the discourse of experiments as it is present in contemporary urban initiatives can be problematized in ways that displace the oppositions introduced above, namely stability/instability, social/technical, local/global. First, experiments inherently rest on a degree of instability, as they are aimed to produce results that are at least partly uncertain. Doing so also implies that the experimental conditions are stabilized, in such a way that results become transferable, and, perhaps more importantly, that convincing proofs can be produced. Consider for instance the transportation app Muni Mobile. The tests that are conducted on this platform act on and perform behaviors that are not known in advance, and the very possibility of producing knowledge about these behaviors rests on the possibility to use a transportation system that will remain the same across time.

Second, and as historians of science working on early experimental practices have convincingly shown (Shapin and Schaffer 1985), scientific experiments are operations that engage in joint technical and social ordering. As they are configured to produce knowledge thanks to the mobilization of technical devices, they also require the assemblages of social collectives able to attest the validity of their outcomes. Extending the notion of experiments to account for certain economic and political interventions does not change this characteristic. Thus, SFMTA's proposal to test autonomous driving in San Francisco is tied to both technical infrastructures ("wifi, charging, smart signals" in the quote above) and particular collectives expected to attest the validity of the tests, including the federal Department of Transportation in charge of validating the proposal.

Third, experiments require demonstration practices that associate local sites of intervention with global scales of action (Latour 1983). Assembling audiences that would attest the validity of the experiment, and defining the ways in which experiments matter and for whom associate situated practices with distant ones. Urban experiments are performed under the gaze of a variety of audiences, including technology companies, investors, or potential future inhabitants.

Once identified as a recurrent topic of urban intervention and made an analytical category, city experiments can now serve as entry points to reflect on the politics of urban innovation without reproducing the oppositions between stability/instability, social/technological, and local/global. Instead, considering experiments as a mode of governing cities will allow us to discuss the politics of urban innovation, and to whom urban innovation is directed.

12.4 Politics and Counter-Politics of Urban Innovation

Analyzing urban initiatives such as the experiments conducted in San Francisco implies that we account for a series of components of these projects. Several components of city experiments can be analyzed, including the identities of the experimenters, the experimental subjects and objects, the perimeter of the laboratories, and the definition of audiences expected to attest the value of the initiative at stake. For our concern here, the experimental entry point offers an analytical lens to explore the politics of urban innovation.

12.4.1 Redefining the Legitimacy of Urban Policy

One can identify a variety of city experiments, which differ according to the ways in which they articulate the roles and identities of experimenters, the entities being experimented with, the perimeter of the laboratory in which experiments are conducted, and the audiences to which they are addressed. One can thus speak of "techno-city", in which a single entity centralizes the conduct of experiments in a controlled and planned manner (Kargon and Molella 2008). Here, an extreme case might be provided by cities that are built from scratch as test-beds—the Korean town of Songdo being a primary example (Halpern et al. 2013). In other situations, experiments are tied to nation-building projects, as, for example, Singapore seeks to turn itself into a laboratory for foreign companies to test technological innovation (Laurent et al. forthcoming).

In San Francisco, experiments are tied to an imagination of the city making innovation a central component of the urban fabric, in which the close relationships between the tech sector and Mayor Lee's vision of the city can then be situated. This is apparent when considering the series of initiatives undertaken by Edwin Lee. In 2012, Lee created an Office of Civic Innovation (OCI) within the Mayor's Office. This Office was the first of its kind in the U.S. and was expected to make sure that the city of San Francisco, "surrounded by innovation in the private sector", "did not just follow behind".[11] One can identify here a variation on the evolutions introduced in the first section of this chapter, as public bodies adopt practices originating from the private sector, while also attempting to lure companies and investors. The evolution might be even deeper though. Consider for instance the "Start-up in Residence" (STIR) program, created by the OCI in 2013. The objective of this program is to connect the city's departments with start-ups in order to craft technological solutions to problems met by the departments. In 2013, 200 applications were sent to the Office, and 6 start-ups were eventually associated with 6 city departments. The contest ended with a "demo day" during which the outcomes of the process were presented to public officials, including the mayor himself, and potential investors—some of them could then be pursued as commercial projects, or inside city departments. Within this process, the OCI helps city departments to identify the problems they want to address, and provide support to interested start-ups. Over the past years, the contest has resulted in several projects that had been used by public bodies, including for instance a prototype built by a partnership between a private company, a non-profit organization and the San Francisco airport services and meant to help blind and disabled people circulate inside the airport.

In an initiative such as STIR, the objective is dual, as it aims both to make city officials think like private actors, and private actors think about urban problems. Here, the experimental intervention offers a format of action that makes this re-alignment possible.[12] Designed as a service expected to articulate public and private

---

[11]Interview, OCI, February 19, 2016.

[12]Another illustration of OCI's activities is an initiative called "Civic Bridge", which "recruits private sector professionals to volunteer 16 weeks of their time to work alongside government

interventions, the OCI's work is not just about delegating public service to private actors, but aims to transform both. As the same official stated, the objective of the program is to "bring start-up thinking into the government", and "the tech ecosystem to think more about civic issues".[13]

Many of the examples introduced above can be read as illustrations of these themes. Projects based on the production and manipulation of transportation or parking data are realized in partnership with a foundation called City Innovate, which has been working closely with the Mayor's office. City Innovate organizes public events such as the annual *Bridge SF* conference, during which leaders from both the public sector and private companies discuss the objectives and practices of civic innovations, and the ways in which both groups can contribute to each other's objectives.[14] City Innovate and the OCI worked in partnership to conduct the Start-up in Residence (STIR) program by jointly selecting eligible start-ups. City Innovate could then also intervene at the end of the process, by acting as a potential investor in the start-ups deemed interesting after the selection phase (the foundation is linked to a venture capital fund and its executive director has an investment banking background). Thus, City Innovate is far more than a broker between public bodies and private actors. It also aims to turn city actors into entrepreneurs, and innovators into both contributors to city policies and potential successful entrepreneurs. Its rationale for intervening with public and private actors of the San Francisco scene is that local policy action needs to be understood in the terms of a series of problems to solve, for which the government itself has no possibility to find answers. As the director of City Innovate said during an interview:

> Most of those problems won't be solved unless you get some collaboration between public, private and academia. (…) San Francisco public agencies will bring a city problem to the lab, and we will talk to the stakeholders (Airbnb, Uber…) to see how they could get involved. (…) We are business focused. We have a network; we choose the most adapted local start-up. (K. S., Founder and Executive Director, City Innovate Foundation, 17/02/2016)

In San Francisco, what the experimental format both facilitates and depends upon is a pervasive intervention of private actors in city affairs, as well as a distributed alignment between private interests and the definition of urban issues.

This evolution of private and public roles in the city is articulated with another one, which makes experiments alternatives to other types of urban intervention that would require costly investments in infrastructure. At the SFMTA Office of Innovation, the OCI or within City Innovate, people would regularly point to a renewed ability to act in the city thanks to small-scale interventions. A member of City Innovate provided telling figures during an interview. She quantified the maintaining costs of cities' subway system as a "$17 billion bill" and rhetorically asked whether one could

---

employees on critical City issues". One of the regularly mentioned examples is that of Google, 6 employees of which volunteered to work with city officials on the analysis of data related to calls in emergency management services, and to search for affordable housing online. (http://www.innovation.sfgov.org/civic-bridge).

[13] Interview, OCI, February 19, 2016.

[14] http://www.bridgesf.city/.

"justify expanding and building new stations" while maintaining the system alone cost that much.[15] An official of the SFMTA Office of Innovation adopted this mode of reasoning as he described the value of the "innovative programs of green bike lanes, red bus lanes, parcels" as follows: "the public started to get the sense that things were happening in their neighborhood—it was in the thousands of dollars, not millions, but brought very visible results".[16] By contrast to costly investments tied to long term planning, experiments allow urban actors to intervene quickly, and display visible outcomes.

The political negotiations that go with this type of intervention request multiple adjustments between public and private actors, and the permanent redefinitions of urban problems and potential solutions (Laurent and Talvard 2017). Described as such, this type of political action offers a stark contrast with practices of local politics in San Francisco, where interest groups are organized into "single-issue lobby groups" that advocate for the issues they care for. This mode of organization has resulted in coalitions that might be unexpected, as, for instance, pro-environment and pro-business groups become allies for the sake of limiting the development of high-rise buildings (Hartman 2002).

Advocacy through single-issue lobby groups has been the topic of lengthy debates in the press,[17] and among the actors of urban policies in San Francisco. In San Francisco, the advocates of urban innovation as it is conducted at the OCI, the SFMTA Office of Innovation, or City Innovation, would speak of the "conservatism" of advocacy politics, which is based on the defense of well-defined interests, at the expense of the permanent redefinition of urban problems and solutions that the experimental format renders possible. In Donald McNeill's term, advocacy politics is part of the "old economy" that is being disrupted by current city policies (McNeill 2016). This opposition also points to an important dimension of the politics of innovation in urban environment, namely the political subjectivities that emerge from innovation projects: who are the political actors expected to intervene in city life? How is their role imagined? Are they imagined as assembled in some collective forms?

12.4.2 Re-assembling Political Subjectivities

When asked with regards to city experiments, the questions above point to particular political subjectivities. Turning people into experimental subjects can take various forms. Pricing experiments are initiatives that turn users of public transportation systems or car drivers into experimental subjects caught in multiple tests. The efficiency of urban policies here is dependent on the ability to manufacture these experimental subjects. This reading is not entirely passive though. Incentive-based systems perform economic modes of reasoning, as inhabitants are expected to weight costs and

---

[15]Interview with M. K., City Innovate, February 17, 2016.

[16]Interview with T. P., SFMTA Office of Innovation, February 10, 2016.

[17]See e.g. "The perils of extreme democracy", *The Economist*, April 20, 2011.

benefits in real-time and adapt their behaviors accordingly. App-based transportation systems use data collected from the users themselves.

Perhaps more importantly, inhabitants are expected to actively engage in experimental practices. Manufacturing innovators has become institutionalized practice in numerous settings, from high education organizations to technology companies (Wisnowski et al. 2019). In the urban context, city policies become innovation policies in that they seek to turn inhabitants into innovators. This evolution can be identified in numerous settings. In Medellin (Columbia), for instance, the narrative of the transformation of the city from the capital of drug to (yet another) capital of innovation is sustained by city policies organized in such ways that inhabitants are expected to be turned into contributors to the city's innovation objective (Talvard 2018). In Singapore, the Smart Nation program seeks to turn Singaporeans into innovators, able to actively intervene in the development of new technologies. When he presented the overall objective of the program, the deputy director of the "Smart Nation Programme Office" drew a contrast between the "traditional" mode of technology development in Singapore, relying on the intervention of foreign companies, and what he hoped could be a path for the development of a new Singaporean citizenry, made of creators and innovators.[18]

Thus, "activating" city dwellers and turning them into innovators has become a common trope in urban policies, possibly mirroring a more general topic of concern in neo-liberal projects of government. This undertaking takes various forms. In Medellin, it is articulated with the would-be transformation of the city alongside a path of urban development that would be "inclusive", and possibly a model for the global south (Talvard 2018). In Singapore, it goes with a problematization of the nation as in need for experimentation—whether it is addressed to foreign companies using the city-state as a suitable laboratory before future extension, or to an internal workforce hopefully turned into participants in technological progress (Laurent et al. forthcoming). In San Francisco, turning citizens into innovators goes through the multiplicity of initiatives whereby inhabitants are invited to intervene in small-scale initiatives at street levels (as in the "Pavement to Park" initiatives or the "Living Innovation Zones"), participate as experimental subjects into the many tests related to the use of data for optimization objectives, use city data to propose new apps for the identification and solving of urban problems. Some of the manifestations of the manufacturing of innovators can be easily connected to more general movements making public bodies adopt the norms of the private sector, as, for instance, the OCI defines its task as that of the transformation of the public administration into an organization made of "intrapreneurs", promoting entrepreneur-like state of mind through which civil servants may think of public policies in the terms of isolated problems for which private companies might have technological answers. But the experimental format in San Francisco also sustains a particular imagination of the city, whereby permanent innovation reconfigures city life as a matter of real-time adjustment of problems and solutions, social groups and their concerns, urban issues and the spatial organization of the city. The "real-time democracy" that emerges from

---

[18]Colleagues and I assisted to this presentation during a field visit in February 2017.

12 Innovation for Whom? City Experiments and the Redefinition ...

these initiatives (Laurent and Talvard 2017) might be the most explicit manifestation of the politics of innovation in San Francisco.

12.4.3 Counter-Experiments and an Alternative City

We can now go back to the oppositions with which we opened our reflection about the politics of innovation in the city. On the first side of the opposition between the tech sector and San Francisco activists, the previous pages have introduced a political project articulating stability/instability, social/technical, and local/global in such ways that innovation becomes a basis for real-time democracy. In San Francisco, city experiments are "social innovation", not in the sense that they would not be "technical" (they can be highly technologized!) but in that they reshape the social fabric of the city in experimental terms, thereby redefining the sources of political legitimacy and envisioning new political subjectivities.

The alternatives that activists propose are not just about the "stability" of urban identities (as opposed to the instability brought about by technological change), "social innovation" (as opposed to technical development) and "local" activism (that would be opposed to global forces). The lens of city experiments is again particularly helpful here, in that it suggests considering activists' interventions as counter-experiments. This expression points to operations that are meant as responses to other experiments, and explicitly meant to displace their aims (Laurent 2011). As in scientific practices, where experimenters might face opponents who built other laboratories, redefine experimental parameters, and eventually propose counter demonstrations (Latour 1993), the urban life can display counter experimental interventions. Two examples are particularly telling in the case of San Francisco.

First, one can regard the Google bus protests as operations aiming to produce public proofs. Using the dual meaning of the word "demonstration", Andrew Barry has shown that public protests can be understood in experimental terms (Barry 1999). Spectacular interventions configure a parallel public space, where collective problems and social identities are redefined. In San Francisco, the Google bus protests were small-scale events, intended to display the connection between the transformation of the city and those who benefited from it—namely wealthy tech sector workers. They were localized, on the streets of San Francisco, and involved only small numbers of people, in some cases only a dozen. But as spectacular demonstrations, they cannot be understood without taking the active construction of audience they rely on into account. The media presence and the social network activities that accompanied the protests made their audience as global as the companies they targeted. As such, the Google bus protests were flexible, small-scale interventions associated with powerful demonstrations, or, in other words, counter-experiments. They were experiments conducted in the city as well as with the city, as they turned the urban space into a site of intervention, where the flows of tech workers could be visibly confronted with collectives associating local inhabitants and global audiences.

A second type of activist interventions in San Francisco provides an illustration of counter-experiments. The Anti-Eviction Mapping Project can be described as a form of "data activism" (Milan and van der Velden 2016), in that its objective is to gather data in order to map increases in rents, narratives of evictions, or ties between initiatives in urban redevelopment and business interests.[19] While it shares with many public bodies and private companies in San Francisco an interest for the production and use of data for experimental practices, the anti-eviction mapping project connects data production, aggregation and use on the one hand, and political representation and collective action on the other hand in a way that strongly differs from those who see San Francisco as the "innovation capital of the world". While the latter, in imagining the city of permanent innovation make data a vehicle for the permanent reformulation of problems and solutions, the anti-eviction mapping project uses them as a tool for displaying one single and major problem—that of the transformation of the city for the benefit of the few. Within this project, the aggregation of data helps activists to gather collectives. They use maps as tools for displaying unacceptable social evolutions and, in parallel, the existence of groups suffering from them. The bus protests made the urban space a site of global demonstration. The anti-eviction mapping project proposes to re-arrange the digital representation of the urban space so that pressing social issues can be displayed, and new collectives can be turned into political actors.

These two experimental interventions offer a stark contrast to the politics of innovation that imagines the city in the terms of real-time democracy. The counter-experiments are also innovation practices, yet at the service of an alternative imagination of political legitimacy and political subjectivities, and ultimately of the city itself. Here, the legitimacy of the urban intervention is tied to the ability to display to whom the transformations of the city are directed, and political subjectivities are shaped in collective forms according to the issues that are made visible. The city becomes less a space defined by the permanent adjustment of small-scale problems and solutions than the outcome of practices associating local inhabitants and global audiences according to concerns about transportation and housing issues that necessarily extend in space and time.

An executive director at the non-profit, Oakland-based organization Ecocity Builders, Kristin Miller described the maps produced by the anti-eviction mapping project as public demonstrations and proofs of the "failure of belief in the city as a common, a city that supports existing residents and new arrivals by integrating them into the collective spaces and systems perhaps best represented by public transportation" (Miller 2014: 62). This quote points to a radical redefinition of the controversies between innovation and its critics in San Francisco. Less than oppositions between stable/instable, social/technical, and local/global, these controversies are revelatory of a clash between different political projects that articulate innovation and society in different ways, and ultimately construe the city in different ways. Real-time democracy, on the one hand, is based on the ability to permanently redefine and adjust urban problems and technological solutions. The counter-experiments that activists

---

[19]See: http://www.antievictionmap.com.

propose, on the other hand, suggest new tools for assembling collectives in the city, whether by targeting the sole benefactors of urban transformations during the bus protests, or by gathering data about the evolutions of the city. The "new class warfare" then appears far wider than the contest over the distribution of capital across the city. It is an opposition about the type of society one might want to live in in the city, and the sociotechnical tools that might be used to realize this collective project.

12.5 Conclusion

The contemporary transformations of cities have been described in numerous analytical languages, including "neo-liberalism", "knowledge economy", or "privatization" (e.g. May and Perry 2016). Such general categories are impetus to further analyze the frictions that technological innovation introduces in cities. Oppositions can be easily identified between the instability introduced by technological change and the stability of urban collectives, technical innovation and social resistance, global forces and local practices. In a city such as San Francisco, which claims to be the "innovation capital of the world", one can locate these oppositions in recent protests that have accompanied the growing influence of the tech sector in the definition of urban policies. Taken at face value, these oppositions risk masking the various layers of the politics of innovation in the city. This chapter has argued that a way to account for the politics of innovation in the city in more nuanced ways is to take the experimental dimension of urban innovation seriously. Used by city actors in San Francisco as elsewhere, the experimental language also offers an analytical lens able to cut across the somewhat simplistic oppositions by which one could be tempted to account for urban controversies related to technological innovation. The objective is then to analyze the conduct of experiments and the type of urban laboratory at stake, rather than considering them ready-made explanatory resources.

When following this approach, one can identify in San Francisco a problematization of the sources of democratic legitimacy based on city experiments, as well as a proposition for the identification of the active participants of urban life - namely those who engage in those experiments. The "real-time democracy" that emerges here is also the outcome of economic ordering processes, as private actors make urban issues a new source of market demand, and, perhaps more fundamentally, as inhabitants are expected to adopt economic modes of reasoning, following incentives, or acting as entrepreneurs to propose new solutions for urban problems. The example of San Francisco offers a contrast, in the same city, to this problematization of innovation, as activists propose to shape new communities to fight against the transformation of the city for the benefit of the few. This alternative problematization is less a "stable", "social" and "local" version of innovation, than a proposition for another politics of innovation, and, ultimately, another society. The particularities of the case of San Francisco can provide lessons for the analysis of the current transformations of the city. They display the interest of studying city experiments as experiments "in" the city, and "with" the city, which can be conducted in different ways (as, for instance, counter-experiments are organized in San Francisco) and, as comparisons with cities like Medellin or Singapore suggest, for the sake of different politics of innovation.

The cases discussed in this chapter display innovation as a site of democratic struggle, not only because of concerns about who can participate in it, who benefit from it, and for the sake of what objectives, but also because innovation shapes individual agencies and collective organizations. Identifying the processes through which these interventions occur, and make alternatives emerge then appears as a particularly important task. The study of city experiments offers a fruitful entry point to undertake such a task.

References

Barry, A. (1999). Demonstrations: Sites and sights of direct action. *Economy and Society, 28*(1), 75–94.

Callon, M., Lascoumes, P., & Barthe, Y. (2009). *Acting in an uncertain world. An essay on technical democracy.* Cambridge: MIT Press.

De Kosnik, A. (2014). Disrupting technological privilege: The 2013–14 San Francisco google bus protests. *Performance Research, 19*(6), 99–107.

Doubleday, R., & Wynne, B. (2011). Despotism and democracy in the United Kingdom: Experiments in reframing citizenship. In S. Jasanoff (Ed.), *Reframing rights: Bioconstitutionalism in the genetic age* (pp. 239–261). Cambridge: MIT Press.

Evans, James, Karvonen, Andrew, & Raven, Rob (Eds.). (2016). *The experimental city.* Routledge: London.

Gieryn, Thomas. (2006). City as truth-spot: Laboratories and field-sites in urban studies. *Social Studies of Science, 36*(1), 5–38.

Goldman, Michael. (2011). Speculative urbanism and the making of the next world city. *International Journal of Urban and Regional Research, 35*(3), 555–581.

Graham, S., & Marvin, S. (2001). *Splintering urbanism. Networked infrastructures, technological mobilities and the urban condition.* London: Routledge.

Halpern, O., LeCavalier, J., Calvillo, N., & Pietsch, W. (2013). Test-bed urbanism. *Public Culture, 25*(2 70), 272–306.

Hartman, C. (2002). *City for sale: The transformation of San Francisco.* University of California Press.

Hiroi, Y. (2019). Science as care: Science and innovation in post-growth society. In S. Lechevalier (Ed.), *Innovation beyond technology* (pp. 301–324). Berlin: Springer.

Jasanoff, Sheila. (1998). The political science of risk perception. *Reliability Engineering & System Safety, 59*(1), 91–99.

Kargon, Robert H., & Molella, Arthur P. (2008). *Invented Edens: Techno-cities of the twentieth century.* Cambridge: MIT Press.

Karvonen, Andrew, & van Heur, Bas. (2014). Urban laboratories: Experiments in reworking cities. *International Journal of Urban and Regional Research, 38*(2), 379–392.

Kitchin, Rob. (2014). The real-time city? Big data and smart urbanism. *GeoJournal, 79*(1), 1–14.

Kusago, T. (2019). Post-disaster community recovery and community-based collaborative action research—A case of process evaluation method for community life improvement. In S. Lechevalier (Ed.), *Innovation beyond technology* (pp. 195–221). Berlin: Springer.

Latour, Bruno. (1983). Give me a laboratory and I will raise the world. *Science Observed, 141,* 170.

Latour, B. (1993). *The pasteurization of France.* Harvard University Press.

Laurent, Brice. (2011). Technologies of democracy: Experiments and demonstrations. *Science and Engineering Ethics, 17*(4), 649–666.

Laurent, B., & Talvard, F. (2017). *Real-time democracy. Imagining the city of permanent innovation.* i3 Working Paper Series, 17-CSI-01.

Laurent, B., Muniesa, F., Doganova, L., & Gasull, C. (Forthcoming). The test-bed island: tech business experimentalism and the imaginary of exception in Singapore. Under review.

Laurent, Brice, & Tironi, Martin. (2015). A field test and its displacements. Accounting for an experimental mode of industrial innovation. *CoDesign, 11*(3-4), 208–221.

Laurent, Brice. (2016). Political experiments that matter: Ordering democracy from experimental sites. *Social Studies of Science, 46*(5), 773–794.

Lezaun, J., & Soneryd, L. (2007). Consulting citizens: Technologies of elicitation and the mobility of publics. *Public Understanding of Science, 16*(3), 279.

Maharawal, Manissa. (2014). Protest of gentrification and eviction technologies in San Francisco. *Progressive Planning, 199,* 20–24.

Marres, N. (2012). *Material participation: Technology, the environment and everyday publics.* Palgrave Macmillan.

May, Tim, & Perry, Beth. (2016). Cities, experiments and the logics of the knowledge economy. In James Evans, Andrew Karvonen, & Rob Raven (Eds.), *The experimental city* (p. 32). London: Routledge.

McNeill, Donald. (2016). Governing a city of unicorns: technology capital and the urban politics of San Francisco. *Urban Geography, 37*(4), 494–513.

Milan, Stefania, & van der Velden, Lonneke. (2016). The alternative epistemologies of data activism. *Digital Culture & Society, 2*(2), 57–74.

Miller, K. (2014). Mapping our disconnect. *Boom: A Journal of California, 4*(2), 62–67.

Millo, Y., & Lezaun, J. (2006). Regulatory experiments: genetically modified crops and financial derivatives on trial. *Science and Public Policy, 33*(3), 179–190.

Mitchell, T. (2005). The work of economics: how a discipline makes its world. *Archives Européennes de Sociologie, 46*(2), 297.

Mitchell, K. (2004). *Crossing the neoliberal line: Pacific Rim migration and the metropolis.* Temple University Press.

Muniesa, F., & Callon, M. (2007). Economic experiments and the construction of markets. In D. MacKenzie, F. Muniesa, & L. Siu (Eds.), Do economists make markets? On the performativity of economics (pp. 163–189). Princeton University Press.

Pinch, T. (1993). Testing: One, two, three … testing! Toward a sociology of testing. *Science, Technology & Human Values, 18*(1), 25–41.

Roy, A. (2003). Paradigms of propertied citizenship: Transnational techniques of analysis. *Urban Affairs Review, 38*(4), 463–491.

Ruphy, S. (2019). Public participation in the setting of research and innovation agenda: Virtues and challenges from a philosophical perspective. In S. Lechevalier (Ed.), *Innovation beyond technology* (pp. 243–261). Berlin: Springer.

SFMTA. (2015). *City of San Francisco: Meeting the smart city challenge.* Notice of funding opportunity DTFH6116RA00002.

Shapin, S., & Schaffer, S. (1985). *Leviathan and the air-pump. Hobbes, Boyle, and the experimental life.* Princeton: Princeton University Press.

Talvard, F. (2018). Can urban 'miracles' be engineered in laboratories? Turning Medellin into a model city for the Global South? In Claudio Coletta, Leighton Evans, Liam Heaphy, & Rob Kitchin (Eds.), *Creating smart cities* (pp. 62–75). London: Routledge.

Tironi, M., & Sánchez Criado, T. (2015). Of sensors and sensitivities. Towards a cosmopolitics of "smart cities"?. *Tecnoscienza: Italian Journal of Science & Technology Studies, 6*(1), 89–108.

Wisniowski, M., Hintz, E., & Kleine, M. S. (Ed.). (2019). *Does America need more innovators?* Cambridge: MIT Press.

Chapter 13
Image of Jurisprudence Reconstructed to Enhance Innovation: Liability Allocation for Improved Predictability

Takehiro Ohya

Abstract Law is generally imaged to be stickler to human rights, often taking its stance to be against technological developments which possibly infringe "humane territory". In this chapter, however, the author tries to show the positive effect of law to enhance innovation, by designing proper allocation of responsibility through legislation. In the case of advancing artificial intelligence (AI) technology, for instance, the "trolley problem" is often used to indicate the difficulty of choice between two alternatives, and thus to show the danger to leave such decision to non-human beings as AIs. But considering that the system of "legal bodies" as companies could be seen as an artificial reality to establish something to hold rights and duties to be liable to the results of their action, we could notice the function of law to establish social institutions apart from the natural order, to sustain or enhance welfare and happiness of the society. Taking example from the problem of traffic accident committed by level 4 auto-driving car, the author tries to discuss the alternatives on the allocation of responsibilities and liabilities, and to show that some of them will surely suppress the further technological innovation, concluding that law may work as a measure for the society to avoid falling into such pitfalls.

13.1 Introduction

To begin with, let us discuss on the doubt some may have, that law can in any way enhance innovation. It is true, for instance in a representative theory of law as Jeremy Bentham's (Bentham 1776) to consider law to be commands of the sovereign to prohibit certain actions by threat of sanction (imprisonment or death penalty, typically),[1] it would be hard to imagine them to have any positive effect on scientific

---

[1] As Bentham wrote, "[T]he efficacy of power is, in part at least, in proportion to the promptitude of obedience: the promptitude of obedience is, in part, in proportion to the promptitude of command: command is an expression of will: a will is sooner formed by one than many" (Bentham 1776: Chap. 2, para. 10), he considered any law to be a command of the sovereign, forced by sanctions.

T. Ohya (✉)
Keio University, Tokyo, Japan
e-mail: t-ohya@keio.jp

© Springer Nature Singapore Pte Ltd. 2019
S. Lechevalier (ed.), *Innovation Beyond Technology*, Creative Economy,
https://doi.org/10.1007/978-981-13-9053-1_13

or technological development. If the owl of Minerva spreads its wings only with the falling of the dusk, insisting that philosophy always appears after something has happened as Hegel put it (Hegel 1821), how about Iustitia, the Roman goddess of law whose eyes are frequently shown covered by blindfold? Is her sword swung blindly in the night?

This doubt may reflect in many representative views from economics toward legal system. One of the early economic theorist Henri de Saint-Simon, commonly counted as utopian socialist, considered that the government would inevitably hinder the function of the industrial class who in their nature tend to enhance the efficiency of the whole society, thus should be limited to the minimum (de Saint-Simon 1816–7). For de Saint-Simon, those who work for the production, not limited to the laborers but including businessmen, managers, scientists, or bankers, should unite to fight against "the idling class", who occupied the government. Herbert Spencer, a representative social Darwinist or precursor of libertarians, shared this view that the scope of the government, and thus law, should be strictly limited (Spencer 1851). Along with his theory on evolution to see everything as developing from simple, undifferentiated homogeneity to complex, differentiated heterogeneity, he predicted the social evolution from the militant depending on the hierarchy and obedience to the industrial consisted from voluntary and contractual relationship. Under this vision, the law should be given its role not more than to ensure contracts to work, which reflects in the idea of many Chicago school economists as Milton Friedman to consider law as the measure to protect economic rights as property to enhance industrial or commercial growth.

My answer to this point is simple: yes, the law or we the lawyers may hardly help enhancing innovation, but we can kill them.[2] We can easily imagine the way to prohibit or obstacle development to be achieved safely. Thus, on the other hand, to realize innovations we need to avoid such a trap. At least to secure that there would not be such kind of unreasonable doubt or trick, we need to do something in law, technology, or their relation.[3] In this chapter, I will try to show how legal framework may effect on the development of certain technology, taking an example from emerging AI (artificial intelligence) and one of its typical implement, autonomous driving cars. Summarizing my conclusion, I will suggest the relation between the framework of risk allocation controlled by law, and the action of agents probably taken under such system, to propose by designing better allocation through legislation we can improve the predictability in our society and can enhance innovation.

---

[2]This expression may be in resonance with the one of Michael Polanyi, quoted by Ruphy (2019).

[3]On the same time, law can be understood as the outcome from political processes. The San Francisco delivery robot story, examined by Laurent (2019), could be considered as the case of conflict between innovation and the legal rules, which probably established on the will of the existing residents. This perspective can lead us to emphasize the importance of public understanding or acceptance, which is supported in the discussion of Kusago (2019), Ruphy (2019), and Hiroi (2019), and (negatively) referred to in Sect. 13.2.3 of this chapter.

13.2 The Legal Problem of Technology Development

13.2.1 The Trolley and AI

Let us start our discussion by introducing the so-called "trolley problem," made famous by Professor Michael Sandel (Sandel 2009). Suppose a trolley loses control while moving. The switch is set for the trolley to steer to the right, but this will hit and kill 5 railway workers. It is possible to move the switch to send the trolley to the left so that these 5 will be saved, but 1 pedestrian will be hit to death instead. In a typical scenario, the conductor is supposed to stand by the switch and decide whether to change the direction and bring 1 person to death intentionally, or to not intervene and thus leave 5 workers to their fate.

This would be a tough dilemma for a human conductor, indicating one's theoretical position over morality. Typically, those who respect utilitarianism of Jeremy Bentham shall choose to change the switch to minimize the loss of life, while a deontologist like Immanuel Kant will refrain himself from intentionally bringing any innocent to death, so that not to change the switch to save the passerby, which eventually cause 5 railway workers' death. In this example Professor Sandel tried to make your ethical standpoint clear, reflecting the choice you will make in the imagined situation. But consider the consequences if the switch was controlled by an AI: This would raise the question of how we should design AI to respond appropriately in such situations.

Such issues reflect one of the fundamental problems in realizing self-driving cars: How should we program the vehicle's AI to properly value human life in a situation when the vehicle needs to choose between hitting 5 pedestrians or applying the emergency brake, which could cause the driver's death? As in the original trolley problem, one can choose not to decide, which will leave 5 people dead, but not by intentional intervention. We may naturally doubt if this default choice is truly neutral or already justified, as does Professor Cass Sunstein's famous criticism against "*status quo* neutrality*" (Sunstein 1993).[4] In the self-driving car scenario, however, we need to note that the first choice—to do nothing and thus hit the pedestrians—would also be the outcome of the program of the AI, which certainly was written by someone. Since the writer of the code, as Professor Lawrence Lessig called (Lessig 1999),[5]

---

[4]Professor Sunstein criticized the wide-spread attitude to put the burden of proof on those who propose to make some change, pointing out that such an attitude presupposed "*status quo* neutrality", which ranked the current situation as just, groundlessly. Rather, he claimed, we need to check the justness and constitutionality of the situation of our human rights protection continuously, sufficiently suspicious on the possible unjustness existing social systems may contain.

[5]Professor Lessig picked up the 4 modalities of regulation or constraint—norms, law, market and architecture—, to warn about the increasing use of the last one. While the architecture, defined as the physical constraints on our activities as locks on doors, certainly limits our possibility or capability of actions, it may hardly be noticed, anticipated, or resisted, as the other modalities of power. Moreover, in the net sphere, though what we can do was given and defined by the codes of many computer programs, the writers will mainly be huge software industries, out of our democratic control. From these elements, our liberty, the possible range of action on the internet and computers, can be intensely affected without our agreement and control, Professor Lessig worried.

made certain choice to be the default, we cannot consider it to be natural. The situation is created, from head to tail, artificially.

A possible attitude against this trouble will be to inhibit AIs to make such choice—the calculations on human-life must be prohibited for automated machines or AIs, since it would endanger human dignity and thus human rights. It could be true, so that the switch will not be changed to cause 5 men's death. If we think that this would be not so much a happy solution, we need to think in a different way.

13.2.2 Negligence Liability

Before moving on, let us make the problem clear. In the area of civil law, most countries share the common principle known as the negligence liability, meaning that those who could control and predict the outcome of the situation shall be held liable.[6] Thus, negative outcomes are assumed to be caused by an agent's *intention* to make harm, or the agent's failure to anticipate and control the situation (*negligence*). Since we can clearly say that intent to cause harm is more blameworthy than negligence, we can consider this principle as to exempt any liability from the action without negligence. In short, we can express this idea shortly as the principle "no negligence, no liability".

In most car accident cases under the current technology, the driver is typically blamed for failing to anticipate expected situations and failing to control his or her car. The driver, we consider, will have sufficient capacity to recognize and make decisions if the situation arose while driving, thus we can put certain responsibility on him to avoid any unhappy event to occur.[7]

Along with the increasing doubt on such capacity to make rational decision, as typically in the cases under developed and complex technologies, we gradually came to modify the principle to introduce certain systems to switch so called "burden of proof": in principle in the lawsuit to claim compensations against the damage caused by the intention or negligence of the defendant, the plaintiff needs to proof the necessary conditions, i.e. that the lawful right or interest of the plaintiff was infringed, the existence of intention or negligence, the existence of damage, and the

---

[6]For instance, the Japanese Civil Code (Act no. 89 of 1896) states in its Article 709, "A person who has intentionally or negligently infringed any right of others, or legally protected interest of others, shall be liable to compensate any damages resulting in consequence".

[7]In reality, however, we may estimate certain cases in which the ordinary negligence liability system fails to give proper and just remedy for the damaged. The typical case will be the accident caused by a stolen car, in which the driver run away to be unknown. To solve this kind of trouble, in Japanese law, the strict liability has been introduced for providers of drive, typically car owners who can manage and control the usage of vehicles, in combination with the compulsory insurance for them (the Act to Secure Compensations for Car Accidents (Act no. 97 of 1955)). While we may consider this to be an example of allocation system of risks arose in the society, to show the basic understanding concerning the framework of legal liability, we will ignore such additional legal schemes in the discussion of this chapter.

causal connection between them. In certain areas, however, this burden of proof was transferred to the defendant by special legislations.

The system of product liability will be a typical case. In the situations where some damages were caused from the defect in manufacturing consumer products, there will exist certain asymmetry between the plaintiff (consumer) and the defendant (manufacture company), where both expertise and factual evidence are mostly monopolized by the latter. To avoid the ordinary negligence liability system to fail, most countries choose to transfer the special burden to the defendants, typically far more strong manufacture companies, to proof their innocence in the manufacturing process.[8]

Even in these cases, however, the principle "no negligence, no liability" has never varied. It is sure that the burden of proof was transferred to the manufacturers. The consumer now no longer needs to prove the existence of manufacturers' negligence, since it is presumed from the damage caused by the product. But the manufacturers can still *negate* their own liability by proving the *non-existence* of their negligence.[9]

From here, we shift to the problem of auto-driving. In the auto-driving level 4 (NHTSA 2013), a car will move autonomously, with no means of interference or control from inside.[10] Thus, there would no longer be a driver, but only a passenger who can only sit in the car and pray there would be no accident. Under the system of negligence liability, such passengers could not be held liable, since they could not control the situation.

But the situation will generally not be different for the manufacturer.[11] At this stage, a car would be driven by deep-learning AI with self-learning capacity. When

---

[8]For instance in Japan, the Product Liability Act (Act no. 85 of 1994) prescribes in its Article 3, "The manufacturer, etc. shall be liable for damages arising from the infringement of life, body or property of others which is caused by the defect in the delivered product which was manufactured, processed, imported, or provided (...), provided, however, that the manufacturer, etc. shall not be liable when the damages occur only with respect to such product".

[9]Same act, Article 4 listed the conditions to prove for the manufacturer to be exempted from the liability for the damage, as "(i) the defect in such product could not have been discovered given the state of scientific or technical knowledge at the time when the manufacturer, etc. delivered the product; or (ii) in case where the product is used as a component or raw material of another product, the defect occurred primarily because of the compliance with the instructions concerning the design given by the manufacturer of such another product, and that the manufacturer, etc. is not negligent with respect to the occurrence of such defect".

[10]Under NHTSA definition, Level 4, "Full Self-Driving Automation" was defined as "The vehicle is designed to perform all safety-critical driving functions and monitor roadway conditions for an entire trip. Such a design anticipates that the driver will provide destination or navigation input, but is not expected to be available for control at any time during the trip. This includes both occupied and unoccupied vehicles. By design, safe operation rests solely on the automated vehicle system", while level 1 provides support for one of the primary vehicle controls (brake, steering, throttle, and motive power), level 2 provides combined and integrated support for plural controls, and level 3 provides full control to free the driver from operating and monitoring the vehicle, without certain occasions in which the system requires him to be back to control (NHTSA 2013). This classification is commonly referred to by the foreign governments (including Japan), and relevant researchers.

[11]We can suppose the service providers in addition, eg. a company to buy auto-driving vehicles to provide them for the use of its customers who paid some rent, but we can consider them to be

the Alpha Go, an AI program to play Go game developed by Google DeepMind to be trained through deep learning technologies, won a game over the world champion professional player (Byford 2016), no one could explain why the program chose certain hands in many situations, but ultimately the program proved that it made the right choices. The manufacturer can set the starting framework for the self-learning process, and control what kind of information the AI will be fed, but no more. By only doing so, it will be very hard to anticipate what decision the manufactured car will make in certain situation, as in the case we prepare our children's learning environment and provide what we expect them to read or study - you can take a horse to the water, but you cannot make him drink. Even under the same learning environment, what each subject will study and how to act in certain situation reflecting the result of learning will depend on the autonomous and self-decisional process of each subject, and thus impossible to perfectly estimate or control. If manufacturers cannot expect the consequences of such learning, they will not have liability, too, from the standpoint of negligence liability system.

13.2.3 Possible Solutions?

Under this situation, we can imagine different types of solutions to the problem, none of which in my opinion are satisfactory. The first will be to dismiss the claims of accident victims as the inevitable and solemn cost of technological development. We will naturally think, however, this "solution" to be very unreasonable and unfair, since he had nothing to do with the occurrence of the accident: he did not, and could not do anything to avoid or stop the accident, but just happened to be its victim. It is unlikely we will choose this option.

The second is to hold users of auto-driving cars completely liable despite their lack of control over the movement. In earlier 3rd century, the Japanese government then sent many missions to Cao Wei (220–266 AD) and Western Jin (265–317 AD) dynasties China, the most advanced nearby country, to establish diplomatic relations to acquire culture, literacy, and technology. The problem was that Japan was separated from the Chinese mainland by the Sea of Japan, which is known to be rough and stormy and cause many shipwrecks. To address the problem, the Japanese government hired an officer named Jisai to sit on the stem of the ship, without cutting his hair or shaving his beard, to keep praying for the ship's safety. An ancient Chinese history book related that if the convoy successfully finished their journey, Jisai would be awarded an enormous prize, but if not, he would be thrown into the storming sea as a sacrifice (Chen 3rd c.). The second solution will make the user into the contemporary version of Jisai, which we will consider to be an extremely unreasonable position with groundless responsibility.

---

mostly equivalents to the manufacturers, in their lack of capacity to anticipate the action of each automated vehicles.

Considering the two options described above to be unjust, and the liability problem difficult to resolve, some lawyers may insist that unless we could find some reasonable solution we shall stop escalating the autonomy of robots or AIs to avoid endangering human dignity. For instance, we should pause at auto-driving level 1–2 (driving support) to protect innocent human beings from blame. While we can understand and be partly sympathetic with these sentiments, choosing this option means abandoning the development of AIs that could help people unable to drive, i.e., the elderly or disabled who are currently alienated from the benefits of driving. We will leave them unable or very hard to move around as they wish, substantially restrict their right to movement which is usually considered as a part of our human rights. We shall note, that if we object to this blame saying that we will change nothing intentionally but to leave the current situation as it is, we will face with the "*status quo* neutrality" criticism from Professor Sunstein.

The fourth alternative, which is rather legally technical, is to amend basic principles to introduce strict liability, under which the manufacturer shall pay for all the loss resulting from accidents, whatever the reason and the amount of damage might be. In fact, we already introduced this principle into our society in certain areas, as in the case in Japan for liability in nuclear power plant accidents, such as the case of Fukushima no. 1 (Mar. 11th, 2011).[12]

However, this principle can result in unexpected and enormous liability for the manufacturer, which in the Fukushima case, was supported by basic de jure monopoly in electricity business, secured by law.[13] But what about car-manufacturers, who are vulnerable to harsh market competition? Such liability may cause large increases in the prices of self-driving cars, potentially pricing them at prohibitive levels.

Where could we find the proper way out?

13.3 Legislative Measures

13.3.1 Establishing Corporations

Here we can introduce a longstanding and technical debate in the theory of civil law: Do corporations (or precisely, juridical persons) exist? Two different views have been

---

[12]The Act for the Compensation Caused by Nuclear Power (Act 147 of 1961) states in its Article 3, Paragraph 1, "In operating reactors, the nuclear company operating the reactor shall be liable to all the nuclear damage caused from operating the reactor; provided, however, that this does not apply to the damage caused by abnormally enormous natural disasters or social disturbances". While the Tokyo Electric Power Co. (TEPCO), the company which operates the Fukushima nuclear power plants tried to claim that the proviso in this article shall be applied to the case emerged from the Great East Japan Earthquake, the Democratic Party of Japan government then refused.

[13]Under the Electricity Business Act (Act no. 170 of 1964), the General Electricity Business to supply electricity to meet general demand was only permitted to the 10 companies separated by their supply area, including TEPCO, until the abolishment of this restriction from April, 2016 (Act no. 47 of 2015).

debated for centuries on this point. The first, typically the Germanistens as Otto von Gierke to consider juridical person to be organic entity, insisted that corporations were real entities, since otherwise we cannot understand them to have rights and duties. A corporation, for instance Keio University, consists of many elements as its campuses, buildings stand on them, persons working and studying in them, etc. Since all of them are certainly real entities existing on earth, the consisted sum, i.e. Keio University, must be a real entity, too. From this view, corporations are existence *per se*, with their own *sui generis* will, apart from the aggregated wills of their members, for instance.

On the other hand, typically the Romanisten civil lawyers as Friedrich Carl von Savigny or Rudolf von Jhering took the other view to deny this idea. They argued, for instance, if we bombed the buildings in the campus into oblivion, wherever they go, or as time goes by and the population of the University turns over completely, we will think that the University still exists somewhere, which shows that the existence of the University is not connected with real entities, but with the fiction we believe that it exists. Under this view, the corporation's will must be a summarization or aggregation of its members confirmed by certain procedure, and nothing more.

The result of the debate was the same as that of many legal debates: unclear. We reached a kind of *Modus Vivendi* in assuming that corporations exist for certain purposes while are fictitious for others. For example, we recognize corporations to have their own rights and duties, independent of those of company owners or shareholders. They are also punishable under criminal law, but not by imprisonment or death penalty. Under Japanese law, companies can contribute to political parties, but cannot vote.

And all these systems and rules are prescribed by each different scheme of law, depending on their purposes and objectives, thus in other words, artificial. This is the most important feature from my perspective: the order of existence is artificial and controllable, potentially flexible for certain objectives and purposes that could vary from area to area, problem to problem.

13.3.2 Designing Risk Allocation

From these unsatisfactory solutions discussed above, we may deduce that if we choose to unexpectedly impose total complete liability, it will cause a chilling effect and unnecessarily delay technological development. Thus, instead, maybe we can find a way to enhance social innovation by limiting and allocating liability to predictable and finite amounts.[14]

A typical way of allocating risk will be insurance, so one possible idea will be to require robots and AIs to be established as corporations and buy insurance to

---

[14]Different from the discussion of Ruphy (2019), the predictability and unpredictability I am discussing in this chapter are not on the application or development of scientific or technological researches, but on their inevitable side effect, namely, the risk of any type of accidents to occur.

cover any damages they cause. At least this solution seems to have three advantages. Firstly, it will help sharing risks necessarily involved in developing new technologies, so that many developers will be released from exaggerated fear of compensation against unexpected damages. Secondly, by securing payment for the damage from the insurances, it will help avoiding some moral panics to occur, and thus increasing social acceptance for the new technology. Thirdly, it will be relatively strong against the uncertainty in the estimation of possible damages caused from the accidents, compared to the strict liability system in which the final supplier of the goods may face with enormous unexpected damages.

The point here seems to be that the designed allocation of risk, an artificial system made through legislation, will change how far each agent—both natural persons and corporations—can challenge for making innovations. If the proposed solution to treat auto-driving vehicles as juridical persons seems to work to eliminate possible barriers in developing new technologies, it owes to the other face of legal studies or jurisprudence, not applying the existing law considered given to the situations, but artificially and intentionally designing the society we would like to live in.[15]

Let me take another example from the area of company finance. The objective to establish a juridical person, typically limited liability company, is to cut the investment away from the company owner's private property. In case the business fails and the company makes bankruptcy, the owner still can keep some of his money to start challenging again. In Japanese financial system, however, it has been common for the banks and other private financial agencies to request the company owner to provide additional security for the loan, usually real property of his own. This is very advantageous condition for those banks, since without seriously evaluating the chance for the business to survive, they can secure their loan by the land price of the owner's real property. Under this custom, however, from the viewpoint of entrepreneurs it would be very dangerous to have bank loan to start new business, since one failure will ruin all of his life getting rid of his all property including his own house. Thus, it was common for them to depend on a public finance agency such as the Japan Finance Corporation, as the safer way.

This tendency would be, however, not much happy for innovations as the development of new and advanced technologies to occur, since all the challenges will be judged from one unified standard and maybe bureaucratic viewpoint, not from different standpoints by diverse investors called "angels" as in the United States.

Considering this problem, the Japanese government recently amended its long standing Civil Code, which was originally enacted in 1898, to prohibit this kind of personal security for business purpose.[16] If it works, we can find a real example

---

[15]On Japanese situation, please note that on the problem of civil liability in traffic accidents caused by auto-driving vehicles the discussion in "the research committee of compensation liabilities in auto-driving" formed in the Ministry of Land, Infrastructure, and Transport, in relation with the Act to Secure Compensations for Car Accidents. The committee published its final report on the issues toward legislation, in March 2018 (http://www.mlit.go.jp/common/001226452.pdf (Japanese)).

[16]The Act to Amend a Part of the Civil Code (Act no. 44 of 2017), which will come into force from April, 2020.

of changing the design of risk allocation to enhance innovation, and some need to improve the self-understanding of lawyers on what we are, and shall, doing.

13.3.3 The Traditional Image of Jurisprudence

Some of the legal researchers, including myself, are trying to make philosophical investigations on legal notions as right, justice, and equality, or considering influence of information technologies on legal and political systems. This field is generally called as the philosophy of law, or Rechtsphilosophy in German, but also called as jurisprudence, especially in Anglo-American tradition. This word, jurisprudence, is consisted of two parts, i.e. "juris-" meaning law and judiciary, and "prudence", wise thinking, to show that it mainly put importance in trial and court procedure up to judgment, as shown in the interpretive theory of representative legal philosopher of the age Ronald Dworkin, to suppose "right answer" (Dworkin 1977a, Chap. 2, 3, 4, and 13) (Dworkin 1977b) on certain case to be judgment made by ideal judge Hercules to realize basic principle of certain society (Dworkin 1986).

This tendency to hail the function of the judiciary could match well with Anglo-American tradition of judge-made law, but even in the United States some criticism appeared, for instance by Professor Jeremy Waldron, to point out that too much respect for judiciary could limit the democratic power of legislation (Waldron 1999). According to him, current situation widely recognized in the world is not the Rawlsian "circumstances of justice" (Rawls 1971: 126–130)[17] in which people with different conception of life seeking coexistence based on human rights protection, but the "circumstances of politics" in which people struggling on the interpretation of the meaning of human rights *ab initio*. To solve this, fundamental debate and decision-making process in parliament must be respected, not undemocratic court adjudication.

Along with the increasing political antagonism and struggles, our bias to judiciary was reviewed in many countries as to the proposal of a new field of study, "legisprudence", which connected "legis", the legislation, with prudence. Professor Luc J. Wintgens is one of the representative scholars to lead this movement into the publication of a global journal, which "focuses on the creation of law, a subject that

---

[17]Rawls tried to specify "the normal conditions under which human cooperation is both possible and necessary" (Rawls 1971: 126), which consist the circumstance where the principle of justice will work. According to him, the conditions may be divided into two parts, objective and subjective, where the former includes such elements as they are "roughly similar in physical and mental powers", "vulnerable to attack, and all are subject to having their plans blocked by the united force of others", or "there is the conditions of moderate scarcity understood to cover a wide range of situations" (Rawls 1971: 126–127), and the latter means that "the parties have roughly similar needs and interests, or needs and interests in various ways complementary, so that mutually advantageous cooperation among them is possible", while "they nevertheless have their own plans of life" (Rawls 1971: 127).

13 Image of Jurisprudence Reconstructed … 295

has been largely underexposed until now"(Wintgens and Hage 2007, p. iii).[18] He depicted the view from the traditional image of jurisprudence, as the following:

> Traditional legal theory takes the law as a given, and limits its theoretical undertakings to law as it is. Law, so it is said, is the result of political decision-making. Legislation as a matter of politics is not rational. Politics is believed to be a power game, resulting in compromises that are framed into a legislative or statutory structure. This power game seems to have its own "logic", the results of which outweigh, most of the time, any other form of logic.

13.3.4 Changing Japanese Society and Legislation

Also in Japan, increasing necessity to investigate on legislation arose from changing political situation. Long in the post-war era, the situation sometimes called as "legislative immobilism" existed in Japan, in which from political antagonism under the Cold War any radical reform through legislation was almost impossible (Ohya 2016). The typical example was the Criminal Code, where its Article 200 to put patricide to death penalty or life imprisonment was judged unconstitutional by the Supreme Court in 1973,[19] but left alone without amendment for more than 20 years.[20] Professor Kōya Matsuo, a famous criminal lawyer, once described this situation as "when legislation stalls like pyramid, interpretation howls as sphinx" (Matsuo 1981: 9).[21]

This tendency, however, was suddenly changed in the 1990's political reform after the end of Cold War to introduce the single non-transferable vote (SNTV) system into the House of Representatives (the lower house). Based on the strong foundation gained from the new election system, the governing party successively proposed rapid reform through legislation, calling it as the "political initiative", up to the constitutional debate in the recent years to officially amend or change interpretation of the current constitution. In the background of this movement was the idea to

---

[18] The journal was published to vol. 6 in 2012, and then was superseded by the journal *The Theory and Practice of Legislation* (2013–), from the same publisher.

[19] The Case for Patricides to be Unconstitutional (the Supreme Court grand bench judgment, April 4th, 1973). The Article 200 then stated that "A person who kills his ascendant shall be punished by the death penalty or imprisonment with work for life", thus limited the statutory penalty on patricides very heavily in comparison with ordinary murder, prescribed in the Article 199. This aggravation was judged too grave so that to lose equity with other penalties, thus unconstitutional infringing the "equality before the law", prescribed in the Article 14 of the Japanese Constitution.

[20] Article 200 of the Criminal Code (Act no. 45 of 1907) was abolished as a part of the colloquialization of the whole Code (Act no. 91 of 1995), which was originally enacted in literary style. From the unconstitutional judgment in 1973 to the abolition, prosecutors voluntarily avoided to apply Article 200, so that to accuse the patricides under Article 199 to prescribe ordinary murders—"A person who kills another shall be punished by the death penalty or imprisonment with work for life or for a definite term of not less than 3 years" (the provision before the 2004 amendment (Act no. 156 of 2004), which increased the minimum term of imprisonment to 5 years).

[21] Kōya Matsuo (1928-2017) was a professor of criminal procedure at the University of Tokyo faculty of law from 1973 to 1989, and was known as a representative scholar in the field. He served as a Special Advisor for the Ministry of Justice (2001–), and a member of the Japan Academy (2005–).

foresee and design the future of society and enhance social innovation artificially by legislation. But the question will be, is it possible, or plausible.

Symbolically, one of the bestsellers in the age in Japan was titled as "the Alteration Plan for Japan" (Ozawa 1993) in the literal translation, while its English version resonates with this—"Blueprint for a New Japan" (Ozawa 1994). The author on the surface, Ichirō Ozawa, had been one of the representative and powerful statesmen in the Liberal Democratic Party (LDP; Jimin-tō), the long-standing government party from 1955 to 93. Though he was rumoured to be the "Kingmaker" of Miyazawa cabinet (1991-93) as the substantive leader of Keisei-kai, the largest faction in the LDP then, he was forced to dash out from it, to make his own "Kaikaku Fōramu 21 (Reform Forum 21)" with Tsutomu Hata (Oct. 1992), ending up to form the Shinsei-tō (Japan Renewal Party; Jun. 1993) as a part of the non-LDP coalition government (Aug. 1993 - Jun. 1994) to terminate the LDP regime. It was while this process that Ozawa published the book to propose the more active commitment to global security, neo-liberal economic policy, and establishment of two-party system politics with the chance of substantive regime-change, to position himself and his colleagues as "reformist" fighting against the old-guards. Though Ozawa and his party was kicked out from the Murayama cabinet (1994–96) under coalition between the LDP, the Socialist Party of Japan, and Shintō Sakigake (the New Party Sakigake), many features of his vision were reflected to, and realized under, Koizumi cabinet (2001–06), including the active commitment to the U.S. "War on Terrorism",[22] and the Privatization of Japanese postal service.[23]

Some of the Japanese legal scholars, including myself, have started committing into the legislative studies under this situation, reached to the publication of 3 volumes of collaborative work between legal philosophers and positive lawyers as a part of the project by the Science Council of Japan (Inoue et al. 2014). This project, however, seems to show some problems or limits of its core ideas, in my opinion.

Along with the progress of legisprudence study, many positive lawyers emphasized their doubt in its goal. If it is the case that legisprudence is to find out the best way to realize ideal social condition by designing necessary legislative measures, we need to know what it is to be ideal social condition in advance, which is considered to be almost impossible to attain, especially in complex and pluralistic current society. We could never form agreement on how to measure efficiency in realizing certain policy, as key index to evaluate certain legislation. Also from the theoretical viewpoint, it is pointed out that we could hardly get the common elements in "good" laws, as "true" something. Is there any similarity between true hero and true liar, or good contract law and good labor law? A legal theorist once asserted that while contract law respects self-decision to pursue one's own profit and thus egoism, labor law depends on association for the laborers to help mutually and thus altruism, so the system of private law stands fundamentally on the fundamental contradiction (Kennedy 1976). Putting aside whether we need to admit such tragic premise, but many lawyers seem to hail a kind of "prescription" theory, where only time will tell

---

[22] The Act on the Special Measures concerning Anti-Terrorism (Act no. 113 of 2001).
[23] The Act on the Privatization of Postal Service (Act no. 97 of 2005).

and by surviving trial by time any law can show its justness, thus to consider judging some legislation to be good or bad in advance is impossible.

13.4 Conclusion: Jurisprudence Revisited

In answering this kind of criticism, we tried to take some different approach in some studies, contrary to the opening passage of *Anna Karenina* —"Happy families are all alike; every unhappy family is unhappy in its own way" (Tolstoy 1877), but all unhappy laws may resemble one another. And if we can grasp some elements to bring any legislation to failure, we can avoid that not to obstacle innovation. Reflecting what we've done in the past from this viewpoint, maybe we can find some earlier challenge in this tendency in such works as Lon L. Fuller's *the Morality of Law* (Fuller 1964),[24] where he asserted 8 conditions which must be filled by anything legitimately called as law. These conditions, however, just provide foundations for the general public to obey the law, not promising that the legislation is efficient, good, just, or anything.

My point in this chapter is similar to this tendency. It could be doubtful for us to find the way to enhance innovation by social scientific measures, but we can find some way to destruct innovation, and avoid them. Especially in the field of technology, it is pointed out and widely acknowledged in my view, that to forecast social reaction, typically how much demand for certain technology will arise, is far more difficult than to forecast how far technological improvement will be achieved in a certain period of time, because the public use of certain technology is very emergent and hard to know beforehand. But since social demand will decide how much new investment will be thrown into the next stage's technological investigation, the difficulty in forecasting social demand will affect achievement forecast to decrease its reliance.

Thus, it could be better to specify the failing condition of scientific and technological investigation to avoid it, by the power of social sciences. At least we can find many useful resources in the field of life or research ethics, considering them as to the way to avoid failing condition as to harm basic human rights.

The consideration how the legal studies can work for enhancing innovation, may bring us to the necessary and desirable change in the legal sphere, from application to allocation, or from interpretation of given law to investigation to create appropriate

---

[24]In considering law as to subject "human conduct to the governance of rules" (Fuller 1964: 74), Fuller concluded that without being (1) sufficiently general, (2) publicly promulgated, (3) prospective (i.e., not applied to the past behavior, but only to future), (4) at least minimally clear and intelligible, (5) free of contradictions, (6) relatively constant, so that they don't continuously change from day to day, (7) possible to obey, and (8) administered in a way that does not wildly diverge from their obvious or apparent meaning, law cannot indicate its subjects how to act in certain circumstances. Fuller called this character as "legality", in his formal theory of natural law.

298   T. Ohya

regulation for the estimated social goals. This maybe is the innovation necessary for the legal study in itself.[25]

Acknowledgements This work was supported by JSPS KAKENHI Grant Number JP26380006.

References

Bentham, J. (1776). *A fragment on government*, London: T. Payne (now in: Bentham, J. (2008) *A comment on the commentaries and a fragment on government* (The Collected Works of Jeremy Bentham), J. H. Burns & H. L. A. Hart (Eds.), Oxford: Clarendon Press).

Byford, S. (2016). Google's AlphaGo AI beats Lee Se-dol again to win Go series 4-1, *The Verge*, Mar. 15th, 2016. Retrieved on June 4, 2018, from http://www.theverge.com/2016/3/15/11213518/alphago-deepmind-go-match-5-result.

Chen S. (3rd c.) Biographies of the Wuhuan, Xianbei, and Dongyi, Book of Wei vol. 30, *Records of the Three Kingdoms*.

de Saint-Simon, H. (1816–7) L'Industrie (now in: Taylor K. (ed., trans.) (1975) *Henri de Saint Simon, 1760–1825: Selected writings on science, industry and social organization* (pp. 158–161). New York, NY: Holmes and Meier).

Dworkin, R. (1977a). *Taking rights seriously*. Cambridge, MA: Harvard University Press.

Dworkin, R. (1977b) No right answer? In P.M.S. Hacker & J. Raz (Eds.), *Law, morality, and society*. Oxford: Clarendon Press.

Dworkin, R. (1986). *Law's Empire*. Cambridge, MA: Belknap Press.

Fuller, L. L. (1964). *The morality of law*. New Haven, CT: Yale University Press.

Hegel, G. W. F. (1821). *Grundlinien der Philosophie des Rechts*. Berlin: Nicolai.

Hiroi, Y. (2019). Science as care: Science and innovation in post-growth society. In S. Lechevalier (Ed.), *Innovation beyond technology* (pp. 301–324). Berlin: Springer.

Inoue, T., Nishihara, H., Ida, M. and Matsubara Y. (eds.) (2014) *Rippōgaku no Furonthia* (the Frontier of Legisprudence) (Vol. 3), Kyōto: Nakanishiya.

Kennedy, D. (1976). Form and substance in private law adjudication. *Harvard Law Review, 89*, 1685–1778.

Kusago, T. (2019). Post-disaster community recovery and community-based collaborative action research—A case of process evaluation method for community life improvement. In S. Lechevalier (Ed.), *Innovation beyond technology* (pp. 195–221). Berlin: Springer.

Laurent, B. (2019). Innovation for whom? City experiments and the redefinition of urban democracy. In S. Lechevalier (Ed.), *Innovation beyond technology* (pp. 265–283). Berlin: Springer.

Lessig, L. (1999). *CODE: And other laws of cyberspace*. New York, NY: Basic Books.

Matsuo, K. (1981). *Dai 4-han no Kankō ni atatte (on the publication of 4th edition), Keiji Soshōhō Hanrei Hyakusen (100 cases of the criminal procedure)* (4th ed., p. 9). Tokyo: Yūhikaku.

NHTSA (National Highway Traffic Safety Administration, United States). (2013). *Preliminary statement of policy concerning automated vehicles*. Retrieved on June 4, 2018, from https://www.nhtsa.gov/staticfiles/rulemaking/pdf/Automated_Vehicles_Policy.pdf.

---

[25]I would like to note that the discussion in this chapter limits itself to the sphere of civil law, thus to the problem of liability to (typically) pay some money to fill the loss of value. We shall keep in mind that in the sphere of criminal law there must arise many problems concerning guilt and responsibility, i.e. sanctions as imprisonment to blame ill action in some sense (legally, ethically, or morally), which will bring much doubt for us whether such system will work against AIs and robots, which we believe lack bodily structure as we the human beings, and thus vulnerability. I would like to keep this point for further discussion, though.

Ohya T. (2016) History and present of legal interpretation in Japan. In Y. Bu (Ed.), *Juristische Methodenlehre in China und Ostasien* (pp. 241–255). Tübingen: Mohr Siebeck.

Ozawa, I. (1993). *Nippon Kaizō Keikaku (the alteration plan for Japan)*. Tōkyō: Kōdansha.

Ozawa, I. (1994) *Blueprint for a new Japan: The rethinking of a nation*. In Rockefeller, J. (introduction), Rubinfein, L. (trans.), Gower, E. (Ed.), Tōkyō: Kodansha International.

Rawls, J. (1971). *A theory of justice*. Cambridge, MA: Belknap Press.

Ruphy, S. (2019). Public participation in the setting of research and innovation agenda: Virtues and challenges from a philosophical perspective. In S. Lechevalier (Ed.), *Innovation beyond technology* (pp. 243–261). Berlin: Springer.

Sandel, M. J. (2009). *Justice: What's the right thing to do?*. New York, NY: Farrar, Straus, and Giroux.

Spencer, H. (1851). *Social statics: Or, the conditions essential to human happiness specified, and the first of them developed*. London: John Chapman.

Sunstein, C. R. (1993). *The partial constitution*. Harvard: Harvard University Press.

Tolstoy, L. (1877). *Anna Karenina* (now in: Tolstoy L. (2000) *Anna Karenina*, Garnett, C. (trans.), Kent, L.J. and Berberova, N. (revised), New York, NY: Modern Library).

Waldron, J. (1999). *The dignity of legislation*. Cambridge: Cambridge University Press.

Wintgens, L. J. & Hage, J. (2007). Editors' Preface, *Legisprudence,* 1(1), Oxford: Harts Publishing, iii–iv.

Chapter 14
Science as Care: Science and Innovation in Post-growth Society

Yoshinori Hiroi

Abstract Science and innovation have been closely connected with the goal of economic growth. But currently, as most of the industrialized countries are experiencing chronic economic stagnation owing to the maturation of material consumption, and the alternative measurement of wealth other than GDP or "happiness studies" is being widely discussed, the fundamental objective of science and technology is put into question and we need a new perspective or value regarding the aim of science and innovation. In this context, I examine the possibility of a "Sustainable Welfare Society," as a relevant social vision that means a society where the well-being of individuals and distributional justice are realized in a sustainable manner under finite natural resources and environment. And in this connection, I take up two policy areas relating to science and innovation—health and renewable energy—, paying attention to the relationships between technological innovation and social environments. Based upon these explorations, I would like to propose "Science as Care" as a possible new direction and conceptualization of science in Post-Growth Society.

14.1 Introduction

Historically, science, technology, and innovation have been closely linked with the goal of economic growth, particularly in the latter half of the 20th century. But currently, as material abundance prevails, most of the industrialized countries are experiencing chronic low-growth (or non-growth) economy. On the other hand, as the finite nature of natural resources and environments at a global level has been recognized, the infinite pursuit of economic growth or expansion itself is put into question. In addition, in recent years, discussions about the meaning of "wealth" have become active and in this context, alternative measurements of wealth other than GDP have been proposed and "happiness" studies have arisen in various academic disciplines.

Y. Hiroi (✉)
Kyoto University, Kyoto, Japan
e-mail: hiroi.yoshinori.5u@kyoto-u.ac.jp

© Springer Nature Singapore Pte Ltd. 2019
S. Lechevalier (ed.), *Innovation Beyond Technology*, Creative Economy,
https://doi.org/10.1007/978-981-13-9053-1_14

If science and innovation have been closely connected with the goal of economic growth as mentioned above, these discussions regarding the meaning of economic growth or measurements of wealth may lead us to rethink the fundamental objective or value of science and innovation. We need a new perspective regarding the aims of science, technology, and innovation.

I have to add here that this topic has a special implication when we think about the Japanese experience. We should say it is symbolic that both "Minamata" and "Fukushima"—one of the most disastrous industrial pollutions in history and also one of the most serious accidents of nuclear power plants—took place in Japan, where "growth-maniac" orientation towards economic growth has been strong and science and technology have been regarded as the most important and effective tools or pathways to achieve the goal of economic growth in the historical background of catch-up economy.

Based upon these concerns, first in this chapter I will review the recent discussions regarding the meaning of economic growth or alternative measurements of wealth and try to put them in a broader historical context since the 19th century. Then I will take up two policy areas of health care and renewable energy, which seem to have close relationships with arising values for science and innovation in post–growth society. Lastly, I will try to conceptualize such a new direction of science and innovation with the idea of "science as care."

14.2 Historical Perspectives of Post-growth Society

14.2.1 Growing Concerns in Alternative Indexes to GDP and "Happiness"

In recent years, the economic growth rates of developed nations have been staying at low levels, with many people suggesting this is "long-term stagnation." Specifically, the average economic growth rate of 39 developed nations has gradually declined from 3.1% in the 1980s, 2.7% in the 1990s, down to 1.6% in the five years between 2011 and 2015 after the so-called Lehman Shock in 2008 and a subsequent short-lived rally (IMF data).

On the other hand, debates on the implications of "affluence" and "happiness" have been increasing in recent years. For instance, at the request of the then French President Sarkozy, prominent economists such as the Nobel laureates Stiglitz and Sen published in 2010 a report on "Alternative Indexes to GDP" (Stiglitz et al. 2010).

Furthermore, given that the true affluence of a country or society cannot be measured from a simple economic viewpoint, Bhutan, a small country in Asia, proposed the concept of "Gross National Happiness (GNH)" and the indexes to measure the state of happiness. Today, GNH is so well-known throughout the world that many

14 Science as Care: Science and Innovation in Post-growth Society

international organizations are referring to the index. In recent years, the United Nations has been issuing an annual report entitled, "World Happiness Report."[1]

By the way, the term "GAH" may not be so well-known as GNH. This is an initiative that Arakawa City in Tokyo, Japan, proposed in 2005, which means "Gross Arakawa Happiness" or the "total amount of 'happiness' of people living in Arakawa City." By trying to achieve a certain level of GAH, Arakawa City tries to improve the performance of its public policies. The city came up with its own happiness indexes to cover six areas and 46 items, including health, welfare, child care, and education. At the same time, Arakawa City is moving ahead with research and policy development related to "GAH," through its resident surveys and in line with each policy challenge such as child poverty. In addition, under the leadership of Arakawa City, a joint initiative called "Happiness League" is being developed as a network of those organizations striving for policy development related to happiness indexes, including cities, towns, villages, and local governments across Japan (currently a little less than 100 cities, towns, and villages are involved). One of the most interesting aspects of this movement is that the implications of "happiness" and "affluence" are being sought at local levels (as opposed to Bhutan pursuing GNH at a national level).

In the meantime, in parallel with policy development initiatives as described above, research called "economics of happiness" or "happiness studies" is becoming active in economics, politics, psychology, and other related academic disciplines.

In the first place, what is the relationship between "economic growth" and people's "happiness"? In a sense, this is the question everyone would ask; however, until recently, there has been little debate or study on the subject except a few pioneering works such as the ones Easterlin wrote (1974). In the recent years, however, efforts to study the relationship between people's subjective or internal "happiness" and the economy are becoming active.

For example, according to limited findings from past studies, some international income comparison data show that for people with annual average income roughly in the range of $10,000–$15,000, the increase in income from economic growth correlates fairly well with the improvement in life satisfaction. As the annual average income goes above that range, however, the correlation between the two parameters gradually weakens to become more randomly distributed (Frey and Stutzer 2002).

As mentioned above, this kind of research has only become active in recent years, and we can say we are still in the initial phase of research. In the first place, surveys of phenomena such as "happiness," which is extremely subjective and difficult to quantify and compare, require particular attention to the accuracy of data and the way of interpretation. However, if we want a hypothetical framework to understand the relationship between economic growth and people's subjective happiness, it would not seem too illogical to imagine the kind of pattern shown in Fig. 14.1.

Figure 14.1 shows that if economic growth or the level of income per capita exceeds a certain level, the correlation between economic growth and the degree of

---

[1] The relationship between economic growth and happiness or well-being, and recent related literature are reviewed and discussed including the topics of sustainability and community by Kusago (2019).

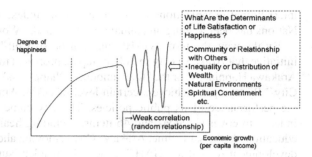

Fig. 14.1 Relationship between GDP per capita and happiness (well-being)

happiness will weaken. Then the question arises regarding what factors will determine the degree of "happiness" (in this case, the averaged degree of happiness of people in a country or region). Those factors may include the following:

(1) Community relationships (the quality of relationships and interactions with others, which is also linked to the so-called social capital).
(2) The degree of inequality or distribution of wealth.
(3) Interactions with the natural environment.
(4) Spirituality (or religious contentment).

I pointed out earlier that science and innovation have been closely linked with the goal of economic growth. Then if the goal of economic growth is no longer regarded as an absolute one, then what are the goals of science and innovation, or the value for which science and innovation are striving? In the case of Fig. 14.1, such goals and value may be something like "science for communities and human interactions," "science for realizing equality or reducing poverty," "science for the sustainability of natural environment," and so forth. It can hardly be said that these goals and value have been clearly defined, so let us continue to give more thought to them in the subsequent discussion in this chapter.[2]

14.2.2 Implications of the Theory of Steady-State Economy

The themes described above can be understood generally as topics relating to "economic growth" and "post-growth society." The debate on "post-growth society" is not a new phenomenon that has emerged for the first time in recent years; in fact, it has a long history. As the first step to exploring the way future science and innovation work, let us briefly review the genealogy of the discussions of "steady-state economy."

---

[2] The discussion regarding the goal or value for scientific innovation is closely linked to the issue of public participation in the setting of research and innovation agenda, which is discussed from a philosophical perspective by Stephanie Ruphy (2019), where the limited character of "market" is also pointed out.

14 Science as Care: Science and Innovation in Post-growth Society

As the starting point for this discussion, let me touch on the theory of "Stationary State" that John Stuart Mill expounded, which we can say is an origine of the theory of steady-state economy. It is noteworthy that modern capitalism rose in around the 16th century, and that Mill wrote the theory in the middle of the 19th century when full industrialization was taking place.

More specifically, in his book *Principles of Political Economy* (1848), Mill argued that the human economy would eventually stop growing and reach a steady state. One thing that intrigues us is that Mill proposed the positive image of people ending up finding true happiness there (in a society that has reached a steady state). Interestingly enough, around the time when Mill created the term "stationary state," the German biologist Ernst Haeckel created the term "ecology" in 1866 which I will take up later in this chapter.

The question is how these theories that make sense even today could emerge in those days. While full industrialization was taking place in those days as mentioned above, agriculture still accounted for the major part of the economy. In his argument, Mill was conscious of the "finite nature of land" (within a country). In other words, Mill's discussion is based on the logic that even if the economy grows, land—which can be rephrased as "nature"—will eventually encounter its finite limits and reach a steady state.

In reality, however, Mill's theory of steady state faded out from mainstream economics, because the structure of the economy shifted from agriculture to industry, later through further accelerating industrialization, and because the plundering of natural resources expanded through the exploitation of colonies. It can be argued that economy or capitalism "took off" from limitations of land. At the same time, the neoclassical economics thinking that human economy would be balanced through the market relationship between supply and demand (as if it was in infinite space) was emerging in the 1870s. In that sense, Mill's argument ended up a remnant of classical economics.

In retrospect, it can be said that "Limits to Growth" which was proposed by the Club of Rome (Meadows et al. 1972), pointed out in more than 100 years later that humankind was facing the problems that had been expressed by Mill's theory of steady state on a global level.

14.2.3 Three Historical Phases of the Theory of Steady-State Economy

In a sense, "Limits to Growth" predicted the oil crisis that would break out the following year. At the same time, it squarely addressed the notion of the "finite nature" of global resources for the first time in the world. Along with its elaborate computer simulations called "World Model," it had a great influence on a number of fields.

In the 1970s when "Limits to Growth" was proposed, the industrialization of developed nations was facing a kind of saturation and resources limitations at a global level, including the oil crises. At the same time, the debate on "alternative indexes to GNP" was occurring, which resembles the situation in recent years. As a whole, it can be said that it was a debate on the theme of "limitations of resources for industrialization."

In the 1980s or later, however, as financial deregulation and economic informatization and globalization progressed, industrialization and economic expansion evolved in developing countries including China. As a result, many people gradually lost interest in discussions like "Limits to Growth." In other words, amid the development of informatization, financialization, and globalization, which is closely linked to technology and innovation, the debate on something like "Limits to Growth," which focused on the problem of "limitations of resources for industrialization," gradually stepped back into the background.

In 2008, however, the aforementioned Lehman Shock or the global financial crisis broke out. Despite a subsequent short-lived rally, the economies of developed nations were moving into a structural slump. In addition, the theory of "decroissance", which advocated the "contraction" of economy and population was becoming active.[3]

Up to this point, we have reviewed the flow of debate, divided largely into three periods or phases: the theory of "steady state" proposed by Mill in the 1840s, the theory of "Limits to Growth" in the 1970s, and a recent series of debates on "alternative indexes to GDP," "happiness", and "decroissance."

If the whole story is seen from a long-term perspective, it can be understood that a different type of "steady-state economy theory" evolved in response to each historical phase of the development of capitalism. In other words, the following phases seem to make sense:

(1) Maturation of "marketization" phase—Transitional phase to "industrialization" → Mill's theory of "steady state" (1848)
(2) Maturation of "industrialization" phase—Transitional phase to "informatization and financialization" → The Club of Rome's theory of "Limits to Growth" (1972) (and the associated debate in the 1970s)
(3) Maturation of "informatization and financialization" phase → Post-growth theory and the theory of "decroissance" in recent years (in the 2000s).

The above phases can be seen as the historical phases of the theory of steady-state economy.

---

[3] The one proposed by the French thinker Serge Latouche is a representative theory of "decroissance" (Latouche 2010). Also, the discussions by the French economist Daniel Cohen regarding economic growth have similar concerns (Cohen 2018).

14.2.4 Possibility of a "Sustainable Welfare Society"

Up to this point, we have reviewed the historical flow of the theory of steady-state economy, which advocates the steady state of economy and population, along with changes in background economic structures. Based on this understanding, what kind of society will we be able to conceptualize, including the way science and technology work?

As one possible concept, I want to consider a vision which can be called a "sustainable welfare society," which is linked to the above-mentioned genealogy of steady-state economy theory.

A "sustainable welfare society" is intended to mean "a society where the well-being of individuals and distributional justice are realized in a sustainable manner under finite natural resources and environment (Hiroi 2001, 2006)."

The point here is that when we develop a vision of future society, the following two elements—"welfare" and "environment"-should be discussed in an integrated manner:

(a) The issue of a "distribution" of wealth ... equality and justice ... the issue of "welfare"
(b) The issue of "total volume" of wealth ... its sustainability ... the issue of "environment".

By the way, how are these two issues interacting with each other in a real society? The interaction is shown in Fig. 14.2 as the international comparison of developed nations. This is a figure that can be called a "sustainable welfare society" indicator. The vertical axis shows the Gini Coefficient, which indicates the degree of inequality (the higher the value, the bigger the inequality). On the other hand, the horizontal axis shows an index for environmental performance. This figure uses a composite index called the environmental performance index (EPI), developed by Yale University, which is a composite index that integrates multiple indexes including environmental pollution, carbon dioxide emissions, natural conservation, and many others. In this figure, the higher the value on the horizontal axis, the higher the value of environmental performance.

Interestingly, if "welfare" and "environment," which are not typically evaluated together, are compared in an integrated manner, some correlation is seen between the two. That is, there are plots of countries like the U.S., Korea, and Japan in the top left area of the figure. In these countries, the level of inequality is generally higher and the level of environmental performance is lower.

On the other hand, countries in the group in the bottom right area have relatively lower inequality and higher environmental performance. Countries in this group include Switzerland, Germany, and other north European countries. It can be said that they are the countries or societies positioned close to the "sustainable welfare society" we are talking about.[4]

---

[4]For more discussions about the theoretical aspects of sustainable welfare society including its implications for developing countries, see Hiroi (2011).

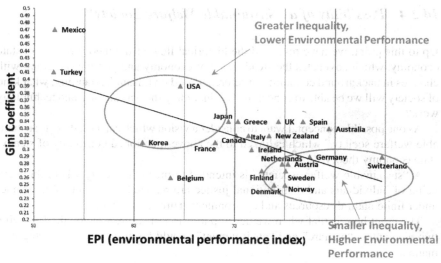

Fig. 14.2 "Sustainable welfare society" indicator: integration of environment and welfare performance

Table 14.1 Integration of welfare, environment, and economy

	Issues or function	Objective
Welfare	Distribution of wealth	Equity (equality, justice)
Environment	Volume of wealth	Sustainability
Economy	Production of wealth	Efficiency growth of GDP

I noted the significance of integrating "welfare" and "environment," and if we add "economy" to this discussion, the topic here can be formulated as a question of how we can achieve the best mix of welfare, environment, and economy, as well as their basic values of equity (equality), sustainability and efficiency as shown in Table 14.1.[5]

Then how do these discussions relate to the meanings of science and innovation? Science and technological innovation have been closely associated with economic growth as we pointed out, and so the relationships or meanings of science and innovation for the objective of welfare and environment in this table have not been fully explored until recently. But as we are now facing a post-growth era or arising val-

---

[5] Complex relationships between environmental protection, technological innovation, and economic developments, as well as various tools to deal with environmental destructions, are widely discussed by Dominique Pestre (2019).

ues of "happiness," community, sustainability and so on, we should put science and innovation in a broader perspective including welfare and environment.

In this section, we examined the meanings of economic growth, the theory of steady-state economy, a vision of sustainable welfare society and their implications for science and innovation. Based on these discussions, I will examine specific policy areas and see how science and innovation work in actual social environments.

14.3 Implications from Two Policy Areas—Healthcare and Renewable Energy

Here I take up two policy areas: healthcare and environment (renewable energy) which have close relationships with the foregoing discussions.

14.3.1 Healthcare

14.3.1.1 U.S. Policies for Biomedical Research and Healthcare Performance

Please look at Fig. 14.3 as a starter for our discussion on healthcare. This figure shows changes in the R&D budget of the U.S. federal government. In 2015, more than half (51.9%) of the enormous R&D budget of $134 billion was spent for national defense-related R&D. This position has been consistent in U.S. science policies after World War II. While the percentage of the national defense-related R&D budget was high particularly in the Cold War in the 1950s, and under the administration of Ronald Reagan in the late 1980s, the baseline trends have remained unchanged till today.

Apart from the military field, the U.S. federal government has been allocating the R&D-related budget overwhelmingly in favor of the healthcare or biomedical research fields. This is another characteristic in postwar U.S. science policies.

The symbolic existence of U.S. science policies is the National Institutes of Health (NIH), arguably the world's largest primary agency responsible for biomedical research. For example, apart from the budget of the Department of Defense, the budget of NIH accounted for 44.9% of the U.S. federal government's total R&D budget in 2015. In addition, as far as basic research is concerned, NIH spent as much as nearly half (49.8%) of the U.S. federal government's total R&D budget (including the military-related budget).

Figure 14.4 shows changes in the U.S. federal government's non-defense R&D budget by field. Standing out in this figure are the size of the budget for the healthcare field and the increase in its percentage particularly in the 1980s or later.

We have reviewed the circumstances surrounding U.S. policies for biomedical research. On the other hand, focusing only on the R&D or innovation side will not

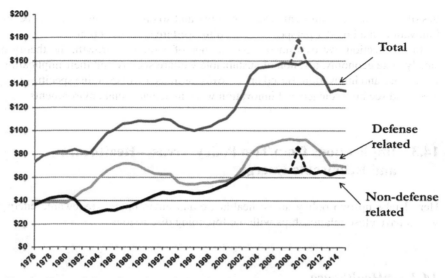

Source: Data of American Association for the Advancement of Science (AAAS)

Fig. 14.3 Changes in R&D budget of the U.S. federal government (actual in 1976 through 2015 in billion dollars)

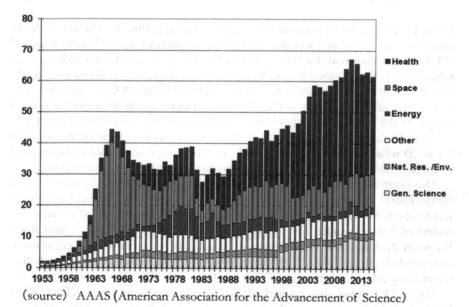

(source) AAAS (American Association for the Advancement of Science)

Fig. 14.4 Historical trend of non-defense R&D Budget of US Federal Government (Fiscal 1953–2015, billion dollars)

14 Science as Care: Science and Innovation in Post-growth Society 311

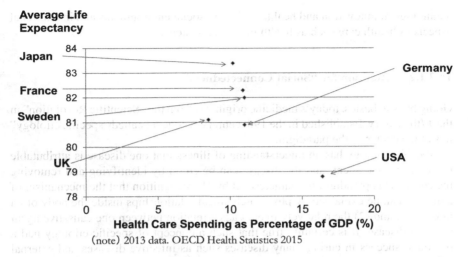

Fig. 14.5 Health care spending against GDP and average life expectancy: international comparison

provide an overall picture in discussing the way healthcare works. Instead, the whole health care system must be looked at from a broader perspective.

Figure 14.5 shows the relationship between total healthcare expenditure and average life expectancy in major developed nations. In this figure, the U.S. stands out among other developed nations in total healthcare expenditure (as a percentage of GDP). Despite that, the U.S. has the lowest average life expectancy.

This indicates that while investing a huge amount of money in the healthcare sector, including the research budget, the U.S. is producing considerably poor performances in terms of health outcomes.

Of course, the level of health in a country or society is determined by a myriad of factors. The overall health outcome is something that can be determined by the consequence of complexly intertwined factors, starting from lifestyles, such as dietary habits and working hours, to inequality, interactions with communities, crime rates, the availability of public health insurance, and so on.

Still, it is certain that some mechanisms are working behind the low healthcare performance in the U.S., including the way lifestyle and community work, inequality, many uninsured individuals due to the inadequate public health care insurance, and its heavy dependence on the market for healthcare, which is leading to price hikes due to "market failures" in healthcare pricing.

At the same time, the circumstances described above at least indicate that "R&D and improvements in individual technologies (or prioritized allocation of budgets and resources to them) are not necessarily considered as the most effective measures for improving the overall level of health outcomes." For these reasons, exploring such themes would lead to the fundamental questions regarding the meaning of science and innovation for health care, and even the meaning of health care itself. At the same time, these topics also require a broader perspective about the relationship between

312 Y. Hiroi

technological innovation and health, including social environments and institutional aspects of health care such as health insurance systems.[6]

14.3.1.2 Attention for "Social Connectedness"

Going back to basics, today's medicine originates from the "Scientific Revolution" in the 17th century. Established in the 19th century, a concept called "specific etiology" lies at the center of the paradigm.

Specific etiology has an understanding of illness that one disease is attributable to one causative agent, and the disease can be cured by identifying and removing the cause. This paradigm is characterized by (1) recognition that the mechanism of a disease can be explained by physico-chemical relationships inside the body of an individual, and (2) the relatively linear causal relation between one causative agent and one disease. It is certainly true that such a concept of specific etiology had a profound success in curing many diseases such as infective diseases and external injuries.

On the other hand, as expressed by the term "modern disease," today's disease structure is changing to a dominance of chronic diseases, including mental disorders like depression. Under such circumstances, it is important to have an understanding that illness is not only caused by internal factors in a body but is also caused by the consequence of a myriad of complicated factors, including psychological factors like mental stress, social factors such as working hours and interactions with communities, economic factors like poverty and inequality, and environmental factors including interaction with nature.

In fact, in the field of social epidemiology, which has become active in recent years, researchers have presented the basic concept of "social determinants of health," and are conducting research and analysis focusing on the very "social" factors surrounding disease and health, including the way public policies work [for details of social epidemiology, see Wilkinson (2005) and Kondo (2005)].

What I pay attention to here also is that this type of research has been increasing rapidly in recent years in many academic disciplines, including humanities, social and natural sciences. This type of research does not regard an individual or agent as a mere independent entity; but regards an individual within the networks of social connectedness including interactions with others. This paradigm also focuses on cooperative behaviors among individuals, empathy, and altruistic behavior with others. This perspective leads to the notion of "Science as Care," which will be discussed later in Sect. 14.4.

---

[6]This understanding echoes the discussion by Robert Boyer (2019) stating that the illness and the medical techniques are socially constructed and the methods for financing and organizing care shape the intensity and direction of medical breakthroughs.

14.3.1.3 "Sustainable Healthcare" and Science/Innovation

Another thing to be discussed here is the relationship between the concept of "sustainable healthcare" and science/innovation.

In all developed nations, aging of the population is progressing at a rapid pace, with Japan as the "front-runner"—Japan's aging ratio (the percentage of the population aged 65 or above) was 27.3% in 2016, the highest in the world. As a result, the country's total healthcare expenditure is increasing at a steady pace. Under such circumstances, there is a great need to know the way healthcare works, by which the quality of healthcare will be improved while the costs will be controlled below an excessively high level. It is in such a context that the concept of "sustainable healthcare" emerges.

In this context, in thinking about the image of sustainable health care, the above Fig. 14.5 can be interpreted as an example of such cost-effectiveness of healthcare at a macroscopic level. In a symbolic sense, the healthcare system in the U.S. shows a pattern that can be called "disease of excess," which stands in contrast to "disease of deficiency" (such as malnutrition) in the old days. Thomas McKeown, a British physician and historian of medicine, used the term "disease of affluence" to express this condition (McKeown 1988).

In the meantime, the following facts suggest that a resources-intensive healthcare and lifestyle will not necessarily result in longevity. In Japan, the so-called "Nagano model" is now drawing attention in the area of health care. Located near the center of Japan, Nagano Prefecture is a region that covers midsize provincial cities and agricultural communities. The 2010 Population Census in Japan found that Nagano Prefecture had the highest life expectancy for both men and women (the highest for men five times in a row, and the highest for women for the first time, overtaking Okinawa Prefecture). It is not too much to say that Nagano Prefecture with the highest life expectancy in Japan is one of the regions in the world enjoying the longest life. On the other hand, the per capita healthcare expenditure of Nagano Prefecture for the elderly aged 75 or above is the fourth lowest in Japan. In other words, Nagano Prefecture realizes healthy longevity at a relatively low healthcare expenditure level, which can be said to be a role model in the aging era of the way "sustainable healthcare" works. In addition, Nagano Prefecture is among prefectures in Japan with the smallest number of healthcare facilities per capita.

With respect to the factors contributing to healthy longevity, Nagano Prefectural government listed the following points in its analysis: (1) the high percentage of working elderly people including agriculture and those who feel motivated in communities (highest in Japan), (2) the high intake of vegetables (highest in Japan), and (3) the involvement of health volunteers' in health promotion and specialists in preventive health activities.

In other words, what has a major significance for longevity or health is factors like everyday interactions with others, involvement in society, and a sense of pride and motivation in life obtained through such activities. These points must be kept in mind when we consider the ultimate purposes or goals of science and innovation and the meaning of medical technology in healthcare.

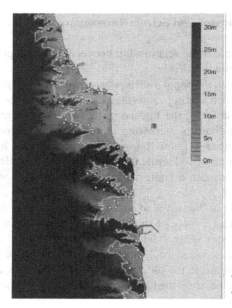

(Source: Hitoshi Takase, et al. (2012), *Warning by Shrines*, Kodansha)

Fig. 14.6 Tsunami line in Tohoku earthquake (3/11/2011) and the geographical location of old Shrines

Based on these discussions, when we consider the meaning of science and innovation in the area of health care, we need a broader perspective which includes various social factors and institutional dimensions such as public health insurance, and the attention to the sustainability of total health care system is significant.

14.3.2 Environment

14.3.2.1 Long-Time Perspective and Locality—Earthquake Prediction and Community Shrines

The other policy area I take up here is the area of environment, particularly the topic of renewable energy.

In the wake of the Great East Japan Earthquake in March 2011, the subsequent tsunami inflicted enormous damage on the areas. Many shrines stood along the border lines marking the arrival of the tsunami (Fig. 14.6).

In August 2011, this topic was aired on a Japanese TV program, "Hodo Tokushu (Japan News Network)," and drew many people's attention. Wataru Kumagai is a journalist who was involved in the coverage of the TV program. After the Earthquake, Kumagai, who had studied the marine environment at graduate school, published with other co-authors a book titled *Warning by Shrines*. To check their damage situation,

14 Science as Care: Science and Innovation in Post-growth Society

he visited 84 tsunami-hit shrines located near the coastline from Minamisoma-shi through Shinchi-machi in Fukushima Prefecture. Called "village shrines," these 84 small shrines had been worshipped and managed by local people for many years. According to his surveys, of the 84 shrines, 17 were washed away or destroyed, but the other 67 shrines were found intact.

In general, the older the shrines are, the fewer they suffer damage from tsunamis. The shrines described in a document titled "Engishiki" (edited in 927 AD) are called "Shikinaisha." Of 100 Shikinaisha in Fukushima, Miyagi, and Iwate, only three were found to have been completely or partially destroyed by the tsunami. Considering the so-called Jogan tsunami that occurred in the year 869 in the Heian period, it seems logical to believe the Jogan tsunami influenced the locations where shrines were built in those days (Takase et al. 2012).

Detailed research is needed to further verify the fact that the locations of shrines and the tsunami-inundated areas overlap with each other. Roughly speaking, it is very likely that people at that time built those shrines, leaving messages to future generations, something like, "Because of the risk of a tsunami arriving up to this point, be sure to evacuate to this shrine in the event of a disaster," or "Be aware that the area from this point to the coastline is dangerous."

This may sound a little exaggerated, but the damage from the tsunami could have been reduced if people had followed the old, simple lesson—"Rush to the nearest shrine or temple in the event of a disaster"—rather than the earthquake prediction and warning system based on modern science such as seismological research.

The above-mentioned journalist, Kumagai, said the following in his summary.

> As is well-known in the press and other media, scientific research shows evidence that tsunami disasters of this scale have occurred at intervals of several hundreds to 1,000 years. Then, what types of disaster prevention measures can we pass on to people 1,000 years in the future? After experiencing this tsunami disaster, we have begun to relook at various disaster prevention schemes and education. However, can those measures remain effective to help society 1,000 years in the future? Look around us, and you will find it difficult to find something that was taken from our predecessors 1,000 years ago.
>
> What I keenly felt through this survey is that we have forgotten, or we do not know, many things about community shrines. For the creation of local communities, I think it is critical to think of community shrines, which have been around for the past 1,000 years, and consider what we can pass on to local communities 1,000 years in the future. (Takase et al. 2012)

The remark of Kumagai, "Disaster prevention measures we can pass on to local communities 1,000 years in the future," reminds me of a movie produced in Denmark titled *Into Eternity* (2009). This is a documentary movie that recorded the construction of a final disposal site of radioactive waste from nuclear power plants in Finland. The title of the movie derives from the fact that the waste will become harmless in 100,000 years.

Conversely, we are passing a thing that will put later generations at risk over the next 100,000 years. In a sense, it can be said that this project runs completely counter to the intentions of the people who built the small local shrines with a message to future generations.

The market economy, or the system of capitalism supported by the market economy, interprets things only standing on a "short" temporal axis, while the long-time perspective is kept aside from the beginning.

In only 200 years (since the energy revolution at the end of the 18th century), modern capitalism is eating up fossil fuels that have accumulated in the earth over the past 300 million years. On the other hand, as an attempt to create a "man-made, infinite" energy source that replaces fossil fuel, a finite natural resource, nuclear power generation, including the above-mentioned radioactive waste, is in fact significantly damaging the life of later generations. Kanuo Mizuno, a Japanese economist, argued that if one can call the former "plundering of the past," the latter can be called "plundering of the future." Mizuno also argued that the housing bubble fanned by financial engineering and subprime loans, which led to the Lehman Shock, was "plundering of the future" taking advantage of the desires of the low-income population (Mizuno 2012).

As mentioned above, modern science or modern people have set aside things like "long-time perspective," "locality," and related traditional knowledge. By reassessing these things, and by relating them to modern science, a new type of "innovation" could be developed. Inspired by this interest, I am now involved in action research called "Chinju-no-Mori (Grove of the Village Shrine)/Natural Energy Community Initiative," which is described below.

14.3.2.2 Challenges with Renewable Energy and "Chinju-no-Mori"

Based on our experience of the nuclear accident after the Great East Japan Earthquake, the shift to decentralized energy systems, particularly to renewable energy, is an unavoidable challenge.

Let us look at the following interesting fact. Japan's energy self-sufficiency rate is no more than the 4 percent level, but 14 prefectures have an energy self-sufficiency rate in excess of 10%. The best five prefectures are: (1) Oita (26.9%), (2) Akita (19.7%), (3) Toyama (17.6%), (4) Nagano (15.4%), and (5) Kagoshima (14.7%). These data are the survey results of the study on the "Sustainable Zone" by Hidefumi Kurasaka, a researcher in environmental policy in Japan. The high percentage in Oita is largely attributed to geothermal power generation at many hot springs. Akita, Toyama, and Nagano have a high energy self-sufficiency rate because of small hydroelectric and biomass power systems that take advantage of their mountainous terrain.

This information reminds me of the fact that the numbers of shrines and temples all around the country are approximately 81,000 and 86,000, respectively. These numbers are huge compared with approximately 10,000 junior high schools across the country. In Japan, shrines and temples in the old days undeniably served as the "centers of local communities." Beyond their roles as religious facilities in the narrow sense, shrines and temples performed economic functions such as "ichi (markets)" being held in their vicinity for commercial activities, education functions like "terakoya (temple schools)," and other functions such as community events typified by "matsuri (festivals)."

Micro hydro electricity test equipment

Fig. 14.7 View of Itoshiro district, Gifu Prefecture

In addition, combined with the concept of "Eight Million Gods (the belief that eight million gods live in nature), these shrines rooted in local areas (including temples, depending on the context) are called "Chinju-no-Mori" (Grove of the Village Shrine).

Interestingly, amid the increasing interest in local communities, there are recent cases in Japan where people began to reevaluate these shrines and temples, in which they had lost interest during the period of high economic growth, as valuable "social resources" in the local community, and use them for their welfare activities, such as child care and geriatric care, and as the place to learn about the environment. I earlier described the fact that many shrines stood along the border lines of the tsunami's impact. Now the importance of shrines or "Chinju-no-Mori" in local communities is being reconfirmed after the Great East Japan Earthquake.

From the concerns described above, the "Chinju-no-Mori/Natural Energy Community Initiative" is intended to combine the development of self-sustaining, renewable energy bases with "Chinju-no-Mori," which used to be local community bases, and also to integrate welfare, environment and intergenerational communications.

14.3.2.3 Development of "Chinju-no-Mori/Natural Energy Community Initiative"

The story mentioned above may sound like a dream-like idea, but some attempts are already under way. For example, in the Itoshiro area, deep in the mountains on the border between Gifu and Fukui prefectures in central Japan, young people from an NPO (non-profit organization) called "Regional Revitalization Organization" are engaged in regional revitalization business through small hydroelectric power generation (Fig. 14.7).

This area is a spot that had prospered from old times as the center of the Hakusan (name of the mountain) belief. In the Edo era, this area was so crowded with religious practitioners and other visitors that they said, "Each day, 1,000 people are coming in 1,000 people are going out, and 1,000 people are staying overnight." However, due to the increasing depopulation in recent years, its population is now below 300, with a little less than 50% of the residents aged 65 or above. In such a situation, the above-mentioned NPO came in and undertook a regional revitalization initiative, with small hydroelectric generation as a profit growth pillar. This business went well, and in 2016, the NPO constructed a small hydroelectric generating facility, powerful enough to export generated electricity to other areas. With the population in the area picking up as a result of the increasing number of immigrants, this project today is drawing nationwide interest.

Mr. Akihide Hirano, vice president of the organization, used to work for a foreign-affiliated consulting company after graduating from a university in Tokyo. But he came to think that there was no better way to solve global issues, such as global environmental issues, than to start addressing local-level issues first. Then, he returned to his hometown and participated in the organization's business. Since then, he has been involved in many activities as a resident of the Itoshiro area.

Around the fall of 2011, the year when the Great East Japan Earthquake occurred, I had a chance to learn about the activities Mr. Hirano and other people were pursuing. It was the time when I was thinking about the feasibility of the above-mentioned attempt to connect renewable energy to "Chinju-no-Mori." I made immediate contact with Mr. Hirano through Facebook, and I received from him the following very impressive reply.

"The Itoshiro area is a village that serves as the center of the Hakusan belief, and we make it a rule that visitors to our small hydroelectric generating facility will also visit the shrine to pray." He added, "Natural energy is all about producing energy with the help of nature's power. We believe the community's involvement in natural energy is the activity to restore regional autonomy and the power of the community."

What I described above is only one such example, but it seems important to design new approaches to tackle contemporary issues, such as natural disasters and energy-related problems, by combining scientific expertise with local traditional culture like "Chinju-no-Mori."

14.4 Science as Care

Up to this point in this chapter, we have discussed the new goal and value for science and innovation in the "post-growth" context (Sect. 14.1), then we examined two policy areas of healthcare and renewable energy (Sect. 14.2). In this Section, based upon the foregoing discussions I explore a possible future vision of science with the concept of "science as care."

14.4.1 Transformation of Science and Care

Going back to basics, "care" is generally regarded as a concept that is related particularly to the fields of elderly care, nursing care, healthcare, education, psychology, and so forth. In the broad sense, it includes the meaning of "hospitality" and "consideration." Furthermore, in the broadest sense, it can be interpreted as a concept that represents almost all the relationships between individuals.

I think this concept of "care" could hold an essential significance when we think about the meaning or value of science and innovation in the post-growth society that we discussed.

If we look back on the basic understanding of science in the historical context of modern science that developed after the so-called Scientific Revolution in the 17th century, each human agent or individual was recognized as an independent, self-contained entity.

In recent years, however, a number of discussions have been taking place in various academic disciplines simultaneously, radically questioning the paradigm of such "individual"-centered view of modern science.

In the field of brain science, for example, an understanding called "social brain" is emerging, which claims that it is interactions with others and social relationships that have essential significance for the formation and evolution of the human brain (Fujii 2009).

In the area of health, according to the framework of modern medicine, human health and illness have been basically regarded as something contained in an individual, and the mechanism of illness has been explained by physicochemical causal relations inside the human body. In contrast, as we mentioned in the discussion on healthcare in Sect. 14.3, a field called "social epidemiology" is rapidly developing. By looking at "social determinants of health," social epidemiology is intended to verify and demonstrate that such factors as interactions with others, connection with the community, and inequality (which are beyond the control of individuals) have definite influences on human health or various types of illness.

In addition to the above, "models beyond individual agents" and the direction of research looking at social relationships, altruistic behavior, and cooperative behavior are developing rapidly in various scientific disciplines. Some of such areas are listed below.

(a) Studies on "social capital" that focus on the quality of trust among people, networks and norms.
(b) Studies in evolutionary biology that look at human altruistic behavior and cooperative behavior.
(c) The development of behavioral economics or neuroeconomics that combine economics and psychology or brain research.
(d) The "happiness" studies relating to the human sense of happiness and its determinants including interactions with others.

Table 14.2 Division of "science" and "care" in the modern scientific paradigm

Science	Care
Split from nature	Interaction with nature or
Control of nature	objects
	Sympathy
Universal or general law	Concerns with individual
	diversity
Aromisnc views of nature	Concerns with relationship
	or total system

[For details, see Putnam (2001), Bowles and Gintis (2011), and Gazzaniga (2009). For socioeconomic backgrounds in which these developments are taking place, see Hiroi (2015)].

If the term or concept of "care" is interpreted to broadly imply the above-mentioned "relationship" between individuals, or between humans and nature and others, it can be said that the viewpoint of "care" is emerging as one of the central concepts in various academic disciplines.[7]

14.4.2 Division and Integration of "Science" and "Care"

In the meantime, "care"-related fields such as nursing care, social welfare, education, and psychology, have often been regarded as lacking in "scientific" rigor and theoretical grounding. Therefore, how to bring "care" closer to "science" has been one of the central issues in those disciplines. To put it differently, the establishment of "care as science" has been a major direction in those areas.

There is no doubt that such an approach is significant. However, considering the above-mentioned development of "science" in recent years, or the historical context of modern science, it seems to be more important to introduce the idea of "science as care."

From the perspective of "division and integration of science and care," this concept can be summarized into a simple matrix as shown in Table 14.2.

There are two major points or axes here. First, the basic direction of modern science can be summarized as a split from nature or control of nature. On the other hand, what holds an essential significance in care is interactions with nature or sympathy.

---

[7]Thus far I have discussed the relationship of "care" with science, mainly paying attention to the meaning of care in its broadest and abstract sense, that is, relationships between agents or individuals. In doing so I have to admit that the more practical or clinical dimensions of care and also the social dimensions of care provisions (including the issues surrounding care providers) are not fully dealt with here, which requires further explorations.

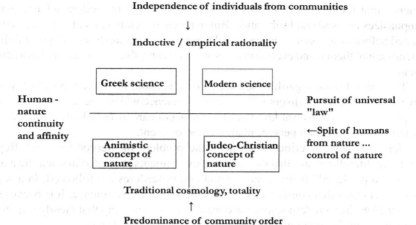

Fig. 14.8 Modern science in history: two coordinate axes

Second, the other basic direction of modern science is empirical rationality directed towards universal law. On the other hand, what has essential significance in care is the diversity of each individual or events which cannot be reduced to general laws.

Figure 14.8 is a summary of such two axes and their historical/social backgrounds.[8] Since the Scientific Revolution of the 17th century, "science" and "care" split from each other, alienated in the frameworks described above.

14.4.3 "Science as Care"

In the above-mentioned new development of science, however, it seems that science and care are now showing signs of fusion and integration again. Such a direction can be summarized into the following points.

The first point is about the possibility of science which can be called "science of relationship." "Science of relationship" is not only about social connectedness or relationships among human agents or individuals, but also about interactions between humans and nature, and inter-generational succession in a long-time perspective.

In this context, the German biologist Ernst Haeckel, who created the term "ecology" in the 19th century, as mentioned in Sect. 14.2, defined "ecology" as the "science of various relationships between organisms and their environment." The idea of

---

[8]These two factors—control of nature by human beings and independent (atomistic) individual—may serve as a basis for the notion of "progress" and the concept of "innovation" as its adapted modern version which are analyzed in depth from epistemological and historical perspectives by Sayaka Oki (2019).

science that focuses on "relationship" was very unique in modern science, which emphasizes elements and substance. But in recent developments of science, as mentioned before, discussions such as social brain in brain research, social epidemiology, social capital theory, and evolutionary biology all carry that "relationship" as a central theme.

The second point regarding science as care is about the direction of "science of diversity." "Science of diversity" is a form of science which does not simply reduce all phenomena to universal law, but as in the act of care, tries to look at the diversity or individuality of each person, phenomenon or event.

Here, we have a serious difficulty—the problem of "reproducibility." Reproducibility literally means that the results of experiments presented in scientific papers can be "reproduced" if the same method and procedures are followed. In a sense, this is a concept that constitutes the foundation of modern science. It is because, as described earlier, modern science is considered as something that clearly articulates "universal law," which must be acceptable across time and space.

However, based on its survey results, *Nature* reported that many researchers perceive that such "reproducibility" is recently in a crisis especially in the fields of biology and medicine. More specifically, of 1,576 researchers who responded to the survey, 52% said that there is a "significant crisis" in reproducibility and 38% said there is a "slight crisis" (*Nature*, 25 May 2016).

In the first place, this theme is a topic relating to the basic principle of what "(modern) science" is all about. Since the Scientific Revolution of the 17th century, the front line of science has moved toward phenomena that are more complex and contain a high level of "individuality," from physical phenomena, life phenomena, to humans. In other words, modern science initially selected areas with higher levels of universality and reproducibility, which could be reduced to a single formula, then gradually broadened the scope of its research subjects.

In that process, the closer the research of "science" came to areas with higher levels of complexity and individuality, such as life phenomena and humans, the tougher the problem of "reproducibility" became. In a sense, this consequence is understandable.

Let us look at a clinical-psychology-related case in which a truant grade school boy gradually came to attend school in a time span of one year thanks to the involvement of people around him in various ways. Finding out what the important factor was in the process of the change is undoubtedly "scientific research." But if one asks if this case is "reproducible," the answer is no. It is because completely replicating the circumstances and conditions which the boy was in is impossible.

The above was an example related to "humans." Let us take another case. Earthquake prediction remains unreliable because so many factors are involved in a phenomenon like the occurrence of an earthquake (including various "individual" characteristics at a certain place). In this case, too, reproducibility is faced with a difficulty.

Under such circumstances, full attention should be paid to the individuality and diversity of a phenomenon on one hand, and the pursuit of reproducibility and universal laws behind them should not be simply abandoned on the other hand. Integrating the two at a higher level is the purpose of "science as care" as "science of diversity."

14.5 Conclusion

In this chapter, we began with the discussion regarding the goal or fundamental value of science and innovation paying attention to its relationships with economic growth and the growing concerns about happiness, well-being or alternative measurements of GDP. Also, we came up with the concept of sustainable welfare society as a possible social vision in the times of post-growth.

Then we picked up two policy areas of health care and renewable energy. Here we found that the social and institutional factors beyond technology played major roles in the outcomes or performances in the area of health care, and the integrations of technological expertise and traditional knowledge or local communities can lead to productive developments in the area of renewable energy.

Based upon these discussions, I proposed the concept of "science as care" as one of the guiding directions of science in post-growth society, which could reconnect science and innovation with surrounding social environments as well as diverse local cultures and communities.

References

Bowles, S., & Gintis, H. (2011). *A cooperative species: Human reciprocity and its evolution.* Princeton University Press.

Boyer, R. (2019). How scientific breakthroughs and social innovations shape the evolution of the healthcare sector. In S. Lechevalier (Ed.), *Innovation beyond technology* (pp. 89–119). Berlin: Springer.

Cohen, D. (2018). *The infinite desire for growth.* Princeton University Press.

Easterlin, R. (1974). Does economic growth improve the human lot? In P. A. David & M. W. Reder (Eds.), *Nations and households in economic growth: Essays in Honor of Moses Abramovitz* (pp. 89–125). New York: Academic Press Inc.

Frey, B. S., & Stutzer, A. (2002). *Happiness and economics.* Princeton University Press.

Fujii, N. (2009). *Sosharu Bureinzu (Social Brains).* NTT Publishing.

Gazzaniga, M. S. (2009). *Human: The science behind what makes your brain unique.* Harper Perennial.

Hiroi, Y. (2001), *Teijo gata Shakai (Steady-State Society).* Iwanami Shoten.

Hiroi, Y. (2006). *Jizoku kanouna Fukushi Shakai* (Sustainable Welfare Society). Chikumashobo.

Hiroi, Y. (2011). Visions of the sustainable welfare society: Extending social quality into an Asian/developmental context. *International Journal of Social Quality, 1*(1), 19–31.

Hiroi, Y. (2015). *Posuto Shihonshugi (Post-Capitalism).* Iwanami Shoten.

Kondo, K. (2005). *Kenko Kkusa Shakai (Society with Health Disparities).* Igaku-Shoin.

Kusago, T. (2019). Post-disaster community recovery and community-based collaborative action research—A case of process evaluation method for community life improvement. In S. Lechevalier (Ed.), *Innovation beyond technology* (pp. 195–221). Berlin: Springer.

Latouche, S (2010). *Farewell to growth.* Polity.

McKeown, T. (1988). *The origins of human disease.* Wiley-Blackwell.

Meadows, D. H., & Meadows, D. L., et al. (1972), *Limits to Growth,* Universe Books.

Mizuno, K. (2012). *Sekai Keizai no Daichoryu (Major tides of global economy).* Ohta Publishing.

Oki, S. (2019). 'Innovation' as an adaptation of 'Progress': Revisiting the epistemological and historical contexts of these terms. In S. Lechevalier (Ed.), *Innovation beyond technology* (pp. 47–62). Berlin: Springer.

Pestre, D. (2019). Environment and social innovation: Why technology never was the solution. In S. Lechevalier (Ed.), *Innovation beyond technology* (pp. 175–194). Berlin: Springer.

Putnam, R. D. (2001), *Bowling alone: The collapse and revival of American community*. Simon & Schuster.

Ruphy, S. (2019). Public participation in the setting of research and innovation agenda: Virtues and challenges from a philosophical perspective. In S. Lechevalier (Ed.), *Innovation beyond technology* (pp. 243–261). Berlin: Springer.

Stiglitz, J. E., Sen, A., & Fitoussi, J. (2010). *Mismeasuring our lives: Why GDP doesn't add up*. The New Press.

Takase, H. et al. (2012). *Jinjha ha Keikoku Suru (Warning by Shrines)*. Kodansha.

Wilkinson, R. G. (2005). *The impact of inequality*. The New Press.